Advanced Topics in End User Computing

Volume 2

M. Adam Mahmood
University of Texas, El Paso, USA

Acquisition Editor:	Mehdi Khosrow-Pour
Senior Managing Editor:	Jan Travers
Managing Editor:	Amanda Appicello
Development Editor:	Michele Rossi
Copy Editor:	Angela Britcher
Typesetter:	Amanda Lutz
Cover Design:	Integrated Book Technology
Printed at:	Integrated Book Technology

Published in the United States of America by
Idea Group Publishing (an imprint of Idea Group Inc.)
701 E. Chocolate Avenue
Hershey PA 17033
Tel: 717-533-8845
Fax: 717-533-8661
E-mail: cust@idea-group.com
Web site: http://www.idea-group.com

and in the United Kingdom by
Idea Group Publishing (an imprint of Idea Group Inc.)
3 Henrietta Street
Covent Garden
London WC2E 8LU
Tel: 44 20 7240 0856
Fax: 44 20 7379 3313
Web site: http://www.eurospan.co.uk

Advanced Topics in End User Computing, Volume 2 is part of the Idea Group Publishing series named *Advanced Topics in End User Computing* Series (ISSN 1537-9310)

ISBN 1-59140-065-1
eISBN 1-59140-100-3

British Cataloguing in Publication Data
A Cataloguing in Publication record for this book is available from the British Library.

Advanced Topics in End User Computing

Volume 2

Table of Contents

Section II: End User System Effects, Outcomes, and Overviews

Section III: Management Attitude, End User Education, and Training

Preface

The End User Computing area continues to grow by leaps and bounds as more and more end users take control of their computing needs. This is causing a friction between the IT department and end user department with each having its own opinion on how to handle the EUC growth. The Journal of End User Computing is contributing to this tremendous growth by encouraging research and publication in the area. The Journal especially welcomes empirical studies on issues related to user-oriented view and IT-oriented view of EUC. The present scholarly book is a collection of some of the best manuscripts published in JEUC during last year. The book is divided into three sections: Section I covers factors that influence end-user selection, commitment, and performance. It includes four manuscripts. The manuscript by Witt and Burke started the section by investigating the applicability of general mental ability and personality test scores in predicting high-performing IT professionals. They compared employees and supervisory responses along technical proficiency, relationship management skills, adherence to documentation standards and requirements, and self-initiated professional development. The results of the study suggest that highly intelligent IT professionals are more likely to be adept in their jobs, among others. The study provides impetus for further research in the area.

The second paper in the section, penned by Turner and Turner, discusses the factors in end-user uptake of computer supported cooperative work (CSCW). The authors claim that this area is mainly neglected in the information systems (IS) literature. They use findings from IS research to structure a meta analysis of uptake issues in the CSCW area supplemented by one of their case studies. Their results show that while there are some factors that seem to be largely specific to CSCW introductions, many of the case study results are very similar to standard IS findings. They conclude by recommending how the two communities of researchers might build on each other's work.

Stone and Henry, in the third paper, use computer-based medical information system end-users in a large hospital as subjects. The theoretical model examined, using the data collected from these subjects, links several antecedents (e.g., past computer experience of the end-user, computer staff support for the computer system, ease of system use, and the degree of system use) to the end user's organizational commitment, mediated by computer self-efficacy and outcome expectancy. The results indicate that past computer experience and the degree of system use positively influence the end user's organizational commitment through both computer self-efficacy and outcome expectancy. The results also show that computer staff support and ease of system use positively impact the end-user's organizational commitment through outcome expectancy. The authors conclude by providing some implications for practicing managers.

Jawahar is the author of the fourth manuscript in this section. He emphasizes that it is important to uncover factors that influence end-user performance because of the significance of this performance to organizational performance. The author claims that prior research has relied mostly on personal factors to predict end-user performance even though several models suggest that both personal and situational factors influence behavior and performance. He examined the influence of both personal and situational factors on end-user performance. The results of the study showed that the three personal factors and four situational factors used in the study, together explained almost 40% of the variance in end-user performance. The author concludes by providing implications for practitioners and researchers and by offering directions for future research.

Section II of the book discusses the effects, outcomes, and quality assessment issues as they relate to end-user systems. McBride and Wood-Harper begin the section by discussing how control has become a major issue in end user computing. The authors claim that the migration of responsibility, resources, and authority from IT departments to user departments as EUC becomes more prevalent is frequently seen as a loss of power by the IT departments and an erosion of cost control by senior management. Such an IT oriented view, the authors suggest, focuses on how EUC causes problems, the additional technology it requires, and the methods and means that should be used to limit, control, and standardize this growth. Authors advocate a user-oriented view of EUC that focuses on the problems it solves, the user's task and the organizational environment it handles. The authors recommend a shift in EUC research away from the technology and the IT-oriented issues towards the political, social and cultural issues associated with the end computing, stating that EUC problems are organizational problems. The authors propose to facilitate such research a dynamic model for EUC in which the progression of EUC within an organization is visualized as a series of inference loops. The authors recommend that the IT people, in order to gain empathy and understanding, look at the EUC phenomenon from the end-user's point of view.

The following research by McGill portrays how organizations rely heavily on systems developed by end users, yet lack of experience and training may compromise the ability of end users to make objective assessments of the quality of these systems. The author investigated the ability of end users to assess the quality of systems they develop. The results of the study confirm that there are differences between the system quality assessed by end user developers and independent experts. In particular, the results of the study suggest that end users with little experience may erroneously consider the systems they develop to be of high quality. The author concludes by discussing some implications of these results.

In the following paper, Karsten started by stating that the working relationship of information technology professionals and end users is an ongoing source of both research and practical concern. The author employed Attribution Theory to examine the causal attributions IS professionals and end users make for successful and unsuccessful user-system outcomes. Results from the study, using a sample of 86 IS professionals and 122 end users, showed no differences in the nature of IS professional and end-user attributions for successful outcomes. The same results, however, did show very significant differences between these two groups following unsuccessful outcomes. Interestingly, post-hoc analysis indicates that for unsuccessful user-system outcomes, the causal attributions of IS professionals and end users who are cross-functional team members are significantly less divergent than the causal attributions of those who are not. The author concludes by discussing the implications of Attribution Theory for IS professional end-user interactions.

Wagner, in the fourth paper in this section, claims that knowledge is receiving recognition as a strategic force in organizations. One form of knowledge capture and maintenance organizations are tempted to use is expert system design by end users. The author discusses difficulties associated with end-user development of expert systems, both in terms of design quality and knowledge content captured in the knowledge base. His analysis of 25 expert systems designed by non-professional developers reveals significant quality and size limitation problems that indicate limited expert system development feasibility by end users. The lack of design quality, the author's research furthermore reveals, may not be easily compensated by a "knowledge advantage" of the end users, as end users may have an advantage in using their knowledge, but not in "knowing" it. The author concludes by offering suggestions for alternate forms of end-user oriented expert system development that consider end user limitations and take advantage of recent developments in information technology.

Morrison, Morrison, Melrose, and Wilson bring this section to a conclusion by discussing a graphical approach for reducing spreadsheet errors. Spreadsheet programs are tools that are widely used by end-user developers in organizations. Recent studies have, the authors claim, shown that spreadsheets often contain significant errors including "linking errors" (e.g., incorrect references to spreadsheet cell values on separate work areas). These errors may affect decisions made out of information provided in these spreadsheets especially those that use distinct work areas spread across several worksheets. The authors describe a code inspection approach that visually represents the structure of a linked spreadsheet and graphically identifies linked cells and their sources. They tested their approach in an experimental study where subjects created a complex spreadsheet. Their results indicate that subjects who used the code inspection approach made significantly fewer errors and experienced no decrease in the spreadsheet production speed or the production process satisfaction.

The third and final section of the book discusses management attitude towards end-user computing, end-user education, and training. Kohli and Gupta start the section by discussing student perceptions of the education and experiences received in Systems Analysis and Design (SA&D) courses taught at academic institutions. The authors themselves conducted an *ex-ante* and *post-hoc* empirical study of students' perceptions in a SA&D course. Their results indicate that after taking the SA&D course and working with a real-life project, the students' perceptions improved in the areas of the applicability of structured methodologies across industries, the importance of computer programming in systems analysis and design process, and the role of advanced technologies in SA&D. Students also recognized the importance of user involvement in system design projects.

Kruck, Maher, and Barkhi, in the second paper in this section, claim it is well documented in the literature that electronic spreadsheet models utilized in many professions to enhance decision-making frequently contain errors. The authors further maintain that limited research has been conducted in the area that systematically identifies potential reasons for these errors, and what procedures can be undertaken to mitigate them. They empirically investigate as to how several important cognitive skills are affected by formalized spreadsheet training. Their results show that one cognitive skill — logical reasoning — significantly increases after a six-week training period. The authors further assert that the greater the increase in logical reasoning skill, the more effectively the subject performed in developing competent spreadsheet models. The authors conclude by recommending that future research should focus on providing different forms of instruction and course materials for subjects with different backgrounds and different levels of expertise.

Winston and Dolgite claim prior research studies show that a positive attitude towards information technology among small business owners appears to be a key factor in achieving high quality IT implementations. The authors conducted case studies with small business owners to extend this area of research. A surprising finding of their research, according to the authors, was that high quality IT implementations resulted with owners who had either a positive or a negative attitude towards IT. They found that, by contrast, owners who had an uncertain attitude about IT and who practiced non-entrepreneurial management style had low quality IT implementations. The authors opined that, based on their research results, small business owners with an uncertain attitude towards IT might experience higher quality IT results in their organizations through practicing a more entrepreneurial or shared management style. They conclude by providing insights for both computer specialists and small business owners planning IT implementations.

Huang concludes the book by describing an innovative training strategy adopted by one mid-size organization to provide its end users with adequate, flexible, and responsive training. The author claims that progressive companies are always looking for ways to provide their end users with timely training and resources as end-user training is becoming increasingly important in today's technology-intensive business environment. The author then compares his innovative three-tier training strategy with other models described in technology training literature. He suggests that managers who supervise technology end users in organizations comparable to the one in his research study may want to use the three-tier strategy in their own training programs to improve end-user skills. The author concludes by suggesting that researchers and scholars may find that the idea of three-tier training generates new opportunities for research.

M. Adam Mahmood

Section I:

Factors Influencing End User Selection, Commitment, and Performance

Chapter I

Using Cognitive Ability and Personality to Select Information Technology Professionals

L.A. Witt
University of New Orleans, USA

L.A. Burke
Louisianna State University-Shreveport, USA

ABSTRACT

In order to achieve competitive advantage, 21st century organizations will make substantial investments in information technology (IT). Effective human resource practices in the IT field will therefore be critical. We investigated the applicability of general mental ability and personality test scores in predicting high-performing IT professionals. Data collected from 94 information technology employees in a service industry firm were compared with supervisory ratings along four orthogonal criteria; technical proficiency, relationship management skills, adherence to documentation standards and requirements, and self-initiated professional development. Results were partially supportive of the hypotheses and provide impetus for further work investigating applications of these tests to predict programmer performance in staffing and selection processes.

INTRODUCTION

The demand continues to escalate for information technology (IT) professionals who create value in project-based work, innovatively solve systems-related problems, and work under inordinate time pressures. Yet, evidence suggests that at least 350,000 information technology jobs remained unfilled in the United States at the start of the decade (Maddern, 2000). Furthermore, it has been estimated to take almost nine months to fill an IT vacancy and get a new IT employee up to speed.

The shortage of IT professionals has spurred many human resource managers to make substantial market-based adjustments to compensation plans in the IT field. Even more progressive companies have introduced a variety of retention incentives, particularly for those working in certain "hot skill areas" such as web design and development, Java programming, E-commerce, multimedia, networking, and Enterprise Resource Planning (ERP) systems (e.g., PeopleSoft, SAP). The IT shortage has also dramatically increased the breadth and/or depth of such skill requirements.

Not surprisingly though, not all IT workers who are hired meet managers' performance expectations, and anecdotal evidence suggests that many managers of information technology professionals find themselves spending a substantial amount of time coaching low performers. Given significant investments in the IT infrastructures and systems development required for competitive advantage in the new business reality, executives can ill afford poor performing information technology professionals. Unfortunately, typical approaches used for selecting IT employees have focused mostly on such ineffective methods as self-reported histories of IT experience or applicant responses in hurried unstructured interviews just to get someone to fill the vacancy.

Many firms have neglected the advances in selection assessment technologies, including inexpensive tests that can be administered in less than 15 minutes, can be processed readily in-house, and deliver reliable job-specific information quickly (Russell, 1999). The most commonly used commercially available test to predict programmer success is the Computer Programmer Aptitude Battery. Unfortunately, it is severely limited (Mahurin, 1992), as it has not been updated since 1964, it predicts success in programmer training courses rather than job performance, and it has adverse impact against minorities.

With escalating salaries and recruiting difficulties, the selection and retention of high-performing IT employees is critical. As such, efforts to improve the selection of information technologists must improve if we are to use our human resources wisely. Fortunately, more rigorous selection strategies and policies exist to increase "person-job" fit and "person-organization" fit for IT employees and promise highly sought-after utility. The purpose of the present study therefore was to investigate the applicability of two commonlyemployed human resource approaches for selecting information technology professionals – general mental ability and personality – with the goal of identifying the most high-performing individuals in this field.

A REVIEW OF THE RELEVANT LITERATURE

Whether labeled cognitive ability, general mental ability (GMA), or "g-factor," the ability to process and analyze information has been shown to predict job performance across a wide variety of jobs (e.g., Hunter & Hunter, 1984; Ree, Earles, & Teachout, 1994). Schmidt and Hunter's review of the literature (1998) substantiated that GMA is a consistent and universal predictor of job performance and learning. GMA influences job performance through its effects on job knowledge (Hunter, 1983; Schmidt, Hunter, & Outerbridge, 1986). Clearly, GMA is likely to predict the job performance of IT workers, who virtually epitomize the knowledge-worker trend in the present business reality. For example, superior mental ability is likely to be related to superior execution of IT tasks, such as coding, design, and problem-solving.

However, GMA is unlikely to explain variance in other elements of an IT worker's job performance. For example, analytical ability may have little to do with a programmer's ability to work with peers, end users, or managers to complete software projects on time and with little re-work. Instead, personality might explain these aspects of performance.

The Five-Factor Model of Personality

Researchers have examined personality-based predictors of work-related outcomes across a variety of organizations (see George, 1992; House, Shane, & Herold, 1996; and Judge, 1992 for reviews). Much of this progress can be attributed to development of one particular personality model, namely, the Five-Factor Model (FFM; Digman & Takemoto-Chock, 1981; Fiske, 1949; Norman, 1963; Tupes & Christal, 1958). The FFM has been well accepted as taxonomy of personality in the field of personality psychology (DeRaad & Doddema-Winsemius, 1999; John & Srivastava, 1999; McCrae & Costa, 1999), despite some criticism (e.g., Butcher & Rouse, 1996).

The dimensions of the FFM are agreeableness, extraversion, conscientiousness, emotional stability, and openness to experience. These five characteristics have been demonstrated to be stable across a multitude of studies (e.g., Costa & McCray, 1988; Costa, McCrae & Holland, 1984; McCrae & Costa, 1987), including some with sources other than the job incumbent (Digman & Takemoto-Chock, 1981; Dunn, Mount, Barrick, & Ones, 1995; McCrae & Costa, 1987).

These traits may be hereditary, providing even more compelling evidence for their stability across language or ethnic groups as well as age and gender (Costa & McCrae, 1992; Digman, 1990; Paunonen, Jackson, Trzebinski, & Forsterling, 1992).

Agreeableness taps an individual's degree of empathy and cooperativeness in a social context. It refers to such traits as flexibility, generosity, sympathy, selflessness, cooperativeness, helpfulness, tolerance, and courtesy (Digman, 1990). Havill, Besevegis, and Mouroussaki (1998) suggested that agreeableness is the primary concept to consider in the assessment of individual differences. Mount, Barrick, and Stewart (1998), however, found that agreeableness is most relevant to job performance in situations where joint action and collaboration are needed. Indeed, work environments having a fairly high level of interpersonal interaction require tolerance, selflessness, and flexibility. Agreeable persons tend to deal with conflict cooperatively or collaboratively, maintain social affiliations, and strive for common understanding (Digman, 1990).

Extraversion refers to a person's predisposition to be active, talkative, sociable, and assertive. As noted by John and Srivastava (1999, p. 121), extraversion reflects an "energetic approach to the social and material world" and is characterized by such traits as assertiveness, activity, positive emotionality, and sociability. Extraverted individuals often have enterprising vocational interests, numerous friendships, and social skills (McCrae & Costa, 1999).

John and Srivastava (1999) described conscientious individuals as being able to maintain socially prescribed impulse control (e.g., delaying gratification, planning, following social norms, prioritizing, and thinking before speaking). Similarly, McCrae and John (1992) described conscientiousness using such adjectives as reliable, responsible, efficient, organized, planful, and thorough. Conscientious individuals often have technical expertise, an organized support network, and long-term plans. (McCrae & Costa, 1999).

Emotional stability refers to the disposition to be optimistic, calm, and well adjusted. McCrae and Costa (1999) noted that persons low in emotional stability suffer from low irrational perfectionistic beliefs, self-esteem, and pessimistic attitudes. With these tendencies, they are predisposed to require considerable emotional support from others, experience less satisfaction and more stress, doubt their abilities, and see themselves as victims (Judge, Locke, Durham, & Kluger, 1998; Hogan & Briggs, 1984).

Individuals high on openness to experience tend to be imaginative, attentive to inner feelings, and possess intellectual curiosity and independence of judgment (Heneman, Judge, & Heneman, 2000). Openness has been associated with such other dispositional traits as unconventionality, autonomy, imagination, creativity, inquisitiveness, and change acceptance (Goldberg, 1992).

Given the established dimensionality of the Five-Factors, researchers have investigated their relationships with job performance (e.g., Barrick & Mount, 1996; Barrick & Mount, 1993; Stewart, 1996). Meta-analytic studies indicate that the Five-Factor Model constructs predict job performance across most, although not all, jobs (Barrick & Mount, 1991; Barrick et al., in press; Hurtz & Donovan, 2000; Salgado, 1997). In summary, a considerable body of work supports the predictive value of the Five-Factor Model, (see Mount & Barrick, 1998), which supports its use as a measure of personality in the current workplace.

HYPOTHESES

Guion (1998) advocated that selection researchers use measures for prediction that are appropriate not only to the work context but also the particular performance dimensions being predicted. Given the purpose of the present study to investigate the applicability for information technology professionals of GMA and personality, job analyses were first conducted to ascertain appropriate performance criteria. Item development was based on the results of our job analyses. Specifically, we interviewed job incumbents, their managers, appropriate human resources representatives, and customers of the programmers about the job and work environment. We also reviewed the performance appraisal forms used to assess incumbent performance. The results of this process yielded four criteria to be used as criterion measures in this study: (a) technical proficiency, (b) relationship management skills, (c) adherence to documentation standards and requirements, and (d) self-initiated professional development.

Hypothesis 1

Technical proficiency reflects the degree to which the IT employee performs the core substantive tasks central to his/her job. Conscientiousness (e.g., Barrick & Mount, 1991; Mount & Barrick, 1995) and GMA (e.g., Hunter & Hunter, 1984) have been found to predict such core measures of job performance. Given the preponderance of prior evidence for using GMA and conscientiousness to predict performance across jobs, we hypothesized similar results for IT workers. In other words, workers predisposed to be reliable, responsible, efficient, planful, achievement-oriented, hardworking, organized, and thorough (i.e., high in conscientiousness) are likely to be more technically proficient than those who are not. Similarly, workers who can process information quickly, anticipate interactions of their work with other modules of code, and understand the big picture (i.e., high in GMA) are likely to be more technically proficient than those who cannot.

Hypothesis 1. GMA and conscientiousness scores are positively related to supervisory ratings of IT workers' technical proficiency.

Hypothesis 2

The second criterion of interest was relationship management, which refers to an IT worker's interpersonal effectiveness. Recent research has shown a strong relationship between agreeableness and interpersonal skills. For example, in a recent study to predict the performance of 79 four-person human resource work teams, the trait of agreeableness predicted interpersonal skills, at both the individual and group levels of analysis (Neuman & Wright, 1999). Similarly, in a study of 110 mid-level managers participating in a university-sponsored management development workshop, agreeableness was related to the use of an integrating, or "win-win," style of conflict resolution (Antonioni, 1998). As such, we expected that cooperative and altruistic (i.e., agreeable) IT workers would thrive in managing relationships at work, such as managing group-based systems projects where conflicts can easily and frequently arise.

Furthermore, in Antonioni's (1998) study, extraversion and conscientiousness were related to an open, exchange-oriented style of conflict resolution. It is not surprising that employees who are active and sociable (i.e., high in extroversion) tend to engage in integrating conflict resolutions and work well with others. Oriented toward follow-up, being organized, and having impulse control and attention to detail, conscientious workers are likely to be effective at relationship management. They are likely to be attentive to the little details that are important to others, careful in planning their words, and hesitant to speak without first thinking of the impact of their comments.

Finally, workers high in emotional stability may be more effective than those low in emotional stability at relationship management. Whereas the optimistic, calm, and well adjusted emotionally stable workers are likely to get along with others, the pessimistic and over-sensitive emotionally unstable workers are likely to encounter problems with others.

Hypothesis 2. Agreeableness, extraversion, conscientiousness, and emotional stability scores are positively related to supervisory ratings of IT workers' relationship management skills.

Hypothesis 3

The third criterion measure, adherence to documentation standards, measures the extent to which IT employees archive and record their work (e.g., document systems problems, technical processes used, programs created or revised, etc.). It is likely that technicians who are high in conscientiousness would be rated high on this criterion. Prudence is central to documenting work, and so simply stated, IT workers who are diligent, exacting, attentive to detail, and predisposed to comply with rules are expected to be rated highly on their ability to maintain documentation standards in their jobs.

Hypothesis 3. Conscientiousness scores are positively related to supervisory ratings of IT workers' adherence to documentation standards.

Hypothesis 4

Our fourth dimension of performance, self-initiated professional development, reflects the information technologist's efforts to seek opportunities for professional improvement. Dispositional research relating to career development and professional improvement-seeking tendencies is scant. However, we suggest that two dimensions of the FFM may be relevant, namely openness to experience and agreeableness. IT workers who are intellectually curious (i.e., high on openness to experience) are likely to pursue continuing education and other self-study opportunities more than others. Agreeableness reflects flexibility, generosity, selflessness, cooperativeness, helpfulness, and tolerance. The helpful and cooperative workers high in agreeableness are more likely to enhance their personal skill sets for the benefit of the company and their co-workers than those low in agreeableness.

Hypothesis 4. Agreeableness and openness to experience scores are positively related to supervisory ratings of IT workers' self-initiated professional development.

We graphically present the relationships predicted in our four hypotheses in Figure 1. We emphasize that we are not proposing a causal model but rather merely illustrating the predicted validity coefficients.

METHOD

Subjects

Ninety-four information technology workers employed by a service-based organization provided complete data. Of these participants, 29.1% were females, and 15.1% were minorities. They averaged 15.96 years (SD = 2.29) of formal education, and the majority (72%) worked in a mainframe environment.

Figure 1: Hypothesized relationships

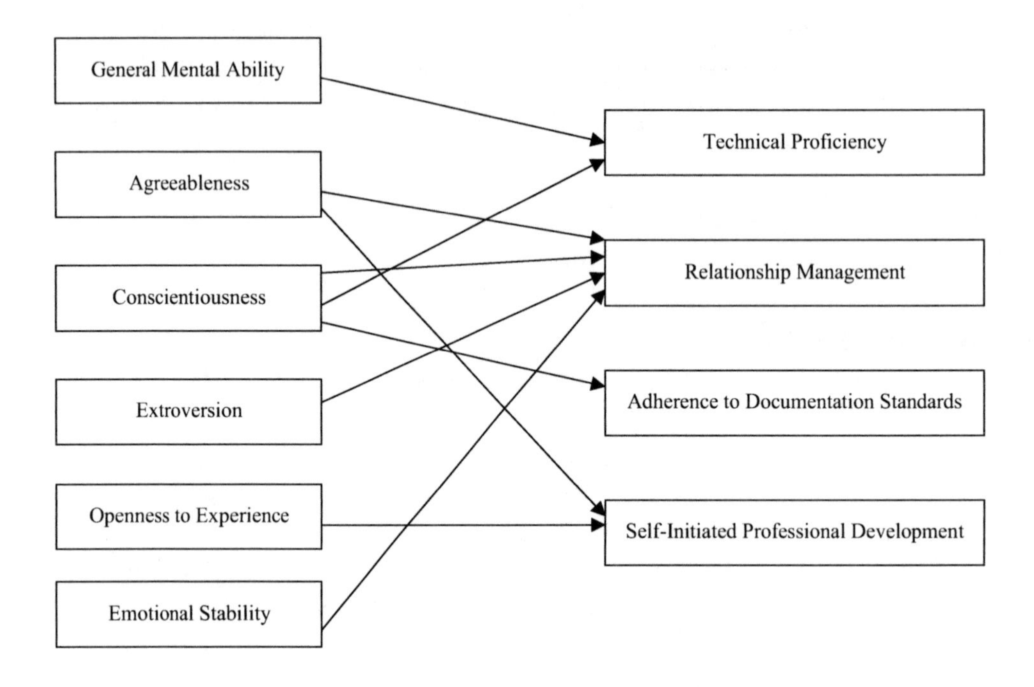

Measures

GMA. The Wonderlic Personnel Test (WPT) was used to measure general GMA. Composed of three types of items—vocabulary, arithmetic reasoning, and spatial relations, the WPT is among the most commonly used measures of GMA and is considered equivalent to other known measures of GMA (Hunter, 1989). Test-retest reliabilities (across test forms) range from .82 to .94, and alternate form reliabilities range from .73 to .95. Other measures of internal consistency (such as the KR-20) range from .88 to .94 (Wonderlic, 1992).

Personality. The Personal Characteristics Inventory (PCI) (Barrick & Mount, 1991) assessed the Five-Factor Model personality dimensions. Unlike other measures based on the FFM, the PCI was developed for use in personnel selection. The PCI presents 120 items: 30 each for conscientiousness and extraversion, and 20 each for agreeableness, emotional stability, and openness to experience. Subjects were asked to rate each item on a three-point, Likert-type scale (from 1 = "disagree" to 3 = "agree"). Coefficient alpha reliability estimates reported in the test manual for this measure range from .82 to .87 for the five dimensions, while the test-retest reliability estimates range from .70 to .82 (Barrick & Mount, 1991). The PCI scales have also demonstrated convergent validity and divergent validity with other Five-Factor measures, such as Goldberg's Adjective Checklist (Goldberg, 1992).

Job Performance. Criterion items were developed on the basis of the job analysis results, as discussed earlier, and in consultation with first-line, middle, and senior managers. Each participating IT employee was rated by his/her first-line supervisor using the following scale: (a) "weak or bottom 10%," (B) "fair or next 20%," (c) "good or next 40%," (d) "very good or next 20%," or (e) "best or top 10%." These responses were scored as 1, 2, 3, 4, and 5, respectively. Principal components factor analysis with varimax rotation was then used to create four orthogonal criterion factors. The resulting factor scores were used to compute subsequent validity coefficients.

Fifteen items composed the first factor to measure technical proficiency (e.g., "(employee name) applies the highest levels of technical skill in completing work requirements"). Eleven items composed the second factor to tap relationship management skills (e.g., "(employee name) develops and maintains positive client relationships"). Six items composed the third factor to measure adherence to documentation standards and requirements (e.g., "(employee name) documents system problems in an accurate and timely manner"). Lastly, three items composed the fourth factor to measure self-initiated professional development (e.g., "(employee name) pursues self-study and continuing education to maintain technical skills").

RESULTS

Descriptive statistics, coefficient alpha reliability estimates, and correlations among the variables are presented in Table 1. As shown there, the scales composed of items using Likert-type response anchors met or exceeded the minimally accepted level of reliability of $\alpha = .70$ (Nunnally, 1978).

To provide rigorous tests of the hypotheses, we employed multiple regression analyses, first entering three demographic variables – age, sex, and tenure in the organization – into the equations. Consistent with our argument that personality explains variance in IT performance beyond that explained by GMA, we added GMA scores prior to conscientiousness to test the first hypothesis and then included it in step one with the demographic variables to test the remaining hypotheses.

Hypothesis 1. As shown in Table 1, GMA ($r = .36, p < .05$), conscientiousness scores ($r = -.18, p < .05$), and agreeableness scores ($r = -.23, p < .05$) were significantly related to the first criterion measure — technical proficiency. The regression analyses revealed that the addition of GMA scores at step two added

Table 1: Descriptive statistics and intercorrelation matrix

Variable	Mean	StD	1	2	3	4	5	6	7	8	9	10	11	12
01. Technical Proficiency	-.01	1.01	(.95)											
02. Relationship Management	.01	1.02	-.01	(.92)										
03. Documentation Standards	.01	1.02	-.01	-.01	(.89)									
04. Self-Development	.03	1.01	.01	-.01	-.02	(.82)								
05. Conscientiousness	2.65	.24	-.18	.27	.09	.12	(.81)							
06. Extroversion	2.08	.37	-.01	-.09	.20	-.04	.15	(.88)						
07. Agreeableness	2.52	.31	-.23	.23	-.03	.16	.44	.22	(.81)					
08. Emotional Stability	2.33	.37	.08	.10	.00	-.16	.45	.34	.35	(.85)				
09. Openness to Experience	2.50	.25	.02	-.17	-.00	.01	.03	.38	.08	.23	(.77)			
10. General Mental Ability	26.08	5.77	.36	-.37	-.00	.10	-.30	.00	-.31	-.04	.31	----		
11. Sex (1 = men; 2 = women)	1.30	.46	-.01	.04	-.13	.27	.30	.01	.13	.07	-.09	-.31	----	
12. Age	39.97	8.58	-.04	-.07	-.28	-.01	-.08	-.25	-.04	-.16	.17	.16	-.17	----
13. Tenure	5.52	5.78	.11	.17	-.32	.12	-.19	-.08	.03	-.09	-.05	.04	-.03	.39

Note: Reliability estimates (α) are presented in the diagonal. Correlations ≥ .17, p < .05; correlations ≥ .25, p < .01.

significant variance (total $R^2 = .06$, $\Delta R^2 = .06$, $p < .05$) over-and-above the variance contributed by the demographic variables. Although agreeableness was not part of the first hypothesis, we then entered agreeableness scores into the equation, because they were more highly correlated with the performance ratings than conscientiousness scores; they contributed no appreciable variance ($\Delta R^2 = .01$, ns). To directly test the first hypothesis, we ran a separate equation without agreeableness. Conscientiousness scores did not contribute unique variance ($\Delta R^2 = .00$, ns) beyond the variance contributed by GMA and the demographic variables in the explanation of technical proficiency.

Hypothesis 2. As shown in Table 1, four predictor measures were significantly related to factor two, relationship management skills, namely conscientiousness ($r = .27$, $p < .01$), agreeableness ($r = .23$, $p < .05$), openness to experience ($r = -.17$, $p < .05$), and GMA ($r = -.37$, $p < .01$) scores. The regression analyses revealed that the addition of conscientiousness scores at step two added significant variance (total $R^2 = .25$, $\Delta R^2 = .06$, $p < .05$) over-and-above the variance contributed by the demographic variables and GMA. The other personality variables did not contribute unique variance to the explanation of relationship management performance.

Hypothesis 3. As shown in Table 1, only extroversion ($r = .20, p < .05$), age ($r = -.28, p < .01$), and tenure ($r = -.32, p < .01$) were significantly related to factor three—adherence to documentation standards and requirements. Extroversion scores did not contribute unique variance ($\Delta R^2 = .02$, ns) beyond the variance contributed by the control variables in the explanation of adherence to documentation standards and requirements.

Hypothesis 4. As shown in Table 1, agreeableness ($r = .16, p < .10$) and emotional stability ($r = -.16, p < .10$) were related to the final criterion measure, self-initiated professional development. The regression analyses revealed that the additional variance brought about by adding agreeableness scores at step two approached significance (total $R^2 = .16, \Delta R^2 = .03, p = .10$) over-and-above the variance contributed by the demographic variables and GMA. Emotional stability entered at the third step (total $R^2 = .23, \Delta R^2 = .07, p < .05$) added unique variance to the explanation of self-initiated professional development.

In summary, our findings were mixed. Results of the regression analyses provided partial support for Hypotheses 1, 2, and 4 but no support for Hypothesis 3.

DISCUSSION AND IMPLICATIONS FOR RESEARCH

Consistent with results of meta-analytic studies that have indicated that the mean observed correlations between FFM scale scores and supervisor ratings of job performance tend not to exceed the teens (e.g., Barrick, Mount, & Judge, in press; Hurtz & Donovan, 2000), our bivariate correlation analyses yielded low correlations between the FFM scale scores and job performance ratings. However, considering the variables together in the regression analyses provided a more accurate picture of the relationships. As hypothesized, GMA scores and technical proficiency were significantly related in our study of IT professionals. Individuals with greater GMA are likely to write code with fewer errors, solve systems problems more effectively, generate solutions more quickly and innovatively and so on, compared to less intelligent associates. Surprisingly, conscientiousness was unrelated to technical proficiency.

Increasingly critical to the success of IT professionals in contemporary organizations are effective relationships. Closeness to the end-user is necessary for definition of project requirements, which when done well reduces subsequent re-work. Similarly, work in project teams requires interpersonal interaction. Our tests of Hypothesis 2 indicated that only conscientiousness contributed unique variance to the explanation of relationship management effectiveness. Oriented toward follow-up, being organized, and having impulse control and attention to detail, conscientious workers were effective at relationship management. This finding supports the argument that personality scores contribute unique variance to an important aspect of job performance well beyond the variance contributed by GMA.

The absence of significant relationships between relationship management and extroversion, agreeableness, and emotional stability, in part, is inconsistent with Hypothesis 2. Yet, IT professionals tend to be more introverted (Fowler, 1999), and thus perhaps the extroverted IT workers can be perceived as overly assertive, inordinately talkative, unnecessarily spontaneous, or even politically motivated. These are characteristics that typically frustrate introverts and therefore, could logically explain the finding of extroverted IT employees being rated as less effective in managing relations at work. Perhaps because much of programmers' work-related interaction is content based, conscientiousness may be the most relevant predictor of relationship management.

While the bivariate correlation between extroversion and adherence to documentation standards and requirements was significant, the regression analysis revealed that extroversion scores contributed no unique variance. Managers insist that effective documentation is important to overall job performance. In computer-related fields, documentation is often "drilled in" as a must-do activity, which conscientious individuals should dutifully execute. Our results suggest that individual differences in conscientiousness did not explain performance differences in adherence to documentation standards and requirements. Subsequent research with other personality and GMA measures may yield more promising results. Recent evidence suggests that biodata selection instruments explain considerable variance in job performance over-and-above the variance accounted for by GMA and the Five-Factor Model constructs (Mount, Witt, & Barrick, 2000). Biodata taps into personal history and behavioral preferences. Accordingly, researchers may find utility in exploring biodata as a predictor of IT job performance.

With regard to Hypothesis 4, the relationships of agreeableness and emotional stability with self-initiated professional development suggests that individuals who are cooperative (high agreeableness) and insecure (low emotional stability) are more likely to seek continuing education or self-study types of activities. In general, selecting workers low in emotional stability would be unwise. However, hiring workers high in agreeableness might be of utility, as they may be predisposed to initiate self-development.

While replication is needed, the study's results are encouraging and have initiated research on the Five-Factor Model with information technology professionals. Conscientiousness, openness to experience, and agreeableness each added unique variance to the explanation of aspects of job performance over-and-above the variance contributed by GMA, sex, age, and organizational tenure.

Several weaknesses of the present study, however, limit the generalizability of the findings and merit attention. The moderately small sample size did not permit cross-validation and poses a potential problem in terms of the stability of the correlation coefficients. Also, participants emanated from only one organization. Yet, a strength of the present study was the development of the job-relevant criterion items, which focused on the aspects of IT job performance critical to organizational success. These content valid items assessed elements of job performance beyond those typically measured, and this may be the first study to assess IT job performance simultaneously looking at these business-critical performance dimensions. Finally, the use of factor analysis to create orthogonal factor scores optimized the amount of variance accounted for by the predictors.

IMPLICATIONS FOR PRACTICE

The present findings have potential implications for both IT supervisors and human resources managers. Put simply, information technology workers cannot be hired "willy-nilly" and expected to deliver superior performance, under increasing time constraints and metamorphosing technologies. Our findings suggest that firms using GMA and personality testing may not only promote better selection of IT workers in certain circumstances but also facilitate more effective utilization and development of human resources in this profession.

Our preliminary findings suggest that highly intelligent IT persons are more likely to be technically adept in their jobs. In addition, conscientious technicians will tend to effectively manage relations in their work environment. Given the increasing collaborative efforts that a worker in this field faces, this finding may have high utility. Lastly, agreeable IT workers may be more apt to seek additional educational or skill building opportunities on their own, which should only enhance their eventual contribution to the firm.

In some ways, our findings call attention to and perhaps further highlight the unique challenges in selecting and managing IT professionals. Thus, universal generalizations and prescriptions for selecting technicians and managing their job performance are potentially dangerous. It is likely that effective IT managers adopt different approaches in coaching and training their employees, based upon their particular personality. For example, managers may more closely monitor the work progress of subordinates low in conscientiousness than those high in conscientiousness. Indeed, adapting different motivational styles to fit the personalities of subordinates is a critical element of managerial performance (Davis, Skube, Hellervik, Gebelein, & Sheard, 1992). Thus, future research may eventually lead to empirically sound approaches for not only selecting but also developing employees in the IT field.

REFERENCES

Antonioni, D. (1998). Relationship between the big five personality factors and conflict management styles. *International Journal of Conflict Management*, 9, 336-355.

Barrick, M. R., & Mount, M. K. (1991). The Big Five personality dimensions and job performance: A meta-analysis. *Personnel Psychology*, 44, 1-26.

Barrick, M. R., & Mount, M. K. (In press). Select on conscientiousness and emotional stability. Chapter to appear in E. A. Locke (Ed.), *Basic Principles of Organizational Behavior: A Handbook*. Blackwell Publishers.

Barrick, M. R., Mount, M. K., & Judge, T. A. (In press). The FFM personality dimensions and job performance: Meta-Analysis of meta-analyses. Invited submission to a special "selection" issue of *International Journal of Selection and Assessment*.

Barrick, M. R., & Mount, M. K. (1993). Autonomy as a moderator of the relationship between the Big Five personality dimensions and job performance. *Journal of Applied Psychology*, 78, 111-118.

Butcher, J. N., & Rouse, S. V. (1996). Personality: Individual differences and clinical assessments. *Annual Review of Psychology*, 47, 87-111.

Costa, P. T., & McCrae, R. R. (1988). From catalog to classification: Murray's needs and the Five-Factor Model. *Journal of Personality and Social Psychology*, 55, 285-265.

Costa, P. T., McCrae, R. R., & Holland, J. L. (1984). Personality and vocational interests in an adult sample. *Journal of Applied Psychology*, 69, 390-400.

Davis, B. L., Skube, C. J., Hellervik, L. W., Gebelein, S. H., & Sheard, J. L. (1992). *Successful manager's handbook*. Minneapolis: Personnel Decisions, Inc.

DeRaad, B., & Doddema-Winsemius, M. (1999). Instincts and personality. *Personality and Individual Differences*, 27, 293-305.

Digman, J. M. (1990). Personality structure: Emergence of the five factor model. *Annual Review of Psychology*, 41, 417-440.

Digman, J. M., & Takemoto-Chock, N. K. (1981). Factors in the natural language of personality: Re-analysis, comparison and interpretation of six major studies. *Multivariate Behavioral Research,* 16, 149-170.

Dunn, W. S., Mount, M. K., Barrick, M. R., & Ones, D. S. (1995). Relative importance of personality and general mental ability in managers' judgements of applicant qualifications. *Journal of Applied Psychology*, 80, 500-509.

Fiske, D. W. (1949). Consistency in the factorial structures of personality ratings from different sources. *Journal of Abnormal and Social Psychology,* 44, 329-344.

Fowler, J. (1999). Understanding IT: A perspective. *Target Marketing*, 22, 68-71.

George, J. (1992). The role of personality in organizational life: Issues and evidence. *Journal of Management*, 2, 185-213.

Goldberg, L. R. (1992). The development of markers for the Big Five factor structure. *Psychological Assessment,* 4, 26-42.

Guion, R. (1998). Some virtues of dissatisfaction in the science and practice of personnel selection. *Human Resource Management Review*, 8, 351-365.

Havill, V. L., Besevegis, E., & Mouroussaki, S. (1998). Agreeableness as a diachronic personality trait. In G. A. Kohnstamm & C. F. Halverson, Jr. (eds.), *Parental descriptions of child personality: Developmental antecedents of the Big 5*. The LEA series in personality and child psychology (pp. 49-64). Mahwah, NJ: Lawrence Earlbaum.

Heneman, H. G., Judge, T. A., & Heneman, R. L. (2000). *Staffing organizations*. Boston: Irwin McGraw-Hill.

Hogan, R. T., & Briggs, S. R. (1984). Noncognitive measures of social intelligence. *Personnel Selection & Training Bulletin,* 5, 184-190.

House, R., Shane, S., & Herold, D. (1996). Rumors of the death of dispositional research are vastly exaggerated. *Academy of Management Review,* 21, 203-224.

Hunter, J. E. & Hunter, R. F. (1984). Validity and utility of alternative predictors of job performance. *Psychological Bulletin,* 96, 72-98.

Hunter, J. E. (1983). A causal model of cognitive ability, job knowledge, job performance, and supervisor ratings. In F. Landy, S. Zedeck, & J. Cleveland (eds.), *Performance Measurement and Theory* (pp. 257-266). Hillsdale, NJ: Lawrence Erlbaum.

Hunter, J. E. (1989). *The Wonderlic Personnel Test as a Predictor of Training Success and Job Performance*. E. F. Wonderlic Personnel Test, Inc.

Hurtz, G. M., & Donovan, J. J. (2000). Personality and job performance: The big five revisited. *Journal of Applied Psychology,* 85, 869-879.

John, O. P., & Srivastava, S. (1999). The "Big Five" trait taxonomy: History, measurement, and theoretical perspectives. In L. Pervin and O. P. John (eds.), *Handbook of Personality: Theory and Research* (Second edition; pp. 102-138). New York: Guilford.

Judge, T. (1992). The dispositional perspective in human resource research. In G. R. Ferris & K. M. Rowland (eds.), *Research in Personnel and Human Resource Management* (Vol. 10, pp. 31-72). Greenwich, CT: JAI Press.

Judge, T. A., Locke, E. A., Durham, C. C., & Kluger, A. N. (1998). Dispositional effects on job and life satisfaction: The role of core evaluations. *Journal of Applied Psychology,* 83, 17-34.

Maddern, S. (2000). High-tech brain drain. *America's Network,* 104, 70-72.

Mahurin, R. K. (1992). Review of the computer programmer aptitude battery. In J. J. Kramer and J. C. Conoley (eds.), *The Eleventh Mental Measurements Yearbook* (p. 225-227). Lincoln, NE: The Buros Institute of Mental Measurements, University of Nebraska.

McCrae, R. R., & Costa, P. T. (1987). Validation of the five factor model of personality across instruments and observers. *Journal of Personality and Social Psychology,* 52, 81-90.

McCrae, R. R., & Costa, P. T. (1991). The neo personality-inventory - using the 5-factor model in counseling. *Journal of Counseling Development,* 69, 637-372.

McCrae, R. R., & Costa, P. T., Jr. (1999). A five-factor theory of personality. In L. Pervin and O. P. John (eds.), *Handbook of Personality: Theory and Research* (Second edition; pp. 139-153). New York: Guilford.

McCrae, R. R., & John, O. P. (1992). An introduction to the five-factor model and its applications. *Journal of Personality,* 60, 175-216.

Mount, M. K., & Barrick, M. R. (1995). *Manual for the Personal Characteristics Inventory.* Libertyville, IL: Wonderlic Personnel Test, Inc.

Mount, M. K., & Barrick, M. R. (1998). Five reasons why the "Big Five" article has been frequently cited. *Personnel Psychology,* 51, 849-857.

Mount, M. K., Barrick, M. R., & Stewart, G. L. (1998). Five-factor model of personality and performance in jobs involving interpersonal interactions. *Human Performance,* 11, 145-165.

Mount, M. K., Witt, L. A., & Barrick, M. R. (2000). Incremental validity of empirically keyed biodata scales over GMA and the five-factor personality constructs. *Personnel Psychology,* 53, 299-323.

Neuman, G. A., & Wright, J. (1999). Team effectiveness: Beyond skills and cognitive ability. *Journal of Applied Psychology,* 84, 376-389.

Norman, W. T. (1963). Toward an adequate taxonomy of personality attributes: Replicated factor structure in peer nomination personality ratings. *Journal of Abnormal and Social Psychology,* 66, 574-583.

Nunnally, J. C. 1978. *Psychometric Theory.* New York: McGraw-Hill.

Paunonen, S. V., Jackson, D. N., Trzebinski, J., & Forsterling, F. (1992). Personality structure across cultures: A multi-method evaluation. *Journal of Personality and Social Psychology,* 62, 447-456.

Ree, M. J., Earles, J. A., & Teachout, M. S. (1994). Predicting job performance: Not much more than g. *Journal of Applied Psychology,* 79, 518-524.

Russell, C. (1999). New technologies improve selection. *HR Focus: Special Report on Recruitment & Retention,* S5-S6.

Salgado, J. (1997). The five factor model of personality and job performance in the European community. *Journal of Applied Psychology*, 30-43.

Schmidt, F. L., & Hunter, J. E. (1998). The validity and utility of selection methods in personnel psychology: Practical and theoretical implications of 85 years of research findings. *Psychological Bulletin,* 124, 262-274.

Schmidt, F. L., Hunter, J. E., & Outerbridge, A. N. (1986). Impact of job experience and ability on job knowledge, work sample performance, and supervisory ratings of job performance. *Journal of Applied Psychology,* 71, 432-439.

Stewart, G. L. (1996). Reward structure as a moderator of the relationship between extraversion and sales performance. *Journal of Applied Psychology,* 81, 619-627.

Tupes, E. C., & Christal, R. E. (1958). Stability of personality trait factors obtained under diverse conditions (USAF WADC Tech. Note No. 58-61). Lackland Air Force Base, TX: U. S. Air Force.

Wonderlic Personnel Test, Inc. (1992). *Wonderlic Personnel Test and Scholastic Level Exam: User's Manual.* Libertyville, IL: Wonderlic Personnel Test, Inc.

Chapter II

Beyond Relative Advantage: Factors in End-User Uptake of Computer Supported Cooperative Work

Susan Turner
Napier University, UK

Phil Turner
Napier University, UK

ABSTRACT

Researchers in Information Systems have produced a rich collection of meta-analyses and models of factors influencing the uptake of information technologies. In the domain of CSCW, however, these models have largely been neglected, and while there are many case studies, no systematic account of uptake has been produced. We use findings from Information Systems research to structure a meta-analysis of uptake issues as reported in Computer Supported Cooperative Work (CSCW) case studies, supplemented by a detailed re-examination of one of our own case studies from this perspective. This shows that while there are some factors that seem to be largely specific to CSCW introductions, many of the case study results are very similar to standard IS findings. We conclude by suggesting how the two communities of researchers might build on each other's work.

INTRODUCTION

This paper considers how far established knowledge in the field of Information Systems (IS) about the dimensions underlying the uptake of new technologies can help researchers and practitioners understand uptake in the specific domain of computer supported cooperative work, hereafter CSCW. CSCW is usually treated as a separate domain by its researchers and practitioners, and the community has yet to develop a systematic model of uptake. As we observe at the beginning of section 2, this is a topic where terminology is often ambiguous, but by 'uptake', we simply mean the sustained use of the technology for real work or domestic purposes.

CSCW has emerged as a separate domain of research and practice since (at least) the 1988 CSCW conference held in the USA. Since then US CSCW and GROUP (group working) conferences have been held biennially, interspersed with a European series of conferences from 1989 onwards. Other specialist conferences and journals flourish, and explicitly CSCW papers are also to be found in the more general human computer interaction literature. The boundaries of the domain have been the subject of debate in the CSCW community, but a key distinguishing element is a focus on people using technology with the primary aim of enhancing or enabling collaborative activity rather than on people who work together using shared tools such as a multi-user database. More recently, studies of the collaborative use of home and mobile applications have been reported, so the CSCW literature is no longer confined to the world of 'work'. While CSCW authors offer a variety of explanations for the success or otherwise of such interventions, there are still no overall models of CSCW uptake. (Grudin's widely-cited discussions of groupware failure and challenges for CSCW systems - Grudin, 1998, 1994; Grudin & Poltrock, 1997 - address some uptake issues, but are more concerned with design challenges rather than the integration of the results of the body of case studies.) By contrast, the IS community has produced many meta-analyses and models of technology uptake, and the literature here is extensive. On the whole, these models are not drawn upon in the CSCW case study literature, although there are some notable exceptions: among others, Kraut *et al.* (1994), Orlikowski (1992), Orlikowski and Gash (1994) and Okamura *et al.* (1994), Baker *et al.* (1999). It is worth remarking that these researchers have their roots in the IS community, in contrast to many CSCW authors whose home disciplines are frequently in sociology, psychology or computer science.

As CSCW researchers and practitioners, we were interested to discover how far the existing IS models and dimensions of end-user uptake (as distinct from organisational acceptance) could account for the heterogeneous collection of CSCW case study findings. IS has a much more mature model of user acceptance than has so far emerged in the study of CSCW and it is reasonable to believe that there are sufficient commonalties between the two disciplines to use insights from the former to inform the latter. A related issue is that decision makers (purchasers, IS managers, systems administrators and so forth) need to be able to anticipate potential problems with user acceptance of CSCW systems.

This chapter first briefly reviews current accounts of uptake in IS, then applies the dimensions identified to a meta-analysis of case studies reporting CSCW introductions. We next explore the applicability of IS models in more detail, using the results of one of our own CSCW case studies and conclude by discussing the overall implications of our findings for IS and CSCW researchers and practitioners.

End-user uptake: perspectives from IS and related fields

One of the persistent problems in synthesising and applying research in this field is the inconsistent use of terminology. Terms which may be taken as meaning uptake include: acquisition, adoption, acceptance, implementation, assimilation, routinization, and, of course, use. While it is clear that some can relate only to specific stages – acquisition, for example, is simply purchasing the technology – others are used much more loosely and inconsistently. Adoption, for example, can mean the decision to purchase, or the routine use of technology by end users. However, rather than being sidetracked into this particular debate, we have adopted a fairly catholic approach to this brief review.

We begin with the classic meta-analysis by Tornatzky and Klein (1982) of 75 innovation adoption papers which identified three key innovation characteristics: compatibility *with* existing practice, relative advantage *over* existing practice and complexity. These were found to have the most consistent relationships to innovation adoption where the innovation is, in the broadest sense, any new technology or practice. A similar meta-analysis was reported by Rogers (1983), who added a number of other dimensions including trialability and observability. IS research has sought to apply these general models to the particular context of new information technology, leading to the identification of a number of extra factors which are held to influence uptake. Davis' (1989) technology acceptance model, for example, argues that user perceptions of usefulness and ease of use have a critical influence on acceptance and usage. Much work (of which Moore & Benbasat, 1991; Hebert & Benbasat, 1994; Miller, Rainer & Harper, 1997; Straub, Keil & Brenner, 1997; Loh & Ong, 1998 are among many other instances) extends the now classic models of Tornatztky and Klein, Rogers, and Davis. To take just two examples, Moore and Benbasat differentiate perceptions of relative advantage, compatibility, ease of use, demonstrability of results, effect on image (of the user), visibility, trialability and voluntariness, while Loh and Ong found that perceived usefulness had a positive relationship not only with perceived ease of use, but also duration of use and user satisfaction.

Agarwal, Prasad and Zanino (1996) and Agarwal and Prasad (1998) have taken a slightly different theoretical base, drawing on the three innovation characteristics identified by Tornatzky and Klein. Their studies relate the adoption of new technology (here meaning use by an individual) to perceptions of relative advantage, ease of use and compatibility with existing values and practice. However, two additional moderating dimensions are proposed: the innovativeness of individual users and the media through which potential users become aware of the technology and its features. A field study showed that innovativeness interacted with perceptions of compatibility, but not the other dimensions. Agarwal and Prasad suggest that the cognitive costs of perceived incompatibility are so high that only more innovative individuals will decide to adopt the technology in question. As for media channels, both relatively impersonal channels such as presentations, videotapes and direct interpersonal channels had an effect on perceptions, interpersonal contact having the greater direct effect.

A further influential explanatory model has been critical mass theory, for example Markus (1987). Critical mass theory predicts that the utility of a communications medium to its users will rise with the number of people using the system, particularly when users are important in some way to each other. The meta-review conducted by Prescott and Conger (1995) finds critical mass as an element in inter-organisational IS uptake but not as a strong factor in intra-organisational technology. Additional intra-organisational characteristics identified by Prescott and Conger include management support, the presence of strong innovation champions, user training, organisational characteristics and organisational fit.

Accounting for end-user uptake: the CSCW perspective

Approaches to reporting case studies in the CSCW literature are heterogeneous in the extreme. Accounts range from 'snap-shot' evaluations to longitudinal studies and from controlled quantitative analysis to ethnographic observations. Furthermore, reports often fail to differentiate between stakeholder groups and rarely identify critical success factors or other metrics in advance. Finally, there are still comparatively few *detailed* case studies to draw upon. As a result of these difficulties we have necessarily adopted a fairly broad-brush approach to this part of the review. Since definitions of uptake, where present, were varied, we have operationally defined uptake simply as 'use'.

We have reviewed over 80 case studies reported between 1994 and 2002 drawing upon the principal CSCW conferences and journals (these include the CSCW, ECSCW, Group and CHI conferences, and CSCW the journal) and the

CSCW streams in more general HCI forums. We include only those studies where technology was introduced into real-life organisations, in contrast to trial use under experimental conditions, or workplace studies of collaborative working unsupported by new technologies. The start date of 1994 was selected so that the technology used to support CSCW was sufficiently mature as not to be a compounding factor in its adoption. Figure 1 maps the findings of those CSCW reports which comment on uptake factors to a number of IS dimensions[1] (these data are presented in more detail in tables 1 through 5 at the end of this paper). These are the basic seven dimensions of Moore and Benbasat (1990, 1991) together with other aspects for which there is support in the literature: user expectations and individual innovativeness (e.g. Agarwal *et al*, 1996, 1998 among others), mandated, championed or discretionary use (e.g. Prescott and Conger, 1995) and critical mass (e.g. Markus, 1987). As can be seen from figure 1 below, many case studies make observations which fit comfortably with relative advantage (24), compatibility (18), ease of use (15), critical mass (6), mandated/championed/ discretionary use (8) and innovativeness (6). There is rather less reported evidence of user expectations (4), demonstrability (3), visibility (1), and user image (1) and none for trialability.

Figure 1: Cited factors in CSCW uptake

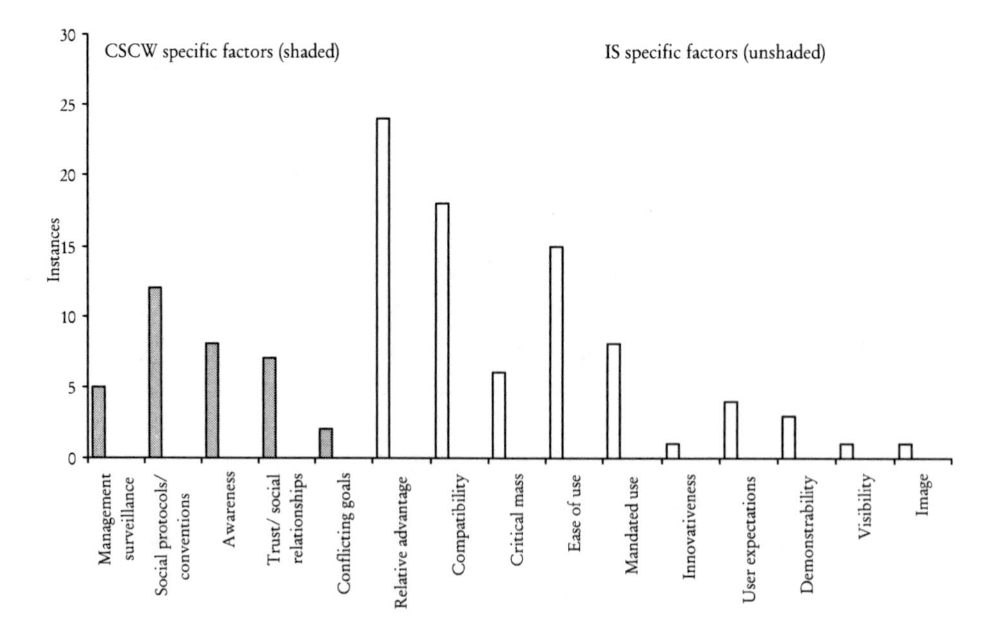

All in all the results of 44 CSCW case study reports (on the evidence reported by their authors) can be accounted for entirely in terms of existing IS models; a further 16 (included in tables 1-7) can be accounted for from a mixture of IS and CSCW dimensions and the remaining 11 more cite CSCW factors alone. The CSCW specific factors are considered below in section 3.1.

CSCW specific dimensions

Those factors found in the above accounts of CSCW uptake which do not fit within the existing IS uptake dimensions are almost entirely related to issues which might be grouped under the umbrella term 'social factors.' (Note that some of these are discussed in the more specialist IS literature, for example Zuboff, 1998 and Rice & Tyler, 1995, but here we are concerned with generic IS uptake models.) These social factors range from concerns over management surveillance to the need for pre-existing social networks. Considering these in turn:

Potential for management surveillance

Concerns about management access to the work of a group or an individual have been identified by a number of authors. Clement (1994) and Lee *et al.* (1997) both note concerns about surveillance and privacy in the deployment of a video-based inter-office awareness tool, while Olson and Teasley (1996) have reported disquiet about the unwelcome potential for monitoring by management with the introduction of collaborative technologies in a distributed automotive design environment. Other related reports are Bowers (1994) and Whittaker (1996).

Trust and the need for a pre-existing network of social relationships

Rocco (1998) argues that trust is a prerequisite for success when a collaborative task involves risk of individualistic or deceitful behaviour by others, presenting empirical data that computer-mediated work can only be successful if an underlying network of social relationships based on face-to-face relationships already exists. Trust is also raised as a factor by Clement (1994), in the context of ownership of information about oneself conveyed through media spaces; Star and Ruhleder (1994) in discussion of the uptake of a shared information system for research biologists, who were reluctant to release valuable early information; Baker *et al.* (1999) noting constraints on the exploitation of high speed networks by media production companies who were potential commercial rivals; and Jancke *et al.* (2001) observing the limited use of an audio-visual link between communal office kitchens. The need for a pre-existing social group *per se* is raised in the studies by Churchill and Bly (1999) of the use of a MUD (Multi-User Dimension) for informal coordination in a software development organisation and O'Connor *et al.* (2001) of a recommender system for moviegoers.

The establishment of social protocols and shared conventions

There are numerous CSCW reports of such issues. Watts *et al.* (1996) report implicit protocols of use in the use of voice loops for shuttle mission control; the development of group norms facilitated the use of an audio-only media space (Hindus *et al.*, 1996); the lack of social conventions impeded use of a system providing awareness of staff whereabouts in an HCI lab (Tollmar, Sandor & Schömer, 1996); common working conventions had to be established between different groups in technologically supported co-working in a ministerial department (e.g., Mambrey & Robinson, 1997; Mark, 1997; Mark *et al.*, 1997; Pankoke-Babatz & Syri, 1997). Lee, Girgensohn and Schlueter, (1997) and Churchill and Bly (1999) note the role of social conventions in the uptake of informal inter-office communication tools; and Grinter (1997b) in her review of workplace studies, cites the development of common social and technical protocols and shared understandings as factors in successful CSCW. Shared conventions were important in overcoming usability flaws in shared workspaces for engineering researchers (Steves *et al.*, 2001). Moving to mobile technologies, a recent study by Longmate and Baber (2002) of the use by students of email and SMS (Short Message Service) for academic-related communication notes that in part, the popularity of SMS could be attribute to its congruence with group norms.

Awareness of what others are doing

The key role of support for the peripheral cues which support mutual awareness is observed by Watts *et al.* (1996) in a study of space shuttle mission control and by Mark, Haake and Streitz (1996) in the context of meeting room support systems. Grinter (1997b) also notes the importance of information afforded by the shared availability of individual work. Similar points are made in the contexts of informal work-based communication via a MUD (Churchill & Bly, 1999); configuration management tools (Grinter, 2000); instant messaging in the work place (Nardi, Whittaker & Bradner, 2000); a shared, electronic multimedia noticeboard for a research group (Greenberg & Rounding, 2001); and in email and SMS communication among students (Longmate and Baber, 2002).

The reconciliation of conflicting goals

The introduction of CSCW can also be obstructed by conflicting goals. Blythin *et al.* (1997) provide an example of this in a banking context, while Herik and

Figure 2: Overlap between IS and CSCW perspectives

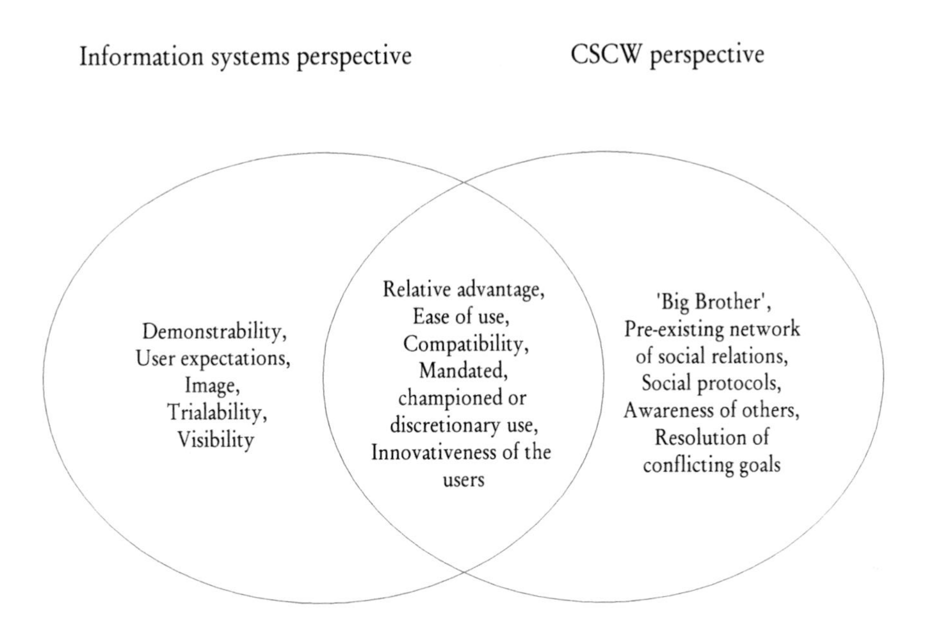

Vreede (1997) observe how a lack of shared goals detracted from the efficacy of group support systems in ministerial policy meetings.

'Missing' IS dimensions in CSCW and the extent of overlap

The CSCW case studies provide no evidence for one of the dimensions identified in the IS literature – trialability – and there is little material on visibility, demonstrability, user expectations and user image. Inevitably, this is partially an artefact of the way the case studies have been reported. We suspect that some of these factors will have been aggregated with more general costs and benefits, but it remains the case that few CSCW researchers have addressed individual characteristics as an element in uptake. Figure 2 is an illustration of the extent to which the dimensions overlap.

So, what does this figure mean? We can speculate that intersection of IS and CSCW perspectives may correspond to the *necessary* conditions of uptake from the viewpoints of the two disciplines. In practice, the separate areas may be more detailed or operationalised aspects of the core dimensions or may reflect the dominating research pre-occupations in the two disciplines. We return to this issue in section 5.

ANALYSING A CSCW CASE STUDY USING THE IS DIMENSIONS

Having demonstrated how established IS models apply to many other CSCW case studies, we now illustrate these issues in more detail in the context of a field study we conducted with a large engineering organisation.

We should stress that the work in question was not undertaken for the purpose of formal hypothesis testing, the construction of new models or the extension or validation of existing theory. Rather, it was a pragmatic pilot trial of collaborative technologies with the dual aims of (i) demonstrating the potential of such technologies for the host organisation and (ii) identifying requirements and issues to be addressed in a more widespread introduction in the organisation or requiring further research. In this approach, the project is typical of much other work in the CSCW community.

The genesis of the CSCW project

The project was concerned to determine what pragmatic combination of low cost, readily available technology and new working practice could meet perceived needs for distributed cooperative working at a major engineering consultancy, hereafter *Metre*. *Metre* operated in the domains of marine engineering, command and control systems and software engineering with clients predominantly from the defence industry. The research discussed in this paper was confined to one particular business area within *Metre*, the Naval Division. Naval Division was largely project-driven with project teams of 3 to 30 or more people, projects typically varying in duration from 6 months to 2 years or more. Team members in some cases were moved to a common location, in others, distributed across several sites. In all such cases, co-ordination was achieved through frequent meetings. Thus travel was a heavy overhead: senior staff and specialist experts (who were shared between projects) were commonly away from their base at least one day a week and frequently as many as four or five days.

At the outset of this study, interviews with senior management elicited the opinion that most staff would be receptive to technological change, although organisational change was recognised to be a more sensitive issue and to require careful handling. There was also some suggestion that since users often did not exploit current technologies to the full, the introduction of CSCW would need to be backed up by substantial training effort. The priorities were seen to be to identify appropriate off-the-shelf facilities, e.g. email and desk-top video conferencing, and then to demonstrate their potential. Their introduction would be the first steps in creating a climate sympathetic to the introduction of CSCW.

Further interviews (25 interviewees) and a substantial questionnaire survey (103 respondents) involving a wide cross-section of staff were undertaken after the initial work with senior management. The overall results showed somewhat mixed expectations of CSCW, but more positive views among senior staff and other frequent travelers. The questionnaires and interviews also generated detailed data about current cooperative activities. A detailed description of the methodology and findings may be found in Turner and Turner (1996).

The pilot introduction of CSCW

Given these preconditions, the next step was to identify a pilot project, which it was hoped would demonstrate the advantages of a move from face-to-face interaction towards technologically supported distributed working. Management at *Metre* selected the Matelot project: the preparation of a huge collaborative bid to upgrade a category of naval warship for the British Ministry of Defence. At its height, Matelot employed a team of some 240 people, who were distributed between sites in Northwest England, Scotland and sites on the south coast of England. Matelot was scheduled to run for 14 months with our trial introduction of CSCW starting three months into the project and lasting eight months.

The tools selected were the then-current versions of Fujitsu DeskTop Conferencing™ (DTC) and Lotus Notes™ DTC supported synchronous working through remote application sharing, a shared electronic whiteboard/flipchart and also includes file transfer. In contrast, Lotus Notes supported asynchronous working by providing a structured, shared information space and integrated email. A number of purpose built Notes applications/databases were also constructed, which were primarily to meet the needs of the project manager. All available users attended a day of demonstrations and hands-on training, with the opportunity to discuss the new tools with developers and the member of *Metre* staff who would be supporting the technology. Several staff could not attend this session and were introduced to the technology individually by the *Metre* support engineer.

The longitudinal evaluation of the pilot

Evaluation methods

The level of input to the evaluation exercise, which could be expected from the users themselves, was severely limited. Further, the work was both security classified and carried out in secure buildings, which meant that ethnographic approaches, with their emphasis on observation of everyday work, were largely impractical. Accordingly, the evaluation techniques planned were:

- structured interviews before the pilot started and towards the end of the trial period, establishing baseline information about users, working practices, and perceptions of the technology;
- minimal records by users of communications to determine patterns of use and changing communication practice;
- automatic logging of technology use;
- unobtrusive observation of the technology in use.

In practice, time constraints on users at Metre prevented the full implementation of even these techniques – very few users logged their communications - so a pragmatic and opportunistic approach had to be adopted. For example, *ad-hoc* training and informal discussion proved a good source of alternative background information.

The structured interviews remained an important source of data. Questions raised with users addressed general issues such as benefits achieved, ease of use and the fit between the technology and the pre-existing working procedures which were derived from the IS and CSCW literature. These were supplemented by follow-up questions to specific issues introduced by users in briefing about the technology prior to its introduction. Each interview concluded with an open-ended question designed to elicit any other outstanding issues.

Results of the evaluation

Despite the apparently promising scope for CSCW, after eight months of continuous availability and technical support the only application to have been used seriously was Lotus Notes email. This had been exploited primarily as a means of transferring files between Northwest England and Scotland. However, users viewed this very positively, several commenting in evaluation interviews that email had been *essential* to the team's work, and that its use for file transfer had avoided many car journeys between Northwest England and Scotland.

Users were asked in interviews to score the technology as a whole for usefulness on a scale of 1 to 5, 5 being the most positive score, before and after use. Somewhat surprisingly, since only email had been used, mean overall perceived usefulness increased from 3.5 to 4.5. The post-experience interviews (conducted with 13 of the original 14 users, and a further 5 who had joined the project during the pilot period) also elicited a number of expressed reasons for the lack of uptake of the remaining tools. Figure 3 is a plot of the five concerns most frequently voiced about the CSCW technology as a whole.

The suggestions elicited from the interviews as to how the pilot might have been improved echo this data. The underlying issues as stated by the interviewees reflect problems with access to the technology (although there is no evidence to suggest that if users had been equipped with individual desktop tools, that the other services would have been used) and its fit with current work practice. Engineering designers at *Metre* used computers as a special purpose tool, rather their primary resource for work. One consequence was that the designers working on the project did not have a computer each. Other work practice related issues reflect that the group selected for the pilot was part of a very much larger project, with established tools, working methods and procedures, and that since much the project's work was security classified, only some of the group's business could be transacted using CSCW running over public communications media.

Analysing the findings

How, then, do the evaluation findings in the particular case of Matelot fit with the IS and CSCW dimensions discussed above?

The influence of *relative advantage* can be seen in the adoption of email. Users specifically commented in evaluation interviews that sending an email was considerably better than driving 120 miles by car simply to deliver an urgent file. Evidence from observation suggests that for other tools, less advantage was

Figure 3: The five most frequently voiced concerns

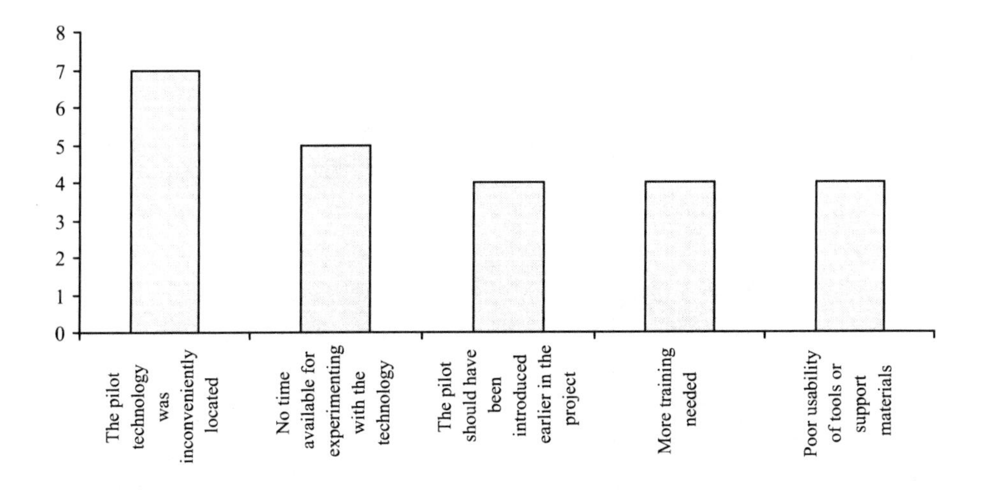

afforded. For example, some users had to travel to the other site for reasons outwith the project work, so would take care of Matelot business in the course of the same trip. This negated much of the potential advantage of synchronous tools such as application sharing.

The *complexity / ease of use* dimension clearly lies behind elicited complaints about the complexity of the Lotus Notes interface, the procedures for starting-up the software, and the manuals supplied to pilot participants.

Lack of compatibility was evident with both the artefacts used and organisational structures, systems and procedures. At Metre, designers exploited a number of design media, computers being but one. For example, designs were frequently realised on multiple sheets of A0 paper (which measure 1680 x 2376 mm), laid out on large tables allowing the designers to move between the representations with ease. It is difficult to imagine how this particular working practice could have been supported during the pilot. The technology was also disjoint from existing computer-based technical and organisational systems, and associated procedures. The pilot project was only part of the larger Matelot enterprise, and procedures and systems had been in place for some time. Among other things, this meant that the technology could not be used when working with members of the wider project, nor indeed with colleagues in other parts of Metre – not all project team members worked on Matelot 100% of their time - a feature which could also be considered as an aspect of *critical mass*. Even entirely within Matelot, work on security-classified materials could not be supported with the technology. All this entailed pilot users on Matelot contending with two incompatible modes of working.

Once again, the use of email produced immediately *demonstrable* results, discussed here under relative advantage, above. Application sharing might have been similarly demonstrable, had other factors not detracted from its usefulness. However, tools such as the Lotus Notes discussion databases would only have produced a useful result after they had been in use for some time by a number of participants (this point is related to *critical mass* but contradicts Prescott and Conger's findings that critical mass is not strong factor in intra-organisational technology.). This immediacy of tangible benefits again maps onto demonstrability of results.

A lack of *trialability* may also have contributed to lack of uptake. While the tools themselves were reasonably supportive of user experimentation, one of the most common comments was that pressure of work meant that there was no spare time at all to do this.

General end-user *expectations* at Metre as elicited from the requirements interviews and the questionnaire, together with expectations of usefulness obtained from the pre-pilot interviews, were a good predictor of the behaviour of the particular group studied in the pilot implementation. The manner in which users conceptualised the applications (*cf.* technological frames, Orlikowski and Gash, 1994) may have had an influence: there is evidence to suggest that users conceptualised the tools as a means for improving the transmission of materials for co-working rather than for collaborative design itself. For example, users would telephone someone at the other site to warn them that a file was about to be sent, email the file, then telephone again to discuss the contents of the file rather than viewing and editing the material together using the application sharing tool. However, incidents such as these may be just as easily explained by the perceived usability problems.

While we have no systematic evidence of the *innovativeness* of the Matelot team, senior staff interviewed at the early requirements stage had mentioned several perceived cultural factors, which may have had a bearing on this trait. For example, many experienced design engineers felt that computers were detrimental to good conceptual design and some of Metre's consultants were former Royal Navy officers who were regarded as 'traditionalists' by their co-workers.

Finally, while a senior manager *championed* the pilot introduction of CSCW, he proved to be too time pressured to maintain enthusiasm.

However, while the low level of exploitation can largely be explained by established IS findings on uptake, there are some further factors involved, which mirror other CSCW fieldwork results. Perhaps the most obvious from the evaluation data is the issue of *shared conventions*. The Matelot project did indeed have shared conventions, but these had been established for some months before the CSCW intervention, and therefore naturally did not encompass how the technology should be used. Moreover, since most of the project was not supported by the new tools, end users in the pilot groups had not only to develop new conventions for themselves, but also to switch to a different set of conventions when working with colleagues in the wider project. *Awareness* was also a factor, not so much as moment-by-moment awareness of co-workers' activity, but evident in the way in which pilot end users would exploit visits to the other site to catch up with events and tacitly remind colleagues of their continued existence, albeit at 200 kilometres distance.

DISCUSSION AND SOME SUGGESTIONS FOR FURTHER WORK

A number of issues arise from the review and analyses we have conducted.

Using the IS uptake literature in CSCW research

It appears to be the case that CSCW research, in the quite proper emphasis on the needs and characteristics of varied stakeholder *groups*, has so far neglected the varied characteristics of the *individuals* comprising those groups. Factors such as individual innovativeness and expectations merit more consideration in researching user behaviour in the context of collaborative technologies, and may help to explain some of the widely differing results between apparently similar CSCW interventions. A further consideration for CSCW research is the apparent explanation of many case study results by IS models. As Plowman *et al.* (1995) note in their review of workplace studies, there is no need to approach the work *ab initio* each time an opportunity to either introduce or evaluate CSCW presents itself. Rather, case studies in this domain could more profitably focus on a deeper investigation of those 'social factors' where there is little empirical evidence from the IS work, rather than establishing yet again that technologies are used most when they afford relative advantage.

Expanding IS models of uptake

Conventional office technologies are increasingly collaboration aware. If generic IS uptake models are to take full account of this, some extension appears to be required. While some of the 'social factors' discussed above may be co-extensive with dimensions such as compatibility (defined in slightly different ways by different authors), others seem to be distinct issues, and would repay systematic investigation in the more formal IS tradition.

ACKNOWLEDGMENTS

This research was supported by the British Department of Trade and Industry and the Engineering and Physical Science Research Council, which we gratefully acknowledge. We also thank the reviewers of an earlier version of this material for their helpful and constructive comments.

REFERENCES

Ackerman, M. S. (1994). Augmenting the organizational memory: A field study of answer garden. In R. Furuta & C. Neuwirth (eds.), *CSCW'94,* (pp. 243-252). New York: ACM Press.

Ackerman, M. S. & Palen, L. (1996). The zephyr help instance: Promoting on-going activity in a CSCW system. In M. J. Tauber *et al.* (eds.), *The*

Proceedings of CHI 96 (pp. 268-275). New York: ACM Press.

Agarwal, R. & Prasad, J. (1998). The antecedents and consequents of user perceptions in information technology adoption. *Decision Support Systems*, 22, 15-29.

Agarwal, R., Prasad, J., & Zanino, M. C. (1996). Training experiences and usage intentions: A field study of a graphical user interface, *International Journal of Human Computer Studies*, *45*(2), 215-241.

Baker, E., Geirland, J., Fisher, T., & Chandler, A. (1999). Media production: Towards creative collaboration using communication networks. *Computer Supported Cooperative Work*, 8, 303-332.

Bardram, J. E. (1997). I love the system - I just don't use it. In S. C. Hayne & W. Prinz (eds.), *Proceedings of Group '97* (pp. 251-260). New York: ACM Press.

Bentley, R., Hughes, J. A., Randall, D., Rodden, T., Sawyer, P., Shapiro, D., & Sommerville, I. (1992). Ethnographically-informed systems design for air traffic control. In *Proceedings of the ACM Conference on Computer Supported Cooperative Work (CSCW'92)* (pp. 123-129). Toronto, Ontario: ACM Press.

Bikson, T. K. & Eveland, J. D. (1996). Groupware implementation: Reinvention in the sociotechnical frame. In M. S. Ackerman (eds.), *Proceedings of CSCW '96* (pp. 428-437). New York: ACM Press.

Blythin, S., Hughes, J. A., Kristoffersen, S., Rodden, T., & Rouncefield, M. (1997). Recognising 'success' and 'failure': evaluating groupware in a commercial context. In S. C. Hayne and W. Prinz (eds.), *Proceedings of Group '97* (pp. 39-46) .New York: ACM Press.

Bowers, J. (1994). The work to make a network work: Studying CSCW in action. In R. Furuta & C. Neuwirth (eds.), *Proceedings of CSCW '94* (pp. 287-298). New York: ACM Press.

Churchill, E. F. & Bly, S. (1999). It's all in the words: Supporting work activities with lightweight tools. In S. Payne (ed.) *Proceedings of Group '99* (pp. 40-49). New York: ACM Press.

Clement, A. (1994). Considering privacy in the development of multi-media communications. *Computer Supported Cooperative Work*, 2, 67-88.

Davis, F. D. (1989). Perceived usefulness, perceived ease of use, and user acceptance of information technology. *MIS Quarterly, 13*(3), 319-340.

Eveland, J. D., Blanchard, A., Brown, W., & Mattocks, J. (1994). The role of "help networks" in facilitating use of CSCW tools. In R. Furuta & C. Neuwirth (eds.), *CSCW '94* (pp. 265-274). New York: ACM Press.

Greenberg, S. & Rounding, M. (2001). The notification collage: Posting information to public and personal displays. In J. A. Jacko, A. Sears, M. Beaudouin-Lafon & R. J. K. Jacob (eds.) *Proceedings of CHI 2001* (pp. 514-521). New York: ACM Press.

Grinter, R. E. (1997a). Doing software development: occasions for automation and formalisation. In J. A. Hughes *et al.* (eds.), *ECSCW'97 - Proceedings of The Fifth European Conference on Computer Supported Cooperative Work* (pp. 173-187). Dordrecht, Kluwer.

Grinter, R. E. (1997b). From workplace to development: What have we learned so far and where do we go. In S. C. Hayne & W. Prinz (eds.), *Proceedings of Group'97* (pp. 231-240). New York: ACM Press.

Grinter, E. (2000). Workflow systems: Occasions for success and failure. *Computer Supported Cooperative Work,* 9, 189-214.

Grudin, J. (1988). Why CSCW applications fail: Problems in the design and evaluation of organization interfaces. In *Proceedings of CSCW '88,* New York: ACM Press.

Grudin, J. (1994). Groupware and social dynamics: Eight challenges for developers. *Communications of the ACM* 37, 93-105.

Grudin, J. & Palen, L. (1995). Why groupware succeeds: discretion or mandate. In H. Marmolin, Y. Sundblat & K. Schmidt (eds.), *Proceedings of ECSCW'95* (pp. 263-278). Dordrecht, Kluwer.

Grudin, J. & Poltrock, S. E. (1997). Computer-supported cooperative work and groupware. In M. V. Zelkowitz (ed.), *Advances in Computing*. (pp. 269-320). Academic Press.

Harper, R. H. R. & Carter, K. (1994). Keeping people apart, *Computer Supported Cooperative Work*, 2, 199-207.

Harper, R. H. R. (1996). Why people do and don't wear active badges: A case study. *Computer Supported Cooperative Work,* 4, 297-318.

Hebert, M. & Benbasat, I. (1994). Adopting information technology in hospitals: The relationships between attitudes/expectations and behavior. *Hospital and Health Services Administration,* 39(3), 369-383.

Hepsø, V. (1997). The social construction and visualiation of a new Norweigan offshore installation. In J. A. Hughes *et al.* (eds.), *ECSCW'97 - Proceedings of The Fifth European Conference on Computer Supported Cooperative Work* (pp. 109-124). Dordrecht, Kluwer.

Herik, K. W. v. d. & Vreede, G.-J. d. (1997). GSS for cooperative policymaking: No trivial matter. In S. C. Hayne & W. Prinz (eds.), *Proceedings of Group'97* (pp. 148-157). New York: ACM Press.

Hindus, D., Ackerman, M. A., Mainwaring, S., & Starr, B. (1996). Thunderwire: A field study of and audio-only media space. In M. S. Ackerman (ed.),

Proceedings of CSCW '96 (pp. 238-247). New York: ACM Press.

Jancke, J. Venolia, G.D., Grudin, J., Cadiz, J.J., & Gupta, A. (2001). Linking public spaces: Technical and spatial issues. In J.A. Jacko, A. Sears, M. Beaudouin-Lafon & R.J.K. Jacob (eds.) *Proceedings of CHI 2001*. (pp. 530-537). New York: ACM Press.

Kraut, R. E., Cool, C., Rice, R. E., & Fish, R. S. (1994). Life and death of new technology: Task, utility and social influences on the use of a communication medium. In R. Furuta & C. Neuwirth (eds.), *Proceedings of CSCW'94* (pp. 13-21). New York: ACM.

Lee, A., Girgensohn, A., & Schlueter, K. (1997). NYNEX portholes: Initial user reactions and redesign implications. In S. C. Hayne & W. Prinz (eds.), *Proceedings of Group'97* (pp. 385-394). New York: ACM Press.

Loh, L. & Ong, Y.-S. (1998). The adoption of Internet-based stock trading: a conceptual framework and empirical results. *Journal of Information Technology,* 13, 81-94.

Longmate, E. & Baber, C. (2002). A comparison of text messaging and e-mail support for digital communities. In X. Faulkner, J. Finlay & F. Détienne (eds.) *Proceedings of HCI 2002* (pp. 69-87). London: Springer,

Losada, M., Sanchez, P., & Noble, E. E. (1990). Collaborative technology and group process feedback: Their impact on interactive sequences in meetings. In Ed., *Proceedings of the Conference on Computer Supported Cooperative Work (CSCW '90),* Los Angeles, California: ACM Press.

Mambrey, P. & Robinson, M. (1997). Understanding the role of documents in the hierarchical flow of work. In S. C. Hayne & W. Prinz (eds.), *Proceedings of Group'97*. New York: ACM Press.

Mark, G. (1997). Merging multiple perspectives in groupware use: Intra- and intergroup conventions. In S. C. Hayne & W. Prinz (eds.), *Proceedings of Group'97*. (pp. 19-28). New York: ACM Press.

Mark, G., Fuchs, L., & Sohlenkamp, M. (1997). Supporting groupware conventions through contextual awareness. In J. A. Hughes *et al.* (eds.), *ECSCW'97 - Proceedings of The Fifth European Conference on Computer Supported Cooperative Work* (pp. 253-268). Dordrecht, Kluwer.

Mark, G., Haake, J. M., & Streitz, N. A. (1996). Hypermedia structures and the division of labor in meeting room collaboration. In M. S. Ackerman (ed.), *Proceedings of CSCW '96* (pp. 170-179). New York; ACM Press.

Markus, M. L. (1987). Towards a "critical mass" theory of interactive media: Universal access, interdependence and diffusion, *Communication Research,* 14, 491-511.

Miller, M. D., Rainer, R. K., & Harper, J. (1997). The unidimensionality, validity and reliability of Moore and Benbasat's relative advantage and compatibility scales. *Journal of Computer Information Systems,* 1, 38-46.

Monk, A.F. & Watts, L. (1999). Telemedical consultation in primary care: A case study in CSCW design. In M.A. Sasse & C. Johnson (eds.) *Proceedings of Interact '99* (pp. 367-374). Amsterdam: IOS Press.

Moore, G. C. & Benbasat, I. (1991). Development of an instrument to measure the perceived characteristics of adopting an information technology innovation. *Information Systems Research,* 2(3),192-222.

Moran, T. P., Chiu, P., Harrison, S., Kurtenbach, G., Minneman, S., & Melle, W. v. (1996). Evolutionary engagement in an ongoing collaborative work process: A case study. In M. S. Ackerman (ed.), *Proceedings of CSCW '96* (pp. 150-159).New York: ACM Press.

Mosier, J. N. & Tammaro, S. G. (1997). When are group scheduling tools useful? *CSCW,* 6, 53-70.

Nardi, B., Whittaker, S., & Bradner, E. Interaction and outeraction: Instant messaging in action. In W. Kellogg & S. Whittaker (eds.) *Proceedings of CSCW'00* (pp. 79-88). New York: ACM Press.

O'Connor, M., Cosley, D., Konstan, J. A., & Riedl, J. (2001). PolyLens: A recommender system for groups of users. In W. Prinz, M. Jarke, Y. Rogers, K. Schmidt & V. Wulf (eds.) *Proceedings of ECSCW 2001* (pp. 199-218). Dordrecht, Kluwer.

Okamura, K., Fujimoto, M., Orlikowski, W., & Yates, J. (1994). Helping CSCW applications succeed: The role of mediators in context of use. In R. Furuta & C. Neuwirth (eds.), *CSCW'94* (pp. 55-66). New York: ACM Press.

Olson, J. S. & Teasley, S. (1996). Groupware in the wild: Lessons learned from a year of virtual collaboration. In M. S. Ackerman (eds.), *Proceedings of CSCW '96* (pp. 419-427). New York: ACM Press.

Orlikowski, W. J. (1992). Learning from notes: Organizational issues in groupware implementation. In J. Turner & R. Kraut (eds.), *Proceedings of the ACM Conference on Computer Supported Cooperative Work (CSCW'92*) (pp. 362-369). Toronto, Ontario: ACM Press.

Orlikowski, W. J. & Gash, D. C. (1994). Technological frames: Making sense of information technology in organisations. *ACM Transactions on Information Systems 12*(2): 174-207.

Palen, L., Salzman, M., & Youngs, E. (2000). Going wireless: Behavior and practice of new mobile phone users. In W. Kellogg & S. Whittaker (eds.), *Proceedings of CSCW'00* (pp. 201-210). New York: ACM Press.

Pankoke-Babatz, U. & Syri, A. (1997). Collaborative workspaces for time deferred electronic collaboration. In S. C. Hayne & W. Prinz (eds.),

Proceedings of Group '97 (pp. 187-196). New York: ACM Press.

Plowman, L., Rogers, Y., & Ramage, M. (1995). What are workplace studies for? In H. Marmolin, Y. Sundblad & K. Schmidt (eds.), *Proceedings of ECSCW'95* Kluwer.

Prescott, M. B. & Conger, S. A. (1995). Information technology innovations: a classification by IT locus of impact and research approach. *Data Base Advances, 26*(2 & 3), 20-41.

Prinz, W. & Kolvenbach, S. (1996). Support for workflows in a ministerial environment. In M. S. Ackerman (ed.), *Proceedings of CSCW '96* (pp. 199-208). New York: ACM Press.

Rice, R. E. & Tyler, J. (1995). Individual and organisational influences on voice mail use and evaluation. *Behaviour and Information Technology,* 6, 329-341.

Rocco, E. (1998). Trust breaks down in electronic contexts but can be repaired by some face-to-face contact. In C.-M. Karat *et al.* (eds.), *The Proceedings of CHI'98* (pp. 469-502). New York: ACM Press.

Rogers, E. M. (1983). *Diffusion of Innovations.* New York: The Free Press.

Rogers, Y. (1994). Exploring obstacles: Integrating CSCW in evolving applications. In R. Furuta & C. Neuwirth (eds.), *CSCW'94* (pp. 67-78). New York: ACM Press.

Sanderson, D. (1994). Mediating collaborative research? *Computer Supported Cooperative Work,* 2, 41-65.

Spellman, P. J., Mosier, J. N., Deus, L. M., & Carlson, J. A. (1997). Collaborative Virtual Workspace. In S. C. Hayne & W. Prinz (eds.), *Proceedings of Group'97* (pp. 197-203). New York: ACM Press.

Star, S. L. & Ruhleder, K. (1994). Steps towards an ecology of infrastructure: complex problems in design and access for large-scale collaborative systems. In R. Furuta & C. Neuwirth (eds.), *CSCW'94* (pp. 253-264). New York: ACM Press.

Steves, M.P., Morse, E., Gutwin, C., & Greenberg, S. (2001). A comparison of usage evaluation and inspection methods for assessing groupware usability. In C. Ellis & I. Zigurs (eds.), *Proceedings of Group'01* (pp. 125-134). New York: ACM Press.

Straub, D., Keil, M., & Brenner, W. (1997). Testing the technology acceptance model across cultures: A three country study. *Information & Management,* 33, 1-11.

Suchman, L. A. & Trigg, R. H. (1991). Understanding practice: Video as a medium for reflection and design. In J. Greenbaum & M.Kyng (eds.), *Design at Work: Cooperative Design of Computer Systems* (pp. 65-89). Hillsdale, NJ: Lawrence Erlbaum Associates.

Tammaro, S. G., Mosier, J. N., Goodwin, N. C., & Spitz, G. (1997). Collaborative writing is hard to support: A field study of collaborative writing. *CSCW,* 6, 19-51.

Tang, J. C. & Isaacs, E. (1993). Why do users like video? *CSCW*, 1,163-196.

Tang, J. C., Isaacs, E. A., & Rua, M. (1994). Supporting distributed groups with a montage of lightweight interactions. In R. Furuta & C. Neuwirth (eds.), *CSCW'94* (pp. 23-34). New York: ACM Press.

Tollmar, K., Sandor, O., & Schömer, A. (1996). Supporting social awareness @ work, design and experience. In M. S. Ackerman (eds.), *Proceedings of CSCW '96* (pp. 298-307). New York: ACM Press.

Tornatzky, L. G. & Klein, K. J. (1982). Innovation characteristics and innovation adoption-implementation: A meta-analysis of findings. *IEEE Transaction on Engineering Management, 29*(1), 28-45.

Turner, S. & Turner, P. (1996). Expectations and experiences of CSCW in an engineering environment. *Collaborative Computing, 1*(4), 237-254.

Van de Ven, A. H. & Delbecq, A. L. (1976). Determinants of coordination modes within organizations. *American Sociological Review,* 41 (April), 322-338.

Watts, J., Woods, D. D., Corban, J., Patterson, E. S., Kerr, R. L., & Hicks, L. C. (1996). Voice loops as cooperative aids in space shuttle mission control. In M. S. Ackerman (ed.), *Proceedings of CSCW '96* (pp. 48-56). New York: ACM Press.

Whittaker, S. (1996). Talking to strangers: An evaluation of the factors affecting electronic collaboration. In M. S. Ackerman (ed.), *Proceedings of CSCW '96* (pp. 409-418). New York: ACM Press.

Whittaker, S. & Schwarz, H. (1999). Meetings of the board: The impact of scheduling medium on long term group coordination in software development. *Computer Supported Cooperative Work,* 8, 175-205.

Zuboff, S. (1998). *In the Age of the Smart Machine.* Oxford: Heinemann.

ENDNOTE

[1] Note that many case studies map to more than one dimension.

APPENDIX: EVIDENCE OF THE IS DIMENSIONS OF UPTAKE IN CSCW CASE STUDIES

Table 1: Relative advantage – perceptions of advantage over the current practice

Authors	CSCW case study summary
Baker *et al.* (1999)	Fast network for media production firms: increased cost but savings in time and enhanced productivity; differential benefits for different industry sectors.
Bardram (1997)	Co-working supported by hospital information systems: factors affecting use included adding minor functionality, which nonetheless adds useful benefits.
Blythin *et al* (1997)	CSCW in banking: amount of extra work was a factor in the limited success of the project.
Churchill and Bly (1999)	Text-based MUD in software organisation: afforded structured but flexible lightweight communication.
Greenberg and Rounding (2001)	Multimedia shared noticeboard for technology research group: used only when extended outside physical environment; flexible communication.
Grinter (1997a)	Software engineering: workflow tools welcomed provided the 'right' work is automated, thus easing tiresome everyday tasks.
Grinter (2000)	Configuration management tools: advantages included time savings, reliable information, support for individual as well as team work.
Hepsø (1997)	Shared work process information for an oil installation: usage was linked to a strong need for asynchronous communication between offshore workers.
Jancke *et al.* (2001)	Audio-video links between communal office kitchens: limited success because few real perceived benefits.
Monk and Watts (1999)	Telemedicine consultations between GPs (with patients) and specialists: a negative factor was the extra work caused by running the equipment.
Mosier and Tammaro (1997)	Group scheduling tools in a geographically distributed department: strong need to streamline meeting organisation.
O'Connor *et al.* (2001)	Group recommender system for movie-goers: some users felt recommendations not sufficiently worth while to justify effort required.
Nardi, Whittaker and Bradner (2000)	Instant messaging among technology developers: less intrusive and more flexible than phone or email.
Olson and Teasley (1996)	Collaborative tools for distributed automotive design: reasons for partial adoption included extra work and lack of incentive to contribute to databases.
Palen, Salzman and Youngs (2000)	New mobile phone users: enhanced mobility, accessibility, safety and coordination with others.
Rogers (1994)	CSCW in a travel centre: a variant of 'extra work', impact of failure to maintain housekeeping procedures much greater than for single user systems.
Sanderson (1994)	Desktop videoconferencing in collaborative research: very limited adoption partially due to lack of need for interactive communication outside meetings.
Spellman *et al* (1997)	CSCW in a large distributed software R&D organisation: factors in success included the need to interact frequently and rapidly.
Star and Ruhleder (1994)	Specialist shared information system for biologists: usage related to perceived usefulness of the information provided.
Steves *et al.* (2001)	Shared workspace for distributed research engineers: many usability problems but a significant improvement over previous collaboration media.
Tammaro *et al* (1997)	Collaborative writing tool for a geographically dispersed department: factors in partial uptake included differential extra work and benefits.
Tang *et al* (1994)	Communication tools applications for software engineers: factors affecting usage included extra effort and extra benefits for those in different buildings.
Whittaker (1996)	Lotus Notes at Lotus: usage in part depended on extent of competition from other communications media.
Whittaker and Schwarz (1999)	Electronic schedulers vs. wallboards for software team coordination: wallboard more 'real', flexible and credible; scheduler better for distributed working and capture of previous versions.

Table 2: Ease of use – as perceived by end users, also perceived complexity

Authors	**CSCW case study summary**
Ackerman and Palen (1996)	Online collaborative help system: success could be partially attributed to its technical simplicity.
Greenberg and Rounding (2001)	Multimedia shared noticeboard for technology research group: trade-off between consumption of screen space and information displayed.
Grinter (1997a)	Software engineering: uptake of workflow tools related to perceived usability/convenience
Grudin and Palen (1995)	Shared diary applications: uptake partially attributed to improved usability
Jancke *et al.* (2001)	Audio-video links between communal office kitchens: negative factors included audio quality and usability generally.
Moran *et al* (1996)	Meeting capture tools: importance of ease of use and understandable representations in uptake.
Nardi, Whittaker and Bradner (2000)	Instant messaging among technology developers: undemanding in use for lightweight communications.
O'Connor *et al.* (2001)	Group recommender system for movie-goers: use discouraged by UI flaws, general ease of use problems.
Palen, Salzman and Youngs (2000)	New mobile phone users: usage constrained by lack of understanding of technology and billing regimes.
Sanderson (1994)	Desktop videoconferencing in collaborative research: very limited adoption partially ascribed to usability problems and a low degree of technical support.
Star and Ruhleder (1994)	Specialist shared information system for biologists: effects of usability and convenience of the application and the underlying operating system on usage.
Steves *et al.* (2001)	Shared workspace for distributed research engineers: many usability problems.
Tang *et al* (1994)	Communication tools applications for software engineers: factors affecting usage included usability and robustness.
Tollmar *et al* (1996)	Support for social awareness in an HCI lab: reports the influence of usability and convenience on uptake.

Table 3: Critical mass – the participation of sufficient users to make use of the system worthwhile

Authors	**CSCW case study summary**
Grudin and Palen (1995)	Shared diary applications: initial usage predicated upon critical mass after which peer pressure may effectively enforce uptake.
Kraut *et al.* (1994)	Two competing video-based communication systems in a research lab: critical mass was the best explanation of why one system survived and the other did not.
Mosier and Tammaro (1997)	Group scheduling tools in a geographically distributed department: otherwise successful use limited by the difficulty of communicating with those not on the system.
Spellman *et al.* (1997)	CSCW in a large distributed software R&D organisation: success factors included overlapping teams such that most people used the tools and a core set of habitual users.
Tollmar *et al.*(1996)	Support for social awareness in an HCI lab: uptake restricted by the unavailability of the system outside the pilot group.
Whittaker (1996)	Lotus Notes at Lotus: critical mass, characterised as diversity of users and large databases, encouraged participation.

Table 4: Compatibility – the degree of 'organisational fit' between the new and old system in terms of working practice, values and needs

Authors	CSCW case study summary
Ackerman (1994)	Organisational memory system for software engineers: reports a need to preserve the visible status of contributing experts.
Ackerman and Palen (1996)	Online collaborative help system: success partially attributed to 'social mechanisms in place for maintaining the sociality'.
Baker *et al.* (1999)	Fast network for media production firms: use governed partially by compatibility with existing modes of working.
Bardram (1997)	Co-working supported by hospital information systems: factors affecting use included ensuring tools supported existing practice and were integrated with existing IS systems.
Bowers (1994)	CSCW in a UK government computer agency: notes *inter alia*, that this depends on sensitivity to existing practice.
Grinter (1997b)	Review of CSCW workplace studies: among other factors in uptake, cites the preservation of status cues.
Grinter (2000)	Configuration management tools: observed to be highly compatible with previous tools and software development practice.
Harper and Carter (1994)	Support for collaboration between architects and engineers in a building project: observes that such ventures only work if collaboration is genuinely desired.
Longmate and Baber (2002)	E-mail and SMS use for academic purposes among students: compatible with existing communications habits.
Monk and Watts (1999)	Telemedicine consultations between GPs (with patients) and specialists: use encouraged by a close fit with current medical practice.
Moran *et al.* (1996)	Meeting capture tools: notes the importance of fit with existing practice.
Olson and Teasley (1996)	Collaborative technologies for distributed automotive design: reasons for partial adoption included the fact that not all tasks were supported by the tools.
Palen, Salzman and Youngs (2000)	New mobile phone users: use encouraged by compatibility with patterns of work and domestic life.
Pankoke-Babatz & Syri (1997)	CSCW for distributed staff in government ministry: shared workspaces successful where the work was not highly prescribed or sequenced. Also a need for shared conventions.
Prinz and Kolvenbach (1996)	CSCW for distributed staff in government ministry: requirement for integration with paper documents, also the need for an evolutionary design and implementation process.
Tammaro *et al* (1997)	Collaborative writing tool for a geographically dispersed department: factors in partial uptake included support for both individual and group working and task complexity.
Tang and Isaacs (1993)	Videoconferencing for software engineers: liked by users because of its support for collaborative process, as contrasted with collaborative product.
Tang *et al* (1994)	Communication tools applications for software engineers: factors affecting usage included integration with existing tools and compatibility with existing privacy norms.

Table 5: Innovativeness of users

Baker *et al.* (1999)	Fast network for media production firms: more use made by companies, which found innovative applications for the technology.
Bowers (1994)	CSCW in a UK government computer agency: a pronounced reluctance to experiment influenced uptake
Okamura *et al.* (1994)	Computer conferencing in a research and development laboratory: expert users both adapted the technology and influenced patterns of use.
Orlikowski and Gash (1994)	Lotus Notes in a management consultancy: individual willingness or otherwise to collaborate as a factor in uptake.
Sanderson (1994)	Desktop videoconferencing in collaborative research: very limited adoption partially ascribed to the individual attitudes, some users unwilling to explore new facilities.
Tammaro et al. (1997)	Collaborative writing tool for a geographically dispersed department: not strictly innovativeness, but disappointing uptake in part due to collaborativeness of individuals

Table 6: Mandated, championed or discretionary use

Baker *et al.* (1999)	Fast network for media production firms: adoption facilitated by change-agents.
Bikson and Eveland (1996)	GDSS at the World Bank: factors influencing use include involvement of a high level champion.
Blythin *et al* (1997)	CSCW in banking: role of management support as a factor in partial success
Churchill and Bly (1999)	Text-based MUD in software organisation: use fostered by *de facto* organisational support.
Eveland *et al* (1994)	CSCW in academic departments: important role of local user experts or product champions in adoption.
Grinter (2000)	Configuration management tools: training and discussion sessions before implementation.
Grudin and Palen (1995)	Observe that upper management advocacy is the key element in large scale adoption.
Hepsø (1997)	Shared work process information for an oil installation: Strong and committed management support a key factor in the success of the project.

Table 7: Less reported evidence

Authors	**CSCW case study summary**
Visibility – perceptions of the tools as visible and salient parts of the change process	
Bikson and Eveland (1996)	GDSS at the World Bank: factors influencing uptake included that the presentation of the new tools was explicitly as a pilot trial.
Demonstrability of results – the immediacy and tangibility of benefits achieved	
Bowers (1994)	CSCW in a UK government computer agency: the 'work to make the network work' was a major factor in adoption.
Moran *et al.* (1996)	Meeting capture tools: the provision of indexing tools was found to offer immediate advantage in the successful introduction of the system.
Tollmar *et al.* (1996)	Support for social awareness in an HCI lab: uptake was restricted by insufficient unambiguous information as to the whereabouts of co-workers.
User expectations – of the system and how it will affect everyday working life	
Grinter (1997b)	Review of CSCW workplace studies: among other factors in uptake, cites the influence of perceptions/expectations.
Harper (1996)	'Active badges' in research laboratories: factors affecting usage included perceptions of the badges as symbolic of organisational loyalties and commitment to the project itself.
Orlikowski and Gash (1994)	Lotus Notes in a management consultancy: differential uptake between stakeholder groups explained in terms of users' 'technological frames' or expectations of purpose.
Palen, Salzman and Youngs (2000)	New mobile phone users: expectations from use of landlines conflicted with design features of mobile phone.
Image – enhancement or the reverse of user image	
Palen, Salzman and Youngs (2000)	New mobile phone users: worries about being seen to have succumbed to peer pressure.

Chapter III

The Roles of Computer Self-Efficacy and Outcome Expectancy in Influencing the Computer End-User's Organizational Commitment

Robert W. Stone
University of Idaho, USA

John W. Henry
Georgia Southern University, USA

ABSTRACT

The study uses data collected by a survey of computer-based medical information system end users in a large hospital in the southeastern United States. The theoretical model examined using this data links several antecedents to the end users' organizational commitment, mediated by computer self-

efficacy and outcome expectancy. These antecedents are past computer experience of the end user, computer staff support for the computer system, ease of system use, and the degree of system use (i.e., percentage of time the system is used by the end user).

The empirical results indicate that past computer experience and the degree of system use positively influence the end user's organizational commitment through both computer self-efficacy and outcome expectancy. These also show that computer staff support and ease of system use positively impact the end user's organizational commitment through outcome expectancy. From these results, conclusions and implications for practicing managers are discussed.

INTRODUCTION

Information technology is present in almost every area of the organization. However, during the last 30 years, there has been an emphasis on the technological attributes of computer systems, often with little concern for human factors. In a job market with high demand for competent computer end users, recruiting and retaining individuals with these skills is crucial to organizational success. One factor influencing the retention of such information technology end users is their commitment to the organization. The research presented below empirically tests a theoretical model regarding the development of organizational commitment among information technology end users. The model links past computer experience, computer staff support, system ease of use, and the degree of system use to the end user's sense of computer self-efficacy, outcome expectancy, and ultimately organizational commitment.

Before proceeding, the definitions of organizational commitment, computer self-efficacy, and outcome expectancy that are used in this research are presented. The first is organizational commitment and it "...(1) includes something of the notion of membership; (2) it reflects the current position of the individual; (3) it has a special predictive potential concerning certain aspects of performance, motivation to work, spontaneous contribution, and other related outcomes; and (4) it suggests the differential relevance of motivation factors" (Brown, 1969, p. 47). Self-efficacy refers to an individual's belief that they have the skills and abilities to successfully complete a specific task (Bandura, 1982; 1986). Outcome expectancy refers to the belief by the individual that completing a specific task leads to a desirable outcome (Bandura, 1986).

The causal mechanisms determining an information technology end user's organizational commitment have not been fully addressed in previous information technology research (Bluestone, 1983; Kiesler, 1983; Cousins, 1981; Walton, 1982; Nelson, 1990; Nelson & Kletke, 1990). Several studies have examined influences such as task complexity, education level, and attitudes of job satisfaction on organizational commitment. In addition, many studies have examined organizational commitment and its antecedents in social science and organizational behavior contexts, but virtually no attention has been given to the organizational commitment of the information technology end user. The purpose of this research is to examine the organizational commitment of the information technology end user based on a model theoretically linking organizational commitment, computer self-efficacy, and outcome expectancy and the antecedents of these expectancies (Bandura, 1986). This is done to allow a clearer understanding of the interrelationships expressed in this model.

The impacts of information technology and its successful acceptance are important to organizations. Typically, however, an information technology implementation places significant emphasis on evaluating the technical implications (e.g., costs, speed, and data handling capacity) of the system with much less attention directed toward individual outcomes (Nelson, 1990; Nelson & Kletke, 1990). Moreover, in many organizational environments, the technology can receive a favorable technical evaluation but be rejected by dissatisfied end users because it may be difficult to use or the interface may be confusing.

Numerous studies in the information technology literature have attempted to describe the variables influencing end users' use and perceptions of information technology (Blackler & Brown, 1985; Blegen, 1993; Counte, Kjerulff, & Salloway, 1985; Glass & Knight, 1988; Pan, Shell, & Schleifer, 1994). However, the isolation of individual controllable antecedents directly associated with the end user's organizational commitment is more meaningful. This is because research in the social sciences and organizational behavior has shown that highly committed employees are desirous of remaining in their job with the organization, working toward its goals, and contributing to higher performance levels (Carey, 1992; Eyob, 1995; Mowday, Porter, & Steers, 1982; Rafaeli & Sutton, 1986; Tomer, 1998). Other research has shown that gaining organizational commitment early in an employee's tenure greatly increases the probability of the desired outcomes mentioned above (Salancik, 1977). Identifying such antecedents facilitates the development of user involvement programs specifically designed to eliminate user resistance to the target system and in this way, increase the end user's organizational commitment. For example, in a study examining the implementation of a computerized hospital management information system, Warnock-Matheron and Plummer (1980) stated that "...preparing the nursing staff for automation is crucial in establishing staff user acceptance and minimizing resistance" (p. 121). The notion of proper pre-implementation practices has been studied extensively and found to nearly always be significant (Cooper & Zmud, 1990).

THE THEORETICAL FRAMEWORK

While several of the constructs in the model employed here are not directly addressed in information technology research, as mentioned above, their interrelationships are discussed in the social science and organizational behavior literature. The two central constructs in the model are computer self-efficacy and outcome expectancy. Self-efficacy theory (Bandura, 1982; 1986) emphasizes the impact of the individual's cognitive state on outcomes such as loss of control, low self-confidence, lowered achievement motivation, and perceptions of future outcomes (Bandura, 1986; Meier, 1985; Seligman, 1990). It determines the individual's level of persistence to learn a task and influences the individual's perceptions of future outcomes. As previously defined, outcome expectancy refers to an individual's belief that task accomplishment leads to a desired outcome. Outcome expectancy is defined as the consequence of an act and not the act itself. Each of these constructs has a separate and distinct impact on individual behavior and affect, although Bandura (1986) states that self-efficacy typically has the larger effect. Self-efficacy also has a direct impact on outcome expectancy (Bandura, 1986; Stone & Henry, 1998). The value of expectancies lies in the notion that not only is there a direct relationship between expectancies and behavioral and affective outcomes, but that the relationship is causal (Sadri & Robertson, 1993). One such outcome is organizational commitment.

The constructs of self-efficacy and outcome expectancy have been mentioned in other literature as correlating with organizational commitment. These studies examined organizational commitment and found that a sense of competence (e.g., self-efficacy) and other "higher order needs" (e.g., outcome expectancy) were directly related to organizational commitment. Further, these studies found that employees exchange commitment for desirable outcomes meeting both intrinsic and extrinsic needs (Koch, 1974; Lum, Kervin, Clark, Reid, & Sirola, 1998; Morris & Sherman, 1981; Steers & Spencer, 1977). Thus, the constructs of computer self-efficacy and outcome expectancy can be theoretically expected to correlate with organizational commitment.

Through computer self-efficacy and outcome expectancy, organizational commitment has a number of antecedents. Past and current work experiences (e.g., past computer experience, degree of system use, and ease of system use) have long been associated with organizational commitment (Steers, 1977). Consistent results have long been found in other studies examining employees' experiences in challenging, yet well defined jobs (Brown, 1969; Marsh & Mannari, 1977; Steers & Spencer, 1977). Further, Stevens et al. (1978) found that employees who experienced a greater dependence on the work of others (e.g., computer staff support) felt more committed to the organization than employees experiencing lesser levels of these factors. Several other studies found similar antecedents influenced behavioral and affective outcomes mediated by self-efficacy and outcome expectancy (Bandura, 1986; Henry & Stone, 1994; 1995; 1999; Stone & Henry, 1998).

Based on this literature, a model was developed examining the dynamic process determining and influencing organizational commitment. It is hypothesized that past computer experience, the degree of current system use, computer staff support, and the ease of system use positively influence computer self-efficacy and outcome expectancy. These expectancies (i.e., computer self-efficacy and outcome expectancy), in turn, are predicted to have direct impacts on organizational commitment. In addition, computer self-efficacy is predicted to have a direct impact on outcome expectancy. The specific hypotheses are stated below and their interrelationships are illustrated in Figure 1.

Figure 1: The theoretical model and hypotheses

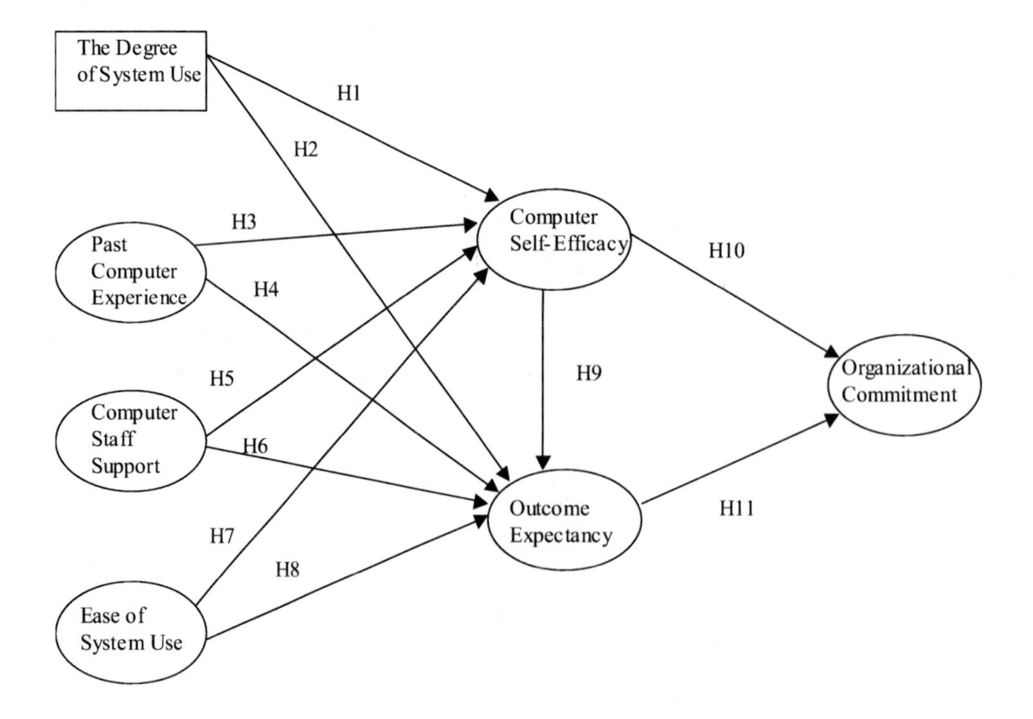

THE HYPOTHESES

As mentioned previously, the literature examined suggests a theoretically grounded model tying the antecedent variables to organizational commitment, mediated by computer self-efficacy and outcome expectancy. The relationships suggested by the model are formally expressed by the hypotheses stated below.

Hypothesis One (H1):	The degree of system use has a positive impact on computer self-efficacy.
Hypothesis Two (H2):	The degree of system use has a positive impact on outcome expectancy.
Hypothesis Three (H3):	Past computer experience has a positive impact on computer self-efficacy.
Hypothesis Four (H4):	Past computer experience has a positive impact on outcome expectancy.
Hypothesis Five (H5):	Computer staff support has a positive impact on computer self-efficacy.
Hypothesis Six (H6):	Computer staff support has a positive impact on outcome expectancy.
Hypothesis Seven (H7):	Ease of system use has a positive impact on computer self-efficacy.
Hypothesis Eight (H8):	Ease of system use has a positive impact on outcome expectancy.
Hypothesis Nine (H9):	Computer self-efficacy has a positive impact on outcome expectancy.
Hypothesis Ten (H10):	Computer self-efficacy has a positive impact on organizational commitment.
Hypothesis Eleven (H11):	Outcome expectancy has a positive impact on organizational commitment.

THE SAMPLE AND PROCEDURES

A questionnaire was distributed to all end users of a computer-based medical information system in a large hospital in the southeastern United States. Its purpose was to collect data to empirically examine the impacts predicted in the theoretical model. The survey was developed with the aid of several hospital administrators. The computer system examined is used by virtually all departments in the hospital to track patient procedures, direct tests to proper locations, maintain diagnosis and physician-specific order sets, provide adequate audit trails, and numerous other healthcare and related activities. The questionnaire contained both demographic information about the participants, their previous and current computer experience,

Table 1: Sample characteristics

Response Rate

Total Questionnaires	Returns	Response Rate
1000	383	38.3%

Gender

Male	Female	No Response
9.1%	81.2%	9.7%

Other Characteristics

Variable	Mean	Median	Minimum	Maximum
Age	36.42	35.00	18	72
Employment Years	7.91	5.00	<1	55

Education

Education Level	Some High School	Graduated From High School or G.E.D.	Some College or Technical Training Beyond High School	Graduated From College	Some Graduate School	Graduate Degree	Did Not Respond
Percentage	0.8	6.3	35.5	36.8	7	6.5	7.1

Position

Position	Director	Manager	Supervisor	Staff	RN	LPNs	Secretary	No Response
Percentage	2.9	8.1	7.3	32.9	22.5	6.8	12.0	7.5

and their perceptions regarding the system and the organizational support for the system. For the statements examining end user perceptions, the participants were provided a Likert-type scale upon which to reply. The scale and weights used were; 1-strongly disagree; 2-disagree; 3-neutral; 4-agree; and 5-strongly agree. A total of 1,000 questionnaires were distributed to all users of this medical information system. A total of 383 usable responses were returned for a 38.3% response rate. The characteristics of the sample formed by these responses are shown in Table 1.

THE MEASURES AND THEIR PSYCHOMETRIC PROPERTIES

All the scales used in the analysis were developed from previously published measures. Adjustments were made to most of the scales modifying them for the specific computer-based medical information system studied. Any additional modifications to the scales are noted below in the discussion of that particular scale. The scale measuring ease of system use was taken as previously published without modifications (Henry & Stone, 1999). The computer staff support measure was modified from a previously published scale of management support (Henry & Stone, 1994). The modification converted the management support scale into a measure focusing on the computer staff helping end users solve problems and make adjustments to the computer system. The item measuring the degree of system use was previously published as part of a computer experience scale (Henry & Stone, 1999). The item asked the respondent to report the percentage of time they spend using the system. The scale measuring past computer experience was a modified version of a published scale by the same name (Stone & Henry, 1998). The modification converted the scale from reporting the amount of prior computing experience to one encompassing the quality of these experiences. The items measuring computer self-efficacy and outcome expectancy were also developed from previously published scales (Henry & Stone, 1995). The computer self-efficacy measure was also modified so the scale was reversed in direction. In other words, individuals with high computer self-efficacy would have low scores on these questionnaire items. These items were reverse-coded before being used in the empirical analysis. Finally, the organizational commitment scale was developed from a previously published scale (Cook & Wall, 1980).

The next step in the empirical analysis was to evaluate the psychometric properties of these measures. The analysis was based on the results from a confirmatory factor analysis, using the structural equations approach Calis (i.e., Covariance Analysis of Linear Structural Equations) in PC SAS version 6.12. A detailed explanation of the confirmatory factor analysis is provided in the appendix. However, the estimation results implied a good fit between the model and the data. Furthermore, the psychometric properties of the measures were evaluated using the standardized path coefficients from this confirmatory factor analysis. The individual questionnaire items, the estimated standardized path coefficients (i.e., factor loadings), and the calculated measures of these psychometric properties are shown in Table 2.

Table 2: The measures, items, factor loadings, reliabilities, and shared variances

Questionnaire Item	Factor Loading	Composite Reliability	Percentage of Shared Variance
Outcome Expectancy		0.94	65%
1. In general, the system makes it easier for me to perform my hospital duties.	0.89		
2. Working with the system leads to a feeling of accomplishment.	0.90		
3. Knowing how to use the system leads to higher quality work.	0.84		
4. Working with the system results in my completing my work on time.	0.85		
5. I believe I am more productive at work when using the system.	0.85		
6. I believe my successful performance with the system increases my chance of promotion.	0.73		
7. I expect the system to be easier to use as time goes by.	0.66		
8. I think I will be able to use the system to produce high quality work.	0.69		
Computer Self-Efficacy		0.76	51%
9. I really have very little sense how the system works.	0.66		
10. If I were sitting before the system, I would not know how to use it.	0.74		
11. I feel incompetent when I try to use the system.	0.74		
Past Computer Experience		0.94	84%
12. My past performance with computers has been good.	0.91		
13. My past experiences with computers have been good.	0.96		
14. My past attitude toward computers has been positive.	0.87		
Computer Staff Support		0.79	56%
15. When I need them, the system staff responds quickly to needed changes in the system	0.73		
16. The system staff is always willing to help me solve problems.	0.84		
17. The system staff is usually able to solve my problems.	0.66		
Ease of System Use		0.83	61%
18. The system is easy to use.	0.76		
19. I like to use the system.	0.83		
20. The system is user friendly.	0.76		
Organizational Commitment		0.88	78%
21. I would think about leaving this hospital if offered the same job with another hospital.	0.81		
22. If another hospital offered me the same sort of job I have now and I was able to keep all the benefits I have now, I would accept the offer.	0.95		

The three initial psychometric properties examined were item reliability, composite reliability, and shared or extracted variance. Item reliability examines how well an individual indicant "loads" on its construct. In other words, it examines the strength of the relationship between an indicant and its construct. Composite reliability measures the degree of internal consistency of all the indicants for the construct. That is, composite reliability is the degree to which the indicants, as a group, measure in common the construct. The percentage of variance extracted is also a measure of reliability. This percentage measures the amount of overall variance in the indicants accounted for by the construct. For additional information about these measures of psychometric properties, see Hair, Anderson, Tatham, and Black (1992).

The interpretation of the confirmatory factor analysis results indicates that the measures used in the study have desirable values of these three properties. Specifically, since the standardized path or factor loading for each indicant to its measure was at least as large as 0.66, item reliability was satisfied (Rainer & Harrison, 1993). Because all the composite reliability coefficients ranged from 0.76 to 0.94, composite reliability was satisfied (Nunnally, 1978). All the average percentages of shared variance were 51% or greater, demonstrating satisfactory levels of this trait (Rivard & Huff, 1988). Due to these desirable values, it can be

Table 3: The squared correlations for pairs of measures

Measure Pair	Squared Correlation
Computer Self-Efficacy-Outcome Expectancy	0.27
Past Computer Use-Outcome Expectancy	0.35
Past Computer Use-Computer Self-Efficacy	0.19
Computer Staff Support-Outcome Expectancy	0.18
Computer Staff Support-Computer Self-Efficacy	0.04
Computer Staff Support-Past Computer Use	0.08
Ease of System Use-Outcome Expectancy	0.10
Ease of System Use-Computer Self-Efficacy	0.00
Ease of System Use-Past Computer Use	0.00
Ease of System Use-Computer Staff Support	0.04
Organizational Commitment-Outcome Expectancy	0.06
Organizational Commitment-Computer Self-Efficacy	0.08
Organizational Commitment-Past Computer Use	0.07
Organizational Commitment-Computer Staff Support	0.02
Organizational Commitment-Ease of System Use	0.00

concluded that convergent validity was satisfied for each measure (Rainer & Harrison, 1993; Igbaria & Greenhaus, 1992).

Discriminant validity was also examined using these results. This examination compared the squared correlation between each pair of measures to their average percentage of shared variances. Discriminant validity is satisfied if, for each measure pair, the average percentages of shared variance are greater than the corresponding squared correlation (Fornell & Larcker, 1981). The squared correlations ranged from 0.00 to 0.35 and are reported in Table 3. Since these squared correlations were less than all the average percentage of shared variance values, discriminant validity was satisfied (Fornell & Larcker, 1981). These results, coupled with convergent validity, imply that the measures satisfied construct validity (Rainer & Harrison, 1993). Thus, the developed measures had desirable psychometric properties.

NON-RESPONSE BIAS

As in the case of any survey research, there is the potential for those individuals returning questionnaires not to accurately represent the population studied (i.e., non-response bias). In order to examine the possibility of non-response bias, the extreme quartiles of the sample, when ordered by questionnaire return date, were studied (Armstrong & Overton, 1977). Specifically, the upper quartile was used to represent or simulate non-respondents and the lower quartile the respondents. The simulated non-respondents and respondents were then compared for differences in their demographics and summated measures. No meaningful differences between the simulated non-respondents and respondents imply an absence of non-response bias in the sample (Armstrong & Overton, 1977). The demographics measured as continuous variables (i.e., age of the respondent and years of employment with the organization) were compared using t-tests. The discrete demographic variables (i.e., gender, educational level, and position in the hospital) were compared between these groups using a chi-square goodness of fit test. Meaningful differences between the simulated non-respondents and respondents, using a 5% significance level, were found for educational level and position in the hospital. The specific values of the test statistics were: age t=-0.31, length of employment at the hospital t=0.26, gender chi-square(6)=6.87, educational level chi-square(4)=24.56, and position in the hospital chi-square(4)=9.65. Inspection of the educational level of the simulated non-respondents and respondents indicated that the primary difference between these groups was found in the respondents with graduate degrees. A full 10% of the simulated non-respondents possessed a graduate degree, while 0% of the respondent group held a graduate degree. Given the link between educational level in the hospital, particularly holding a graduate degree, and position, this likely influenced the meaningful difference between these groups for the position variable as well.

Because of the significant differences for these two demographic variables, additional tests were performed. The constructs measured using multiple questionnaire items were captured by summing the values of the individual items. These summated measures were then analyzed using multiple analysis of variance along with the continuous, single item measure of the degree of system use. The results of this analysis showed no significant differences either individually or as a group. The F-statistic for each measure were: computer self-efficacy $F(1,162)=0.18$, outcome expectancy $F(1,162)=0.30$, past computer experience $F(1,162)=0.38$, computer staff support $F(1,162)=0.03$, ease of system use $F(1,162)=0.29$, degree of system use $F(1,162)=0.39$, and organizational commitment $F(1,162)=1.06$. Wilks' Lambda was used to measure the group significance of these measures. Its value was 0.98, producing an F-statistic with 7 and 156 degrees of freedom equal to 0.38. Thus, the measures used in the analysis did not differ in a significant way between the simulated non-respondents and respondents. It is these measures and their interrelationships that are at the heart of the analysis. Since these measures did not demonstrate significant differences between the simulated non-respondents and respondents, non-response bias should not present a serious problem in the sample or the study.

THE ESTIMATION OF THE MODEL

The theoretical model shown in Figure 1 was estimated using Calis in PC SAS version 6.12. The estimation method used was maximum likelihood. The fit of this model to the data was good. The specific details of the estimation results are discussed in the appendix. The results pertaining to the theoretical model are shown in Figure 2 and summarized below.

Based on the results, several general statements are possible. All paths from the measures to their indicants that were free to vary had estimates that were statistically significant at a 1% level. All but one disturbance term had an estimated standard deviation that was statistically significant at a 1% level. The one indicant with an insignificant estimate for the standard deviation of the disturbance term was associated with organizational commitment. Several of the paths among the measures had estimated values that were statistically significant and sufficiently large to be meaningful. Measures having significant paths to both computer self-efficacy and outcome expectancy were past computer experience and the degree of system

Figure 2: The empirical results of the estimated model using standardized path coefficients

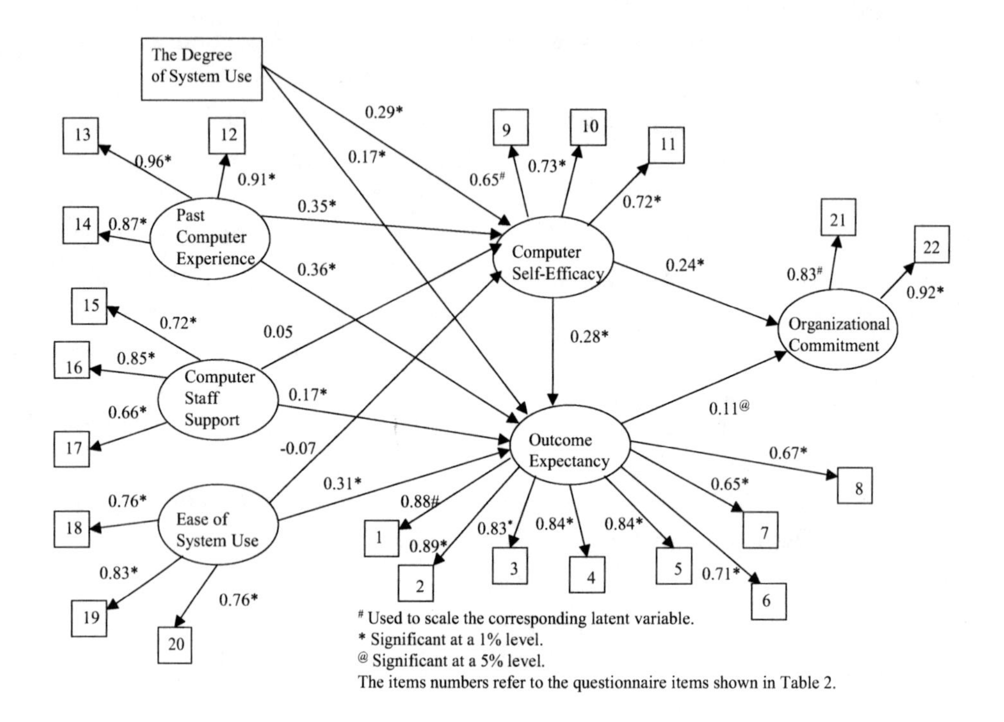

use. Ease of system use and computer staff support had significant impacts on outcome expectancy, but not on computer self-efficacy. Computer self-efficacy had a significant path to outcome expectancy. Both computer self-efficacy and outcome expectancy had significant impacts on organizational commitment.

CONCLUSIONS AND MANAGERIAL IMPLICATIONS

When interpreting and drawing implications based on these empirical results, one must be aware of the study's limitations. It must be remembered that the data used to test the theoretical model and hypotheses were drawn from a single organization concerning a single computer-based system. While the results are appropriate for this organization and system, it is not necessarily the case in other settings. Additional studies across organizations and different systems are required to be able to reach more general conclusions and implications regarding these hypothesized interrelationships. Within these limitations, the following conclusions and implications are presented.

The consequences of strong employee commitment to the organization have implications for individuals and work groups as well as the organization as a whole. At the individual level, organizational commitment has been found to result in greater effort at work, reduced absenteeism, turnover, and tardiness (Mowday, et al., 1982). For example, Mowday et al. (1982) found that the level of commitment among branch bank employees was related to higher levels of performance. Several other studies also indicate that organizations composed of highly committed employees benefit through members' extra efforts in pursuit of organizational goals, greater commitment to the organization's mission and goals, lower levels of turnover, absenteeism, and tardiness (Angle & Perry, 1981; Tomer, 1998).

Given the desirable impacts of having highly committed employees, a key question is how can organizations improve the organizational commitment of its employees? Knowledge of the antecedents to organizational commitment enables organizations to manage these behaviors and attitudes of employees (Colbert & Kwon, 2000). There are cases reported in the literature establishing links between individual and organizational variables to organizational commitment. For example, Morris, Shinn, and DuMont (1999) found that management support (e.g., computer staff support) impacted organizational commitment. Importantly, the research presented above focused not only on these antecedents, but the causal process by which these variables influence organizational commitment. Using the theoretical model, improvements in organizational commitment are accomplished through manipulating the controllable antecedents to computer self-efficacy and outcome expectancy, and ultimately impacting organizational commitment.

The theoretically proposed and empirically found linkages between organizational commitment and both computer self-efficacy and outcome expectancy are consistent with results reported in the literature. For example, while studying healthcare employees, O'Neill and Mone (1998) indicated that a relationship exists between self-efficacy and organizational commitment. Similarly, in a study of U.S. Army soldiers, Jex and Bliese (1999) identified collective efficacy as a moderator of a relationship between task significance and organizational commitment. McNeese-Smith (2001) found that, in a healthcare environment, one outcome expectancy measure for nurses (i.e., patient care) was related to organizational commitment.

Using these empirical results, there are several approaches to increase an employee's commitment to the organization. Hiring employees with computer experiences similar to those needed by their current organization and providing additional experiences through a high degree of system use improve the employee's organizational commitment through increasing the employee's computer self-efficacy and outcome expectancy. In the design process for the development of computer systems, making sure that these systems are easy to use improves the organizational commitment of employees through positively impacting their outcome expectancy. Similarly, providing support for the computer system and its users increases these employees' outcome expectancy and ultimately organizational commitment. In other words, easy to use systems and/or providing system support help users identify the desirable outcomes from system use. This, in turn, leads to an increase in organizational commitment.

REFERENCES

Angle, H., & Perry, J. (1981). An empirical assessment of organizational commitment and organizational effectiveness. *Administrative Science Quarterly*, (26), 1-14.

Armstrong, J. S. & Overton, T. S. (1977). Estimating Nonresponse Bias in Mail Surveys. *Journal of Marketing Research,* (XIV: August), 396-402.

Bandura, A. (1986). *Social Foundation of Thought and Action: A Social Cognitive Theory*. New Jersey: Prentice-Hall.

Bandura, A. (1982). Self-efficacy mechanism in human agency. *American Psychologist* (37), 122-147.

Blackler, F. & Brown, C. (1985). Evaluation and the impact of information technologies on people in organizations. *Human Relations* (38:3), 213-231.

Blegen, M. A. (1993). Nurses' job satisfaction: A meta-analysis of related variables. *Nursing Research, 42*(1), 36-41.

Bluestone, I. (1983). The human factor: Some effects of the computer revolution on labor. *Computers and People,* 32, 12-14.

Brown, M. E. (1969). Identification and some conditions of organizational involvement. *Administrative Science Quarterly,* 14, 346-355.

Carey, J. M. (1992). Job satisfaction and visual display unit (VDU) usage: An explanatory model. *Behaviour & Information Technology*, *11*(6), 338-344.

Colbert, A. E. & Kwon, I. G. (2000). The factors related to the organizational commitment of college and university auditors. *Journal of Managerial Issues, 12*(4), 484-492.

Cook, J. & Wall, T. D. (1980). New work attitude measures of trust, organizational commitment, and personal need non-fulfillment. *Journal of Occupational Psychology*, 53, 39-52.

Cooper, R. B. & Zmud, R. W. (1990). Information technology implementation research: A technology diffusion approach. *Management Science, 36*(2), 123-140.

Counte, M. A., Kjerulff, K. H., Salloway, J. C., & Campbell, B. (1985). Implementing computerization in hospitals: A case study of the behavioral and attitudinal impacts of a medical information system. *Journal of Organizational Behavior Management*, 6, 109-122.

Cousins, P. (1981). Closing the gap between technology and the people who use IT. *Training and Development Journal*, 10, 45-52.

Eyob, E. (1995). Managing the motivation of information technology staff for higher organizational productivity and employee job satisfaction. *Journal of International Information Management, 3*(1), 27-33.

Fornell, C. & Larcker, D. F. (1981). Evaluating structural equation models with unobservable variables and measurement error. *Journal of Marketing Research*, (XVIII), 39-50.

Glass, C. R., & Knight, L. A. (1988). Cognitive factors in computer anxiety. *Cognitive Therapy and Research,* 12, 351-366.

Hair, Joseph F. Jr., Rolph E. Anderson, Ronald L. Tatham, & William C. Black. (1992). *Multivariate Data Analysis with Readings* (3rd ed.). New York: Macmillan Publishing Company.

Henry, J. W. & Stone, R. W. (1999). End user perceptions of the impacts of computer self-efficacy and outcome expectancy on job performance and patient care when using a medical information system. *International Journal of Healthcare Technology Management*, 1, 103-124.

Henry, J. W. & Stone, R. W. (1995). A structural equation model of job performance using a computer-based order entry system. *Behaviour and Information Technology, 14*(3), 163-173.

Henry, J. W. & Stone, R. W. (1994). A structural equation model of end-user satisfaction with a computer-based medical information system. *Information Resources Management Journal*, *7*(3), 21-33.

Igbaria, M. & Greenhaus, J. H. (1992). Determinants of MIS employee's turnover intentions: A structural equation model. *Communications of the ACM*, 35, 35-49.

Jex, S. M. & Bliese, P. D. (1999). Efficacy beliefs as a moderator of the impact of work-related stressors: A multilevel study. *Journal of Applied Psychology, 84*(3), 349-361.

Keisler, S. (1983). New technology in the workplace. *Public Relations Journal*, 39, 12-14.

Koch, J. L. (1974). Need environment congruity and self-investment in organizational roles. *Sociology of Work and Occupations*, 1, 175-196.

Lum, L., Kervin, J. Clar, K. Reid, F., & Sirola, W. (1998). Explaining nursing turnover intent: Job satisfaction, pay satisfaction, or organizational commitment? *Journal of Organizational Behavior*, *19*(3), 305-320.

Marsh, R. M. & Mannari, H. (1977). Organizational commitment and turnover: A prediction study. *Administrative Science Quarterly*, 22, 57-75.

McNeese-Smith, D. K. (2001). A nursing shortage: Building organizational commitment among nurses. *Journal of Healthcare Management, 46*(3), 173-186.

Meier, S. T. (1985). Computer aversion. *Computers in Human Behavior*, 1, 171-179.

Morris, J. & Sherman, J. D. (1981). Generalizability of an organizational commitment model. *Academy of Management Journal*, 24, 512-526.

Morris, A., Shinn, M., & DuMont, K. (1999). Contextual factors affecting the organizational commitment of diverse police officers: A levels of analysis perspective. *American Journal of Community Psychology, 27*(1), 75-78.

Mowday, R. T., Porter, L. W., & Steers, R. M. (1982). *Employee-Organization Linkages*. San Diego: Academic Press, Inc.

Nelson, D. L. (1990). Individual adjustment to information-driven technologies: A critical review. *MIS Quarterly,* 14, 79-98.

Nelson, D. L., & Kletke, M. G. (1990). Individual adjustment during technological innovation: A research framework. *Behaviour & Information Technology, 9*(4), 257-271.

Nunnally, J. (1978). *Psychometric Methods* (2nd ed.). New York: McGraw-Hill.

O'Neill, B. S. & Mone, M. A. (1998). Investigating equity sensitivity as a moderator of relations between self-efficacy and workplace attitudes. *Journal of Applied Psychology, 83*(5), 805-816.

Pan, C. S., Shell, R. L., & Schleifer, L. M. (1994). Performance variability as an indicator of fatigue and boredom effects in a VDT data-entry task. *International Journal of Human-Computer Interaction, 6*(1), 37-45.

Rafaeli, A., & Sutton, R. I. (1986). Word processing technology and perceptions of control among clerical workers. *Behaviour and Information Technology,* 5, 31-37.

Rainer, R. Kelly, Jr. & Allison W. Harrison (1993). Toward development of the end user computing construct in a university setting. *Decision Sciences Journal, 24*(6), 1187-1202.

Rivard, S., & Huff, S. L. (1988). Factors of success for end-user computing. *Communications of the ACM,,* 31, 552-561.

Sadri, G. & Robertson, I. T. (1993). Self-efficacy and work-related behaviour: a review and meta-analysis. *Applied Psychology: An International Review,* 42, 139-152.

Salancik, G. R. (1977). Commitment and the control of organizational behavior and belief. In B.M. Staw & G. R. Salancik (eds.). *New Directions in Organizational Behavior.* Chicago: St. Clair Press.

Seligman, M. E. P. (1990). *Learned Optimism.* New York: Alfred A. Knopf, Inc.

Steers, R. M. (1977). Antecedents and outcomes of organizational commitment. *Administrative Science Quarterly*, 22, 46-56.

Steers, R. M., & Spencer, D. G. (1977). The role of achievement motivation in job design. *Journal of Applied Psychology*, 62, 472-479.

Stevens, J. M., Beyer, J., & Trice, H. M. (1978). Assessing personal role, and organizational predictors of managerial commitment. *Academy of Management Journal,* 21, 380-396.

Stone, R. W. & Henry, J. W. (1998). Computer self-efficacy and outcome expectations and their impacts on behavioral intentions to use computers in non-volitional settings. *Journal of Business and Management, 6*(1), 45-58.

Tomer, J. F. (1998). Organizational capital and joining-up: Linking the individual to the organization and society. *Human Relations, 51*(6), 825-846.

Walton, R. E., (1982). Social choice in the development of advanced information technology. *Human Relations,* 35, 1073-1084.

Warnock-Matheron, A. & Plummer, C. (1980). Introducing nursing information systems in the clinical setting. In M. J. Ball, K. J. Hannah, U. Gerdin Jelger, & H. Peterson (eds.) *Nursing Informatics: Where Caring and Technology Meet.* (pp. 115-127). New York: Brunner/Mazel.

APPENDIX—STATISTICAL DETAILS

The Confirmatory Factor Analysis

The confirmatory factor analysis estimated paths between each measure of a construct (i.e., theoretical latent variable) to each of its questionnaire items. Each measure was exogenous in the model and scaled by setting its standard deviation equal to one. The measures of the latent constructs were also allowed to pair-wise correlate. The individual items in each measure were reflective and affected by a random disturbance term. Each disturbance term was free to vary with a path between it and the indicant set equal to one. The estimation method used was maximum likelihood in Calis (i.e., Covariance Analysis of Linear Structural Equations) in PC SAS version 6.12.

The overall fit of the model to the data was good. The goodness of fit index was 0.92 and adjusted for degrees of freedom it was 0.90. The root mean square residual was 0.04. The chi-square statistic was statistically significant at a 1% level and had a value of 363.66 with 194 degrees of freedom. The normed chi-square statistic was 1.87. Bentler's comparative fit index was 0.97. The incremental fit indexes (i.e., Bentler and Bonett's normed and non-normed indexes and Bollen's normed and non-normed indexes) ranged from 0.92 to 0.97. These results and the relatively large sample size, even with the undesirable significant chi-square statistic, imply a good fit between the model and the data (Hair, Anderson, Tatham, and Black, 1987).

The Estimation of the Model

As in the confirmatory factor analysis, the model was expressed so that all the questionnaire items measured only their own construct. All indicants were reflective of their measures. Each indicant was also impacted by a disturbance term that was free to vary with an associated path to the indicant set equal to one. The measures of past computer experience, computer staff support, and ease of system use were exogenous in the model. Each had its standard deviation set equal to one. For these measures, the associated path between each indicant and its measure was free to vary. The degree of system use, measured as the percentage of time spent using the system, was an observable, exogenous variable. The three remaining measures in the model were endogenous. For these three measures, the path from the measure to one of its indicants was set equal to one in order to scale the measure. The endogenous measures were also influenced by disturbance terms free to vary with associated paths to the measure set equal to one. The hypotheses were expressed as paths between appropriate measures.

The model was estimated using Calis in PC SAS version 6.12. The estimation method was maximum likelihood. The resulting goodness of fit index was 0.91 and when adjusted for the degrees of freedom in the model it was 0.88. The root mean square residual was 0.08. The chi-square statistic was 454.40 with 217 degrees of freedom. It was also statistically significant. The normed version of the chi-square statistic was 2.09. Bentler's comparative fit index was 0.96 and the incremental fit indexes (i.e., Bentler & Bonett's and Bollen's normed and non-normed indexes) ranged from 0.90 to 0.96. These results, even given the significant chi-square statistic, indicate a good fit between the model and the data, particularly when considering the size of the sample used (Hair, Anderson, Tatham, and Black, 1992).

Chapter IV

Personal and Situational Factors as Predictors of End User Performance

I.M. Jawahar
Illinois State University, USA

ABSTRACT

End-user computing (EUC) has the potential to enhance productivity. However, for this potential to be realized, end users must learn EUC skills and perform at high levels. Because of the significance of end user performance to organizations, it is important to uncover factors that influence end user performance. However, prior research has relied almost exclusively on person factors to predict end user performance even though several models suggest that both person and situational factors influence behavior and performance. This limitation of previous research was overcome by examining the influence of both person and situational factors on end user performance. The three person factors and four situational factors investigated in this study, together, explained almost 40% of the variance in end user performance. Suggestions to enhance end user performance are offered, and directions for future research are discussed.

INTRODUCTION

The emergence of end user computing (EUC) can be traced to the proliferation of microcomputers, increased organizational computing needs, and the availability of sophisticated user application tools (Shayo, Guthrie, & Igbaria, 1999). EUC has the potential to influence productivity, competitiveness and profits. Consequently, computer literacy requirements have skyrocketed for clerical and support staff (Bowman, Grupe, & Simkin, 1995) and for many middle and senior management positions (Olsten, 1993).

Several scholars have acknowledged end user training as an essential contributor to the productive use of computer systems in organizations (Compeau & Higgins, 1995; Davis & Bostrom, 1993; Rivard & Huff, 1988). The practitioner literature also supports the view that training is essential for effective use of computer technology. Testimonials to the importance of training are common features in the popular press (Finley, 1996; Warner & Smith, 1990). Because training can affect the success or failure of EUC in organizations (Bostrom, Olfman, & Sein, 1990; Rivard & Huff, 1988), training employees to use information technology productively has become a high priority in many organizations (Aggarwal, 1998; Finley, 1996). Since the primary purpose of introducing new technology is to improve productivity, organizations expect their employees to learn and apply EUC technology to increase their job performance and contribute to organizational effectiveness.

To date, user satisfaction has served as the most popular measure in the literature for measuring EUC success (Igbaria & Nachman, 1990; Mahmood, Burn, Gemoets & Jacquez, 2000; Munro, Huff, Marcolin & Compeau, 1997). Use of user satisfaction as the primary measure of EUC success is based on the implicit assumption that satisfied users perform better than dissatisfied users (Amoroso, 1992). Unfortunately, evidence to support this assumption is lacking. Equating user satisfaction with end user computing success is problematic because it does not tell us anything about productivity. Munro et al. (1997) aptly noted that a better measure of EUC success than user satisfaction is necessary to justify the substantial investments in end user technologies and in end user training. Given that the primary reason organizations computerize their operations is to improve productivity, competitiveness and profits (Harrington, McElroy & Morrow, 1990), unless end users learn the skills and utilize those skills to improve their job performance, the expected benefits of EUC are unlikely to accrue.

This article is organized into five sections inclusive of this introductory section. A selected review of research on end user performance is presented in the second section. In the third section, hypotheses are developed. The methodology and results are presented in the fourth section. In the final section, I will offer suggestions to enhance end user performance, and discuss avenues to extend research on end user performance.

A Selected Review of Research on End User Performance

Studies have investigated the influence of attitudes (e.g., Jawahar & Elango, 1991; Jawahar & Elango, 1998; Kennedy, 1975; Kernan & Howard, 1990; Szajna, 1994), aptitudes (e.g., Evans & Simkin, 1989; Szajna & Mackay, 1995), learning styles (e.g., Bohlen & Ferratt, 1997), cognitive styles (e.g., Davis & Davis, 1990), experience (e.g., Dambrot, Silling, & Zook, 1988; Harrison & Rainer, 1992), education (e.g., Davis & Davis, 1990), age (e.g., Czara, Hammond, Blascovich, & Swede, 1989), and sex (e.g., Harrison & Rainer, 1992) on end user performance.

Although a number of factors have been examined, the preponderance of research on end user performance has focused on attitudes toward computers to predict end user performance. However, these studies have generally reported inconsistent results (e.g., Kennedy, 1975; Kernan & Howard, 1990; Marcoulides, 1988; Mawhinney & Saraswat, 1991; O'Quin, Kinsey, & Beery, 1987; Roszkowski, Devlin, Snelbecker, Aiken, & Jacobsohn, 1988, Szajna, 1994). About one half of the studies that examined the relationship between attitudes and end user performance have reported a relationship. While some these studies reported a positive relationship (e.g., Jawahar & Elango, 1991; Nickell & Pinto, 1986; Roszkowski, et al., 1988), others have reported a negative relationship (e.g., Hayek & Stephens, 1989; Marcoulides, 1988; Mawhinney & Saraswat, 1991; Rosen, Sears & Weil, 1987). Alternatively, roughly one half of the studies failed to find a relationship between attitudes and end user performance (Kennedy, 1975; Kernan & Howard, 1990; O'Quin, Kinsey & Beery, 1987; Szajna, 1994; Szajna & Mackay, 1995).

At least three reasons could be offered for the inconsistent results reported by prior research. First, the review of prior research indicates that many previous studies have used the constructs of computer anxiety and negative attitudes toward computers, interchangeably. These two constructs are distinct and consequently, are not interchangeable. Indeed, factor-analytic investigations indicate that computer anxiety and negative attitudes toward computers should be treated as separate constructs (Kernan & Howard, 1990). Second, items such as "Computers are a blessing to mankind," "Computers make it possible to speed up scientific progress and achievements," and "Computers are becoming necessary to the efficient operation of large businesses" reflect the spirit of the "attitudes toward computers" measure (Lee, 1970). Given the spirit of the items used to measure the construct, the rationale for expecting "attitudes toward computers" to be related to end user performance is not clear. Just because a person has favorable attitudes toward computers does not automatically mean that he or she would be willing to work with computers. Willingness to work with computers could result in a higher rate of system utilization leading to a higher level of end user performance. Willingness to work with computers is captured by Rafaeli's (1986) Attitudes Toward Working with Computers Scale. Attitudes toward working with computers are likely to evidence a more consistent relationship with end user performance than attitudes toward computers. Finally, besides attitudes, a myriad of individual difference factors has the potential to influence end user performance.

Development of Hypotheses

In this study, I investigated the second and third assertions. Specifically, the effects of attitudes toward working with computers and those of two well-established individual difference constructs, goal setting and self-efficacy on end user performance were examined. The rationale for investigating these constructs is presented next.

Person Factors

Attitudes Toward Working With Computers. As argued earlier, it is possible for a person to have favorable attitudes toward computers in general and yet have negative or unfavorable attitudes toward working with one in the workplace. Additionally, according to the behavioral intentions model of Ajzen and Fishbein (1980), behaviors or outcomes can be best predicted by attitudes that specifically relate to those behaviors than by more global and general attitudes. Attitude toward working with computers is much more specific and relevant to performance of tasks that require the use of computer skills than the more general, attitudes toward computers. Individuals who hold favorable attitudes toward working with computers are more likely to practice and learn EUC skills, and evidence higher levels of performance on tasks that require the use of those skills than those who hold less favorable attitudes. Indeed, Jawahar and Elango (1991) reported that attitudes explained 7% of the variance in end user performance.

H1: Attitudes toward working with computers will be positively related to end user performance.

Goal Setting. The positive effect of goal setting on task performance is one of the most robust and replicable findings in the psychological literature (Locke & Latham, 1990; Locke, Shaw, Saari, & Latham, 1981). Literally, hundreds of studies have been conducted on goal setting with a range of subjects including children, factory workers, managers, engineers, and scientists (Locke & Latham, 1990, pp. 40-62). Research on goal setting has documented that specific and difficult or challenging goals lead to higher levels of performance than the absence of goals or easy goals or "do your best" goals (Locke et al., 1981). Locke and Latham (1990) have shown that goal setting when combined with feedback or knowledge of results leads to high levels of performance. Thus, goal setting is most likely to improve task performance when the goals are specific and sufficiently challenging, and feedback is provided to show progress in relation to the goal.

Setting goals that are specific and challenging is particularly important when the task is complex or novel. Learning software packages is likely to be challenging to most individuals; consequently, individuals who set specific and challenging goals to learn and use new end-user computing technology are more likely to outperform those who do not set such specific and challenging goals. Only one study has examined the effects of goals on end user performance. In this study, goal setting explained 11% of the variance in end user performance.

H2: Goal setting (i.e., setting specific and challenging goals) will be positively related to end user performance.

Self-efficacy. Self-efficacy is the belief in one's ability to effectively complete a task or exhibit a specific behavior (Bandura, 1982, 1977). Bandura (1982, 1977) has shown that self-efficacy beliefs are primarily shaped by performance accomplishments, vicarious experiences, verbal persuasion, and physiological states; and Jawahar, Stone, and Cooper (1992) have illustrated the mechanism through which self-efficacy beliefs affect behavior and outcomes.

Theory and research on self-efficacy suggests that, in contrast to individuals with low levels of self-efficacy, the highly efficacious are less apprehensive of change, set more challenging goals, exert more effort, persist in the face of difficulty, and achieve higher levels of performance (Wood & Bandura, 1989). Prior research has also documented the predictive utility of self-efficacy in diverse settings (Jawahar et al., 1992; Stajkovic & Luthans, 1998).

Self-efficacy can be considered a potential antecedent of training effectiveness, because individuals who enter training believing they are capable of mastering the training content are likely to learn more during the training. For instance, in one study, Gist, Schwoerer, and Rosen (1989) studied managers and administrators undergoing two types of training in the use of computer software. Trainees with higher self-efficacy prior to training performed better than their low self-efficacy peers on a timed computer task at the end of training. Thus, highly efficacious individuals who believe that they can effectively use new end-user computing technology are likely to outperform those with low levels of efficacy beliefs.

H3: Self-efficacy will be positively related to end user performance.

As mentioned earlier, previous research focused almost exclusively on person factors for predicting end user performance. The omission of situational factors is a major limitation of previous research because situational factors also have the potential to affect end user performance. Situational factors could influence end user performance directly, and also through their effects on person factors. After all, the prediction that inhibiting situational conditions could adversely affect performance is straightforward and has been expressed in several theoretical models of performance (e.g., Peters & O'Connor, 1980; Schneider, 1978; Terborg, 1981). Situational factors that restrict or constrain performance are referred to as situational constraints. These include factors beyond the control of individual employees (e.g., faulty equipment, lack of resources, time constraints) that restrict the range of individual performance. Research has reported the existence of situational constraints (e.g., Peters, O'Connor, & Rudolph, 1980; Peters, Chassie, Lindholm, O'Connor, & Kline, 1982), and the adverse effects of situational constraints on performance has been documented in laboratory studies (e.g., Hatcher, Prus, Englehard, & Farmer, 1991) and in field studies (e.g., Steel & Mento, 1986).

Unlike previous studies that relied *exclusively* on individual difference factors to predict performance (e.g., Jawahar & Elango, 2001; Roszkowski, et al., 1988), this study also investigated the effect of situational factors on end user performance. Although it is widely accepted that factors in the situation or environment affect behaviors and outcomes, there is no framework of situational variables that lists situational variables that are accepted to be universally useful from which to sample. Typically, situational factors chosen for investigation are study-specific. Situational factors examined in prior research on end user performance, and situational factors relevant to the context of the study and to organizational settings were chosen for investigation. The situational factors of complexity of training, software user-friendliness, opportunity to practice and time constraint met these criteria and were included in this study (for more details see Jawahar, in press).

SITUATIONAL FACTORS

Complexity. Studies have examined the effects of job characteristics on worker adjustment to end-user computing systems (Buchanan & Bessant, 1985;

Olson, 1982) and on success of end-user computing systems (Cheney, Mann, & Amoroso, 1986). However, the more important question of how characteristics of training per se, such as complexity of training, affects performance has not been addressed. Clearly, the complexity of "training to use new technology" is likely to affect worker adjustment and the assimilation of the technology in the workplace. When employees are trained in new end-user computing skills, perceived complexity of training will significantly influence how well trainees learn and use those skills (Tannenbaum & Yukl, 1992). For instance, if training to use the new technology is perceived to be difficult and complex, one can anticipate low performance without much variance in performance levels of employees. A perception of complexity is likely to affect performance directly, and indirectly through its effect on motivation by lowering expectancy beliefs (Vroom, 1964).

H4: Perceptions of complexity of training (to use software packages) will be negatively related to end user performance.

Lack of Opportunity to Practice. Lack of opportunity to practice in the training environment and in the post-training environment is likely to affect how well trainees learn and use their newly acquired skills to perform their jobs. While the importance of practice for learning new skills is widely acknowledged (Tannenbaum & Yukl, 1992), training and work environments differ in the extent to which they provide trainees opportunities to practice newly acquired skills. For instance, Ford, Quinones, Sego, and Speer (1991) studied Air Force technical trainees after they completed training and found significant differences in opportunity to apply the training and also noted wide variations in the lengths of time before trainees first performed the tasks for which they had been trained. Opportunities to practice newly acquired skills are likely to strengthen learning and influence how well trainees use those skills. In a study of IRS managers, Pentland (1989) found that attempts to practice trained computer skills immediately upon returning to the job had a major impact on long-term retention. These studies suggest that the opportunity to practice trained skills will significantly influence how well trainees learn and perform with those skills. Conversely, lack of opportunity to practice newly acquired skills is likely to inhibit learning and performance on tasks that require the use of those skills.

H5: Perceptions of lack of opportunity to practice the newly acquired skills will be negatively related to end user performance.

Time Constraint. In one study, Peters, O'Connor, and Rudolf (1980) used the critical incidents method to identify situational constraints relevant to performance outcomes. In that study, 62 subjects employed in a wide variety of jobs identified situational variables that adversely affected performance. Peters, et al. identified time availability as a potent situational constraint. Trainees are likely to become frustrated and not learn as well when they are expected to learn and become proficient in new skills in a short amount of time. The time allotted to learn and become proficient in new skills is likely to affect how well trainees learn and use their skills. Consequently, trainees who perceive time constraints are likely to evidence lower levels of performance relative to those who do not perceive such time constraints.

H6: Perceptions of time constraint to learn and use software packages will be negatively related to end user performance.

Lack of Software User-friendliness. End user performance is likely to be facilitated by user friendliness of software packages. Trainees' motivation to learn and use software packages is likely to be high when those software packages are perceived to be easy to understand and to use. Alternatively, lack of software user-friendliness is likely to hinder acceptance (e.g., Davis, Bagozzi, & Warshaw, 1989) and actual use (e.g., Igbaria, Iivari, & Maragahh, 1995) of the software. In turn, actual use is likely to affect performance. In one study, Bloom and Hautaluoma (1990) found that software with user-friendly features (e.g., error messages, HELP commands, summarized on-screen menus) led to better performance than software without such features. To the extent software packages are perceived as confusing and difficult to understand and to use, they are likely to constrain and debilitate end user performance.

H7: Perceptions of lack of user-friendliness of software packages will be negatively related to end user performance.

METHOD

Subjects

Subjects were 345 undergraduate students enrolled in two different sections of a Management Information Systems (MIS) course taught by the same instructor at a large state university. Because of incomplete responses, the final sample was reduced to 310 subjects. Of the 310 subjects, 145 were male and 165 were female.

The age of 90% of subjects ranged from 20 to 24. Students in MIS courses have been used as acceptable surrogates for end users in many previous studies (e.g., Bohlen & Ferratt, 1997; Evans & Simkin, 1989; Palvia, 1991).

Management Information Systems Course

In this required course, subjects attended one theory class period and two lab periods each week during the 15-week semester. Subjects were taught database concepts and how to use a database software package during the ninth through the thirteenth week of the semester. In the ninth week, subjects were introduced to database concepts during the theory class period. During the lab periods of the ninth week, subjects were taken to the lab to get a hands-on experience with the software. During the next four weeks (weeks 10, 11, 12, & 13), subjects had to complete one assignment per week. The instructor explained the database concepts during the theory class period. During the first lab period of weeks 10, 11, 12, and 13, students worked with a tutorial that exposed them to concepts and commands necessary to complete the assignment for the week. During these lab periods, three to four graduate assistants were available in the lab to answer students' questions and help them work through the tutorials. The second lab period of weeks 10, 11, 12 and 13 was designated for completing the assignments. Students were handed their assignments as they entered the lab and the graduate assistants were instructed to collect the assignments at the end of the lab period. Although the graduate assistants were available to answer questions, students had to complete assignments on their own. Each assignment was worth 25 points.

Study Design and Procedure

Data for this study were collected in three phases. In the ninth week of the semester, a questionnaire was administered (during the theory class period) to students enrolled in the MIS course to measure the dispositional variables of attitudes toward working with computers, self-efficacy, and goal setting. In addition, subjects were requested to provide demographic information (e.g., sex, age), their social security number and section number but not their names. They were assured of confidentiality and informed that only the investigator (not the instructor) would have access to their responses. In the tenth week of the semester, the situational constraint variables of complexity, lack of opportunity to practice, lack of software user-friendliness, and time constraint were measured using a questionnaire that also requested social security number and section number. In order to avoid self-serving bias, subjects' perceptions of situational constraints were measured after they were exposed to the database software but before they received the score on their first database assignment. At the end of the fourteenth week, scores on the four assignments obtained from the instructor were matched with subjects' social security numbers for data analysis purposes.

Measures

Independent Variables: Attitudes toward working with computers were measured with a 10-item scale (a=.88) with scale points of 1 - completely disagree, 2 - strongly disagree, 3 - disagree, 4 - neither disagree nor agree, 5 - agree, 6 - strongly agree, and 7 - completely agree. Rafaeli's (1986) Attitudes Toward Working with Computers Scale was modified so that items would be relevant to the subjects. Sample items included "I would like to use computers to do part or all of my work," and "Working with computers is an enjoyable experience." Goal setting was measured with 5 items (a=.7) to ascertain the extent to which subjects set specific and challenging goals with respect to performance. Sample items included "I have set a specific goal, in terms of a grade, for this course," "I have set a challenging goal, in terms of a grade, for this course," and "I have set a specific and challenging goal, in terms of a grade, for this course." Goal setting was measured with a seven-point scale with the same anchor points as those used to measure attitudes toward working with computers. The methodology used by Bandura and his colleagues (e.g., Bandura, 1982; Zimmerman, Bandura, & Martinez-Pons, 1992) was used to measure self-efficacy. Self-efficacy was measured using 5 items (a=.71) and subjects rated their perceived self-efficacy on a 7-point scale with scale points of 1 – not well at all, 3 – not too well, 5 – pretty well, and 7 – very well. Sample items included "I can learn to effectively use the word processing software package," "I can learn to effectively use the spreadsheet software package," and "I can learn to effectively use the database software package."

To measure perceptions of situational factors, a 7-point scale with scale points of 1 - completely disagree, 2 - strongly disagree, 3 - disagree, 4 - neither disagree nor agree, 5 - agree, 6 - strongly agree, and 7 - completely agree, was used. Complexity was measured with 3 items (a=.81) and sample items included "The training to use the database software was very complex," and "The instructor explained how to do the assignments, clearly." Three items were used to measure lack of opportunity to practice (a=.71). Sample items included "The assignments provided me with ample opportunity to use the database software," and "I was able to use the software whenever I wanted to practice." Time constraint was measured with 4 items (a=.72), and sample items included "I did not have enough time to complete the assignments," and "I would have learned more if I had more time to work on the assignments." Lack of software user-friendliness was measured with 2 items (a = .7). The items used were "This database software package is very confusing," and "This database package is user-friendly (easy to understand and use)." Reliability of measures ranged from .7 to .86. Reliability of .7 or higher is considered as acceptable for social science research (Nunnally & Bernstein, 1995, p. 265).

Dependent Variable: The database assignments were graded from an objective key and thus did not require any judgment on the part of the grader. Four graduate assistants graded the assignments and recorded the scores. To check the reliability of grading, the four graduate assistants were asked to independently grade a random sample of assignments using the objective key. Reliability of grading was very high and varied from .85 to .91. Each student had 4 scores, one for each assignment, and the 4 scores were highly correlated with correlations ranging from .83 to .89. Consistent with prior research (e.g., Jawahar & Elango, 2001; Kernan & Howard, 1990; Mawhinney & Saraswat, 1991) the 4 scores were added and the total score was used as the dependent variable. The total score ranged from 45 to 100 with an average of 78.34.

RESULTS

Since multiple independent variables were examined, Tolerance and Variance Inflation Factor (VIF) values were computed to check for multicolinearity. Tolerance value is 1 minus the proportion of the variable's variance that is explained by the other predictors; thus a high tolerance value indicates little colinearity. VIF is the reciprocal of the tolerance value; thus small VIF values indicate low intercorrelation among variables. Tolerance values above .10 and VIF values below 10 indicate absence of multicolinearity (Hair, Anderson, Tatham, & Black, 1992, p. 48). Tolerance values exceeded .8 and VIF values ranged from 1.08 to 2.0 indicating that multicolinearity was not a problem. The data also met all of the assumptions of regression.

Hypotheses Testing

An optimum strategy of statistical inference controls for, and balances type I and type II errors. According to Cohen and Cohen (1983, p. 177), this objective can be accomplished by using sets of independent variables as the primary units of analysis and t-testing for significance only those independent variables whose sets have given rise to significant Fs. Therefore, hypotheses testing proceeded as follows. First, the contribution to end user performance of person factors entered as a set and situational factors entered as a set was tested for significance at a =.05 level with the appropriate standard F test. Both the sets significantly contributed to end user performance. Next, all the independent variables were entered in a regression equation and t-values and significance levels that correspond to the regression coefficients were used for hypotheses testing. When all the variables are in the equation, the regression coefficients, t-values and significance levels will be the same, regardless of the order in which the variables were entered in the regression equation (Pedhazur & Schmelkin, 1991, pp. 417-418). The t-test for each individual regression coefficient was used to test individual hypothesis. Means and standard deviations of independent variables, and regression results of hypothesis testing are presented in Table 1. Both R^2, squared zero-order correlations and sR^2, squared semi-partial correlations are reported. sR^2 values indicate the variance in performance that is unique to each independent variable (Cohen & Cohen, 1983).

As predicted in hypothesis 1, attitudes toward working with computers were positively related to end user performance (see Table 1, $R^2 = .081$, $sR^2 = .036$, $\beta = .082$, $p < .001$). The general attitudes of attitudes toward computers were not related to end user performance. Likewise, goal setting was positively related to end user performance ($R^2 = .124$, $sR^2 = .068$ $\beta = .186$, $p < .01$) as predicted in hypothesis 2. Support for hypothesis 3 was obtained as self-efficacy was positively related to performance ($R^2 = .26$, $sR^2 = .137$, $\beta = .419$, $p < .001$). The three dispositional variables of attitudes toward working with computers, goal setting, and self-efficacy when entered as a set explained 32% of the variance in end user performance.

As predicted in hypothesis 4, perceived complexity of training to use database software was negatively related to end user performance (see Table 1, $R^2 = .107$, $sR^2 = .044$, $\beta = -.228$, $p < .001$). Hypothesis 5 was not supported as the relationship between lack of opportunity to practice and end user performance ($R^2 = .065$, $sR^2 = .014$, $\beta = -.062$, $p = .161$) failed to reach significance. As hypothesized (hypothesis 6), perceived time constraint was negatively related to performance ($R^2 = .087$, $sR^2 = .04$, $\beta = -.119$, $p < .01$). And, as predicted in hypothesis 7, lack of software user-friendliness was negatively related to end user performance ($R^2 = .058$, $sR^2 = .029$, $\beta = -.095$, $p < .01$). The four situational constraints of complexity, lack of opportunity to practice, time constraint, and lack of software user-friendliness when entered as a set explained about 17% of the variance in end user performance. Together, the dispositional variables and situational constraints, that is the entire model, explained 40% of the variance in end user performance.

Table 1: Means, standard deviations, and summary of regression results

Hypo.	Independent Variable	M	SD	R^2	sR^2	Stand. Beta β	t value	p value
	Person Factors							
1	Attitudes toward working with computers	4.9	.86	.081	.036	.082	2.183	.000
2	Goal setting	5.2	.71	.124	.068	.186	4.349	.003
3	Self-efficacy	4.9	.76	.261	.137	.419	11.224	.000
	Situational Factors							
4	Complexity	4.32	.98	.107	.044	-.228	-5.595	.000
5	Lack of opportunity to practice	3.77	1.45	.065	.014	-.062	-1.403	.161
6	Time constraint	4.98	1.01	.087	.040	-.119	-2.710	.008
7	Lack of software user-friendliness	4.98	1.2	.058	.029	-.095	-2.342	.004

Note: R^2 values are squared zero-order correlations. sR^2 values are squared semi-partial correlations and indicate the variance in performance that is unique to each independent variable.

DISCUSSION

Two reasons served as the impetus for this study: first, the inconsistent relationship reported between attitudes and end user performance; second, and more importantly, the lack of research investigating the effects of both person and situational factors on end user performance. As expected, attitudes toward working with computers predicted end user performance, whereas the general attitudes of attitudes toward computers did not. This result provides a partial explanation for the inconsistent relationship reported between attitudes and end user performance in previous research. As hypothesized, attitudes toward working with computers, goal setting, and self-efficacy were positively related to end user performance. Perceptions of situational factors of complexity, time constraints, and lack of software user-friendliness negatively influenced end user performance. The dispositional and situational factors explained 32% and 17% of the variance, respectively, and together they explained 40% of the variance in end user performance. The amount of variance in end user performance explained in this study compares very favorably with that explained by other studies (e.g., Evans & Simkin, 1989; Konvalina, Stephens, & Wileman, 1983). For instance, Evans and Simkin (1989) used 34 independent variables and their stepwise multiple regression models accounted for only 24% of the variance in end user performance. In this study, 40% of the variance in end user performance was explained with just 7 variables.

A potential limitation of these and many other studies on end user computing (e.g., Bohlen & Ferratt, 1997) is the use of end user surrogates as subjects. Subjects in studies 1 and 2 fit Rockart and Flannery's (1983) descriptions of non-programming and command level end users; and therefore, results should generalize to those populations. Measuring situational factors subjectively in the form of perceptions as opposed to objectively could be construed as a potential limitation. Not only have many studies on EUC used perceptual measures (Al-Jabri & Al-Khaldi, 1997; Sankar & Marshall, 1993; Shayo, Guthrie, & Igbaria, 1999) but one could argue that perceptions of constraints are likely to have more influence on behavior and performance than the objective presence or absence of constraints per se.

Implications for Practitioners and Researchers

The results suggest that managers can increase end user performance by implementing goal setting, by shaping end users' attitudes toward working with computers, and by enhancing end users' self-efficacy beliefs. Self-efficacy beliefs can be enhanced through direct experience, vicarious experiences, and verbal persuasion (Bandura, 1982). Managers should use all three avenues to enhance self-efficacy beliefs. For instance, to enhance self-efficacy beliefs through direct experience, managers should begin by assigning tasks that can be easily performed by the end user. The next set of tasks should require the use of more difficult and complex end user computing skills. By methodically increasing the level of difficulty and complexity of tasks, managers can build and strengthen end users' efficacy beliefs. To enhance self-efficacy beliefs through vicarious experience, managers should identify effective end users as role models and persuade others to emulate those role models. Managers could also enhance efficacy beliefs by persuading end users to learn and apply computing skills. This can be accomplished by expressing confidence in end users' ability to do so. Additionally, managers should work closely with trainers and end users to identify potential constraints in the training and in the post-training environment and remove those constraints. At the very least, trainees should be taught how to effectively cope with those constraints. There is ample evidence that individuals do poorly in situations they believe exceed their coping abilities, whereas they behave assuredly when they judge themselves capable of managing otherwise intimidating situations (Bandura, 1982,1977). Enhancing coping-efficacy will not only strengthen computer-related self-efficacy beliefs, it will also have a direct influence on end user performance and the effective use of computer-based technologies in organizations.

Strong support for goal setting by these data suggests that trainers should set specific and challenging goals with respect to both learning and transfer. Learning goals involve the material to be learned by trainees during the training program. Also, by working with managers, trainers should identify specific work assignments that provide opportunities to apply skills taught in the training program and set transfer goals. Transfer goals involve applying skills learned in the training program to the job. Both learning and transfer goals should be specific and challenging. To evaluate accomplishment of transfer goals, managers and trainers should monitor end users to see if they are applying skills learned in the training program to complete job assignments that require the use of those skills. Rewards can be used to institutionalize the application of skills learned in the training program by end users to their job environments.

Specific attitudes are likely to be more easily influenced than general attitudes. Moreover, study data yielded support for attitudes toward working with computers, a specific attitude, but not attitudes toward computers, a general attitude. Therefore, trainers and managers should focus on enhancing specific attitudes such as attitudes toward specific computer applications or software packages. Implementing goal setting and strategies to enhance efficacy beliefs are likely to have a positive influence on end users' attitudes toward working with computers. Favorable attitudes toward working with computers can also be shaped by explicating how knowledge of specific computer applications and the proper application of that knowledge can help employees accomplish their work in a more productive manner and enhance their contributions to the organization.

Of the situational variables examined, complexity of training ($sR^2 = .044$) and lack of software user-friendliness ($sR^2 = .04$) appear to have the most detrimental effect on end user performance. Support for situational constraints suggests that trainers and managers should design computer education and training programs that are moderate in complexity, choose software packages that are user-friendly, and provide ample time to practice newly trained computer skills. In general, trainers and managers should require trainees to identify potential constraints in the training and in the work environment and make a concerted effort to remove those constraints. If those constraints cannot be eliminated or minimized, at the very least, trainees should be taught how to effectively cope with those constraints (Bandura,

1982). Enhancing coping-efficacy may be just as important as improving computer-related self-efficacy for facilitating end user performance.

In this study, the effects of a few theoretically relevant dispositional factors and situational constraints were examined. Future research should try to uncover other person and situational factors with potential to influence end user performance. Given that recent research has found personality to be a significant predictor of performance in diverse occupations (see Gatewood & Field, 1998), future research should examine the relationship between personality and performance of end users. For instance, openness to experience, one of the factors of the 5-factor personality model (McCrae & Costa, 1987) may be expected to positively influence end user performance. Another fruitful avenue of future research would be to examine the effects of situational facilitators on end user performance. For instance, situational factors such as EUC support perhaps in the form of "help desk" and organizational rewards are likely to enhance end user performance.

CONCLUSION

The primary purpose of introducing new technology is to improve productivity and organizational competitiveness. Organizations that introduce new end-user computing technologies expect their employees to learn and effectively use those technologies to enhance performance. Consequently, identifying person factors and situational conditions that facilitate (or debilitate) performance on tasks that require the use of skills taught in computer education and training programs has both theoretical significance and practical relevance.

REFERENCES

Aggarwal, A. K. (1998). End user training - revisited. *Journal of End User Computing*, 10(3), 32-33.

Ajzen, I., & Fishbein, M. (1980). *Understanding Attitudes and Predicting Social Behavior*. Englewood Cliffs, NJ: Prentice-Hall.

Al-Jabri, I. M., & Al-Khaldi, M. A. (1996). Effects of end user characteristics on computer attitude among undergraduate business students. *Journal of End User Computing, 9*(2), 16-22.

Amoroso, D. L. (1992). Using end user characteristics to facilitate effective management of end user computing. *Journal of End User Computing, 4*(4), 5-15.

Amoroso, D. L., & Cheney, P. H. (1991). Testing a causal model of end user application effectiveness. *Journal of Management Information Systems, 8*(1), 63-89.

Bandura, A. (1982). Self-efficacy mechanism in human agency. *American Psychologist*, 37, 122-147.

Bandura, A. (1977). *Social Learning Theory*. Englewood Cliffs, NJ: Prentice-Hall.

Bloom, A. J., & Hautaluoma, J. E. (1990). Anxiety management training as a strategy for enhancing computer user performance. *Computers in Human Behavior*, 6, 337-349.

Bohlen, G. R., & Ferratt, T. W. (1997). End user training: An experimental comparison of lecture versus computer-based training. *Journal of End User Computing*, 9(3), 14-27.

Bostrom, R. P., Olfman, L., & Sein, M. K. (1990). The importance of learning style in end user computing. *MIS Quarterly, 14*(1), 100-119.

Bowman, B. J., Grupe, F. H., & Simkin, M. G. (1995). Teaching end user applications with computer-based training: Theory and an empirical investigation. *Journal of End User Computing, 7*(2), 12-18.

Buchanan, D. A., & Bessant, J. (1985). Failure, uncertainty, and control: The role of operators in a computer integrated production system. *Journal of Management Studies,* 22, 292-308.

Cheney, P. H., Mann, R. I., & Amoroso, D. L. (1986). Organizational factors affecting the success of end-user computing. *Journal of Management Information Systems,* 3, 65-80.

Cohen, J., & Cohen, P. (1983). *Applied Multiple Regression/Correlation Analysis for the Behavioral Sciences*. Hillsdale, NJ: Lawrence Erlbaum Associates.

Compeau, D. R., & Higgins, C. A. (1995). Application of social cognitive theory to training for computer skills. *Information Systems Research, 6*(2), 118-143.

Czara, S. J., Hammond, K., Blascovich, J. J., & Swede, H. (1989). Age related differences in learning to use a text-editing system. *Behavior and Information Technology, 8*(4), 309-319.

Dambrot, F. H., Silling, S. M., & Zook, A. (1988). Psychology of computer use: Sex differences in prediction of course grades in a computer language course. *Perceptual and Motor Skills*, 66, 627-636.

Davis, D. L., & Davis, D. F. (1990). The effect of training technique and personal characteristics on training end users of information systems. *Journal of Management Information Systems*, 7, 93-110.

Davis, F. D., Bagozzi, R. P., & Warshaw, P. R. (1989). User acceptance of computer technology: A comparison of two theoretical models. *Management Science*, 35, 982-1003.

Evans, G. E., & Simkin, M. G. (1989). What best predicts computer proficiency? *Communications of the ACM, 32*(1), 1322-1327.

Finley, M. (1996). What's your techno type – and why you should care? *Personnel Journal*, January, 107-109.

Ford, J. K., Quinones, M., Sego., & Speer, J. (1991). Factors affecting the opportunity to use trained skills on the job. Paper presented at the Annual Conference of the Society of Industrial and Organizational Psychology, St. Louis, Missouri.

Gatewood, R. D., & Field, H. S. (1998). *Human Resource Selection* (4th edition). Fort Worth, Texas: The Dryden Press.

Gist, M. E., Schwoerer, C. E., & Rosen, B. (1989). Effects of alternative training methods on self-efficacy and performance in computer software training. *Journal of Applied Psychology*, 74, 884-891.

Hair, J. F., Anderson, R. E., Tatham, R. L., & Black, W. C. (1992). *Multivariate Data Analysis with Readings* (3rd ed.). New York: MacMillian Publishing Company.

Harrington, K. V., McElroy, J. C., & Morrow, P. C. (1990). Computer anxiety and computer based training: A laboratory experiment. *Journal of Educational Computing Research, 6*(3), 343-358.

Harrison, A. W., & Rainer, R. K. (1992). The influence of individual differences on skill in end user computing. *Journal of Management Information Systems, 9*(1), 93-111.

Hatcher, L., Prus, J. S., Englehard, B., & Farmer, T. M. (1991). A measure of academic situational constraints: Out-of-class circumstances that inhibit college student development. *Educational and Psychological Measurement,* 51, 953-962.

Hayek, L. M., & Stephens, L. (1989). Factors affecting computer anxiety in high school computer science students. *Journal of Computers in Mathematics and Science Teaching,* 8, 73-76.

Igbaria, M., & Iivari, J., & Maragahh, H. (1995). Why do individuals use computer technology? A Finnish case study. *Information and Management*, 29, 227-238.

Igbaria, M., & Nachman, S. (1990). Correlates of user satisfaction with EUC. *Information and Management, 19*(2), 73-82.

Jawahar, I. M. (in press). The influence of dispositional factors and situational constraints on end user performance: A replication and extension. *Journal of End User Computing.*

Jawahar, I. M., & Elango, B. (1988). Predictors of performance in software training: Attitudes toward computers versus attitudes toward working with computers. *Psychological Reports*, 83, 227-233.

Jawahar, I. M., & Elango, B. (2001). The effects of attitudes, goal setting and self-efficacy on end user performance. *Journal of End User Computing, 13*(2), 40-45.

Jawahar, I. M., Stone, T. H., & Cooper, W. H. (1992). Activating resources in organizations. In R. W. Woodman & W. A. Pasmore (eds.), *Research in Organizational Change and Development,* 6, 153-196. JAI Press.

Kennedy, T. C. S. (1975). Some behavioral factors affecting the training of naïve users of an interactive computer system. *International Journal of Man-Machine Studies*, 7, 817-834.

Kernan, M. C., & Howard, G. S. (1990). Computer anxiety and computer attitudes: An investigation of construct and predictive validity issues. *Educational and Psychological Measurement*, 50, 681-690.

Konvalina, J., Stephens, L., & Wileman, S. (1983). Identifying factors influencing computer science aptitude and achievement. *AEDS Journal, 16*(2), 106-112.

Lee, R. S. (1970). Social attitudes and the computer revolution. *Public Opinion Quarterly*, 34, 53-59.

Locke, E. A., & Latham, G. P. (1990). *A Theory of Goal-Setting and Task Performance.* Englewood Cliffs, NJ: Prentice-Hall.

Locke, E. A., Shaw, K. N., Saari, L. M., & Latham, G. P. (1981). Goal-setting and task performance: 1969-1980. *Psychological Bulletin*, 90, 125-152.

Mahmood, A. A., Burn, J. M., Gemoets, L. A., & Jacquez, C. (2000). Variables affecting information technology end-user satisfaction: A meta-analysis of the empirical literature. *International Journal of Human-Computer Studies*, 52, 751-771.

Marcoulides, G.A. (1988). The relationship between computer anxiety and computer achievement. *Journal of Educational Computing Research*, 4, 151-158.

Mawhinney, C. H., & Saraswat, S. P. (1991). Personality type, computer anxiety, and student performance. *Journal of Computer Information Systems*, 8, 110-123.

McCrae, R. R., & Costa, P. T. (1987). Validation of the five-factor model of personality across instruments and observers. *Journal of Personality and Social Psychology,* 52, 81-90.

Munro, M. C., Huff, S. L., Marcolin, B. L., & Compeau, D. R. (1997). Understanding and measuring user competence. *Information and Management*, 33, 45-57.

Nickell, G., & Pinto, J. (1986). The computer attitude scale. *Computers in Human Behavior*, 12, 301-306.

Nunnally, J. C., & Bernstein, I. H. (1994). *Psychometric theory* (3rd ed.). New York: McGraw-Hill, Inc.

Olson, M. H. (1982). New information technology and organizational culture. *MIS Quarterly*, 6, 71-99.

Olsten Corporation (1993). Survey of changes in computer literacy requirements for employees as reported in "Computer skills are more critical, but training lags," *HR Focus*, 70 (5), 18.

O'Quin, K., Kinsey, T. G., & Beery, D. (1987). Effectiveness of microcomputer-training workshop for college professionals. *Computers in Human Behavior*, 3, 85-94.

Palvia, P. (1991). On end user computing productivity. *Information and Management*, 21, 217-224.

Pedhazur, E. J., & Schmelkin, L. P. (1991). *Measurement, Design and Analysis: An Integrated Approach.* Hillsdale, New Jersey: Lawrence Erlbaum Associates.

Pentland, B. T. (1989). The learning curve and the forgetting curve: The importance of time and timing in the implementation of technological innovations. Paper presented at the Annual Academy of Management Meetings, Washington, DC.

Peters, L. H., Chassie, M. B., Lindholm, H. R., O'Connor, E. J., & Kline, C. R. (1982). The joint influence of situational constraints and goal setting on performance and affective outcomes. *Journal of Management, 8*(2), 7-20.

Peters, L. H., & O' Connor, E. J. (1980). Situational constraints and work outcomes: The influence of a frequently overlooked construct. *Academy of Management Review*, 5, 391-397.

Peters, L. H., O' Connor, E. J., & Rudolf, C. J. (1980). The behavioral and affective consequences of performance-relevant situational variables. *Organizational Behavior and Human Performance*, 25, 79-96.

Rafaeli, A. (1986). Employee attitudes toward working with computers. *Journal of Organizational Behavior*, 1, 89-106.

Rivard, S., & Huff, S. L. (1988). Factors of success for end user computing. *Communications of the ACM, 31*(5), 552-561.

Rockart, J. F., & Flannery, L. S. (1983). The management of end user computing. *Communications of the ACM, 26*(10), 776-784.

Rosen, L. D., Sears, D. C., & Weil, M. M. (1987). Computer phobia. *Behavior Methods, Instruments and Computers*, 19, 167-179.

Roszkowski, M. J., Devlin, S. J., Snelbecker, G. E., Aiken, R. M., & Jacobsohn, H. G. (1988). Validity and temporal stability issues regarding two measures of computer aptitudes and attitudes. *Educational and Psychological Measurement*, 48, 1029-1035.

Sankar, C. S., & Marshall, T. E. (1993). Database design support: An empirical investigation of perception and performance. *Journal of Database Management, 4*(3), 4-14.

Schneider, B. (1978). Person-situation selection: A review of some ability-situation interaction research. *Personnel Psychology,* 31, 281-297.

Shayo, C., Guthrie, R., & Igbaria, M. (1999). Exploring the measurement of end user computing success. *Journal of End User Computing, 11*(1), 5-14.

Stajkovic, A. D., & Luthans, F. (1998). Self-efficacy and work-related performance: A meta-analysis. *Psychological Bulletin, 124*(2), 240-261.

Steel, R. P., & Mento, A. J. (1986). Impact of situational constraints on subjective and objective criteria of managerial job performance. *Organizational Behavior and Human Decision Processes*, 37, 254-265.

Szajna, B. (1994). An investigation of the predictive validity of computer anxiety and computer attitude. *Educational and Psychological Measurement, 54*(4), 926-934.

Szajna, B., & Mackay, J. M. (1995). Predictors of learning performance in a computer-user training environment: A Path-analytic study. *International Journal of Human-Computer Interaction, 7*(2), 167-185.

Tannenbaum, S. I., & Yukl, G. (1992). Training and development in work organizations. *Annual Review of Psychology*, 43, 399-441.

Terborg, J. R. (1981). Interactional psychology and research on human behavior in organizations. *Academy of Management Review,* 6, 569-576.

Vroom, V. H. (1964). *Work and Motivation.* New York: Wiley.

Warner, L., & Smith, T. (1990). Computer training: Necessity not luxury. *Management Accounting, 68*(3), 48.

Wood, R. E., & Bandura, A. (1989). Impact of conceptions of ability on self-regulatory mechanisms and complex decision-making. *Journal of Personality and Social Psychology*, 56, 407-415.

Zimmerman, B. J., Bandura, A., & Martinez-Pons, M. (1992). Self-motivation for academic attainment: The role of self-efficacy beliefs and personal goal setting. *American Educational Research Journal, 29*(3), 663-676.

Section II:

End User System Effects, Outcomes and Overviews

Chapter V

A Dynamic Model of End-User Computing

Neil McBride
De Montfort University, UK

A. Trevor Wood-Harper
University of Salford, UK

ABSTRACT

Control is a major issue in end-user computing. The migration of responsibility, resources and authority from IT departments to user departments is frequently seen as a loss of power by the IT departments and an erosion of cost control by senior management. Reactions to this situation tend to focus on technology and formal control mechanisms. This chapter contrasts such an IT-oriented view with a proposed, alternative user-oriented view. An IT-oriented view of EUC focuses on the problems it causes, the technology it requires, the methods that should be used and the means of limiting, controlling and standardizing. A user-oriented view of EUC focuses on the problems it solves, the user's task and the organizational environment. The chapter advocates a shift in EUC research away from the technology and the IT issues towards the political, social and cultural issues associated with the users. EUC problems are, in the main, organizational problems requiring a research approach which addresses dynamic issues emerging over a period of time. As a basis for such research, the chapter proposes a dynamic model for EUC in which the progression of EUC within an organization is visualized as a series of inference loops.

INTRODUCTION

The advent of end-user computing (EUC) catalyzed by increasingly simple technology and increasingly sophisticated users has brought with it both solutions to problems within the information technology (IT) departments and new problems. While providing one solution to the so-called applications backlog, it has created new problems of control for the IT department which, in some cases, has led IT departments to avoid supporting EUC, and consider outsourcing end-user training, the support of PCs and networks and the help desk. EUC has led to an increase in the work load of the IT department, a growing application backlog as EUC systems require repair and support from the IT department, and increasing conflict between users and the IT department as the IT department seeks to rein in the uncontrollable proliferation of EUC.

At the heart of these problems lies the issue of control of EUC. Robson (1997, p382) refers to EUC as user-controlled computing. Responsibility, resources and authority over IS moves away from IT departments into user departments. EUC within the organization is affected by politics, culture and power within the organization. Reasons for the proliferation of EUC may include the wish to wrest control of IT from the IT department and to concentrate power within particular departments. The shift of control over IT resources to user departments has been associated with the duplication of computer applications, incompatibility and lack of integration, and low quality systems (Taylor et al., 1998). However, over-control of EUC by the IT department leads to alienation of end users and conflict (Beheshtian & Van Wert, 1987). Many organizations consider the solution to the lack of control of EUC to be the exertion of more control from the center. This IT-centered view of EUC sees EUC as a problem to be solved through standards, auditing, and financial control mechanisms which seek to make end users behave like IT professionals. Literature within the EUC field emphasizes the need for management of EUC by the IT department through the use of restrictions on users (Alavi, 1988; Behseshtian & Van Wert, 1987; Ngwenyama, 1993; Taylor et al., 1998).

This chapter firstly defines the IT-oriented approach to EUC control based on published research (Taylor et al., 1998). This is then contrasted with a user-oriented approach to EUC. A research agenda for studying EUC development from a user-oriented point of view is developed and supported by a model. It is concluded that research in EUC needs to address user motivations and the dynamics of end-user development within an organization.

An IT-Oriented Approach to EUC

If inadequately managed, EUC may become a source of problems. Valuable resources within IT are diverted to support amateur users who produce badly-written systems of no strategic value. There is a constant battle to halt the proliferation of various and incompatible platforms, to control spending, and to deal with problems caused by bad design and non-professional approaches to application development.

Figure 1: Case Study: BIS Health Care

BIS Health Care is a wholly owned subsidiary of BIS UK. Based at Swindon, it is the European center for pharmaceutical manufacturing, employing 600 people on four sites. The IT Department consists of three sections:

1. Operations: Deals with running of the mainframe, management of user authorizations, and support of mainframe applications;
2. Database: Manages the Health care customer and product databases.
3. Information Center: Provides user support for in house mainframe applications and user programmed mainframe applications, particularly user programmed database queries. Limited support of some PCs for technical users in the Research and Development areas has been provided in the past.

IT operations centered around the support of a mainframe running DOS /VSE.

In the last year, as a result of the reorganization of European operations of BIS, the mainframe has been moved to Reading. This has catalyzed a move towards increasing use of PCs, which is causing serious problems for the Information Center. The nature of the average user has changed. Rather than in-depth technical support for a few specialist packages, broad support is now required for users with limited computer knowledge. The number of calls to the Information Center has increased dramatically, leaving the staff over-stretched.

The number of PCs within BIS Health Care is unknown. Many departments have purchased PCs for staff on internal capital budgets without the knowledge of the IT department. Requests by the IT department for information on numbers of PCs have been ignored, and new PC users are 'emerging from the woodwork almost daily'.

Relationships between users and the IT department are difficult. One user described the IT Department as 'a bunch of user un-friendly, customer un-focused techno-freaks.'

The case study described in figure 1 illustrates some of the problems. An IT department focused on mainframe and large systems alienates the individual end user whose needs are not being met. The availability of cheap PC technology provides a means for those users to take control of their computing needs. Through word-of-mouth and by example, the use of small packages spreads throughout the organization. IT finds itself faced with needs for support from a whole class of users who were previously excluded from organizational computing. The IT department is ill-prepared to meet the needs of the changing customer base. End users consequently seek support elsewhere including non-IT departments and informal networks (Govindarajulu & Reithel, 1998).

The response of IT to such loss of control may be to adopt an authoritarian attitude by creating organizational rules for the use of PCs; for example, removing hard disks from PCs on client-server networks so that users must store applications on a central server; placing restrictions on the purchasing of computers; blocking access to organizational databases unless the EUC applications which may derive data from these databases have been audited and approved; and refusing to support non-standard systems and software. Such IT-oriented solutions arise from the perception that the control of EUC is an IT problem. It is not seen that the IT department's problem may be the user's solution. Discussion of an EUC research study will further illustrate this.

The questions addressed in Taylor et al. (1998) concern some of the problems of EUC and conclude that part of the solution lies in the adoption of a systems development methodology by the end users. Based on case studies of 34 organizations, they identify duplication of effort, low quality of end user developed systems and the lack of training of end user developers as key problems. The research focused on IT departments and interviewing IT staff about EUC. This work provided a widespread and intensive survey of EUC within UK organizations from an IT viewpoint. It highlights the IT-oriented focus of EUC research.

The questions addressed in this work concerned the nature of EUC development and included:

- How is the development and maintenance of end-user computing applications carried out?
- How is the quality of end-user computing projects assured?
- How are end-user computing projects supported by the IT department?

These questions reflect the concerns of the IT professionals which may not be those of the users. The researchers used the case study material to identify several strategies for using information systems methodologies in the development of end-user computing projects; end users should develop and maintain systems to the same standards as IT departments and they should adopt a 'cut-down' version of the IT department's methodology, tailored with the help of IT advisors to be contingent with the end-user department's needs. There is an underlying assumption that the solution to EUC problems is the same as that for IT department computing problems, namely the application of methods and standards; EUC problems will be solved if end users become closet IT professionals. The advantages given for the adoption of methodologies in EUC are the reduction of duplication of effort and maintenance problems, the improving of quality, security and recovery and the aligning of IT department and EUC systems (Taylor et al., p. 93). These may have been seen as advantages from the point of view of IT who are interested in how computing is done. They may not be of relevance to users who are interested in what is done and why.

In summary, an IT-oriented view of EUC focuses on the problems it causes, the technology it requires, the methods that should be used and the means of limiting, controlling and standardizing. A good outcome from EUC is defined in terms of the technical quality of the resulting application, the extent to which it follows the rules laid down by IT and the extent to which it integrates with IT's technology strategy.

A User-Oriented Approach to EUC

If an IT-oriented view of EUC focuses on the problems that EUC causes, a user-oriented view focuses on the solutions it provides. Control remains with the users and EUC problems are treated as organizational problems, not IT problems. For example, the duplication of applications and the redundancy of data that is often associated with EUC may be seen not as a result of a lack of IT standards and methods to be resolved by the imposition of control by IT, but rather as a symptom of an organizational problem. System duplication indicates organizational failure, not lack of involvement by IT. In one hospital, duplicate systems emerged as a result of organizational culture and politics; different specialties wished to assert their autonomy through the development of their own applications, and the control of their own data, raising barriers with other specialties and management (Hackney & McBride, 1995). Duplication of effort may arise from the hierarchical structures prevalent in organizations. Solutions to the duplication of systems may involve the restructuring of the organization and the establishing of better communication channels.

End users tend to develop computer systems to solve problems of immediate concern to them. These immediate problems need rapid solutions, so time is a significant factor. End users cannot wait for IT to produce systems (Fahy & Murphy, 1996). End users may be uncertain as to the solution to the problem and wish to experiment. EUC may involve establishing information needs in order to reduce task uncertainty (Blili et al., 1998). The focus of the end user is on the goal and not the means to the goal. In user-oriented EUC, quality considerations should focus on the quality of the solution and the resulting benefits rather than the quality of the tool produced to achieve that solution. An IT-oriented focus on code quality, documentation, backup and recovery misses the point of the end user system.

End-user training is a key issue in EUC. Igbaria and Zviran (1996) suggest that computer experience and training are key to effective EUC. Ngwenyama (1993) recognises the problem of end-user competence and proposes a solution based on collaborative action learning. Zinatelli et al. (1996) identify computer experience and computer training as key factors in encouraging EUC sophistication. While there is little argument about the importance of training and experience, the nature of that training is open to debate. Some authors advocate an IT-oriented view which focuses on training in the technology, methods and standards. Taylor et al. (1998) suggest training users in MicroSSADM which is a reduced and simplified version of SSADM (Structured Systems Analysis and Design Method). Other authors advocate training in tools and IS concepts (Alavi et al., 1988; Beheshtian & Van Wert, 1987). User-oriented EUC training should focus on identifying problems and solutions and evaluating potential IT tools. Rather than training that seeks to turn an end user into an IT professional, training should focus on making end users better at their tasks through the effective use of information systems, whether these are existing systems or are built by the end user. IT issues such as database management, backup and recovery should be handled automatically by the end-user computing tool or handled sensitively in the background by IT professionals.

The use of a systems development methodology by end users may be regarded as an attempt to impose an IT culture on end users. This culture may be foreign to the users (Ward & Peppard, 1996; Peppard & Ward, 1998). An IT-oriented view of the advantages of the use of a methodology in EUC may be interpreted by users as reasons for not using a method. Table 1 offers a possible user-view of each of the advantages given for the suggested use of methodologies by Taylor et al. (1998).

A thesis of this chapter is that the control of EUC should remain with the user, and that IT involvement should be limited to providing advice, perhaps through the mechanism of information centers (Gunton, 1988; DeVargas, 1989; Khan, 1992), only if requested. Attempts by IT to control EUC and enforce an IT-oriented approach are likely to generate resentment and fail. Alavi et al. (1988) suggest that EUC control should be enforced through line management and not by IS personnel. Beheshtian and Van Wert (1987) argue that, while IT should suggest standards and controls, it cannot be expected to enforce them since it is unlikely to have the authority or the resources. If IT is to be involved in EUC, it may be done by relinquishing control of IT staff to the users. Govindarajulu and Reithel (1998) found

Table 1: Contrast between IT's view and the user's view of the use of methodologies in EUC

IT View	User View
Reduces duplication	Removes my autonomy and ownership of the data.
Reduces difficulty of maintenance	Removes dependency on me as the system expert, reduces the extent to which I am needed to understand the problem and my creative solution to it.
Improves quality	Reduces creative input, reduces my ability to develop an evolving solution which reflects who I am (my role in the organization) and my ability to develop my skills.
Improves security	Reduces accessibility of system, reduces my ability to gain kudos by spreading my clever ideas around the department
Improves backup and recovery	Increases time wasted on non-essential, technical activities, which I don't want to worry about because they are not part of the problem I am working on.
Aligns IT department and EUC	Allows IT to interfere with the way I work, increases IT's power and control which I am trying to break free of, reduces my independence.

that 62% of organizations in their survey had decentralized support for EUC by placing IT staff in user departments. In user-oriented EUC, control of computing activities is taken away from IT which signals that EUC is an organizational issue, not an IT issue.

The removal of EUC control from IT, or any centralized authority, may enhance the risk of complications: system redundancy, data duplication, lack of data integrity. However, this may bring with it increased creativity, the extension of organizational knowledge, and greater opportunity of the creation of strategic information systems (Davenport, 1994; McBride et al., 1997). Effective solutions may be embedded in everyday experience and local knowledge; open experimentation by end users should be encouraged; ideas should emerge from deviations from standards and from initiatives outside IT's development agenda (Ciborra, 1994).

In summary, a user-oriented view of EUC focuses on the problems it solves, the user's task and the organizational environment. Technology is provided unobtrusively as a background tool supporting the end user in delivering business benefit. A good outcome from EUC is defined in terms of the business quality of the solution provided by the end user (the extent, for example, to which it reduces costs, increases efficiency and increases customer satisfaction), and the extent to which it contributes to business goals.

Research Questions for User-Oriented EUC

We argue that a reframing of EUC research is required. Both the subject and the method of research need to change. EUC needs to be viewed from a user's point of view as well as an IT point of view. While IT-oriented research is important, too much of the survey work within information systems has solicited only the views of IS practitioners and largely ignored the views of users (Galliers et al., 1994). While IT-oriented research on EUC focuses on IT problems (Taylor et al., 1998), user-oriented EUC focuses on end-users needs (Fahy & Murphy, 1996). Important areas of research concern the user's motivation, the nature of user tasks, and the role of the user within the organization. The IT-oriented research questions of Taylor et al. (1998) are replaced by user-oriented questions:

- What has motivated the user to start EUC?
- What are the user's objectives in doing some programming?
- What is the user's attitude to computing, to the IT department, to information?
- What is the primary focus of the problems the end user is tackling?
- What are the problems that EUC solves?
- How do those problems relate to the business's corporate objectives?
- Why do end users ignore standards and guidelines?

Research in EUC should focus on motivation, attitudes, the development of experience and the triggers which cause or promote end-user computing developments. EUC emerges over time. Therefore, a research approach is required which addresses the dynamic issues and discovers the emerging patterns and influence on the end user's activities and attitudes. Static studies based on surveys or interviews will not reveal the complex and developing interactions which change the way computing is carried out within an organization. Longitudinal studies are required which build up a history of the development of EUC within an organization and demonstrate the emerging, cyclical patterns (Weick, 1979). Static studies, even when taking a case study approach (Taylor et al., 1998; Zinatelli, 1996) may not provide the rich detail required to interpret EUC development.

EUC arises from the complex relationships between groups, individuals and technologies. The motivation for EUC needs to be determined and the effect of EUC on user motivation analyzed. EUC may increase satisfaction in work through providing self-expression, self-determination and intrinsic job satisfaction. Users can influence job design and determine their own information requirements. They can increase their skills, deriving satisfaction from the expression of those skills and from self-expression. It can be argued that EUC leads to greater job variety, complexity, autonomy and responsibility which may lead to greater job satisfaction (Katz & Kahn, 1978).

Interpretive studies are required which seek to examine the dynamics of EUC. These studies must ask how end users produce change in their environment and identify areas of organizational change requiring further attention. The user of IT in mediating such change needs to be examined. EUC studies must understand how end users interpret their organizational environment and impose structure on it; how they differentiate between figure and ground (Weick, 1979), that is between what is seen as interesting, important and worthy of focused attention and the background information that is assumed, taken for granted or ignored. The use of EUC may help in retaining and formalizing the end-users' interpretive structures; their understanding of their roles, processes and customers.

A Dynamic Model of EUC

The progression of EUC within an organization may be visualized as a series of inference loops (Weick, 1979) which develop over time. Effects within loops are amplified and small factors may take on great significance as EUC evolves. The following describes a theoretical model which seeks to explain the interactions which influence EUC within an organization, described in terms of inference loops. The attributes describe discrete events; the arrows connect events and represent influence. Weick (1979) also describes these events as variables which can have a variety of values. These inference loops bear some similarity to the causal maps used in comprehensive situational mapping (CSM) (Offodile & Acar, 1993; Georgantas & Acar, 1995). In CSM, nodes represent influencing functions or attributes and arrows represent influence vectors and are given a signed magnitude. However, in CSM, causal maps support decision-making whereas Weick's inference loops support sense-making in complex social situations within organizations.

Technology Improvement

A key element of EUC is the availability of the technology. EUC requires cheap technology that is easy to use. Figure 2 illustrates possible inference loops based on the following attributes:

- Technology Accessibility. The ease of procurement and use of IT, influenced by the low cost of workstations, the ease of implementation and the ease of end-user system development.

- Technology Availability. The extent to which the end user has access to PCs and workstations.
- Technology Awareness. The knowledge that the end user has of what IT is available and how it can influence her work tasks.
- Technology Acceptability. The extent to which the use of IT is an accepted part of work practice and is embedded in the end-user's tasks; the extent to which the use of IT is a natural element of the end-user's role and the extent to which IT use is an organizational norm.
- Management Support. The extent to which management encourages the use of IT by their sub-ordinates and the extent to which they encourage end-user developments and initiatives. This will be influenced by the management's awareness of the technology.
- Technology Spread. The extent to which IT spreads with the organization. This might be examined by looking at changes in the number of users that have PCs or workstations on their desk.
- Technology Development. The way the technology is used within the organization, the maturity of information systems support, the development of the technology platform, the provision of better development tools.
- Technology Publicity. The extent to which the organization is exposed to publicity about changing technology in the popular and trade press, through word of mouth, through supplier advertising including supplier visits and trade fairs.

The availability of the technology is necessary but not sufficient for the uptake of EUC. There must be group acceptance of the technology, and the establishing of an environment in which the use of computers is seen as socially acceptable. Social acceptability may emerge from management support, strengthened by the rules, norms and interpretations placed on the technology. We must ask: how does the management interpret the role of information technology within the organization and its use by end users?

Figure 2 illustrates the positive influence of the attributes on each other. For example, increased technology availability and technology publicity may lead to increased technical awareness and consequently increased management support. It should be noted that the figure also suggests a decrease in one attribute will lead to a decrease in another. Thus, reduced technology availability and reduced technology publicity may lead to reduced technical awareness and consequently reduced management support.

Figure 2: Technology development (+ indicates one attribute causes increase in another, - indicates one attribute reduces another)

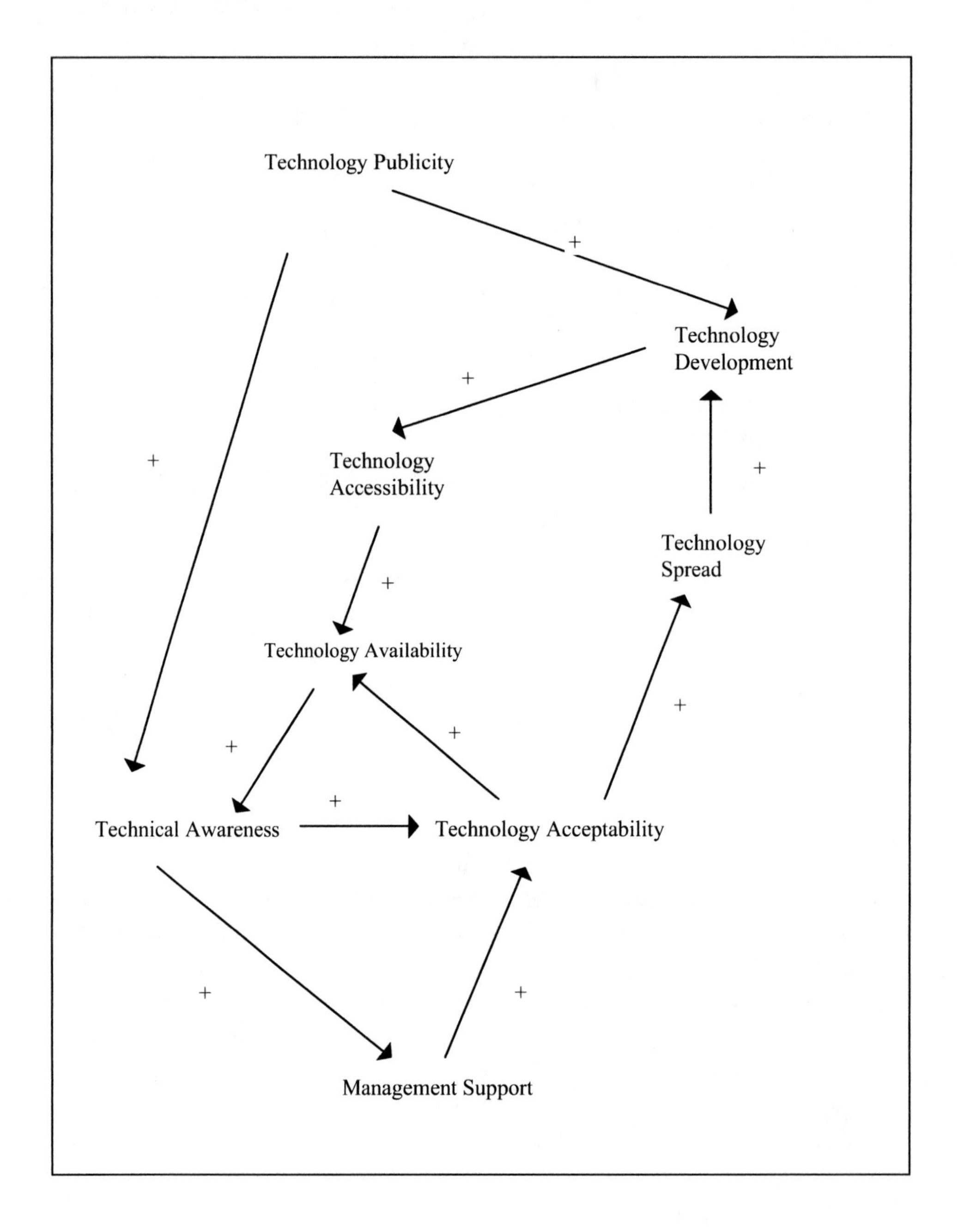

IT Department Involvement

The role of the IT department is crucial to the development of EUC. Figure 3 identifies some suggested causal influences based on the following attributes:

- Demand from Users. The demand for new IT development from users as represented by development project requests, information system usage, involvement of end users in systems development.
- IT Department Overload. The size of the gap between the number of requests for development, maintenance and support work from end users and the available development resources, both staff and capital, to meet the demand.
- IT/User Culture Gap. The extent to which the IT and business functions within the organization are aligned in terms of strategy, organizational goals, empathy, professional respect, geographical location and knowledge of the business.
- IT Support. The level of IT support provided to users to enable them to fulfil their organizational roles effectively and efficiently, as perceived by the end users themselves.
- EUC Development. The extent of development of end-user systems within the organizations and its departments, as suggested by the number of users involved, the amount of time spent by users in system development, the size of the resulting systems, the extent of usage of those systems and the importance of the systems to the organization.
- Autonomy. The extent to which the end users have control over their IT budget, the selection of IT systems, the way they carry out business processes and the outcomes of those business processes.
- Time Required. The amount of time required to deliver a new information system development, in terms of actual time needed which is affected by the size and complexity of the system, and elapsed time which is also affected by the availability of resources and the waiting period before a project can begin.
- Competitor Activity. The extent to which the organization's competitors are using IT to develop new services and enhance existing services.
- Customer Expectation. The perception of customers as to the level of service the organization should provide and the types of service. This is influenced by what competitors are providing and by their use of IT.
- Service Demand. The demands placed on the organization in terms of the volume, level, quality and complexity of service provided.
- Problem Complexity. The complexity of the problem for which end users are developing a computer-based solution, considered in terms of number of data items, algorithm complexity, number of processes and interactions.

- Solution Searching. The amount of effort expended by end users in researching the use of information systems to provide solution to business problems.

Figure 3: IT department involvement (+ indicates one attribute causes increase in another, - indicates one attribute reduces another)

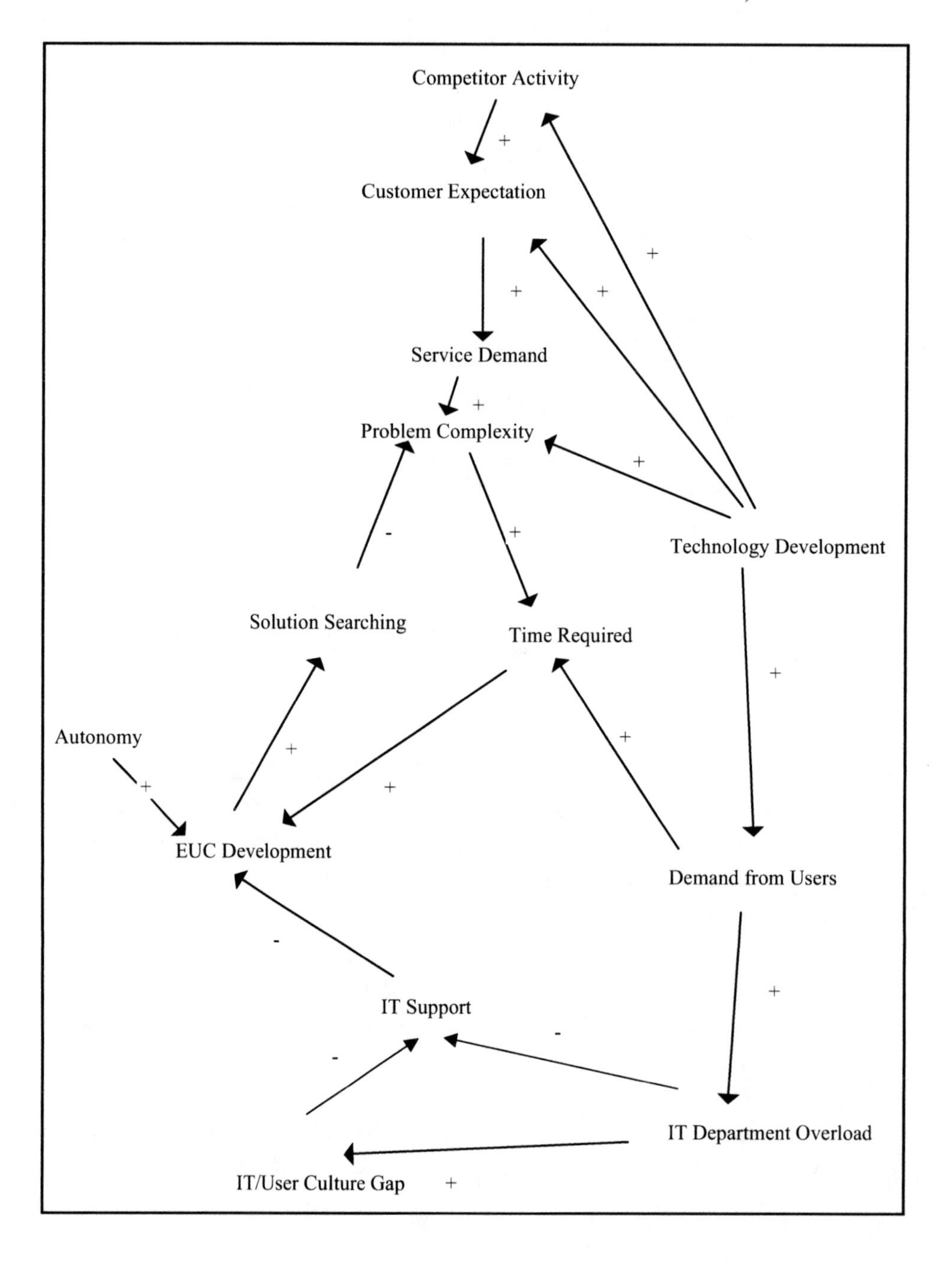

Technology improvement may lead to increased demand for IT services. This, in turn, may lead to IT distancing itself from the user in order to minimize the resources being directed away from major operational IT projects. However, in a dynamic environment the effect of a factor may change suddenly. For example, while initially the lack of IT support increases EUC activity since demands for systems are not being met by IT, when the end user subsequently hits development problems, the absence of IT support may act as an inhibitor of EUC since the user cannot proceed without advice and expertise which is not forthcoming.

The motivation for EUC lies in the need for end users to overcome problems which affect their day-to-day processes. The complexity of the problem leads to an increase in EUC as the problem-solvers seek to develop solutions which reduce complexity and make the operational situation manageable. Problem complexity may be influenced by the availability of improved technology which leads to greater demands from customers. End users require rapid solutions to problems. Often time limitations motivate the user to undertake her own system development. Both problem complexity and IT overload may be seen as increasing the time needed for a problem to be solved. Increased waiting may increase the motivation to carry out EUC.

Power Distribution

A third series of inference loops (figure 4) hypothesizes the effect of EUC on power. In addition to the attributes described above, the following attributes are suggested:

- Control of Resources. The extent to which the end user controls the hardware and software platforms and applications. The extent to which the end user controls the development and usage of local computer systems.
- Development of New Knowledge. The rate at which the end user takes on new knowledge and develops new skills through attending training courses and developing new systems.
- Computer Competence. The overall level of IT understanding of the users as shown through the usage and development of information systems.
- Strategic Applications. The number of applications built by the end user which have a significant effect on the organization's business success. The extent to which particular applications built by the end user are influential within the organization and have high visibility.
- Power. The perceived influence of end users on the distribution of resources, the decision-making process, and the strategic direction of the organization.

Figure 4: Power distribution (+ indicates one attribute causes increase in another, - indicates one attribute reduces another)

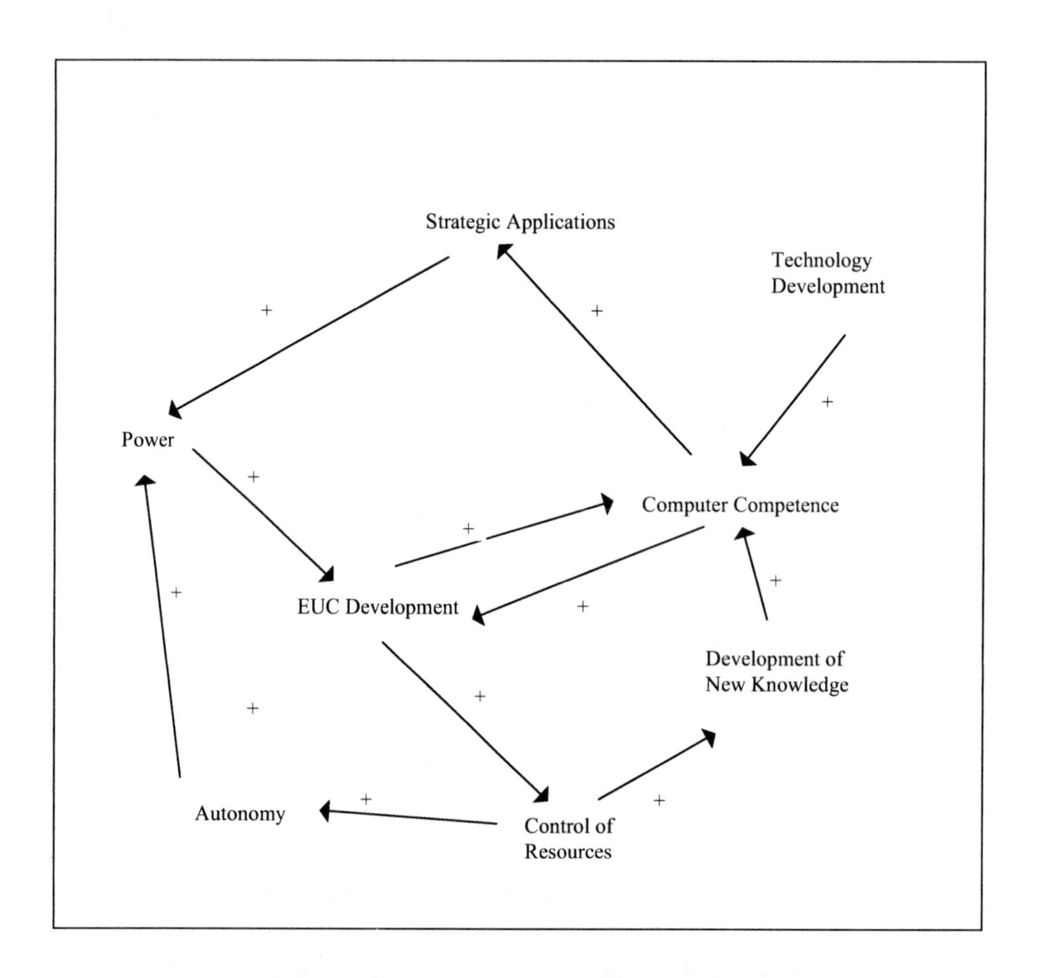

Increased EUC may result in increased control of resources by the end user. This may lead to increases in autonomy and power within the user community. Furthermore, the expansion of EUC may lead to increased computer competence. This may, in turn, lead to the development of new strategic applications by end users which may increase their power base within the organizations.

Research Strategy

The above model is based on our understanding of the important issues in EUC, drawn from both the literature (Alavi, et al., 1988; Hackney and McBride, 1995; Taylor et al., 1998) and our own experience. As such, the model is untested:

research is needed to develop it. Since the model describes the influences of factors on EUC over a period of time, the progression of these inference loops may be best studied through case studies developed over time to provide an historical analysis of the progression of EUC. Interviews should be conducted with end users at intervals over a period of time. The gathering of local knowledge, local stories and local meaning (Colville et al., 1999) will enable an understanding of these phenomena to be built up. We are not advocating that the attributes within the inference loops be necessarily treated as quantitative measurables. They may be used as conceptual guides, sensitizing the researcher to themes that should be developed in the storytelling. We see this as a way of interpreting and understanding processes, rather than developing objective measures. However, we recognize that the model of EUC may be investigated quantitatively by seeking to measure the change in each variable over time.

These studies need to recognize the importance of external influences on the development of EUC, the intimate link between EUC development and organizational dynamics and the effect of feedback. As a result of case study research, these models may provide a practical basis for directing resources towards EUC, developing an appropriate organizational culture and optimizing the use of information and communication technologies within the organization.

CONCLUSION

The advent of Internet technology and the development of Intranets as the basic information infrastructure for an increasing number of organizations may accelerate a sea-change in approaches to IT management. Intranets offer end users increased freedom from IT-oriented control of organizational computing. Instead of being dependent on centrally defined menus and systems, end users are free to select the systems they want and to develop their own personalized information environments. End users may develop home pages which contain information sources which are relevant to their organizational roles, rather than using company-wide systems which may not be of significant value.

The scale of this change may catalyze such a change in information management that end-user computing becomes the dominant form of organizational computing. A user-oriented view of EUC may become essential for both researchers and practitioners. The technological view of EUC control, centered around standards, methods and technological audits may not be an appropriate approach to a series of problems which concern organizational context, culture and politics.

EUC problems are, in the main, organizational problems requiring a research approach which addresses dynamic issues emerging over a period of time (Watson

& Wood-Harper, 1996). EUC research must draw out the organizational issues which drive EUC. A user-oriented view may enable a focus on user tasks and problems and the way IT can serve the user and solve the user's problems, not on the technology and the way the user can serve the technology. User-oriented EUC research may lead to alternative approaches to IT development and support. This may involve the use of component technology, the development of tailorable, evolving systems, and the use of disposable software to solve immediate problems. Flexibility and tailorability may be more important than structure and method. User-oriented EUC should be judged on business value and problem-solving success, not methodological rigor. New EUC research should be business-focused rather than technology-focused, understanding the motivations for EUC and the nature of successful outcomes.

In order to gain empathy and understanding, IT departments must view the development of EUC within an organization from the user's point of view. If the IT department understands the user's motivation, both explicit and tacit, it may be able to provide help both technically and managerially. That help must be anticipatory and unobtrusive. This chapter identifies a research need, the outcome of which will help IT departments to understand EUC and respond appropriately.

REFERENCES

Alavi, M., Nelson, R. R., & Weiss, I. R. (1988). Managing end user computing as a value-added resource. *Journal of Information Systems Management,* Summer 1988, 26-35.

Behshtian, M. & VanWert, P. D. (1987). Strategies for managing user developed systems. *Information and Management,* 12, 1-7.

Blili, S., Raymond, L., & Rivard, S. (1998). Impact of task uncertainty, end user involvement and competence on the success of end-user computing. *Information and Management,* 33, 137-153.

Ciborra, C. (1994). The grassroots of IT and strategy. In Ciborra, C & Jelassi, T, John Wiley (eds.), *Strategic Information Systems: A European Perspective* (pp. 3-24). .

Colville, I. D., Waterman, R. H., & Weick, K. E. (1999). Organizing and the search for excellence: Making sense of times in theory and practice. *Organization, 6*(1), 129-148.

Davenport, T. H. (1994). Saving IT's soul: Human centered information management. *Harvard Business Review,* March-April 1994, 119 - 131.

Devargas, M. (1989). *Introducing the Information Center*. NCC Blackwell.

Fahy, M. & Murphy, C. (1996). From end user computing to management developed systems. In Coelho, J. D., Jelassi, T., Konig, W., Krcmar, H., & O'Callaghan, R. (eds.), *Proceedings of the 4th European Conference on Information Systems* (pp. 127 – 142).

Galliers, R. D., Merali, Y., & Spearing, L. (1994). Coping with information technology? How British executives perceive the key information systems management issues in the mid-1990s. *Journal of Information Technology, 9*(3), 223-238.

Georgantzas, N. C. & Acar, W. (1995). *Scenario-Driven Planning: Learning to Manage Strategic Uncertainty*. Quorum Books.

Govindarajulu, C. & Reithel, B. J. (1998). Beyond the information center: An instrument to measure end user computing support from multiple sources. *Information and Management,* 33, 241-250.

Gunton, T. (1988). *End User Focus*. Prentice Hall.

Hackney, R. & McBride, N. K. (1995). The efficacy of information systems in the public sector: Issues of context and culture. *International Journal of Public Sector Management, 8*(6), 17 - 29.

Igbaria, M. & Zviran, M. (1996). Comparison of end user computing characteristics in the US, Israel and Taiwan. *Information & Management,* 30, 1-13.

Katz, D. & Kahn, R. L. (1978). *The Social Psychology of Organizations*. Chichester: John Wiley.

Khan, E. H. (1992). The effects of information centers on the growth of end user computing. *Information & Management,* 23, 279-289.

McBride, N., Lander, R., & McRobb, S. (1997). Post-modernist information management. *Proceedings of the 7th Annual Business Information Technology Conference,* Manchester Metropolitan University, November 5-6 1997.

Ngwenyama, O. K. (1993). Developing end user's systems development competence. *Information & Management,* 25, 291-302.

Offodile, O. F. & Acar, W. (1993) Comprehensive situation mapping for robot evaluation and selection. *International Journal of Operations and Production Management, 13*(1), 71-80.

Peppard, J. & Ward, J. (1999). 'Mind the gap': Diagnosing the relationship between the IT organization and the rest of the business. *Journal of Strategic Information Systems,* 8, 29 - 60.

Robson, W. (1997). *Strategic Management and Information Systems.* London: Pitman.

Taylor, M. J., Moynihan, E. P, & Wood-Harper, A. T. (1998). End user computing and information system methodologies. *Information Systems Journal,* 8, 85-96.

Ward, J. & Peppard, J. (1996). Reconciling the IT/ business relationship: a troubled marriage in need of guidance. *Journal of Strategic Information Systems,* 5, 37-65.

Watson, H. & Wood-Harper, A. T. (1996). Deconstructing contexts in interpreting methodology. *Journal of Information Technology, 11*(1), 36-51.

Weick, K. (1979). *The Social Psychology of Organizing.* New York: McGraw-Hill.

Zinatelli, N., Cragg, P. B., & Cavaye, A. L. M. (1996). End user computing sophistication and success in small firms. *European Journal of Information Systems* 5, 172-181.

Chapter VI

A Comparison of End User and Expert System Quality Assessments

Tanya J. McGill
Murdoch University, Australia

ABSTRACT

Organizations rely heavily on applications developed by end users, yet lack of experience and training may compromise the ability of end users to make objective judgments about the quality of their applications. The study reported on in this chapter investigated the ability of end users to assess the quality of applications they develop. The results confirm that there are differences between the system quality assessments of end user developers and independent expert assessors. In particular, the results of this study suggest that end users with little experience may erroneously consider the applications they develop to be of high quality. Some implications of these results are discussed.

INTRODUCTION

User developed applications (UDAs) form a significant proportion of organizational information systems (McLean, Kappelman, & Thompson, 1993) and the ability to use end user development tools is often a position requirement instead of an individual option (Brancheau & Brown, 1993). The benefits that have been claimed for user development of applications include better access to information and improved quality of information, leading to improved employee productivity and performance. However, the realization of these benefits may be put at risk because of problems with information produced by UDAs that may be incorrect in design, inadequately tested, and poorly maintained.

Despite these risks, organizations generally undertake little formal evaluation of the quality of applications developed by end users (Panko & Halverson, 1996). In the majority of organizations the only measures of whether an application is suitable for use are user developers' subjective assessments of their applications. Yet purely subjective, personal evaluations of UDA quality could be at wide variance with actual quality. Lack of experience and training may compromise the ability of end users to make objective judgments about the quality of their applications, but it appears that many end users do lack experience and training in both use of system development tools and in systems development procedures (Cragg & King, 1993).

There has been little empirical research on user development of applications (Shayo, Guthrie, & Igbaria, 1999), and most of what has been undertaken has used user satisfaction as the measure of success because of the lack of objective measures available (Etezadi-Amoli & Farhoomand, 1996). The fact that vital organizational decision making relies on the individual end user's assessment of application effectiveness suggests that more insight is needed into the ability of end users to assess the success of their own applications, and that as well as user satisfaction additional criteria of success should be considered.

Research on the relationship between experience or training and the success of UDAs has been inconclusive. Some studies have found positive impacts (Crawford, 1986; Nelson & Cheney, 1987; Raymond & Bergeron, 1992) and some have found negative impacts (Amoroso, 1986; Crawford, 1986; Janvrin & Morrison, 2000). Yaverbaum and Nosek (1992) speculated that computer training increases one's expectations of information systems, and hence may actually cause negative perceptions. This may be the case for both training and experience in the UDA domain and may go some way to explaining the lack of conclusive results in the literature.

There have been many calls for the development of more direct and objective measures of UDA effectiveness (Al-Shawaf, 1993; Edberg & Bowman, 1996;

Igbaria, 1990; Rivard, Poirier, Raymond, & Bergeron, 1997). There have also been some attempts to move away from the use of user satisfaction as the major indicator of UDA success and to adopt a software engineering approach with a focus on application quality rather than user satisfaction. Edberg and Bowman (1996) compared the quality of UDAs with applications developed by information systems professionals, and found UDAs to be of significantly lower quality. Rivard and her colleagues (1997) noted that although the conceptual definitions of quality from the software engineering literature are appropriate for UDAs, the operationalizations in terms of software metrics are not. They, therefore, attempted to capture both the user perspective and the more technical aspects of UDA quality through a validated assessment instrument to be completed by end user developers (Rivard et al., 1997). However, none of these studies have compared user and expert assessments of UDA quality, nor looked at the roles of experience and training in end users' ability to assess the quality of applications. This paper describes a study, which uses direct examination of applications to compare users' and experts' assessments of UDAs.

RESEARCH QUESTIONS

As discussed above, reliance on end user perceptions of UDA quality may be problematic because users may not only lack the skills to develop quality applications but may also lack the knowledge to make realistic determinations about the quality of applications that they develop. A user developer may be pleased with the quality of their 'creation' and its contribution to their decision-making activities when in fact the application includes serious errors such as incorrect formulae (Edberg & Bowman, 1996). End user developers who are unaware of quality problems in their applications may make errors in tasks or make poor decisions, which, in turn, could impact on organizational performance.

The potential for a user developer's perceptions to be colored by ignorance indicates the need for research assessing the ability of end users to evaluate the quality of the products of their own application development work. This can be accomplished by comparing user developers' perceptions of application quality with independent expert assessments.

The primary research question investigated in this study was:

> How do user developer assessments of the quality of applications they have developed differ from independent expert assessments?

As discussed earlier, in previous studies that have related computing experience and training to EUC success the dependent variable used has mainly been user satisfaction and the results have not been conclusive. Whilst Crawford (1986) found that greater user developer experience was associated with higher levels of satisfaction, Al-Shawaf (1993) did not find any relationship between development experience and user satisfaction, and Amoroso (1986) found that the lower the level of programming skills and report building skills reported, the higher was the satisfaction. Janvrin and Morrison (2000) found that their more experienced subjects were less confident that their applications were error free.

Crawford (1986) also found that higher levels of training were generally associated with lower levels of user satisfaction, while Raymond and Bergeron (1992) found microcomputer training to have a significant positive effect on satisfaction with decision making, and Nelson and Cheney (1987) concluded that there is generally a positive relationship between computer-related training that a user receives and his or her ability to use the computer resource.

Hence in this study the second research question to be answered was:

How do experience and training influence differences between user developer and independent expert assessments of UDAs?

It was hypothesized that:

(1) End user assessments of UDA quality will not be consistent with expert assessments of UDA quality when the user developer has little experience with application development using the chosen tools.

(2) End user assessments of UDA quality will not be consistent with expert assessments of UDA quality when the user developer has had little training in use of the chosen tools.

METHOD

The study was conducted with Masters of Business Administration (MBA) students participating in a business policy simulation over a period of 13 weeks as part of a capstone course in Strategic Management. All subjects had at least 2 years of previous professional employment.

The general applicability of research findings derived from student samples has been an issue of concern. However, Briggs et al. (1996) found MBA students to be good surrogates for executives in studies relating to the use and evaluation of technology, suggesting that the students who participated in this study can be considered as typical of professionals who would be involved in user development of applications in organizations. The opportunity to undertake the study in a relatively controlled environment where all applications had similar requirements and there was minimum confounding by extraneous variables, was considered worth trading off against the greater generalizability that may have been obtained from a field study.

The Game

The Business Policy Game (BPG) (Cotter & Fritzche, 1995) simulates the operations of a number of manufacturing companies. Participants assume the roles of managers, and make decisions in the areas of marketing, production, financing and strategic planning. Typical decisions to be made include product pricing, production scheduling and obtaining finance.

In this study the decisions required for the operation of each company were made by teams with 4 or 5 members. Decisions were recorded twice a week and the simulation run immediately afterwards so that results were available for teams to use during the next decision period. Each team was free to determine its management structure but in general the groups adopted a functional structure, with each member responsible for a different area of decision-making. The simulation accounted for 50% of each subject's overall course grade.

The User Developed Applications

The subjects developed their own decision support systems using spreadsheets to help in their decision-making. Decision support systems were developed either by individuals to support their own area of responsibility or by several members of a team. Where several members of a team worked on one application, each was responsible for one worksheet that related to their area of responsibility. The unit of the analysis in the study was an individual's application. If they wished, the subjects were able to use simple templates available with the game as a starting point for their applications, but they were not constrained with respect to what they developed, how they developed it, or the hardware and software tools they used. The majority of applications were developed in Microsoft Excel© but some subjects also used Lotus 1-2-3© and Claris Works©. The spreadsheets themselves were not part of the course assessment, so there were no formal requirements beyond students' own needs for the game. The fact that development of applications was optional and unrelated to the purposes of this study reduces the artificiality of the study situation.

Procedure for Data Collection

Each subject was asked to complete a written questionnaire and provide a copy of their spreadsheet on disk after eight 'quarterly' decisions had been made (4 weeks after the start of the simulation). This point was chosen to allow sufficient time for the development and testing of the applications. The majority of completed questionnaires and spreadsheets were collected in person during the time when subjects were submitting their decisions but where this wasn't possible subjects were sent a follow up letter with a reply paid envelope. Ninety- one questionnaires were distributed and 79 useable responses were received giving a response rate of 86.8%.

The Instrument

The questionnaire consisted of two sections. The first section asked questions about the subjects and their previous training and experience with spreadsheets, and the second section asked questions about the spreadsheet they had developed. Spreadsheet experience was measured in years and subjects were subsequently categorized (based on the spread of experience in the sample) as low experience (0 – 4 years experience), medium experience (5 – 8 years experience) or high experience (9+ years experience). Previous spreadsheet training was measured using a 4-item 5-point Likert-type scale from Igbaria (1990) which asked for level of training received in each of 4 types of training (college or university; vendor; in-company; self study). Scores for the 4 types of training were summed and subjects were subsequently categorized as low training (score less than 6), medium training (score of 7 - 9) or high training (score of 10 or more).

System quality relates to the quality of the information system itself and is concerned with matters such as whether or not there are 'bugs' in the system, the consistency of the user interface and ease of use. In this study, system quality was operationalized based upon the instrument developed by Rivard et al. to assess specifically the quality of user-developed applications (Rivard et al., 1997). Rivard et al.'s instrument was designed to be suitable for end user developers to complete, yet to be sufficiently deep to capture their perceptions of components of quality.

Seven of the eight dimensions of quality in Rivard et al.'s instrument could be considered for these applications. These were reliability, effectiveness, portability, economy, user-friendliness, understandability, and maintainability. The verifiability dimension was not included because the processes being examined in the questionnaire items relating to verifiability were not applicable to the environment in which the development was done. A number of individual items were also not included either because they were not appropriate for the applications under consideration (e.g. specific to database applications) or because they were not amenable to expert assessment (e.g. required either privileged information about the subjects' performance in the game or access to the hardware configurations on which the spreadsheets were originally used). Minor adaptations to wording were also made to reflect the terminology used in the BPG and the environment in which application development and use occurred.

The resulting system quality scale consisted of 40 items, each scored on a Likert scale of 1 to 7 where (1) was labeled 'strongly agree' and (7) was labeled 'strongly disagree' (see Appendix 1 for a list of the items). Measures for each of the quality dimensions were obtained by averaging the values of the criterion variables relating to that dimension. An overall application quality measure was obtained by averaging the seven quality dimension scores. This is consistent with the approach used by Rivard et al. The instrument had a Cronbach's alpha of 0.82.

Independent Expert Assessment of System Quality

Two independent assessors using the same set of items also assessed the system quality of each UDA. Both assessors were information systems academics with years of experience teaching spreadsheet design and development. Before assessing the study sample, the assessors spent a substantial amount of time familiarising themselves with the BPG and then completed four pilot evaluations of applications not included in the study sample. Differences were discussed and adjustments made to ensure consistency between the assessors. Assessments of the actual UDAs were then undertaken. The quality ratings of the two independent assessors were highly correlated ($r = 0.73$, $p = 0.000$).

RESULTS

Of the 79 subjects 78.5% were male and 21.5% female (62 males, 17 females). Their ages ranged from 21 to 49 with an average age of 31.8. Subjects reported an average of 5.9 years experience using spreadsheets (with a range from 0 to 15 years).

Table 1 indicates that the subjects had received relatively little spreadsheet training. More than 50% of the subjects had received no in-company or vendor training and just under 50% had received no college or university training. Self-study was the predominant means by which students had acquired their knowledge of spreadsheets.

The first research question considered how end user developer assessments of application quality might differ from those of the independent experts. To address this question, the mean scores for each quality dimension as assessed by the user

Table 1: Summary of the subjects' previous spreadsheet training

Training Source	*Level of Training*										
	Mean	Number in each category									
		(1) None		(2)		(3)		(4)		(5) Extr. Intensive	
		N	%	N	%	N	%	N	%	N	%
College or University	2.0	46	58.2	8	10.1	6	7.6	11	13.9	7	8.9
Vendor	1.5	62	78.5	3	3.8	4	5.1	5	6.3	4	5.1
In-company	1.7	52	65.8	6	7.6	12	15.2	7	8.9	1	1.3
Self study	3.3	8	10.1	8	10.1	26	32.9	23	29.1	13	16.5

developers were compared with the independent assessments (Table 2). The scores for each quality dimension as assessed by the user developers were compared statistically with the independent assessments using paired samples t-tests.

There were significant differences on five of the quality dimensions. The user developers rated the effectiveness and portability of their applications significantly lower than did the independent assessors (t=-2.67, p=0.009; t=-3.55, p=0.001) and rated reliability, understandability and user-friendliness significantly higher than did the independent assessors (t=7.25, p=0.000; t=4.58, p=0.000; t=4.06, p=0.000). However, the overall assessments of quality were not found to be significantly different as the above differences canceled out. The rankings of mean quality across the dimensions were also considered. The applications were ranked highest on portability and lowest on reliability by both the user developers and the independent assessors, but the other dimensions were ranked differently. A Spearman rank order correlation test showed the rankings to be not significantly correlated (rho = 0.607, p = 0.148).

Several individual questionnaire items stood out in illustrating problems that many end user developers had in recognizing quality problems with their applications. These are shown in Table 3. If end user developers have serious misconceptions such as these, it could pose significant risks to the security and integrity of organizational data and to the quality of organizational decision-making.

The second research question considered whether experience and training might influence differences between user developer and independent expert assessments of user-developed applications. The role of experience was consid-

Table 2: A comparison of the mean user developer assessments of each quality dimension with the independent expert assessments for each quality dimension

Quality dimension	*User developer assessment*			*Independent expert assessment*			*Significance*
	Mean	*SD*	*Ranking*	*Mean*	*SD*	*Ranking*	
Economy	3.85	1.75	2	4.27	0.71	3	p=0.058
Effectiveness	3.77	1.29	5	4.29	1.03	2	p=0.009
Maintainability	3.56	1.44	6	3.29	1.25	4	p=0.228
Portability	3.91	1.31	1	4.51	0.68	1	p=0.001
Reliability	3.06	0.90	7	2.19	0.65	7	p=0.000
Understandability	3.83	0.83	3	3.20	0.71	5	p=0.000
User-friendliness	3.81	0.94	4	3.18	0.81	6	p=0.000
Overall quality	3.68	0.80		3.57	0.60		p=0.380

Table 3: System quality instrument items on which there were major differences of opinion

	% of applications for which end user developers agreed	*% of applications for which expert assessors agreed*
Unauthorized users could not easily access all the data or a part of it	35.4	16.7
Each user owns a unique password	29.5	9.0
This system automatically corrects certain types of errors at data-entry time	35.0	0.0
This system always issues an error message when it detects an error	26.0	0.0
The system performs an automatic backup of the data	26.3	0.0
The system never modifies a cell without asking for a confirmation and getting a positive response	32.9	5.1

ered first. End user developers were categorized according to the number of years of spreadsheet experience they had: low experience (0 – 4 years; N = 29), medium experience (5 – 8 years; N = 29) and high experience (9+ years; N = 21). Table 4 shows the mean end user quality assessments of the applications for the 3

Table 4: A comparison of the assessments of each quality dimension across the low, medium and high experience groups

Quality dimension	*Low Experience*		*Med. Experience*		*High Experience*		*Significance*
	Mean	*Std. dev.*	*Mean*	*Std. dev.*	*Mean*	*Std. dev.*	
Economy							
End user developer	4.03	1.64	3.86	1.50	3.57	2.18	0.654
Expert assessors	4.24	0.73	4.16	0.77	4.48	0.58	0.294
Difference	-0.21	1.94	-0.30	1.80	-0.90	2.25	0.433
Effectiveness							
End user developer	4.07	1.19	3.41	1.32	3.85	1.27	0.141
Expert assessors	4.24	1.04	4.07	1.21	4.69	0.58	0.103
Difference	-0.17	1.64	-0.68	2.01	-0.82	1.40	0.367
Maintainability							
End user developer	3.75	1.55	3.86	1.09	2.88	1.52	0.037 [LH, MH]
Expert assessors	3.14	1.24	3.26	1.35	3.58	1.10	0.450
Difference	0.63	2.00	0.62	1.86	-0.70	1.53	0.022 [LH, MH]
Portability							
End user developer	4.02	1.43	3.79	1.09	3.83	1.49	0.797
Expert assessors	4.41	0.89	4.54	0.49	4.59	0.56	0.650
Difference	-0.40	1.66	-0.68	1.19	-0.76	1.62	0.652
Reliability							
End user developer	3.31	0.82	3.13	0.94	2.66	0.87	0.040 [LH]
Expert assessors	2.20	0.69	2.06	0.64	2.34	0.61	0.329
Difference	1.11	0.96	1.02	1.14	0.32	0.90	0.018 [LH, MH]
Understandability							
End user developer	4.16	0.69	3.80	0.74	3.45	0.98	0.011 [LH]
Expert assessors	3.18	0.68	3.12	0.83	3.37	0.61	0.476
Difference	1.02	1.06	0.66	1.23	0.08	1.23	0.026 [LH]
User-friendliness							
End user developer	3.95	1.05	3.92	0.71	3.47	1.00	0.145
Expert assessors	3.12	0.83	3.18	0.90	3.28	0.66	0.808
Difference	0.83	1.54	0.73	1.14	0.19	1.29	0.225
Overall quality							
End user developer	3.89	0.79	3.68	0.68	3.38	0.90	0.086
Expert assessors	3.50	0.62	3.48	0.64	3.76	0.49	0.221
Difference	0.38	1.06	0.20	1.11	-0.38	0.99	0.043 [LH]

[LH] *Significant difference in means ($p<0.05$) between the low experience and high experience groups*

[MH] *Significant difference in means ($p<0.05$) between the medium experience and high experience groups*

experience groupings, the mean independent assessments, and also the mean difference between the end user developer and independent assessment for each application.

In order to analyze the differences in quality assessments between end users with different experience levels, these were compared across the groups using ANOVA. In cases where ANOVA indicated significance differences, the Bonferroni test was used to perform pair wise comparisons to determine the exact nature of the difference. The results provide support for Hypothesis 1.

The end user developers with low experience considered their applications to be of higher quality on all dimensions than did the end user developers with high experience. There were significant differences in end user quality assessments across the experience groups for maintainability (F=3.45, p=0.037), reliability (F=3.36, p=0.040) and understandability (F=4.80, p=0.011). In each of these cases, Bonferroni tests showed that the quality assessments for the applications of the low experienced end users were significantly higher than those of the high experienced end user developers. However, no differences between the experience groupings were found in the independent assessments of quality.

A comparison of the difference scores between the 3 groups further supports what the results of the end user assessment comparison suggested. On each dimension and on overall quality the low experience group had either the largest positive difference or least negative difference. This pattern of differences suggests that the low experience group perceived applications of equivalent quality (as assessed independently) to be of better quality than did the high experience group. That is, they tended to overestimate the quality of their applications relative to the high experience group. The differences between groups were significant for overall quality (F=3.27, p=0.043) and for the following quality dimensions: maintainability (F=4.02, p=0.022), reliability (F=4.24, p=0.018) and understandability (F=3.84, p=0.026).

The role of training in the ability of an end user developer to make objective assessments of application quality was considered by comparing the 3 groupings of end user developers: low training (training score <=6; N=20), medium training (score 7–9; N=35) and high training (score >=10; N=23). Table 5 shows the mean quality assessments by the end user developers, the independent assessors and also the mean difference between the end user developer and independent assessment for each application. In order to analyze the differences in quality assessments between end users with different training levels these were compared across the groups using ANOVA. The results do not provide support for Hypothesis 2 as no significant differences were found between end users with low, medium and high levels of training with respect to end user developer quality ratings, independent

Table 5: A comparison of the assessments of each quality dimension across the low, medium and high training level groups

Quality dimension	*Low Training*		*Med. Training*		*High Training*		*Significance*
	Mean	*Std. dev*	*Mean*	*Std. dev*	*Mean*	*Std. dev*	
Economy							
End user developer	3.90	1.65	3.77	1.82	3.83	1.75	0.966
Expert assessors	4.32	0.67	4.20	0.75	4.32	0.70	0.761
Difference	-0.42	1.84	-0.43	2.16	-0.50	1.89	0.990
Effectiveness							
End user developer	3.75	1.33	3.62	1.28	3.96	1.26	0.624
Expert assessors	4.15	1.05	4.30	1.09	4.41	0.95	0.722
Difference	-0.40	1.81	-0.66	1.79	-0.45	1.66	0.844
Maintainability							
End user developer	3.74	1.22	3.27	1.56	3.78	1.38	0.330
Expert assessors	3.40	1.15	3.01	1.36	3.65	1.07	0.152
Difference	0.35	1.76	0.26	2.13	0.15	1.72	0.942
Portability							
End user developer	3.75	1.36	3.99	1.27	3.78	1.37	0.768
Expert assessors	4.31	1.04	4.58	0.55	4.57	0.41	0.338
Difference	-0.56	1.49	-0.59	1.56	-0.70	1.41	0.946
Reliability							
End user developer	3.16	0.93	2.82	0.70	3.33	1.08	0.097
Expert assessors	2.20	0.63	2.15	0.69	2.22	0.64	0.919
Difference	0.95	1.04	0.67	0.87	1.07	1.32	0.355
Understandability							
End user developer	4.07	0.69	3.78	0.75	3.70	1.03	0.337
Expert assessors	3.18	0.66	3.19	0.75	3.26	0.76	0.918
Difference	0.94	1.02	0.59	1.03	0.40	1.60	0.363
User-friendliness							
End user developer	3.93	0.80	3.74	0.93	3.79	1.10	0.762
Expert assessors	3.26	0.77	3.16	0.95	3.16	0.62	0.902
Difference	0.67	1.10	0.57	1.55	0.61	1.30	0.967
Overall quality							
End user developer	3.74	0.75	3.57	0.76	3.74	0.88	0.642
Expert assessors	3.55	0.63	3.51	0.63	3.66	0.56	0.688
Difference	0.19	1.05	0.05	1.13	0.08	1.13	0.902

quality ratings or difference scores on any of the quality dimensions. However it is interesting to note that the difference scores showed a similar (though not significant) pattern to the difference scores for the experience groupings with the low experience group having larger positive or less negative scores on all dimensions but reliability.

DISCUSSION

This study investigated the ability of end users to assess the quality of the applications they develop. The results indicate that there are some differences between the system quality assessments of end user developers and independent expert assessors, and also differences between quality assessments of end users with low and high levels of experience. In particular, the results of this study suggest that user developers with little experience may rate applications of equivalent quality more highly than do experienced user developers. Whilst the findings should be considered preliminary because of the use of MBA student subjects, the results raise concerns about the heavy reliance of organizations on users' perceptions of their own applications. These findings should be followed up by field studies evaluating UDAs in organizations.

Can User Developers Assess the Quality of Their Applications?

User developer assessments of overall application quality were not found to be significantly different from the independent assessments. This is because some of the differences at the quality dimension level are in different directions and partially cancel out. There were significant differences on five of the quality dimensions. The user developers rated the effectiveness and portability of their applications significantly lower than did the independent assessors. It is interesting that the user developers were more critical with respect to the effectiveness of applications than the independent assessors were. Of all the quality dimensions considered, effectiveness was the dimension of most immediate importance to the user developers, and the dimension about which they received the most feedback via the BPG reports, and hence it is the dimension about which they could be expected to be most critical.

The questionnaire items on portability related to two criteria: portability across hardware, and portability across organizational environments. User developer assessments differed significantly from the independent assessments only with respect to portability across different hardware platforms. This appears to result from a lack of awareness of just how portable applications developed in Microsoft Excel© currently are. The fact that both the end user developers and the independent assessors ranked portability highest amongst the dimensions suggests that the difference is not too problematic.

The user developers rated the reliability, understandability and user-friendliness of their applications significantly higher than did the independent assessors. Spreadsheets are the first introduction to application development for many end users, and in general end users have not been trained in systems analysis and design and tend to overlook issues such as reliability and auditability (Ronen, Palley, & Lucas, 1989). The differences in reliability and understandability assessments are consistent with the findings of Nelson (1991), who identified the major skill deficiencies of end users as being in technical and information system product areas, and with those of Edberg and Bowman (1996) who found major data integrity problems with the end user applications in their study. Rivard et al. (1997) noted that they would not be surprised to find user attitudes quite impervious to the more technical dimensions of application quality as the more 'technical' dimensions of quality would be expected to preoccupy computer professionals but probably not end users unless they have been trained to focus on them. However, the fact that reliability was the lowest ranking dimension for user developers as well as the independent assessors provides some hope that user developers are gaining insight into the weaknesses of their applications.

The difference in assessments of user-friendliness between the user developers and the independent assessors could be because the familiarity user developers gain with their applications during development may color their perceptions of their application's user-friendliness. As many UDAs are used by end users other than the developer (Bergeron & Berube, 1988) this could cause problems.

There might also be a self-evaluation effect. Doll and Torkzadeh (1989) speculated on the 'bias' of end user developers but didn't empirically investigate it. McGill et al. (1998) provided preliminary evidence of this 'bias' in the UDA domain by showing that end users exhibited an increased degree of satisfaction with a spreadsheet application that they had developed themselves compared with another end user using the same application.

The Effect of Experience

Level of spreadsheet experience appeared to play an important role in the ability of end user developers to assess system quality. Those end users with little experience rated the quality of their applications higher on all dimensions than did the user developers in the high experience group. The differences between end user assessments of quality and independent assessments were also either larger (if positive) or less negative, for the low experience group. This suggests that lack of experience seriously impedes the ability of user developers to be objective about the quality of their applications. The quality dimensions for which the differences between experience levels were significant were the more technical dimensions of maintainability, reliability and understandability. It seems that despite Rivard et al.'s (1997) concerns about end user awareness of the technical dimensions of quality, with experience comes some increase in awareness.

It is interesting to note that no relationship was found between level of spreadsheet experience and the independent expert quality assessments. Those with more experience did not develop higher quality applications. Perhaps despite being more aware of the limitations of their applications they did not aim to develop quality applications. This could suggest a lack of awareness of the consequences of using applications of low quality (Ronen et al., 1989). A lack of concern for consequences might be exacerbated by two factors in this study. Firstly, the applications did not form part of the formal assessment for the course, and secondly, the subjects were aware that the applications would only be required for a limited period of time (the duration of the simulation). However, these circumstances are often mirrored in the workplace with no external controls being placed on development and with end users developing applications that they believe will only be used once and then using them repeatedly (Kroenke, 1992). It can only be hoped that despite the fact that their applications were not of significantly better quality, the additional insight into the quality of their applications would lead high experience end users to treat their results with more caution.

The Effect of Training

In this study, level of spreadsheet training did not appear to play a role in determining either the ability of end user developers to assess system quality or system quality itself. The differences between the end user developer perceptions of quality and the independent assessments were not significantly lower for those end user developers in the highest training group. Both the amount of training that the subjects had received and the types of training could explain the results. As Table 1 shows, the subjects had received relatively little training and the major means of training was self-study. It has been suggested that when end users are self-taught the emphasis is predominantly on how to use the software rather than broader analysis and design considerations (Benham, Delaney, & Luzi, 1993). Thus, the subjects in this study may not have received training of a type conducive to reflection on system quality. As self-training has been shown to be the major form of training in a number of studies (e.g. Amoroso & Cheney, 1991; Benham et al., 1993; Chan & Storey, 1996) the results of this study may highlight potential problems in a wide range of organizations.

The fact that no relationship was found between amount of previous spread-sheet training and the independent quality assessments may also relate to the amounts and types of training received. Preliminary results of Babbitt, Galletta and Lopes's (1998) study of spreadsheet development by novice users suggested that end users whose training emphasizes planning and testing of spreadsheets will develop better quality spreadsheets. However, it is also possible that despite the training the subjects may previously have had they did not consider it important to develop applications of high quality. Future research should investigate the role of type of training in both application quality and end user perceptions of application quality.

CONCLUSION

The results of this study cast some doubts on the ability of end users to make realistic determinations of the quality of applications they develop. Those subjects with little experience erroneously considered their applications to be of higher quality than subjects with more experience did. This may compromise the effectiveness of end users as application developers and could have major consequences when the systems developed are used to support decision making in organizations. Also of concern, is the fact that no relationship was found between spreadsheet experience or training and the independent assessments of quality. Those user developers who would be expected to able to be more realistic in assessing the quality of their applications were, however, not developing applications of higher quality.

Given the increasing importance of user developed applications to organizational decision-making it is essential that organizations be aware of the potential problems and that steps are taken to address them. Organizations must recognize that end user developers may perceive the information from an application to be suitable to support decision making when, in fact, technical design and implementation flaws have introduced serious errors.

With the majority of organizations imposing no quality control procedures on user developers (Bergeron & Berube, 1990; Cale, 1994; Panko & Halverson, 1996), a number of authors have suggested that training may be the most effective tool for minimizing risks associated with end user computing (Cragg & King, 1993; Edberg & Bowman, 1996; Nelson, 1991). However, as the results of this study show, increasing levels of training is no guarantee of improvements in quality. Future research should target the role of training that emphasizes application development methods and procedures, especially in the area of quality assurance. Intelligent application development tools such as the one proposed by Shah and Lawrence (1996) could also increase the quality of UDAs by embedding the necessary knowledge about the more technical aspects of system quality. Unless proficiency in developing applications is increased, organizations risk incurring considerable costs.

REFERENCES

Al-Shawaf, A.-R. H. (1993). An investigation of the design process for end-user developed systems: An exploratory field study. Unpublished Ph.D., Virginia Commonwealth University.

Amoroso, D. L. (1986). Effectiveness of end-user developed applications in organizations: An empirical investigation. Unpublished Ph.D., University of Georgia.

Amoroso, D. L., & Cheney, P. H. (1991). Testing a causal model of end-user application effectiveness. *Journal of Management Information Systems, 8*(1), 63-89.

Babbitt, T. G., Galletta, D. F., & Lopes, A. B. (1998). Influencing the success of spreadsheet development by novice users. *Proceedings of the Nineteenth International Conference on Information Systems*, 319-324.

Benham, H., Delaney, M., & Luzi, A. (1993). Structured techniques for successful end user spreadsheets. *Journal of End User Computing* (Spring), 18-25.

Bergeron, F. & Berube, C. (1988). The management of the end-user environment: An empirical investigation. *Information & Management,* 14, 107-113.

Bergeron, F. & Berube, C. (1990). End users talk computer policy. *Journal of Systems Management* (December), 14-16, 32.

Brancheau, J. C. & Brown, C. V. (1993). The management of end-user computing: Status and directions. *ACM Computing Surveys, 25*(4), 450-482.

Briggs, R. O., Balthazard, P. A., & Dennis, A. R. (1996). Graduate business students as surrogates for executives in the evaluation of technology. *Journal of End User Computing, 8*(4), 11-17.

Cale, E. G. (1994). Quality issues for end-user developed software. *Journal of Systems Management* (January), 36-39.

Chan, Y. E. & Storey, V. C. (1996). The use of spreadsheets in organizations: Determinants and consequences. *Information & Management,* 31, 119-134.

Cotter, R. V. & Fritzche, D. J. (1995). *The Business Policy Game*. Englewood Cliffs, NJ: Prentice-Hall.

Cragg, P. G. & King, M. (1993). Spreadsheet modelling abuse: An opportunity for OR? *Journal of the Operational Research Society, 44*(8), 743-752.

Crawford, J. B. (1986). An investigation of strategies for supporting and controlling user development of computer applications. Unpublished Ph.D., University of California, Irvine.

Doll, W. J. & Torkzadeh, G. (1989). A discrepancy model of end-user computing involvement. *Management Science, 35*(10), 1151-1171.

Edberg, D. T. & Bowman, B. J. (1996). User-developed applications: An empirical study of application quality and developer productivity. *Journal of Management Information Systems, 13*(1), 167-185.

Etezadi-Amoli, J. & Farhoomand, A. F. (1996). A structural model of end user computing satisfaction and user performance. *Information & Management,* 30, 65-73.

Igbaria, M. (1990). End-user computing effectiveness: A structural equation model. *OMEGA, 18*(6), 637-652.

Janvrin, D. & Morrison, J. (2000). Using a structured design approach to reduce risks in end user spreadsheet development. *Information & Management, 37*(1), 1-12.

Kroenke, D. (1992). *Management Information Systems*. Watsonville, CA: McGraw-Hill.

McGill, T. J., Hobbs, V. J., Chan, R., & Khoo, D. (1998). User satisfaction as a measure of success in end user application development: An empirical investigation. In M. Khosrowpour (ed.), *Proceedings of the 1998 IRMA Conference* (pp. 352-357). Boston, USA: Idea Group Publishing.

McLean, E. R., Kappelman, L. A., & Thompson, J. P. (1993). Converging end-user and corporate computing. *Communications of the ACM, 36*(12), 79-92.

Nelson, R. R. (1991). Educational needs as perceived by IS and end-user personnel: A survey of knowledge and skill requirements. *MIS Quarterly, 15*(4), 503-525.

Nelson, R. R. & Cheney, P. H. (1987). Training end users: An exploratory study. *MIS Quarterly,* 11, 547-559.

Panko, R. R. & Halverson, R. P. (1996). Spreadsheets on trial: A survey of research on spreadsheet risks. *Proceedings of the Twenty-Ninth Hawaii International Conference on System Sciences,* 2, 326-335.

Raymond, L. & Bergeron, F. (1992). Personal DSS success in small enterprises. *Information & Management,* 22, 301-308.

Rivard, S., Poirier, G., Raymond, L., & Bergeron, F. (1997). Development of a measure to assess the quality of user-developed applications. *The DATA BASE for Advances in Information Systems, 28*(3), 44-58.

Ronen, B., Palley, M. A., & Lucas, H. C. (1989). Spreadsheet analysis and design. *Communications of the ACM, 32*(1), 84-93.

Shah, H. U. & Lawrence, D. R. (1996). A study of end user computing and the provision of tool support to advance end user empowerment. *Journal of End User Computing, 8*(1), 13-21.

Shayo, C., Guthrie, R., & Igbaria, M. (1999). Exploring the measurement of end user computing success. *Journal of End User Computing, 11*(1), 5-14.

Yaverbaum, G. J. & Nosek, J. (1992). Effects of information system education and training on user satisfaction. *Information & Management,* 22, 217-225.

APPENDIX 1

Questionnaire Items used to measure System Quality

Economy

- The system increased my data processing capacity

Effectiveness

- The system provides all the information it should

Maintainability

- This system provides the capability to import data from other applications
- It is possible to copy parts of the system (outputs or data) into other systems or to link with other systems

Portability

- The system can be run on computers other than the one presently used
- The system could be used in other similar organisational environments, without any major modification

Reliability

- Unauthorised users could easily access all the data or a part of it
- Each user owns a unique password
- Unauthorised access is controlled in several parts of the system
- Errors in the system are easy to identify
- Each password limits the access to specific parts of the system
- This system (rather than the spreadsheet package) automatically corrects certain types of errors, at data-entry time
- Should an error arise, the system provides the capability to perform some checking in order to locate the source of error
- This system (rather than the spreadsheet package) always issues an error message when it detects an error
- All outputs provided by this system are required

- The data entry sections provide the capability to easily make corrections to data
- Outputs provided by this system are comprehensive
- The system contains all the information required to produce comprehensive outputs
- The system does not destroy any information without asking for a confirmation and getting a positive response
- The system provides default values in the data-entry section
- The system performs an automatic backup of the data
- Data is labelled so that it can be easily matched with other parts of the system
- The system never modifies a cell without asking for a confirmation and getting a positive response
- Corrections to errors in the system are easy to make

Understandability

- The same terminology is used throughout the system
- Data entry sections are organised in such a way that the data elements are logically grouped together
- The data entry areas clearly show the spaces reserved to record the data
- The format of a given piece of information is always the same, where ever it is used in the system
- Headings provide information related to the nature of data in the system (e.g.: emp-no = employee number)
- The system is broken up into separate and independent sections
- Each section has a unique function
- Each section includes enough information to help you understand its functioning
- The documentation provides all the information required to use the system
- Message presentation is always the same (position, terminology, style..)
- The documentation explains the functioning of the system

User-friendliness

- Using the system is easy, even after a long period of non-utilisation
- The system is easy to learn by new users
- The outputs are easy to understand
- The terms used in data-entry sections are familiar to users
- Queries are easy to make

Chapter VII

A Matter of Perspective: The Role of Casual Attribution in the Assessment of User-System Outcomes

Rex Karsten
University of Northern Iowa, USA

ABSTRACT

The working relationship of information systems (IS) professionals and end users is an ongoing source of both research and practical concern. This study employs Attribution Theory to examine the causal attributions IS professionals and end users make for successful and unsuccessful user-system outcomes—end user attempts to use an information system to get the information needed to complete system-dependent, work-related tasks. Eighty-six IS professionals and 122 end users participated. The results show no differences in the nature of IS professional-end user attributions for successful outcomes, but very significant differences between them following unsuccessful outcomes. Post hoc analysis indicates that for unsuccessful user-system outcomes, the causal attributions of IS professionals and end users who are cross-functional team members are significantly less divergent than the causal attributions of those who are not. The implications of Attribution Theory for IS professional-end user interaction are discussed.

INTRODUCTION

Effective interaction among information systems (IS) professionals and end users is an essential ingredient in IS success (Joshi, 1992). As the impact of information technology on personal and organizational success becomes even more apparent to workers, the need for and extent of IS professional-end user interactions are expected to intensify (Joshi, 1992; Tapscott & Caston, 1993). Unfortunately, IS professional-end user interaction in many IS settings too often results in mutual frustration and blame laying rather than effective problem solving behaviors (Concord, 1999; MORI, 1999).

This study seeks to shed additional light on the IS professional-end user relationship through the application of Attribution Theory (Heider, 1958; Kelley, 1973). Attribution Theory (AT) is a cognitive-perceptual theory of human information processing that has provided research insights in a variety of pertinent organizational settings (Brown & Jones, 1998). AT directly addresses how individuals explain (i.e., how they attribute) the causes of their own and others' performance in mutually dependent, interactive contexts (Brown, 1984; Green & Mitchell, 1979). Prior research in relevant organizational settings suggests that causal attributions have consequences of relevance to IS professional-end user interaction (Brown & Jones, 1998). For example, causal attributions can influence information-seeking strategies (Harrison, West, & Reneau, 1988), problem-solving responses to poor performance (Kaplan & Reckers, 1985), and information system use (Kelley, Compeau, & Higgins, 1999; Magal & Snead, 1993).

This study differs from prior research in its application of AT to IS professional-end user interaction in a post-implementation IS context. It is specifically concerned with IS professional and end user attributions following end user attempts to use an information system to complete system-dependent, work-related tasks. Growing dependence on IS support for work-related tasks has in turn led to an escalating demand on IS professionals to respond quickly and appropriately to end user needs (Tapscott & Caston, 1993). Unfortunately, recent surveys indicate IS professional-end user interaction in this important context is frequently unproductive and of practical as well as research concern (Concord, 1999; MORI, 1999).

To respond appropriately in such situations, IS professionals must be able to determine why a user-system outcome is perceived as a success or failure by end users. Misunderstandings by IS professionals as to why end users perceive IS support to be successful or unsuccessful can be a source of mutual confusion and frustration (Goodhue, 1988). AT research has demonstrated that *why* a person believes an event occurs–the causal attribution for the event–provides the impetus for decisions and actions that follow. AT research has also identified biases that can disturb the attribution processes of mutually dependent, interacting individuals. In short, the application of AT to similar working relationships has provided insights of relevance to IS professional-end user interaction (Brown, 1984; Brown & Jones, 1998).

Therefore, the purpose of this exploratory research is to apply AT to IS professional-end user interaction in an important organizational context. In doing so, this study measures and compares the causal attributions of IS professionals and end users for successful and unsuccessful user-system outcomes in IS-dependent organizations. An overview of AT and an attribution analysis of the IS professional-end user relationship provide the theoretical background for this research.

OVERVIEW OF ATTRIBUTION THEORY

Attribution Theory is one of the most powerful and thoroughly researched areas in social psychology (Hughes & Gibson, 1987). Applied in organizational contexts, AT has provided insight into leader-member interaction and performance feedback (Green & Mitchell, 1979; Martinko & Gardner, 1987), job performance evaluation (Greenhaus & Pasuraman, 1993; Watson Dugan, 1989), supervisor responses to poor auditor performance (Kaplan & Reckers, 1985), group performance outcomes (Brown, 1984), and information seeking strategies in production variance investigations (Harrison et al., 1988).

In the IS realm, AT has been used to explicate decision support system usage (Hughes & Gibson, 1987), race and gender differences in job performance and IS career success (Igbaria & Wormley, 1995; Igbaria & Baroudi, 1995), measurement bias (Hawk & Aldag, 1990), and end-user involvement (Magal & Snead, 1993). More recently, AT has provided insight into individuals' rejection of information technology (Henry & Martinko, 1997), failed IS projects (Brown & Jones, 1998), and individual reactions to ERP systems (Kelley et al., 1999).

The Attribution Process

AT is a theory about how people make causal explanations. AT has shown that *why* we believe an event occurs influences our response to that event (Harrison et al., 1988; Kaplan & Reckers, 1985). Accordingly, the more accurately we are able to infer (i.e., attribute) the cause of an event, the more appropriate and effective our subsequent responses are likely to be (Kelley, 1973).

AT offers insight into social interaction through its concern with both *self perception*—how we explain our own behavior—and *social perception*—how we explain the causes of the observed behavior of others (Kelley, 1973). While individuals typically combine information in a logical manner to form attributions about their own and others' behavior, AT research has demonstrated that attribution biases can distort the causal attribution process (Kelley & Michela, 1980). The AT terms and constructs relevant to this study are summarized in Figure 1 and are discussed in more depth in the following sections:

Attribution Biases

Attribution bias occurs when a perceiver systematically distorts (e.g., under uses or over uses) an otherwise proper procedure (Hewstone, 1989). For example, *actor-observer bias* is the robust and "pervasive tendency" (Jones & Nisbett, 1972: 80) of *actors* (the individuals performing a task) and *observers* (the

Figure 1: Attribution theory terms and constructs

Causal Attribution:	The perceived cause of a performance outcome; *why* a person believes an outcome or event occurred.
Locus of Causality:	An important causal *dimension* of an attribution. Describes where on an internal-external continuum a causal attribution is placed. A focal point for the operation of AT biases.
Internal Attributions ← Personal or dispositional causes; effort or ability	*causal dimension* → *External Attributions* Environmental or situational causes; other individuals
Actor:	The individual performing a task.
Observer:	The individual monitoring task performance.
Actor-Observer Bias:	The pervasive tendency of actors to make external attributions and observers to make internal attributions for the same task performance outcome.
Self-Serving Bias:	The strong tendency of individuals to take personal responsibility for success and deny responsibility for failure.
Psychological Distance:	A lack of empathy or understanding between mutually dependent, interacting individuals. Psychological distance promotes actor-observer bias.
Performance Expectations:	Performances consistent with personal expectations tend to be attributed to internal causes, while performances inconsistent with expectations tend to be attributed to external causes.

persons monitoring the performance) to have sharply divergent perceptions of the causes of an actor's performance outcome. Actors and observers have different information available to them and tend to process it differently. Information about the environment is naturally more salient and easier for actors to monitor than is their own behavior, and attention is likely to be directed outward. For the observer, the situation is reversed, and the actor is more likely to be the focus of attention. The difference in focus biases the actor towards situational factors and away from personal factors, while having an opposite effect on the observer (Regan & Totten, 1975). Consequently, actors tend to over attribute their performance to external, environmental causes (e.g., task difficulty, misfortune, or other individuals) while observers tend to over attribute that same performance to causes internal to the actor (e.g., effort, ability, other personal characteristics).

When performance outcomes involve attributions for success or failure, causal analysis may be further influenced by *self-serving bias* (Zuckerman, 1979). Self-serving bias describes the strong tendency of individuals to take credit for success and deny responsibility for failure. Individuals tend to attribute successful performances to internal, personal causes and unsuccessful performances to external, environmental causes. Self-serving bias influences causal attributions to the extent the outcomes of interest have implications for self-esteem (Zuckerman, 1979).

Two additional attribution moderators that appear relevant to IS professional-end user interaction warrant mention. *Psychological distance*—a lack of empathy and understanding between mutually dependent, interacting individuals—appears to promote actor-observer bias (Regan & Totten, 1975). *Performance expectations* can also moderate causal inference. When a person's task performance is consistent with his/her expectations, that performance outcome is more likely to be attributed to internal factors. When performance outcomes are inconsistent with expectations, external factors are more likely to be inferred (Hewstone, 1989).

Casual Attributions

The biases described reflect a distinction between causes that are internal or external to a person (Lalljee, 1981). The *locus of causality* dimension, which describes where an attribution is placed on this internal-external continuum, is of central concern to AT and a focal point for the operation of the biases described above. Prior AT research has shown that it is the internal or external dimension of an attribution (i.e., its locus of causality) rather than the specific causal attribution, that influences actions taken in response to an observed performance (Green & Mitchell, 1979; Harrison et al., 1988; Weiner, 1985).

Consequences of Attributions

Studies of mutually dependent, interacting individuals have found that attributions can influence subsequent information-seeking strategies (Harrison et al., 1988) and actions taken in response to observed performances (Kaplan & Reckers, 1985). Biased attributions may also encourage individuals to provide self-enhancing or self-protecting explanations that may not accurately reflect the causes of system success or failure (Brown & Jones, 1998).

Harrison et al. (1988) found that supervisors (i.e., observers) tended to make significantly more internal attributions for unfavorable subordinate performance than did subordinates (i.e., actors), results consistent with other research on the actor-observer and self-serving biases. The causal dimension of the attributions also influenced the subsequent information seeking strategies of study participants. Supervisors sought to confirm their initial internal attributions by soliciting internal information relative to the subordinate, while subordinates sought external evidence to confirm their more external attributions.

Importantly, related research has indicated that individuals strongly prefer "case-building" information-seeking strategies that confirm the accuracy of their initial attributions regardless of preexisting evidence to the contrary (Snyder & Swann, 1978; Snyder & White, 1981). Based on their findings, Harrison et al. (1988) suggested that supervisors and subordinates may come to divergent attributions for poor performances that cause friction in the relationship. This friction may be intensified when supervisors and subordinates search for information regarding the cause of failure that tends to confirm their disparate hypotheses. The culmination of biased causal reasoning may be disagreements between the interactors regarding the appropriate responses and corrective measures to be taken.

In another study concerned with actor-observer bias, stronger internal attributions by auditors toward a subordinate were highly associated with "action-responses" directed toward subordinates (Kaplan & Reckers, 1985). When auditors attributed poor subordinate performance to internal factors, their reactions were directed toward changing something about the subordinate (e.g., attitude or effort) rather than the situation.

A case study of IS professionals and end users participating in a failed IS project suggests that participants employed self-serving attributions designed to preserve self-esteem when faced with perceived project failure (Brown and Jones, 1998). The case study authors concluded that IS project participants, whose social identities and self-esteem are tied to the work they perform, are likely to use self-serving explanations to distance themselves from project failure. Unfortunately, self-serving explanations may result in divergent narratives that tend to simplify events and attribute cause to external factors, including the actions of others. Brown and Jones (1998) caution that few situations are reducible to a single cause, and that biased attributions may obscure the real reasons for IS failures.

Attribution Analysis Applied to IS Professional-End User Interaction

When end users fail to get the information they need to complete a system-dependent task, AT-based analysis suggests IS professionals and end users are likely to come to different conclusions for the similar performance outcomes. End users, with a "natural" perceptual focus on the environment coupled with a need to protect their own status, appear inclined to attribute unsuccessful user-system outcomes to external, system-related factors. In contrast, IS professionals, with a "natural" focus on the user and a considerable personal stake in the IS, may attribute the same outcomes to factors internal to the user, such as a lack of effort or ability. In addition to hindering the search for the actual cause(s) of user-system failure, these divergent initial attributions may lead to friction between IS professionals and users, particularly if both parties subsequently employ information seeking strategies that attempt to confirm hypotheses each considers inappropriate or threatening. AT research has suggested that when moderators such as self-serving bias and actor-observer bias come together concerning a performance failure, "...performance appraisal interaction may degenerate into a reciprocal blame-placing sequence, with frustration the typical emotional response for both [parties]" (Sims & Gioia, 1984, p. 67).

While performance failures are obviously of great concern, attributional divergence may play a detrimental role in the assessment of successful user-system outcomes as well. For example, IS professionals may presume that successful outcomes are due to superior system design, while users may view this same success as due to exceptional system-related skills or effort put forth on their part. Both are likely to be at least partially correct. If IS resources allocated for maintaining user-system success were subsequently directed toward system enhancement rather than continued user training, users may view such a response to *their* successful user-system outcome as less than appropriate. Thus, attribution biases may limit the full appreciation of all causes of IS success as well as failure.

In sum, for *unsuccessful* user-system outcomes, the attributions of IS professionals are likely to be more internal than the attributions of end users. If biases are evident following *successful* user-system outcomes, causal attributions of IS professionals should tend to be more external than the attributions of end users. These suppositions are phrased as testable hypotheses in the following section.

METHODOLOGY

Sample

End users and IS professionals from five different organizations were surveyed. Surveying multiple organizations provided the opportunity to determine if different approaches to IS development or acquisition, end-user support, or other organizational differences influenced study findings. Moreover, if study effects are obtained across diverse end users and IS professionals in different organizational settings, the external validity of the study increases (Cook & Campbell, 1979). The brief descriptions of the organizations that follow illustrate some of the basic differences among the participating organizations.

Organization 1 is a multi-campus college system with local, decentralized information services departments. The information system employed was purchased from a commercial vendor. Organization 2 is a grocery distribution firm, Organization 3 is a large, metropolitan hospital, Organization 4 is an international manufacturing firm, and Organization 5 is a regulated public utility. In contrast to Organization 1, the other participating organizations have centralized information services departments and information systems developed in-house.

Though diverse, the organizations do have several important factors in common. The end users and IS professionals surveyed regularly used or provided support for, respectively, each organization's information systems. The information systems in all five organizations provide comparable decision-making support for similar system-dependent tasks (e.g., retrieving information and/or generating reports regarding student, customer, client, or patient status). Likewise, end users could only obtain the decision-making information necessary to complete work-related tasks via each organization's IS.

Study participation was voluntary and anonymity guaranteed. The participating organizations identified potential study participants as belonging to either the end user or the IS professional category. Though it is conceivable that IS professionals could be end users as well, none of the study participants belonged to both categories. Survey questionnaires were distributed on-site and returned by mail. In addition to collecting demographic and other work-related data, the questionnaire asked participants to attribute causes for successful and an unsuccessful user-system outcomes, as described in the following section.

User-System Outcomes

Since it was not possible to manipulate performance outcomes in these busy organizations, participants were asked to recall situations in which it was necessary for *end users* to use the organization's information system to get the information needed to complete an important work-related task. End user operation of the information system was defined as a successful user-system outcome when, *according to the end user*, it provided the information necessary to *complete* the work-related task, and as an unsuccessful user-system outcome when it did not.

Each end user was asked to recall at least one successful and one unsuccessful user-system outcome in which he or she had actually participated (i.e., was the *actor*). Each IS professional was also asked to recall at least one successful and one unsuccessful user-system outcome, as reported by an end user, that he or she had actually witnessed (i.e., was the *observer*). Following the recall of user-system outcomes perceived and reported as successful by end users, study participants indicated the most likely cause or causes and the causal dimension (i.e., whether the cause or causes were internal or external to the end user) of the successful outcomes. Participants provided identical information following the recall of unsuccessful user-system outcomes.

Measures

The consensus in the literature is that causal dimensions yield more information than the assessment of specific causal explanations (Kent & Martinko, 1995).

Measuring the dimension along which causal explanations vary permits the identification and comparison of a potential myriad of causal explanations for an event.

In this study, after making causal attributions for successful and unsuccessful user-system outcomes, participants were asked to indicate the causal dimension of the attributions using the Causal Dimension Scale II (CDSII). McAuley, Duncan and Russell (1992) have provided psychometric support demonstrating the internal consistency and construct validity of the CDSII across diverse research domains. Though the entire CDSII was administered to protect the psychometric integrity of the measure, the three-item Locus of Causality Subscale was of primary interest to this study. The subscale, modified to reflect IS professional and end user viewpoints, is displayed in Figure 2. Subscale items allowed individuals to indicate where on an internal/external continuum, relative to the end user in this study, that causal attributions fall. In other words, an IS professional *or* end user described as making internal attributions would be inferring the locus of causality to be *internal to the end user*. In similar fashion, external attributions by IS professionals *or* end users would infer the locus of causality to be *external to the end user.* Participants completed the CDSII twice—once following the recall of at least one successful outcome, and once following the recall of at least one unsuccessful outcome. If participants recalled multiple outcomes, each locus of causality score provides the participants' overall, prevailing perceptions of where on the internality/externality continuum the causes of multiple successful or unsuccessful user-system outcomes fall. The complete measure is available from the author.

All scale items employed a 1 to 7 point Likert scale. The mean score on the three-item scale was then used to compare the internality/externality dimension of IS professional and end user causal attributions for successful and unsuccessful user-system outcomes. A low score would indicate that the perceived outcome cause or causes were attributed by IS professionals or end users as more likely due to something internal to the end user, while a high score would indicate the perceived cause or causes were more likely due to something external to the end user. The main dependent variables of initial interest represented each respondent's locus of causality score for successful user-system outcomes (i.e., Locus of Success) and unsuccessful user-system outcomes (i.e., Locus of Failure). The study evaluated the following hypotheses:

Hypothesis 1: For successful user-system outcomes, the causal attributions of IS professionals will be significantly more external (to the end user) than the causal attributions of end users.

Hypothesis 1 tests for bias under conditions of success. Both self-serving bias and actor-observer bias might influence the causal attribution process of end users and IS professionals for successful performance outcomes. Self-serving biases may appear as both IS professionals and end users are motivated to take credit for successful user-system outcomes (Weary Bradley, 1978; Zuckerman, 1979). In today's business environment, successful information system use is often a key to

Figure 2: Locus of causality subscale

End User (IS Professional) versions of subscale items:
Is the cause something:

1. That reflects an aspect of yourself (the user)	1 2 3 4 5 6 7	That reflects an aspect of the situation
2. Inside of you (the user)	1 2 3 4 5 6 7	Outside of you (the user)
3. About you (the user)	1 2 3 4 5 6 7	About others

internal attributions ← → *external attributions*

personal as well as organizational success (Tapscott & Caston, 1993). Rather than share credit with the information system, Hypothesis 1 predicts end users will seek primary responsibility for the positive outcome and attribute the cause of success to internal factors (e.g., the effort or ability necessary to operate the system). IS professionals, however, will seek personal credit by emphasizing the important role of external factors (e.g., the support provided by "their" information system) in the successful user-system outcome.

On the other hand, actor-observer bias is the pervasive tendency of actors to attribute their performance, whether *favorable* or *unfavorable*, to external, environmental factors, while observers tend to attribute that same performance to factors internal to the actor (Jones & Nisbett, 1972). Following successful outcomes, then, actor-observer bias may work to lessen the divergence in attributions expected to occur when individuals invoke self-serving bias (Harrison et al., 1988). Self-serving bias, however, is one of the most robust findings in AT research (Weary, Stanley, & Harvey, 1989), and successful user-system outcomes play an important role in the achievement of personal and organizational rewards (Tapscott & Caston, 1993). Consequently, Hypothesis 1 predicts the attributions of IS professionals will tend toward external causes, while the attributions of end users will tend toward internal causes following successful user-system outcomes.

Hypothesis 2: For unsuccessful user-system outcomes, the causal attributions of IS professionals will be significantly more internal (to the end user) than the causal attributions of end users.

Hypothesis 2 tests for bias under conditions of failure. Self-serving bias and actor-observer bias seem even more likely to influence the attribution processes of IS professionals and end users engaged in causal reasoning about unsuccessful user-system outcomes. User-system failures are serious matters in information-reliant organizations and should have significant implications for the self-esteem of both parties. The greater the threat to self-esteem, the more likely an individual is to invoke self-serving bias (Zuckerman, 1979). Therefore, both end users and IS professionals should tend to attribute user-system failure to causes outside themselves. In the end user-system dyad of interest here, both groups seem to have a convenient "scapegoat."

End users may be inclined to "blame the system" rather than themselves, while IS professionals may tend to attribute responsibility for failure to the end user, rather than to "their" system.

Moreover, actor-observer bias works *with* self-serving bias following unsuccessful performance outcomes (Harrison et al., 1988). While actor-observer bias stems from perspective-induced differences in available information and perceptual focus rather than self-protection motivation, both biases are compatible. Thus, Hypothesis 2 predicts that end user (i.e., actor) attributions will tend to be externally oriented, while the attributions of IS professionals (i.e., observers) will be internally oriented following user-system failure.

RESULTS AND DISCUSSION

As displayed in Table 1, 371 end users and IS professionals were surveyed, with 208 (56%) individuals returning completed questionnaires. By category, 122 of 230 end users (53%) and 86 of 141 IS professionals (61%) participated in the study. Table 1 shows that the percentage of responses received were similar for all five organizations.

Table 2 shows the means, standard deviations, and ranges of study variables. While the sample consisted of significantly more females than males, extensive statistical analysis revealed no main or interaction effects by gender. Since the study drew participants from five different organizations, additional preliminary analysis was conducted to determine if organizational differences significantly influenced study outcomes. For example, Organization 1 provides decentralized IS support services, while the other organizations offer centralized IS support. When IS support services are decentralized, IS professionals will presumably be closer to end users physically, administratively, and conceptually than their counterparts in organizations with centralized IS support (Goodhue, 1995). It is reasonable to suspect that closer working relationships might also influence the participants' perceptions of responsibility for user-system outcomes. Extensive statistical analysis, however, revealed no significant differences in causal attributions between centralized and decentralized IS professionals, or between centralized and decentralized end users.

Table 1: Response rates

	End Users			IS Professionals			Overall
Org	Surveyed/Returned		%	Surveyed/Returned		%	%
1	112	56	50%	37	22	60%	52%
2	30	18	60%	34	20	59%	59%
3	36	18	50%	20	12	60%	54%
4	24	15	63%	20	12	60%	61%
5	28	15	54%	30	20	67%	60%
Total	230	122	53%	141	86	61%	56%

Table 2: Descriptive statistics for study variables

Continuous variables:

Variable (scale)	Mean	SD	Min	Max	N
Locus of Success (1 internal – 7 external)	3.97	1.48	1	7	208
Locus of Failure (1 internal – 7 external)	4.32	1.76	1	7	208
Perceptions of Users (1 unsuccessful – 7 successful)	5.11	1.31	1	7	208
Age (Years)	39.45	7.91	22	64	204
Work Experience (Years)	17.65	8.64	1	50	207
Years in Organization	10.46	7.39	1	33	208
Years in Current Position	6.42	5.42	1	30	203
Education (Years)	15.48	2.16	12	22	206
Computer Experience (Years)	12.21	6.50	2	31	208

Categorical variables:

Variable	N	(%)	Variable	N	(%)
Category:			Team Membership:		
End Users	122	(59)	Yes	102	(49)
IS Professionals	86	(41)	No	97	(47)
			No Response	9	(4)
Gender:					
Male	79	(38)			
Female	129	(62)			

With the exception of Team Membership, discussed further in the additional analyses section, none of the organizational or individual variables analyzed demonstrated main or interaction effects. Consequently, only those variables that are critical to testing hypotheses are of demographic interest, or are otherwise relevant to the discussion of the research findings are included in the following tables.

Comparisons by Category

Table 3 displays the results of t-test comparisons of several study variables by category (end users vs. IS professionals). As the t-test results for the Perceptions of Users variable demonstrate, there was no significant difference between end user and IS professional responses (end user mean=5.16, IS professional mean=5.04, p=.524) to the statement "most users are successful when using the information system to get the information they need" (1-7 Likert scale, 1=strongly disagree, 7=strongly agree). If the initial perceptions of IS professionals and end users as to historical user-system success were significantly different, it would make the interpretation and comparison of their attributions for user-system outcomes difficult. In effect, the case could be made that each recalled end users of differing competency. The similar, positively oriented perceptions of both groups regarding previous end user success with IS alleviated this concern.

There were no significant differences (p=.558) in mean age, with members of both groups approximately 39 years old. The years of overall work experience were nearly identical (end user mean =17.8, IS professional mean = 17.4, p= .708), as were years of experience in their current organization (end user mean= 10.7, IS professional mean = 10.0, p= .504). On average, end users have been employed in their current position approximately 2.5 years longer than have IS professionals (end user mean = 7.4, IS professional mean = 4.9, p= .000).

End users and IS professionals did differ significantly, though not dramatically, in mean total years of education (end user mean = 15.2, IS professional mean = 15.8, p=.038). However, the major areas of study identified by IS professionals and end users were very dissimilar. Nearly all responding IS professionals had two-

Table 3: Comparisons by category, t-test results

Variable	Category	N	Mean	SD	t-value	Sig
Perceptions of Users	End Users	122	5.16	1.31	.525	.524
	IS Professionals	86	5.05	1.30		
Age (Years)	End Users	118	39.17	7.62	-.595	.558
	IS Professionals	86	39.84	8.31		
Work Experience (Years)	End Users	121	17.84	8.03	.386	.708
	IS Professionals	86	17.37	9.47		
Years in Organization	End Users	122	10.75	7.63	.660	.504
	IS Professionals	86	10.06	7.05		
Years in Current Position	End Users	120	7.43	6.21	.3.285	.000**
	IS Professionals	83	4.95	3.55		
Education (Years)	End Users	120	15.23	2.40	-1.985	.038*
	IS Professionals	86	15.83	1.72		
Computer Experience (Years)	End Users	122	10.09	5.51	-6.060	.000**
	IS Professionals	86	15.21	6.64		

* $p < 0.05$; ** $p < 0.001$

year (19.8%), four-year (46.5%), or post-bachelors degrees (20.9%) in management information systems, computer science, or closely related fields. None of the end users surveyed possessed similar, technically oriented degrees. IS professionals also reported significantly more years of computer experience than did end users (end user mean = 10.01, IS professional mean = 15.2, $p = .000$).

In sum, the results indicate the sample consisted of two distinct groups whose members are well-educated and similar in age, work and organizational experience. Differences did exist, as expected, in the areas of technical education and computer experience. Thus, the categories of IS professional and end user appear clearly defined and appropriate.

Tests of the Hypotheses

The 3-item Locus of Causality Subscale from the CDSII (McAuley et al., 1992; Russell, 1982) was used to measure the dependent variables Locus of Success and Locus of Failure, respectively, involved in the tests of Hypotheses 1 and 2. The internal consistency of the subscale for both Locus of Success (Cronbach's alpha = .84) and Locus of Failure (Cronbach's alpha = .93) was well within the acceptable range according to Nunnally (1978).

Table 4 displays the results of t-test analyses for Hypotheses 1 and 2. As can be seen from Table 4, t-test analysis revealed no significant differences between IS professionals and end users on the dependent variable Locus of Success (end user mean = 3.98, IS professional mean = 3.94, $p = .864$). These results indicate that Hypothesis 1—the prediction that IS professional attributions for a *successful* user-system outcome would be significantly more external than end-user attributions for such an outcome—was not supported, with the mean scores of both groups hovering around the neutral midpoint of the scale. Besides not differing in attributions, they appeared willing to share the credit for the successful outcome.

Table 4: T-test results for hypotheses 1 and 2

Hypothesis 1 (dependent variable = Locus of Success):					
Category	N	Mean	SD	t-value	Sig.
End Users	122	3.98	1.5	.17	.864
IS Professionals	86	3.94	1.4		
Hypothesis 2 (dependent variable = Locus of Failure):					
Category	N	Mean	SD	t-value	Sig.
End Users	122	5.04	1.5	8.16	.000**
IS Professionals	86	3.28	1.5		

** $p < 0.001$

Attribution Theory may offer possible explanations for the results. The exhibition of self-serving biases—in this case, a bias toward self-enhancement—has been described as dependent upon the degree to which self-esteem concerns are aroused by an outcome (Zuckerman, 1979). As discussed earlier, end users were perceived as generally successful when using the IS. Consequently, successful user-system outcomes meet performance expectations. Taking credit for expected success may not have been sufficient to motivate significant self-enhancement tendencies in members of either category.

Hypothesis 2—the prediction that IS professional attributions would be significantly more internal than end user attributions for unsuccessful user-system outcomes—was supported. IS professionals and end users did differ significantly on the dependent variable Locus of Failure (end user mean = 5.04, IS professional mean = 3.28, $p = .000$). Inspection of the means for each category indicates that the difference was also in the predicted direction, with the IS professional mean below (i.e., more internal) and the end user mean above (i.e., more external) the midpoint of the 7-point Likert scale.

Several explanations for this finding are suggested. From a motivational standpoint, there are clear self-esteem concerns under conditions of user-system failure that would encourage the use of self-serving bias (Zuckermann, 1979). When user-system failure occurs, it is reasonable to assume that both end users *and* IS professionals are strongly motivated to protect themselves from blame, and consequently to infer causation away from themselves.

Actor-observer bias (Jones & Nisbett, 1972) may also have produced, or perhaps amplified, the disparate causal inferences of end users and IS professionals faced with unsuccessful user-system outcomes. Since IS professionals have less information about end users' performance over time than they do about the system's, the IS professionals may have assumed the observed failure was consistent with past end user performance when using an IS, and thus inferred causes internal to the end user. The end users, on the other hand, may have had personal performance information that encouraged attributions to other, external circumstances.

IS professional and end user performance expectancies may have also played a role in the formation of divergent attributions for unsuccessful outcomes. As discussed above, both IS professionals and end users may have reasonably expected the users to employ the system successfully, given the well-educated, computer-experienced end users in the study sample. When faced with an unexpected, unsuccessful outcome, however, AT research has demonstrated that individuals will direct their attention toward potential causes about which they are least informed (Bell, Wicklund, Manko, & Larkin, 1976). Given the training and perspectives of IS professionals and end users, it seems plausible that end users may be inclined to blame external factors (e.g., "the system"), while IS professionals tend to blame end users.

Additional Analyses

Additional analyses of the study sample by user-system outcome indicated one significant, non-hypothesized interaction effect of considerable interest. Study participants were asked to indicate if they were members of regularly scheduled work teams composed of both IS professionals and end users. Post hoc analysis indicated the variables Category and Team Membership demonstrated a significant interaction effect *only* following unsuccessful user-system outcomes (Locus of Failure). Table 5 displays the results of the ANOVA based on the 199 study participants who provided their team membership status. Category exhibited a significant main effect (p=.000) and a significant interaction effect with Team Membership (p=.030). Team membership did not exhibit a significant main effect.

Table 5 also shows the cell means for team members compared with those who indicated they were not. End users who belonged to such teams had substantially lower (i.e., more internal) Locus of Failure scores (mean=4.80) than did end users who did not belong to such teams (mean=5.31).

Table 5: Locus of failure by category and team membership

ANOVA results:

Source	Sum of Squares	DF	Mean Square	F	Sig.
Main Effects	160.827	2	80.414	34.807	.000**
Category	149.109	1	149.109	64.542	.000**
Team Membership	0.572	1	0.572	0.248	.619
Category X Team Membership	10.997	1	10.997	4.751	.030*
Explained	171.804	3	57.268	24.788	.000
Residual	450.502	195	2.310		

Cell means, team members vs. nonmembers:

	End Users		IS Professionals	
Team Membership Status (N)	Mean	N	Mean	N
Team Members (102)	4.80	48	3.45	54
Nonmembers (97)	5.31	66	2.99	31

* p < 0.05; ** p < 0.001

In turn, IS professionals who belonged to such teams had higher Locus of Failure scores (mean=3.45) than did IS professional who were not team members (mean=2.99). In sum, the failure attributions of IS professionals and end users that were members of mixed teams were less divergent than the attributions of IS professionals and end users that were not.

The lack of significant influence on causal attributions by other measures of IS professional-end user interaction makes the Team Membership results intriguing. For example, neither the frequency of informal, social interaction, nor the frequency of formal, work-related interaction was significantly associated with participant attributions for user-system outcomes. Also, as noted previously, Organization 1 provides decentralized IS support services that should foster close working relationships between IS professionals and end users (Gooodhue, 1995). However, the causal attributions of the "decentralized" IS professionals and end users were not significantly different from the attributions of their "centralized" counterparts. In this sample at least, only interaction in a team context appeared to reduce the significant "gap" in IS professional end-user perceptions of responsibility for unsuccessful user-system outcomes. The fact that attribution differences were reduced suggests another possible benefit of team membership. Perhaps when interacting as members of a team, IS professionals and end users are inclined to become less distant psychologically, less likely to evidence actor-observer bias, less self-serving, and less likely to lay blame as well. If team members spend less time and energy on "self-defense," more time should be available for accomplishing team objectives. Though the limitations of this study preclude any conclusive interpretation of the team membership effect, the results do suggest that future research into this aspect of IS professional-end user interaction may be enlightening.

CONCLUSIONS, IMPLICATIONS, AND LIMITATIONS

IS professionals and end users appear willing to share credit for success, but come to decidedly different conclusions regarding the causes of user-system failure. The significant difference in attributions for unsuccessful outcomes between IS professionals and end users from different organizations suggests that actor-observer bias, self-serving bias, or both had an influence on study participants. Evidence from other organizational settings has found divergent attributions to be a source of friction between mutually dependent, interacting individuals. Extrapolating from the AT literature, end users may view the information-seeking strategies and responses of IS professionals as inappropriate, since they are not likely to be directed at ascertaining and resolving what end users perceive to be the "real" cause(s) of failure. Thus, AT principles and research seem to offer useful insight into potential sources of friction in IS professional-end user interaction. Friction between IS professionals may be exacerbated by the fact that expectations based on initial causal attributions can "set the stage" for future expectations, and tend to be perpetuated even in the face of unexpected outcomes (Magal & Snead, 1993). If, based on prior experience, IS professionals expect end users' lack of ability to be the most likely cause of user-system failure, it will take a great deal of evidence to convince them to the contrary. Given the fact that IS professionals and end users typically meet under severe time and other resource constraints, fewer opportunities to disconfirm expectations are likely to exist (Robey, Farrow, & Franz, 1989). In sum, unsuccessful user-system outcomes appear to encourage divergent causal attributions, which in turn may encourage information-seeking strategies or responses IS professionals and end users view as inappropriate from their perspectives. Biased causal attributions appear to be likely sources of difficulty when IS professionals and end users interact.

The implications for practice are several. This research suggests IS professionals need to periodically evaluate the nature of the causal attributions made and information-seeking strategies employed when responding to end user problems. As discussed, causal attributions form the basis for future expectations, and individuals are inclined to employ "case-building" strategies that may not only be a source of friction when interacting with end users, but may also hinder the search for the real, and likely multiple, reasons for failure (Brown & Jones, 1998). In this vein, IS professionals would do well to remember that end user explanations for failure are likely to be simplistic and biased toward self-protection (Brown & Jones, 1998). In short, an understanding and awareness of these motivational and perceptual biases should help IS professionals avoid many of the perspective-induced "traps" identified by AT research. Finally, study findings tentatively suggest that placing IS professionals and end users on the same team may be a way to reduce attributional divergence and, hopefully, some of the misunderstanding and frustration that such differences can engender.

The limitations of this study suggest future research. While the study sample was deliberately chosen for its heterogeneity, final analysis indicates that the IS professionals and end users were quite homogeneous in terms of average age (nearly 40 years), work experience (about 17 years), and years in the organization (about 10). It would be useful to determine if the differences found here represent IS professionals and end users with historically "entrenched" views of each other and the causes of user-system outcomes. For example, are IS professionals and end users new to the work force more or less likely than older, more experienced employees to diverge in the fashion demonstrated here? If so, how does the causal attribution process change over time?

The locus of causality was of primary interest to this exploratory research because of its central concern in AT and its role in attribution biases. Though the analysis of causal dimensions is posited to yield more information regarding causal reasoning than the assessment of specific causal explanations, the explanations themselves seem worthy of investigation and may provide added insights into the IS professional-end user relationship (Kent & Martinko, 1995).

Finally, while study results suggest IS professionals and end users are susceptible to attribution biases, the influence of conflicting causal attributions on subsequent interactive behavior has been hypothesized based on prior AT research on individuals in similar working relationships. The actual influence of attributions on the actions and responses of interacting IS professionals and end users remains to be explored. In conclusion, both study findings and limitations warrant a call for the continued application of Attribution Theory in IS contexts.

REFERENCES

Bell, L. G., Wicklund, R. A., Manko, G. & Larkin, C. (1976). When unexpected behavior is attributed to the environment. *Journal of Research in Personality,* 10, 316-327.

Brown, A. D. & Jones, M. R. (1998). Doomed to failure: Narratives of inevitability and conspiracy in a failed IS project. *Organization Studies, 9*(1), 73-88.

Brown, K. A. (1984). Explaining group poor performance: An attributional analysis. *Academy of Management Review, 9*(1), 54-63.

Cook, T. D. & Campbell, D. T. (1979). *Quasi-Experimentation.* Boston: Houghton Mifflin Company, 28-30.

Concord Communications (1999). Concord network rage survey. [Online] Available: http://www.concord.com/library/network_rage/ [Aug.16].

Goodhue, D. (1995). Understanding user evaluations of information systems. *Management Science, 41*(12), 1827-1844.

Goodhue, D. (1988). I/S attitudes: Toward theoretical and definitional clarity. *Data Base,* Fall/Winter, 6-15.

Green, S. & Mitchell, T. R. (1979). Attributional processes of leaders in leader-member interactions. *Organizational Behavior and Human Performance,* 23, 429-458.

Greenhaus, J. H. & Pasuraman, S. (1993). Job performance and career advancement prospects: An examination of gender and race effects. *Organizational Behavior and Human Decision Processes,* 55, 273-297.

Harrison, P. D., West, S .G. & Reneau, J. H. (1988). Initial attributions and information seeking by superiors and subordinates in production variance investigations. *Accounting Review, 63*(2), 307-320.

Hawk, S. R. & Aldag, R. J. (1990). Measurement biases in user involvement research. *OMEGA, International Journal of Management Science, 18*(6), 605-613.

Heider, F. (1958). *The Psychology of Interpersonal Relations.* New York: John Wiley & Sons.

Henry, J. W. & Martinko, M. J. (1997). An attributional analysis of the rejection of information technology. *Journal of End User Computing*, Fall, 3-17.

Hewstone, M. (1989). *Causal Attribution.* Cambridge: Basil Blackwell Inc.

Hughes, C. T. & Gibson, M. L. (1987). An attribution model of decision support systems (DSS) usage. *Information and Management,* 13, 119-124.

Igbaria, M. & Baroudi, J. J. (1995). The impact of job performance on career advancement prospects: An examination of gender differences in the workplace. *MIS Quarterly*, March, 107-123.

Igbaria, M. & Wormley, W. M. (1995). Race differences in job performance and career success. *Communications of the ACM, 38*(1), 82-92.

Jones, E. E. & Nisbett, R. E. (1972). The actor and observer: Divergent perceptions of the causes of behavior. Chapter 5 in Jones et al (eds.) *Attribution: Perceiving the Causes of Behavior*. Morristown, NJ: General Learning Press.

Joshi, K. (1992). Interpersonal skills for cooperative user-analyst relationships: Some research issues. *Data Base*, Winter, 23-25.

Kaplan, S. E. & Reckers, P. (1985). An examination of auditor performance evaluation. *Accounting Review, 60*(3), 477-487.

Kelley, H., Compeau, D. & Higgins, C. (1999). Attribution analysis of computer self-efficacy. *Proceedings of the 1999 Americas Conference of Information Systems,* 782-784.

Kelley, H. H. (1973). The processes of causal attribution. *American Psychologist,* 28, 107-128.

Kelley, H. H. & Michela, J. L. (1980). Attribution theory and research. *Annual Review of Psychology,* 31, 457-501.

Kent, R. L. & Martinko, M .J. (1995). The Measurement of attributions in organizational research. In Martinko, M. (ed.), *Attribution Theory: An Organizational Perspective* (pp 17-33). Delray Beach, FL: St. Lucie Press.

Lalljee, M. (1981). Attribution theory and the analysis of explanations. In Antaki, C. (ed.), *The Psychology of Everyday Explanations* (pp.119-138). London: Academic Press.

Magal, S. R. & Snead, K. C. (1993). The role of causal attributions in explaining the link between user participation and information system success. *Information Resources Management Journal,* Summer, 8-19.
Martinko, M. J. & Gardner, W. L. (1987). The leader/member attribution process. *Academy of Management Review, 12*(2), 235-249.
McAuley, E., Duncan, T. E., & Russell, D. W. (1992). Measuring causal attributions: The revised causal dimension scale (CDSII). *Personality and Social Psychology Bulletin, 18*(5), 566-573.
MORI-Market and Opinion Research International (1999). Compaq survey: Rage against the machine. [Online] Available: http://www.compaq.co.uk/rage/ [Aug 16].
Nunnally, J. C. (1978). *Psychometric Theory.* New York: McGraw-Hill.
Regan, D. T. & Totten, J. (1975). Empathy and attribution: Turning observers into actors. *Journal of Personality and Social Psychology, 32(*5), 850-856.
Robey, D. Farrow, D. L., & Franz, C. R. (1989). Group process and conflict in system development. *Management Science, 35*(10), 1172-1191.
Russell, D. (1982). The causal dimension scale: A measure of how individuals perceive causes. *Journal of Personality and Social Psychology, 42*(6), 1137-1145.
Sims, H. P. & Gioia, D. A. (1984). Performance failure: Executive response to self-serving bias. *Business Horizons*, Jan/Feb, 64-71.
Snyder, M. & Swann, W. B. (1978). Hypothesis-testing in social interaction. *Journal of Personality and Social Psychology, 36*(11), 1202-1212.
Snyder, M. & White, P. (1981). Testing hypotheses about other people: Strategies of verification and falsification. *Personality and Social Psychology Bulletin, 7*(1), March, 39-43.
Tapscott, D. & Caston, A. (1993*). Paradigm Shift.* New York: McGraw-Hill.
Watson Dugan, K. (1989). Ability and effort attributions: Do they affect how managers communicate performance feedback information? *Academy of Management Journal, 32*(1), 87-114.
Weary, G., Stanley, M. A. & Harvey, J. H. (1989). Attribution. New York: Springer-Verlag.
Weary B. G. (1978). Self-serving biases in the attribution process: A re-examination of the fact or fiction question. *Journal of Personality and Social Psychology,* 36, 56-71.
Weiner, B. (1985). An attributional theory of achievement motivation and emotion. *Psychological Review, 92*(4), 548-573.
Zuckerman, M. (1979). Attribution of success and failure revisited, or: The

motivational bias is alive and well in attribution theory. *Journal of Personality,* 47, 245-287.

Chapter VIII

Knowledge Management through End User Developed Expert Systems: Potential and Limitations

Christian Wagner
City University of Hong Kong, China

ABSTRACT

Knowledge is receiving recognition as a strategic force in organizations. Correspondingly, one form of knowledge capture and maintenance organizations are tempted to use is expert system design by end users. The chapter discusses difficulties associated with end-user development, both in terms of design quality and knowledge content. An analysis of 25 expert systems written by non-professional developers reveals significant quality and size limitations that indicate limited feasibility of end-user expert system development. Furthermore, the lack of design quality may not be easily compensated for by a "knowledge advantage" of the end users, as end users may have a performance advantage in using their knowledge, but not in "knowing" it. The chapter then offers suggestions for alternate forms of end-user oriented expert system development that considers end-user limitations and takes advantage of recent developments in information technology.

BACKGROUND

Growing Need for Knowledge Based Systems

Knowledge is enjoying widespread attention as a strategic tool for the competitiveness of firms. The topic has been widely covered, both in the management research literature, (e.g., Alavi & Leidner, 1999; Davenport et al., 1998; Zack 1999a, 1999b; Ruggles, 1999; Burns et al., 1999; Nonaka & Takeuchi, 1995) and the popular press, (e.g., Davenport & Marchand, 1999, "In Praise of Knowledge" *Economist*, May 27, 1995, 20). Several of these studies have emphasized that knowledge creation and management is not simply the capture and storage of information. Knowledge management also requires the storage and processing of associations (rules) through which meaning can be derived from the information. And, to follow the argument of Nonaka and Takeuchi, knowledge should be stored in explicit, observable form.

Presently, the pre-eminent information technology vehicle for the explicit representation of knowledge in managerial applications is the expert system (or knowledge based system). Thus, knowledge explication would require massive expert system development. Given the existing demands placed on the systems development function, the implication is that at least part of the expert system development effort will have to be completed by end users. This creates a dilemma. On one hand, the bottleneck in knowledge acquisition is well acknowledged (Holsapple & Raj, 1994). On the other hand, one of the truisms of expert systems development is that the domain expert should not be his or her own knowledge engineer (Hayes-Roth et al., 1983), a heuristic based on Johnson's *paradox of expertise* (Johnson, 1983).

Despite common wisdom condemning end user expert system development, there are numerous accounts of successes with this development approach. For example, Du Pont (Feigenbaum et al., 1988; McNurlin, 1987) reported positive experiences with end-user created solutions 10 years ago when development tools were more primitive than today. So did Eastman Kodak (Huntington, 1989), and so did the US Navy (Griesser & Tubalkain, 1992). The number of applications ranged from a few tens (US Navy) to more than 1,000 (DuPont), the size per application from tens of rules to several hundred. Lubrizol has users participate in expert system development by letting them build the underlying decision tables (*I/S Analyzer*, 34, 3, March 1995, 12-15). In addition, several of today's development "languages" have become much more user friendly, (e.g., visual design of trees as in Exsys' Rulebook software) and are now targeting end user developers rather than professional developers. These trends are paralleled by a numerous university curricula offering courses on expert systems to their business (!) students, who are likely not going to be professional developers.

Clearly, end user expert systems development enjoys at least a successful niche presence. Yet a recent survey on end user computing sophistication (Blili et al., 1996), did not even consider to ask participants about the use of 5th generation expert system tools. Hence, it seems that most companies do not even consider this approach, while those who do, are successful (or at least claim success). Will therefore those companies who embrace user-developed expert systems become knowledge based firms, while the many others will not? And, what are the limits to end user developed systems? Accounts of successes, such as those of DuPont, Kodak, or the Navy, are not sufficient to help us answer this question, as they are always presented at the macro level (company totals for the number of systems developed, number of rules per system, average pay-back). They report little about the difficulties end user developers face in actually creating their systems.

Special Problems of End User Developed Expert Systems

In a recent study, Panko (1998) addressed the issue of spreadsheet errors and their potential impact on organizations. He reports a picture of unacceptably high error rates and significant bottom-line impact related to these errors. If a similar pattern emerged in expert system development by end users, it would already be concerning. However, expert system development adds several additional elements of complexity, compared to spreadsheet development, which can potentially result in even higher error rates, namely:

- Expert systems carry out qualitative (logic based) reasoning using (frequently) non-numeric symbols whose semantics can be defined by user rules. Spreadsheets are largely quantitative with well-established semantics.
- Expert system developers will usually have little training in the "language" of expert systems, which might be a derivative of first order logic, or a similar logic-oriented language. In contrast, spreadsheet developers can rely on many years of training and expertise in the common "language" of spreadsheets, arithmetic.
- Most expert system shells separate development from use. That is, the knowledge base will be developed in an editor or other development environment (with limited error checking). After completion of the knowledge base, it will then be executed. This separation of development and use makes verification and correction of errors significantly more tedious, if not difficult than in spreadsheets, which are more WYSIWYG in nature and which provide instantaneous feedback on the correctness of a formula, or on the impact of a number change.

- Rule-based expert systems frequently adopt a backward reasoning approach whose logic is not at all obvious to inexperienced developers, or to developers with experience in traditional programming languages.

Taken together, these characteristics add extra complexity, which affects knowledge extraction and formalization (extraction and formalization of "rules" or such), representation (especially in a backward reasoning environment), validation (in the absence of WYSIWYG and instantaneous confirmation), and learning/usage (logic with user definable semantics versus algebra). Consequently, higher error levels are to be expected than for more typical end user applications such as spreadsheets, and special attention needs to be drawn to key sources of errors.

Overview of the Study

Given the apparent difficulty of end user expert system development on one hand, and the increased demand for end user developed expert systems on the other hand, the decision was made to investigate the feasibility of this form of knowledge base creation. Two questions were addressed. First, ***are end users able to develop expert systems that are structurally of sufficient quality*** to represent the knowledge they are supposed to (knowledge formalization and representation), and secondly, ***are experts capable of expressing their reasoning*** sufficiently to create valuable knowledge bases (knowledge acquisition)?

The first question was investigated by assessing the quality and size of end user developed knowledge bases. The purpose was to determine the limits for size and reliability of end user created solutions and thus to assess how far end user expert system development can go. The second question was addressed through the review of research in the area of tacit and implicit reasoning. Its purpose was to find evidence for whether end-user developers can develop expert systems that convey useful business knowledge, regardless of design quality.

The rest of the chapter is organized as follows. First, an empirical analysis of end user developed applications is introduced, together with metrics for expert system quality. This is followed by a more detailed analysis of the problems encountered in end user development. The purpose of this section is to illustrate to the reader which aspects of the development process create difficulties for the inexperienced developer. Thereafter, the issue of knowledge explication is discussed. The last section extrapolates the findings to determine the limits of end user developed expert systems and discusses alternative approaches to capture the valuable knowledge of end users.

DEVELOPMENT BY END USERS: EMPIRICAL ANALYSIS OF KNOWLEDGE BASE DESIGNS

End User Development of Expert Systems

End user developers in our consideration are professionals or managers whose primary function is not information systems development. These individuals will usually select a lower-end development environment (e.g., Knowledge Garden, Expert Builder, Exsys Corvid, XpertRule, M.4), based on simplicity and cost, and will choose application areas according to their own knowledge and interests. To study this form of development and the problems associated with it, 25 expert system development projects were analysed. The systems were written as individual in-class projects by MBA students (84% part-time students with full-time professional or managerial jobs). Average work experience exceeded five years. The course was a Year 2 (2-year program) elective in management support systems for students who had taken at least one prior course in information systems, and some course-based, hands-on software development experience. Course participants chose problem areas to develop systems based on their individual interests, but according to problem feasibility criteria, as outlined in Waterman (1986). To enable them to develop expert systems, course participants received approximately 15 hours of instruction, covering both methodology (e.g., development life cycle) and implementation issues. The instruction duration was similar to that of courses offered in industry (usually 2 to 3 days, as for instance at Knowledge Garden, URL http://*www.kgarden.com*). Despite these hours of instruction, virtually all participants were novices with respect to the task.

The project counted for 25% of the participants' course grade, thus offering a strong incentive to do well. Participants also had the ability to do well, as they received clearly formulated evaluation guidelines, including a diagnostic sheet. Participants also submitted milestone reports and received feedback on their milestone reports with respect to fulfillment of the evaluation criteria.

The programming environment was Teknowledge's M.4, successor to one of the early commercial shells, M.1. Its inference engine permits both rule based and frame based reasoning (through class definitions), as well as probabilistic reasoning. M.4 operates under MS-Windows. (Teknowledge recently changed its product strategy and does not offer M.4 anymore, but instead focuses predominantly on solutions based on its knowledge technologies.)

Metrics for Quality Measurement

Measuring software quality has long been recognized as a complex issue. In the software engineering literature therefore, quality is often very broadly defined as conformance to specifications (Crosby, 1984), and is operationalized through attributes such as those identified by McCall et al. (1977). These guidelines are useful for professional software development, but much less so for end user development, where specifications may only exist (vaguely) in the end user developer's head.

This study, therefore, adopted an approach to measure three criteria which are applicable to a variety of development projects, whether systems professional or end user. The first criterion, *completeness*, is related to the content of the software to be created. The second criterion, *decomposition*, reflects good design thinking, but also strongly impacts maintainability of the knowledge base. The last criterion, *probabilistic reasoning*, reflects a key aspect of expert systems, namely their heuristic nature. As is the practice in measurement of software quality, quality criteria (at least two of them) were measured through different operationalizations (metrics).

The first quality criterion was *completeness*. Unfortunately, it is almost impossible for end-user developed applications to assert whether they are "complete", or what their level of completeness is. Consequently, two measures were chosen. One was the absolute size of the knowledge base measured through number of rules. Size can be considered a surrogate for richness of the knowledge base, as it determines the number of conditions the knowledge base can handle. This, however, is true only for two knowledge bases of the same level of decomposition (discussed below). The second, operationalization, was a measure of the presence of "holes" in the knowledge base, a determination of knowledge base incompleteness. A knowledge base hole exists when there are conditions for which the knowledge base has no response, even though they belong to its domain. For example, the knowledge base may offer investment advice for when the stock market goes down or goes up, but not advice for a stable market. If common wisdom (Johnson, 1983; Hayes-Roth et al., 1983) were to prevail, this quality criterion should be compromised by end-user developed systems.

The second criterion was *decomposition*. Decomposition is widely accepted as a design principle in software development (Myers, 1978; Parnas, 1972), and in database design (Bernstein, 1976; Date, 1990; Ullman, 1980), and now also in expert system development (Coenen & Bench-Capon, 1993; Hicks, 1994-95). Design rules, such as modular design or use of structured programming concepts, or database normalization (Date, 1990) are illustrations of this concern. Fundamentally, designers are advised to design systems so that components that belong together are associated with each other (cohesion), and that those that do not belong together are separated (decoupling). Yet, while these concepts are well accepted in professional systems development, they might not be at all intuitive to end user developers. To measure decomposition, three metrics were used, namely (largest) number of premises in a rule, levels reasoning within the knowledge base, and the use of OR connectors, all of which will be described in more detail in the next section. Although this criterion might be perceived as less important for user developed applications, violations of rules of decomposition will limit growth and hamper maintenance, and therefore limit the use of the developed systems as an organizational asset. Stockdale and Wood (1992) also identified the issue of knowledge base structuring as an area of weakness for end-user developed systems.

The third criterion was the use of *probabilistic reasoning* within the knowledge base. Part of the appeal of expert systems is their ability to incorporate an aspect of expert reasoning which is reflected in approximate reasoning, use of heuristics, and pursuit of multiple paths. As professionals in their field of expertise, the individuals participating in this study were aware of non-deterministic concepts. In fact, they had received formal instruction about heuristic reasoning and the mechanisms of probabilistic reasoning within expert systems. They therefore had "motive and means." Would they then follow through, and in fact implement this form of reasoning in their systems?

Were useful criteria left out in this analysis of the quality of user-developed systems? Likely. For once, the study did not measure the content quality of each knowledge base. Thus, a knowledge base could "score highly" but at the same time be simple in its advice capability, if the developer chose such a direction. Knowledge bases were not allowed to be trivial, but there was clearly a range of content quality. However, it was impossible to prescribe to study participants which area to build a system for, because the purpose of the exercise was to let them build a system for an area they were highly familiar with. Hence, there was no uniformity in the knowledge base content and no well justifiable way to assess content quality *per se* (the issue of knowledge content, therefore, will be addressed in this chapter in more general terms based on research into people's ability to express their knowledge). Also left out were typical measures such as bugs that would not allow a knowledge base to execute. A minimum qualification for all systems was that they were executable. Overall then, the quality measures used in this study covered—although not completely—the two defect areas associated with the knowledge based view of software maintenance (Coenen & Bench-Capon, 1993), *content* and *structure*. Together with the probabilistic reasoning criterion, they were thus expected to provide a multi-faceted insight into the quality of user developed systems.

Subject Performance

All 25 projects were evaluated according to the six measurement criteria. The results are listed in Table 1. Table 1 shows an overall wide range of values for the six metrics, representing different level of sophistication, and development effort. In total, quality concerns were detected in 80% of the projects. 8 of 25 projects had

Table 1: Project summary data

Project No.	Application	Max. Number of Premises	Number of Rules	Number of Levels	Use of OR	Prob. Reasoning?	Holes in the KB?
1	Help desk	5	47	2	No	No	Yes
2	Help desk	4	57	3	No	No	No
3	Help desk	5	24	2	No	No	Yes
4	Help desk	3	39	3	Yes	No	No
5	Employee evaluation	9	26	2	No	No	No
6	A/V equipment selection	5	108	2	No	No	Yes
7	Equipment selection	5	44	3	Yes	Yes	Yes
8	Dining out selection guide	4	75	3	No	No	No
9	Employee morale advisor	4	86	4	No	No	Yes
10	Blackjack advisor	4	128	4	Yes	Yes	No
11	Travel advisor	4	83	3	Yes	Yes	No
12	Financial aid advisor	5	87	4	Yes	Yes	No
13	Software explanation	3	59	4	No	No	No
14	Order audit	4	35	3	Yes	Yes	No
15	Insurance profiling	3	95	3	No	No	No
16	NFL wager advisor	8	37	2	Yes	Yes	Yes
17	Space system architecture planner	3	175	5	No	Yes	No
18	Risk assessment	3	32	4	No	No	No
19	Computer configuration	3	244	4	No	No	No
20	General problem solver	6	109	3	Yes	Yes	No
21	Clothing "catalog" (intelligent DB)	5	155	2	No	No	Yes
22	SBA loan eligibility advisor	7	30	2	No	Yes	No
23	Medical advisor	2	51	3	No	Yes	No
24	Help desk	4	33	3	No	Yes	Yes
25	WWW advisor	19	91	3	Yes	No	No

Average No. of Premises	Average No. of Rules	Average No. of Levels	Total with OR	Total with Prob.'s	Total with Holes
5.1	78.0	3.0	7	11	8

missing rules, 5 gave strong indications of poor decomposition, and 14 lacked probabilistic reasoning. At the same time, knowledge bases were not insignificant in size, with an average of 78 rules each. Looking at the table one might wonder what levels of performance are acceptable. For some criteria, the answers are simple. Holes for instance, are not acceptable at all. For other criteria there are no such hard-and-fast rules. Hence, the next section will discuss good and less good performance parameters and will highlight particular design weaknesses.

END USER DEVELOPMENT DIFFICULTIES

Completeness Problem: Holes in the Knowledge Base

Although the systems developed as part of the exercise were of considerable size (average 78 rules), almost 1/3 had missing rules. As a result, such a system frequently answers "I don't know" (or the equivalent in "expert system language") to an inquiry. This occurs because the system does not contain a rule that governs the combination of conditions specified by the user. Although likely to be expected from an unfinished prototype, this is not necessary. Holes are frequently due to an oversight, where part of a range of values is not covered. This is an easy mistake for end users who frequently do not use knowledge formalization techniques, such as representation in decision tables. Holes become even more likely and more difficult to detect when the system is not well decomposed and, therefore, every rule contains many premises (see below). Other holes exist because the novice developer assumes that specific conditions or combinations of conditions just cannot occur and therefore can be left out.

Decomposition Problem: Flat Knowledge Base

A "flat" knowledge base, like a flat organization, has few layers. The number of layers or levels in a knowledge base can be determined as follows. The top-level goal is at level 0. Rules that will satisfy the goal are level 1, rules that are called by level 1 rules become level 2 rules, and so on. At one point, there are no further calls to rules (the expert system then asks the user or consults a database). The highest level of rules then describes the depth of the knowledge base. The minimum level of depth for a knowledge base is 1 (it can be 0, if the knowledge base contains no rules at all, but a knowledge base without rules does not really qualify as such). While flatness is desirable in modern organizations, it is not necessarily desirable in knowledge bases. Especially when the knowledge base gets larger, we should expect more than one or two levels of reasoning. In fact, none of the projects listed in Table 1 contains only one level. Nevertheless, an obvious example of a flat knowledge base is, for instance, Project No. 21 with 155 rules and only two reasoning levels. A flat knowledge base is the result of little decomposition of the application problem. Figure 1 demonstrates differences of depths and corresponding rules by means of a credit card application problem. (Note that for ease of reading, the rule syntax in the example does not follow M.4 syntax entirely, especially with respect to capitalization and arithmetic expressions).

In the example, the same knowledge is represented by one "flat" rule (somewhat of a misnomer, since it is not the rule that is flat, but the knowledge base it belongs to) versus four "deep" rules. The "flat" rule has six premises, while the knowledge base it is part of contains only one level, compared with two levels for

Figure 1: Flat versus deep knowledge base

```
Rule Flat-1:
IF      Income > 3000
AND     Income > 3 * Debt_Service
AND     Home_Owner = Yes
AND     Years_at_Residence > 2
AND     Job = Yes
AND     Years_at_Job > 2
THEN    Approval = Yes CF 100.

Rule Deep-1:
IF      Finances = Stable
AND     Home = Stable
AND     Employment = Stable
THEN    Approval = Yes CF 100.

Rule Deep-Finance-1:
IF      Income > 3000
AND     Income > 3 * Debt_Service
THEN    Finances = Stable.

Rule Deep-Home-1:
IF      Home_Owner = Yes
AND     Years_at_Residence > 2
THEN    Home = Stable.

Rule Deep-Employment-1:
IF      Job = Yes
AND     Years_at_Job > 2
THEN    Employment = Stable.
```

the "deep" rule. At first, a comparison between the two representations appears to be in favor of the flat one. While it is a little longer (6 premises), one "flat" rule replaces four "deep" ones. If each premise is multi-valued, however, (e.g., Home_Owner = Yes, Home_Owner = No) and has different corresponding outcomes, the flat knowledge base becomes quickly less favorable. While rules remain long, they also become plentiful.

Rule length is a disadvantage of flat design. Although any two rules may only differ in a single attribute value (e.g., Home_Owner=Yes vs. Home_Owner=No), each rule has to be written and maintained. Longer rules are, unfortunately, also more difficult to verify than shorter ones.

The flat design's second weakness, its need for more rules, may be illustrated quantitatively through the following example. If we consider the scenario in Figure 1 and assume that there are two values for each premise, then the results are as follows:

- Flat design (six premises) results in 2^6 rules = 64 rules.
- Deep design (one rule with three premises, three rules with 2 premises each) results in $2^3 + 3 * 2^2$ rules, for a total of 20 rules.

Of course, the larger the number of significant values (e.g., more than two significant values of income or years-with-employer), the more pronounced the differences become. Again, more rules typically means more development, maintenance, and verification effort. This is where holes easily appear in the knowledge base. When the number of rules becomes large (i.e., 64), one of them is easily forgotten. In the deep design, fewer rules have to be written. Furthermore, much fewer rules are written at each level, which simplifies verification even more.

A third disadvantage is the lack of intermediate results. This disadvantage is based on a feature of expert systems, which lets them remember intermediate reasoning results of an inference, regardless of the final outcome of the inference. The intermediate results can then be used for other inferences during the same session. Unfortunately, the flatter the knowledge base, the smaller the number of intermediate results. In the Figure 1 scenario, for instance, the flat knowledge base reaches only one type of conclusion, namely whether to approve. The deep knowledge base, by comparison, also concludes the financial, home, and employment situation. Although, we should not expect much performance (speed) improvement from them, intermediate results are potentially useful in explaining expert system recommendations to a user. For example, success of rule Deep-Finance-1 may prompt the explanation "the applicant's financial situation meets the approval criteria."

Among the projects listed in Table 1, there are several knowledge bases, which are in apparent need of further decomposition. Project No. 6, for instance, consists of 108 rules, yet has only two levels. Project No. 25 possesses three levels, but also rules, with too many premises (up to 19 in one rule). In contrast, Project No. 23 is highly decomposed. It has no rule with more than two premises, contains 51 rules, organized in three levels of reasoning.

Given the disadvantages associated with flat knowledge bases, why would designers actually create them? Novice developers report that flat knowledge bases are easy to design. The developer sets up a "rule template" and then produces variants, often simply through "cut-and-paste". This procedure can initially quickly produce a small knowledge base that deals with some of the relevant case scenarios. It is only later that the developer realizes how difficult it is to complete the knowledge base and to detect any existing errors in it. In contrast, creating a deep knowledge base requires more initial insight and planning. The developer has to understand how to decompose the knowledge of the domain and then implement the knowledge in decomposed form. This, of course, requires more understanding of design principles, and is a skill that end user developers will rarely develop.

Decomposition Problem: Rule Coupling Through OR

Some designers may consider the use of OR within knowledge base rules an efficient mechanism to reduce the overall number of rules. And it can be. After all, the use of OR allows us to combine two sets of premises that result in the same conclusion, as illustrated in Figure 2. In fact, even the M.4 manual exemplifies the use of OR in knowledge bases. In our set, 7 out of 25 projects used OR statements in rules. Yet, before two sets of premises are combined, we need to ask whether they actually belong together. Are they related in meaning other than their simply inducing the same conclusion? The two premises in rule Approval-1 in Figure 2, for instance, have little in common and they are not related. Premises should be considered related if they refer to the same condition and differ only in the value for that decision, (e.g., IF Home=Very_Stable OR Home=Stable THEN ...). Again, concepts of programming and database design advise us not to combine unrelated elements. In programming, this would be considered coupling (7). When rule premises are coupled, as in rule Accept-1 in Figure 2, the second, independent premise is much harder to detect during knowledge base verification or modification. For example, when all statements relating to Finances need to be changed, the "hidden" second premise in Accept-1 may be overlooked. Alternatively, if the developer decides that the first premise does not apply anymore, he or she may accidentally remove the entire rule, thus eliminating also the second premise.

A representation without OR has further advantages if combined with probabilistic reasoning. When premises are separated, one can attach a certainty factor to the conclusion of each separated rule and increase the cumulative confidence factor for a conclusion, as more and more evidence is gathered. The details of this approach are discussed further in the next sub-section.

When developers use OR, it is often not to shorten the knowledge base, but because inexperienced developers draw analogies to traditional programming where both AND and OR are common. If AND is used in expert systems, then why not also OR? It requires some experience for novice developers to realize that writing a new rule (with the same conclusion) is identical to attaching a premise with an OR, so that the use of OR is, in fact, unnecessary. Unfortunately, when rules have too many premises, the attachment of an extra condition with an OR becomes seemingly more efficient then writing an extra rule.

Lack of Probabilistic Reasoning

End user developers often do not seem to realize that the knowledge they represent is probabilistic instead of "hard and fast". As a result, rules that should be described using confidence factors are stated as certain (see the example in Figure 5, rule Approval-100). For example, the majority of projects ($^{14}/_{25}$) listed in Table

Figure 2: Use of logical or statement

Knowledge representation using OR:

Rule Accept-1:
IF Home = Very_Stable
OR Finances = Very_Stable
THEN Approval = Yes.

Same knowledge representation without use of OR:

Rule Accept-10:
IF Home = Very_Stable
THEN Approval = Yes.

Rule Accept-11:
IF Finances = Very_Stable
THEN Approval = Yes.

1 were programmed in deterministic form, even after multiple reminders to consider probabilistic reasoning. Two reasons were given for this type of representation. First, based on their verbal comments, developers apparently truly believed their tasks were non-probabilistic, even when they were obviously not. This, by itself, is an interesting issue. Experts may recognize that the rules they know do not work all the time, and are comfortable in applying "back-up" rules, if the most likely ones do not work. At the same time, they seem to feel uncomfortable in operationalizing this method of reasoning in the form of most-likely rules with high probability values and less-likely rules with low probabilities. Second, being novices, the developers considered the introduction of meaningful confidence factors too difficult. They simply found it difficult to attach a specific probability (or certainty) value to a rule. It should be noted here that even experienced developers may find the assignment of factors representing the probabilistic nature of the experts' knowledge difficult. However, they typically see the problem as one of determining the most appropriate probability values (or certainty factors) so that final conclusions are presented with meaningful probability numbers.

End-User Expertise: Knowing More Than They Can Tell?

One potential advantage of end-user developed knowledge bases is that end users are the source of domain expertise. Thus, instead of explaining their knowledge to a knowledge engineer, end user developers can save the intermediate step of trying to "educate" another person who then implements the knowledge. The more direct process of end user development would, therefore, hopefully create a richer and more accurate knowledge base. Consequently, weaknesses in structural design would be compensated for by strength in knowledge and value of that knowledge. The question, then, is how able are end users to elicit their own knowledge?

Waterman (1986) provides an insightful example of knowledge acquisition, which may illustrate the issue. In Waterman's example, an insurance claims expert is interviewed by a knowledge engineer to elicit and formalize the expert's knowledge. The expert, after reading the case detail, quickly gives an estimate of financial liability without explanation. Probed by the knowledge engineer during the subsequent discussion, the expert explains his assessment, describing algorithms and heuristics used, as well as assumptions made. In the end, the expert's lengthy computations result in a financial liability figure almost identical to the value determined prior without explanation (difference of about 1%).

The example suggests at least two points. First, the expert may use different reasoning mechanisms for the same problem, a fast and efficient data or case based reasoning format to solve the problem, and a formal, rule-based reasoning format to generate explanations. After all, if the same reasoning were used, results would be identical. Second, experts are expert in what they do, not necessarily in explaining (which is more the expertise area of teachers and university faculty). An expert may not be able to provide explanations for all of his or her reasoning. While being able to solve the problem, he or she will not be able to explain the necessary rules or heuristics to do so.

Evidence for the existence of unexplainable "tacit" knowledge has mounted in recent years. The existence of tacit knowledge was put forward a long time ago, however, by Polanyi (1966). Polanyi's views of tacit knowledge can be stated as follows:

> Tacit knowledge is a set of facts and rules, of which only the resulting (i.e., implied) facts are observable by the knowledge owner. The resulting component, called *Term 2*, is considered *specifyably known*. The unobservable component (*Term 1*) is considered *tacitly known*.

For example, a loan officer might review the facts of a loan application and reject the application. When asked "why did you reject it?," she cannot give a meaningful explanation ("it did not warrant acceptance"), because she is not aware why she rejected it.

Term 2 (specifyably known): loan rejection, (fact).

Term 1 (tacitly known): facts, such as monthly income, monthly debt service, rule stating "reject an application if monthly debt service exceeds 20% of monthly income."

Evidence for Tacit Knowledge and Implicit Reasoning

Empirical evidence for the phenomenon "knowing more than being able to tell" has emerged from multiple task areas. For example, in several experiments, Lewicky et al. (1987, 1988) found that subjects were able to improve their performance in cognitive tasks over thousands of trials, but were unable to explain the rule that governed their performance, even when offered rewards for explaining, amounting to $100. In another study, Reber and Lewis (1977) found that through task performance subjects became better at the task as well as better in explaining their performance (explication), however that their performance increase surpassed their improvement in explaining the performance. In yet another study, Mathews at al. (1989) demonstrated empirically that when a subject group, while learning a task, explained its knowledge to a control group, the control group performed at about half the level of accuracy of the first group. These examples point to an important shortcoming of the expert (our end user) working alone, and stress the need for a knowledge engineer not simply as a knowledge implementer, but as a knowledge creator who observes the expert's behavior and translates observations into rule (or similar) form.

An example may illustrate this issue further. Let us assume, a person is asked how to add two numbers. The person's answer could be, "for as long as the first number is greater than zero, decrement it by one and increment the second number by one. Once this process of counting down and counting up is finished, the second number will reflect the total." Let us also assume, that same person is asked to calculate the result of 3 + 4. He or she will likely reply "7", but will likely not apply the rule just described, but instead simply recall the result from memory. Being able to recall results from memory with accuracy and consistency will suggest the use of a rule (such as that given earlier). Yet, even if unable to provide a rule for how to add up numbers, many people will be able to carry out arithmetic correctly through recall from memory. Similar principles are at work when an expert, as in Waterman's example, quickly gives an estimate that seemingly requires a complex formula to determine it. The expert recalls a fitting case from memory (an "anchor") and adjusts it to reflect the differences between the recalled solution and the characteristics of the task ("adjustment"). Compare Tversky and Kahneman (1974) for the value and perils of this reasoning heuristic. An empirical study by Wagner (2000) identified non-linearities in the processing of mathematical data, which suggests the existence of "data driven" rather than "rule driven" reasoning.

The discrepancy between the ability to complete the task and "knowing the rule" is supported through the findings of Reber et al. (1980). This study found that "knowing the rule" hindered subjects' task performance compared to simple pattern matching performance. In the study, subjects learned the problem task experientially. Having achieved a reasonable performance level, they were told the "rule" by which the pattern matching problem was solved. Yet, being told the rule (which in many cases did not match with subjects' own understanding of the task) slowed their performance.

This and related results (Perruchet et al., 1990) suggests that people often simply "don't know" their own knowledge. More than being unable to explain, they simply have no complete understanding or a partially incorrect understanding of the underlying principles. This is different from the argument made by Johnson (1983) and many of the issues discussed by Gaines (1987). While to an outside observer it appears as a set of carefully crafted rules, expert knowledge might better be described as a fairly complete and consistent set of case based solutions (some of which the experts can explain). Irgon et al. (1990) support the argument in their analysis of the development of five expert systems. In one of the development cases, the experts frequently frustrated knowledge by providing highly specific cases, when the knowledge engineers were looking for general principles and rules.

In summary, then, the end user's domain knowledge might not be in a form that is immediately useful for implementation into an expert system. Even if an expert can describe a rule by which the reasoning is supposedly carried out, it may not at all describe the expert's reasoning mechanism. Hence, the end user's best knowledge, the knowledge that goes beyond routine problem solving and textbook knowledge, might only be discovered (!) through a knowledge elicitation and interpretation process, which involves a skilled knowledge engineer as well.

IMPLICATIONS FOR KNOWLEDGE MANAGEMENT

The discussion so far has revealed shortcomings in end-users' ability to construct quality knowledge and has suggested a further inability to express key problem solving knowledge as well. The implications of both these concerns are discussed below.

Limits to Knowledge Base Structural Quality

The projects analyzed here were of considerable size, yet they also exhibited a range of problem symptoms. Size is seemingly easier to generate than good design. Lack of probabilistic reasoning indicates that developers did not fully capture the essence of expert reasoning. Missing rules point to end user difficulties in the systematic validation of knowledge bases. Poor decomposition is evidence that developers ignored, willingly or unwillingly, knowledge base decomposition principles (thus creating future maintenance and enhancement headaches). Taken together, end user expert systems make trade-offs that qualify them as "throw-away", systems that might work at the present, but lack the features that allow them to easily grow and be maintainable.

These quality concerns were encountered even though all individuals had been previously instructed in knowledge base decomposition, probabilistic reasoning, use of OR, and knowledge base verification. In addition, all projects had gone through one prior development iteration (participants submitted an early version for review and comments).

LIMITS TO KNOWLEDGE BASE SIZE

With knowledge base design and maintenance being time-consuming tasks, there are obvious limits to the maximum size knowledge base a developer can create. If an end user spends about as much time per year on expert system development as the participants did in this exercise (about 50 hours on average), the resulting systems should also be of similar size. That size, around 80 rules on average, is very much in the range of systems developed at DuPont or Eastman Kodak. And while it is considerable already, 80 rules are not enough to capture significant amounts of expertise. By comparison, American Express' Authorizer's Assistant contains about 850 rules, Coopers and Lybrand's Expertax about 3000 rules, DEC's XCON system about 10,000 rules. Also, the professional systems contain well-written rules, where one well-written rule may represent the same knowledge as several poorly written ones.

The above discussion does not imply that a larger knowledge base is automatically a better or more knowledge rich knowledge base. This was demonstrated earlier in the discussion of flat vs. deep knowledge bases. By comparison, the developers of XCON, for instance, measure size and complexity in terms of the number of rules, but in addition consider the number of conditions per rule, the number of conclusions per rule, and the number of attributes per condition element (Barker & O'Connor, 1989). With respect to richness, XCON is also interesting because its size fluctuated up and down. Periods of increase in rule size were followed by a re-organization effort in which the knowledge base size shrank, although the contained knowledge did not. Yet, all else being equal (i.e., two knowledge bases with the same depth), the system with more rules will contain more knowledge and will provide more reasoning capability.

Expert Capabilities

The discussion of tacit versus explicit reasoning suggests another implication for end-user developed systems. End-user experts need to be able to express their knowledge. Hence, end users should have either a high level of awareness of their knowledge, or should be trained in knowledge "explication" before engaging in any such development effort. Alternatively, a case-based development process would need to be employed, which lets experts solve cases, while a rule induction system interprets the experts' actions and constructs rules from the observed data points.

Does Type of Domain Matter?

One potential source of poor designs might, of course, be related to the choice of problem domain or the type of system built. As pointed out, for instance, by Waterman (1986) and Mallach (1994), there are "good" expert system problems and less good ones. In order to steer subjects away from less good problems, they had to have their problem choice approved and had to formally argue for the problem's suitability, using Waterman's criteria. Projects topics are listed in Table

1. While there is little data available to suggest any strong patterns, it appears that the least sophisticated designs coincided with the helpdesk system applications. The typical weaknesses in these systems were flat knowledge bases (long rules) with corresponding holes in the knowledge base (3 out of 5). None of the projects dealt with toy problems. The least "expert" system was probably Project 8 (Dining out selection guide), yet it had a lengthy knowledge base. Another project, Project 16 (NFL Wager advisor) whose subject area might suggest a "toy application" was based on the developer's complex wagering system, which he had developed and successfully used over many years.

Good Knowledge in Poorly Designed Knowledge Bases?

Does poor knowledge-base design imply a poor knowledge base? Of course not. A poorly designed knowledge base with holes and other structural deficiencies may nevertheless capture a valuable portion of a company's business rules. Yet, the scenario of an end-user designed structurally poor, but knowledge-rich expert system is not all too likely. A weakly structured knowledge base will have difficulty in representing deep knowledge, which is knowledge with many layers of structure where the result of one layer becomes the input of another. This type of knowledge is, however, a reflection of true expertise and one of the targets of end user developed expert systems. Another, more suitable type of knowledge might be categorized as "clever" knowledge. This would be knowledge that is simple in structure, but only known to few people and, therefore, of high value. Examples might include "smokers buy more furniture", "beware of Greeks bringing gifts", or "the murderer always returns to the scene of the crime" (some of these rules are less widely known and less clever than others). If knowledge of this type can be captured and propagated throughout the organization, it can provide broad value.

And yet, all other factors being equal, even with this type of knowledge, a well designed knowledge base will be more valuable than a poorly designed one, because its structural quality will lead to better knowledge quality. There will be fewer holes, leading to less frustration on the side of other users using the expert system. There will also be fewer chances that appropriate rules do not fire, due to design problems. Finally, the maintainability of a well-structured knowledge base will allow it to change and grow.

Need for a New Paradigm

The findings strongly suggest that there are significant limitations faced by an end-user-oriented development paradigm. These shortcomings are present both in the structure of the programs (the expert systems), and in the formalization of the knowledge. Domain experts are, after all, not software engineers, nor decision theorists. Consequently, a new paradigm is needed which recognizes these inherent limitations, and defines a development approach, which is robust enough to accept the limitations. Table 2 summarizes elements of such a new paradigm, all of which are discussed below.

Recent developments in software engineering are one source for possible remedies. First, software engineering in the age of e-business is quickly moving to component-based solution (e.g., Baster et al., 2001). The components are re-usable objects with well-defined interfaces and communication protocols (namely via message passing). Second, new development approaches such as "extreme programming" make use of elaborate test facilities that can "automatically" test code as it is developed (e.g., Jeffries, 1999).

A component-based approach will be a must for the development of large, intelligent systems for the future. Whether components are individual intelligent agents, or objects in a larger knowledge-based system, they need to be highly decoupled, so that individual experts can design them without concern for the structure of an overall program. Domain experts should never be asked to develop these components (i.e., write code), they should, however, define the knowledge

Table 2: Expert weaknesses and remedies

Weakness	**Remedy**
Structural weaknesses	Expert never responsible for knowledge base design, but only for knowledge formalization of individual knowledge components.
Small knowledge bases only	Component based design where each expert is only responsible for a small knowledge base component. A professional software engineer designs interfaces to other components.
Lack of probabilistic reasoning	Determine probabilistic nature through repeated "experiments" where one or multiple experts provide case based solutions, and recommendations are aggregated.
Lack of explicit rule knowledge (knowing more than they can tell)	Train end users to raise awareness of their own knowledge. Engage experts in providing data (i.e., findings), not in the definition of decision rules.
Errors in the knowledge base	Experts never write rules sets, but only express judgments, from which rules are abstracted. Rules are later verified by providing alternate scenarios to the experts, where earlier "rules" need to be confirmed.

that is encapsulated in each of the components in a machine-interpretable form. To reiterate an earlier example, the expert might define the concept "stable finances", or "stable employment". Elicitation of the key concepts, and their content definition might follow the approach suggested by Gaines and Shaw (1999). Encapsulation of the knowledge and implementation of the inter-object communication would then possibly require the work of a software engineer. Alternatively, this new breed of expert systems would simply consist of knowledge components that support very localized solutions, with the knowledge integration being carried out by a knowledge worker. It would offer less support (at least at first), but avoid some of the structural problems inherent in current end-user developed expert systems.

Given that domain experts do not necessarily think in form of rules, and especially not in form of probabilistic rules, the new paradigm will need to abstract rules from data, and probabilities from variances in recommendations. One way of abstracting rules from data is obviously through data mining of transactional data (e.g., Lin & McClean, 2001). However, even if there is no data available from transaction systems, data can be generated by approaching one or more experts with repeated problems for which they have to offer a solution. The resulting data set can then be used to abstract (or "induce") rules. Any variations between expert judgements should not be "averaged out", but can allow the definition of probabilistic reasoning concepts.

Errors in the knowledge base, as found in this study can be addressed by "extreme" forms of testing (Jeffries, 1999), which will result in experts being confronted with "their" knowledge applied by the system to other tasks. The expert can then verify the system's finding, or not, upon which an exception handling mechanism would have to process the deviation.

CONCLUSIONS

As more and more firms recognise that it is easier to collect large amounts of data than to make sense out of that data, they look for intelligent information technologies to support that activity. Creating intelligent systems at a large scale will, however, remain a difficult endeavour. All "famous" intelligent information systems have been the product of costly professional development efforts. And, as this study indicates, there is little chance that similar successes can be achieved through end-user developed systems. End-user development will be limited in content, quality, and size and will not scale up. Ten 80-rule expert systems do not contain the same knowledge as one 800 rule system, and the development of one large system requires significantly more effort, planning, and developer ability than that of many small ones (Gallagher, 1988). Companies that look for new ways to create and manage knowledge will have to search for alternative means to achieve this goal. Yet while some new technologies promise knowledge discovery (data mining) and knowledge management (groupware), even their application has obvious limits, capturing maybe just "clever knowledge." Nevertheless, the positive payback organizations such as Kodak or the Navy have received from larger numbers of smaller systems should not be forgotten in the decision whether to decentralize expert system development.

Interestingly enough, although user-developed decision support systems have become commonplace and are well supported through tools such as spreadsheets or visual databases, the same is certainly not true for knowledge-based system development. But without the tools to formalize and represent knowledge at large scale by those who own that knowledge, moving towards a knowledge-based organization will be difficult. Spreadsheets allowed end users to become decision support system developers. Which new technology will enable end users to become knowledge system developers?

New developments in software engineering, largely brought about by the need for faster development of systems to be used by end users (web based applications), demonstrate the possibility of a new approach to end-user (co-)developed systems. This new paradigm would not attempt to make domain experts better developers, but to take the need for significant development out of the process, thus bridging the "business-technology gap" (Baster et al., 2001).

REFERENCES

Alavi, M. & Leidner, D. E. (1999). Knowledge management systems: Issues, challenges, benefits. *Communications of AIS, 1*(7), 2-41.

Barker, V. & O'Connor, D.E. (1989). Expert systems for configuration at digital: XCON and beyond. *Communications of the ACM, 32*(3), 298-318.

Baster, G., Konana, P., & Scott, J. E. (2001). Business components: A case study of bankers Australia limited trust. *Communications of the ACM 44*(5), 92-98.

Blili, S., Raymond, L., & Rivard, S. (1996). Definition and measurement of end user computing sophistication. *Journal of End User Computing, 8*(2), 3-10.

Burn, J., Marshall, P., & Wild, M. (1999). Managing knowledge for strategic advantage in the virtual organisation. *Proceedings of the 1999 ACM SIGCPR Conference on Computer Personnel Research,* 19-26.

Coenen, F. & Bench-Capon, T. (1993). *Maintenance of Knowledge-Based Systems*. London: Academic Press.

Crosby, P. (1984). *Quality without Tears: The Art of Hassle Free Management.* New York: McGraw-Hill.

Date, C. J. (1990) *An Introduction to Database Systems* (5th edition). Reading: Addison-Wesley.

Davenport, T. H., Long, D. W. D., & Beers, M. C. (1998). Successful knowledge management projects. *Sloan Management Review*, Winter, 43-57.

Davenport, T. H. & Marchand D. A. (1999). Is KM just good information management?. *Financial Times*, March 3, 2-3.

Dologite, D, Mockler, R. J., Ragusa, J. M., Lobert, B., & Banavara, N. (1994). Is there a successful knowledge-based system developer profile? *Heuristics, 15*(2), 73-83.

Feigenbaum, E., McCorduck, P., & Nii, H. P. (1988). *The Rise of the Expert Company*. New York: Times Books.

Francioni, J. M. & Kandel, A. (1988). A software engineering tool for expert system design. *IEEE Expert*, 33-41.

Gaines, B. R. & Shaw, M. L. G. (1999) Embedding formal knowledge in active documents. *Communications of the ACM, 42*(1), 57-63.

Gaines, B. R. (1987). An overview of knowledge-acquisition and transfer. *International Journal of Man-Machine Studies,* 26, 453-472.

Gallagher J. P. (1988) *Knowledge Systems for Business*. Englewood Cliffs, NJ: Prentice Hall.

Griesser, J. & Tubalkain, T. (1992). Building a distributed expert system capability. In Turban, E. & Liebowitz, J. (eds.), *Managing Expert Systems*. Hershey: Idea Group Publishing.

Hayes-Roth, F., Waterman, D. A., & Lenat, D. (1983). *Building Expert Systems*. Reading: Addison-Wesley.

Hicks, R. C. (1994-95). Deriving appropriate rule modules for rule-based expert systems. *Journal of Computer Information Systems*, 20-25.

Holsapple, C. W. & Raj, V. S. (1994). An exploratory study of two KA methods. *Expert Systems, 11*(2), 77-87.

Huntington, D. (1989). Real time process control expert system implementations. *AI Review*, Menlo Park: American Association for Artificial Intelligence.

Irgon, A., Zolnowski, J., Murray, K. J., & Gersho, M. (1990). Expert system development: A retrospective view of five systems. *IEEE Expert*, 25-40.

Jeffries, R. (1999). Extreme testing. *Software Testing and Quality Engineering*. 23-26.

Johnson, P. E. (1983). What kind of expert should a system be. *Journal of Medicine and Philosophy,* 8, 77-97.

Lewicky, P., Czyzewska, M., & Hoffman, H. (1987). Unconscious acquisition of complex procedural knowledge. *Journal of Experimental Psychology: Learning, Memory, and Cognition,* 13, 523-530.

Lewicky, P., Hill, T., & Bizot, E. (1988). Acquisition of procedural knowledge about a pattern of stimuli that cannot be articulated. *Cognitive Psychology,* 20, 24-37.

Lin, F. Y. & McClean, S. (2001). A data mining approach to the prediction of corporate failure. *Knowledge Based Systems, 14*(1), 189-195.

Mallach, E. G. (1994). *Understanding Decision Support Systems and Expert Systems*. Boston: McGraw-Hill.

Mathews, R. C., Buss, R. R., Chinn, R., Stanley, W. B., Blanchard-Fields, F., Cho, R.-J., & Druhan, B. (1989). The role of implicit and explicit processes in learning from examples: A synergistic effect. *Journal of Experimental Psychology: Learning, Memory, and Cognition,* 15, 1083-1100.

McCall, J. A., Richards, P. K., & Walters, G. F. (1977). Factors in software quality assurance. *RADC-TR-77-369*, Rome: Rome Air Development Center.

McNurlin, B. (1987). A three-year strategy for expert systems. *EDP Analyzer, 25*(3).

Myers, G. J. (1978). *Composite/Structured Design*. New York: Van Nostrad Reinhold.

Nonaka, I. & Takeuchi, H. (1995). *The Knowledge Creating Company: How Japanese Companies Create the Dynamics of Innovation.* New York: Oxford University Press.

Olson, D. L., Schellenberger, R. E., & Mechitov, A. I. (1995). Teaching knowledge base consistency and completeness. *Journal of Computer Information Systems*, 7-12.

Panko, R. (1998). What we know about spreadsheet errors. *Journal of End User Computing,* 10, 15-21.

Parnas, D. L. (1972). On the criteria to be used in decomposing systems into modules. *Communications of the ACM, 15*(12), 1053-1058.

Perruchet, P., Gallego, J., & Savy, I. (1990). A critical reappraisal of the evidence for unconscious abstraction of deterministic rules in complex experimental situation. *Cognitive Psychology,* 22, 493-516.

Reber, A. S. & Lewis, S. (1977). Toward a theory of implicit learning: The analysis of the form and structure of a body of tacit knowledge. *Cognition,* 5, 333-361.

Reber, A. S., Kassin, S. M., Lewis, S., & Cantor, G. W. (1980). On the relationship between implicit and explicit modes in the learning of a complex rule structure. *Journal of Experimental Psychology: Human Learning and Memory,* 6, 492-502.

Ruggles, R. (1998) The state of the notion: Knowledge management in practice, *California Management Review, 40*(3), 80-89.

Stockdale, A. & Wood, M. (1992). Building a small expert system for a routine task. *Management Decision, 30*(3), 46-49.

Tversky A. & Kahneman D. (1974). Judgment under uncertainty: Heuristics and biases. *Science*, 185, 1124-1131.

Ullman, J. (1980). *Principles of Database Systems.* Stanford: Computer Science Press.

Wagner, C. (2000). The illusion of knowledge. In Steffen Hölldobler (ed.), *Intellectics and Computational Logic* (pp. 347-359)., Kluwer: Academic Publishers.

Waterman, D. A. (1986). *A Guide to Expert Systems.* Reading: Addison-Wesley.

Zack, M. H. (1999a). Competing on knowledge. In *2000 Handbook of Business Strategy*. Faulkner & Gray, 81-88.

Zack, M. H. (1999b). Developing a knowledge strategy. *California Management Review*. 41(3) 125-145.

Chapter IX

A Graphical Approach for Reducing Spreadsheet Linking Errors

Charles M. Morrison
University of Wisconsin–Eau Claire, USA

Joline Morrison
University of Wisconsin–Eau Claire, USA

John Melrose
University of Wisconsin–Eau Claire, USA

E. Vance Wilson
University of Wisconsin–Milwaukee, USA

ABSTRACT

Spreadsheet programs are deceptively simple tools that are widely used by end user developers in organizations. However, recent studies have shown that spreadsheets often contain significant, decision-affecting errors. One study that addressed "linking errors," i.e., incorrect references to spreadsheet cell values on separate work areas, found these errors to be a major error source in complex spreadsheets that use distinct work areas spread across multiple worksheets. This paper describes a code inspection approach that visually represents the structure of a linked spreadsheet and graphically identifies linked cells and their sources. We tested this approach in an experimental study where subjects created a complex spreadsheet. Results indicate that subjects who used the approach made significantly fewer errors and experienced no decrease in speed of spreadsheet production or satisfaction with the production process.

INTRODUCTION

Spreadsheets are widely used in business to develop simple "scratch pad" or throwaway applications, as well as to develop large and complex applications that guide critical corporate decisions (Panko, 1998; Panko, 2000). Managers typically create spreadsheets rather than personal databases for large, data-intensive applications because they perceive spreadsheets as being easier to use and because they are more familiar with spreadsheets.

When spreadsheets were first introduced, developers solved complex problems using a single large worksheet. An elaborate worksheet might involve hundreds or even thousands of columns and rows, and often the spreadsheet developer found it difficult to keep track of what was going on in distant regions of the spreadsheet. As spreadsheets evolved, vendors enabled users to partition large spreadsheets by creating inter-linked worksheets that allow results from one worksheet to act as inputs for calculations in another worksheet. Today, related worksheets are combined into sets called workbooks. Links between different worksheets are called inter-worksheet links, and workbooks with links among worksheets are called **three-dimensional** spreadsheets. Every major spreadsheet vendor now supports three-dimensional spreadsheets with inter-workbook links. These links allow users to decompose complex spreadsheets into smaller worksheets that are more easily understood. Unfortunately, three-dimensional spreadsheets also introduce potential for inter-worksheet linking errors (Janvrin & Morrison, 2000).

For example, suppose a user mistakenly thinks one or more cells on one worksheet are linked to another worksheet, when in fact the actual data values were copied. If data values are changed on the source worksheet, the values on the destination (target) worksheet do not change, and incorrect data appears on the target sheet. Similarly, a user might delete a cell or a range of cells on a source worksheet that are linked to a second target worksheet without realizing that the cells were linked to the target sheet. If the worksheet uses relative addressing, the data values that are now located where the deleted cells were located are used in the link references on the target sheet. No error appears in the target sheet that referenced the deleted cells, but the linked values on the target sheet are now wrong. (Typically, an error message appears in a referenced cell only if an entire column or row is deleted.)

Moreover, it is very difficult to maintain, audit, and validate complex three-dimensional workbooks. When a developer has to modify a complex three-dimensional workbook, it can take hours or even days to deduce how the original workbook was constructed. Modifications can introduce new linking errors when the developer changes or deletes some of the originally linked cells. While similar errors can occur when all data is placed on a single large worksheet, three-dimensional spreadsheets have enabled spreadsheet applications to become even larger, more complex, and more prone to errors.

A related problem exists when a manager has to make a decision based on an employee's spreadsheet analysis. How can a manager quickly determine that an employee's workbook was properly constructed? Should a manager spend hours or days validating the workbook? The answer to the last question depends on how much an organization has to lose if an incorrect decision is made, but the bottom line is that if the decision is critical, a manager is under significant pressure to validate the workbook.

One approach to addressing these concerns is to use code inspection techniques and tools to identify errors (Panko, 2000). To explore and evaluate code inspection techniques, we developed a method for identifying linked cells by providing a visual cue in both the linked source and target cell. We also developed a method for documenting complex linked spreadsheets by enabling users to graphically display each worksheet as a process that has directed lines representing inputs and outputs to the other worksheets. The graphic display is directly linked to the contents of an opened workbook file, so that as changes are made in the underlying worksheets, these changes are automatically reflected in the graphical data flow diagram (DFD) representation. This provides a validation tool to help developers identify errors. This research is important to the growing body of literature that focuses on methods for identifying and reducing spreadsheet errors.

The next section presents background literature describing the spreadsheet error problem, solution approaches, and our motivations for developing a visual code inspection approach for identifying spreadsheet-linking errors. Section 3 describes our visual code inspection approach, and Section 4 describes a research study performed to assess the value of the approach. Section 5 discusses the results of the study, and presents our conclusions and future research directions.

BACKGROUND LITERATURE

Experimental studies addressing error rates in end-user spreadsheets indicate that 30 to 50 percent of all spreadsheets contain at least one error (Panko & Halverson, 1996). Studies on operational spreadsheets (e.g., Cragg & King, 1993; Davies & Ikin, 1987; Lerch, 1988) indicate that errors are both prevalent and costly. Spreadsheet errors have been identified as falling into one of three categories (Panko & Halverson, 1996): mechanical errors (typing the wrong value or pointing to the wrong cell when making a link), logic (entering an incorrect formula), and omission (leaving something out).

Panko (2000) suggests three approaches for reducing spreadsheet errors: creating and enforcing systematic spreadsheet development methods; using development tools that help developers avoid errors; and using code inspection tools that help developers detect errors. The following paragraphs explore these approaches.

Spreadsheet Development Methods

Planning and design activities for end-user developed applications such as spreadsheets tend to be unstructured or non-existent (Brown & Gould, 1987; Salchenberger, 1993). Ronen, Palley and Lucas (1989) suggest that several attributes of spreadsheets, such as non-professional developers, shorter development life cycles, and ease of modification, tend to preclude a formal spreadsheet analysis and design process. Research studies on spreadsheet development approaches indicate that most spreadsheets are developed using an iterative approach, with little to no formal planning or design (Cragg & King, 1993; Davis and Ikin, 1987; Salchenberger, 1993). Almost all published spreadsheet design approaches agree on one principle: the importance of keeping spreadsheet work areas small. This makes errors easier to find, limits the damaging effects of errors, and makes spreadsheets easier to understand and maintain.

Small work areas are supported in all major spreadsheet packages through the use of modular worksheets that can be linked using cell references. Lerch (1988) noted that mechanical error rates rose dramatically when cell formulas contained references to other cells. It follows that linked worksheets introduce the possibility of inter-worksheet linking errors, which are references in cell formulas to the wrong cells in different worksheets. Janvrin and Morrison (2000) performed a study to investigate linking errors where subjects created a complex workbook with ten separate worksheets and sixty-six linked cells. The subjects made an average of nine errors per workbook; and 84% of these were linking errors. The following actions were noted to cause linking errors:

- Accidentally deleting a cell, range of cells, column, or row in one worksheet that were referenced by another sheet;

- Mistakenly thinking a range in one sheet is linked to another sheet when in fact actual data values were copied;
- Linking a source worksheet cell to the wrong target worksheet cell.

To mitigate linking errors, Janvrin and Morrison proposed a data flow diagram (DFD) approach for visually designing three-dimensional workbooks. Each DFD process corresponded to a single worksheet. Links among worksheets were represented by directed flows between processes. Their premise was that designing a complex workbook by visually displaying the worksheets along with their inputs and outputs would reduce inter-worksheet linking errors. Their experimental study demonstrated significantly reduced errors with equivalent development times for groups using the DFD design approach when compared to ad-hoc control groups. Unfortunately, the DFD group had reduced confidence in their solutions and doubted they would continue using the approach because they perceived it to be difficult and time consuming, which suggested that automating the design process might improve user confidence and reduce resistance to the design methodology. This finding suggested a need to investigate approaches for automating the DFD design methodology.

Spreadsheet Development and Inspection Tools

Spreadsheet development tools are used to avoid errors during the development process, and inspection tools detect errors after they are made (Panko, 2000). Development tools can address syntax errors, like using the wrong data type in a predefined function, or performing an illegal operation like dividing by zero. Predefined spreadsheet templates to support common tasks like creating balance sheets or income statements can also be considered as development tools.

Inspection tools seek to make the underlying logic of the spreadsheet more visible. Inspection tools primarily involve different ways of presenting the spreadsheet to the user. Different options include presenting formulas next to cells or making formulas readily available to code inspectors. Displaying formulas has not proven to significantly decrease error rates, probably because interpreting the formulas requires an in-depth understanding of the spreadsheet problem domain and layout, and because a large spreadsheet involves many formulas. This premise was confirmed in an experimental study conducted by Galletta et al. (1997), where subjects were asked to perform a code inspection on a spreadsheet with seeded errors. Subjects who had a spreadsheet displaying formulas did not perform significantly better than subjects who inspected spreadsheets that did not display formulas.

For example, Microsoft Excel provides an "Auditing" feature that enables spreadsheet developers to trace precedents and dependents for each cell value. We are not aware of any formal studies evaluating the efficacy of this auditing tool. Research findings by Galletta et al. (1997) suggest that to effectively use this tool to discover improper dependencies, the code inspector must have a detailed understanding of the meaning of each cell. Since the information underlying each dependency must be uncovered with a separated mouse click, the auditing process for a workbook with many worksheets and with many linked cells would probably be time consuming and tedious. Additionally, precedents and dependents among cells on the same page can be difficult to interpret because their indicators often lie on top of one another when several values contribute to a single cell, as in the case of a column sum. The shortcomings of current code inspection tools motivated us to try to develop a simpler way of displaying linked cell precedents and dependents. Our approach is to allow code inspectors to observe visual patterns in linked cells and detect omitted links, rather than provide the high degree of detail supplied by including complete formulas or complete details for all linked cell precedents and dependents.

A Visual Code Inspection Approach for Representing Linked Workbooks

Spreadsheet design is usually an iterative process. Developers create an initial worksheet, add additional worksheets, and then go back and modify the worksheets. Our original plan was to create a CASE (Computer Assisted Software Engineering) tool that would allow developers to design the workbook graphically using a DFD approach (Ronen, Palley and Lucas, 1989; Janvrin and Morrison, 2000) by first creating processes representing worksheets, and then linking these processes using linked cell references. When the user created a new process, the tool would create the corresponding worksheet in Excel. When the developer created a link between two worksheets, the link would be reflected on the graphical design diagram. However, when end-user spreadsheet developers pilot-tested our initial prototypes, they always reverted to their former development approach of creating the worksheets in Excel, then creating the links between the worksheets. At the same time, the developers expressed an interest in using the graphical display as a code inspection tool for auditing complex workbooks with many worksheets. To aid in the code inspection process, we added visual cues within the worksheets to denote link sources and targets to aid in code inspection. These cues only showed inter-worksheet links (links among cells on different worksheets), and underlying information about the links was automatically displayed on the screen, and did not require an explicit user action to retrieve.

Figure 1: DFD overview representation

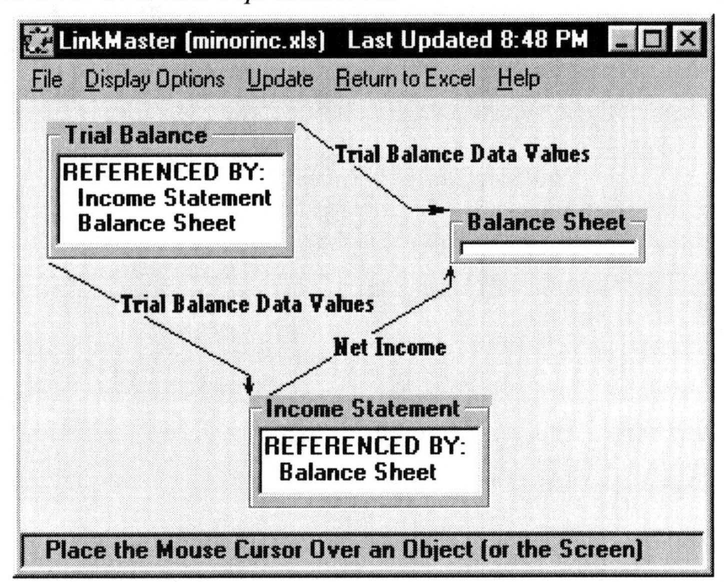

The following paragraphs describe our visual code inspection approach using a multi-sheet workbook that contains worksheets representing a trial balance, income statement, and balance sheet. Figure 1 shows the DFD overview representation of this workbook provided by our code inspection tool. (A demonstration version of the Microsoft Excel Add-In tool that supports this approach is available at http://mike.uwec.edu/anonymous/LinkMaster)

The Trial Balance worksheet provides data values that are linked to both the Income Statement and Balance Sheet worksheets. Net Income is calculated in the Income Statement worksheet, and the result is linked to the Balance Sheet. This view can be displayed at any time, and the view is automatically regenerated when the Update menu choice is selected to display the current worksheets and their associated links. The linking lines can be displayed or hidden. The spreadsheet developer can optionally add link labels to describe the nature of the data that is passing from one worksheet to another.

Visual cues for link sources or destinations appear on individual worksheets. Figure 2 shows the Trial Balance Worksheet, which provides data values for the Income Statement and Balance Sheet.

Link sources are indicated with comment tick marks in the upper right corner of the cells. When the developer moves the mouse pointer over a commented cell, the link target address appears as a ToolTip. This visual cue enables the spreadsheet developer to easily see which cells are linked to other worksheets. Omitted links can be visually identified by pattern recognition: the spreadsheet developer knows

Figure 2: Link source cells

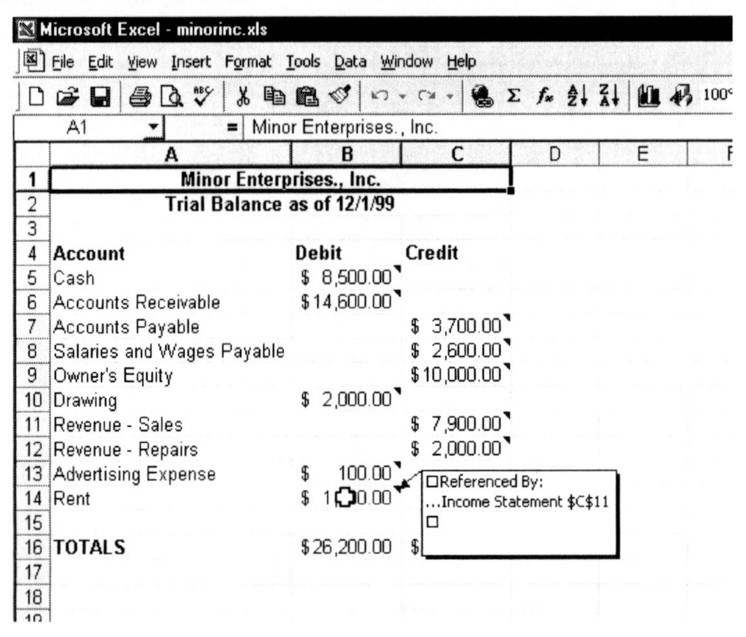

that all of the values on the Trial Balance should be used as source data values. If one of the cells is missing a tick mark, the developer knows that a link has been inadvertently missed or deleted.

Figure 3: Income statement worksheet showing linked source and target cells

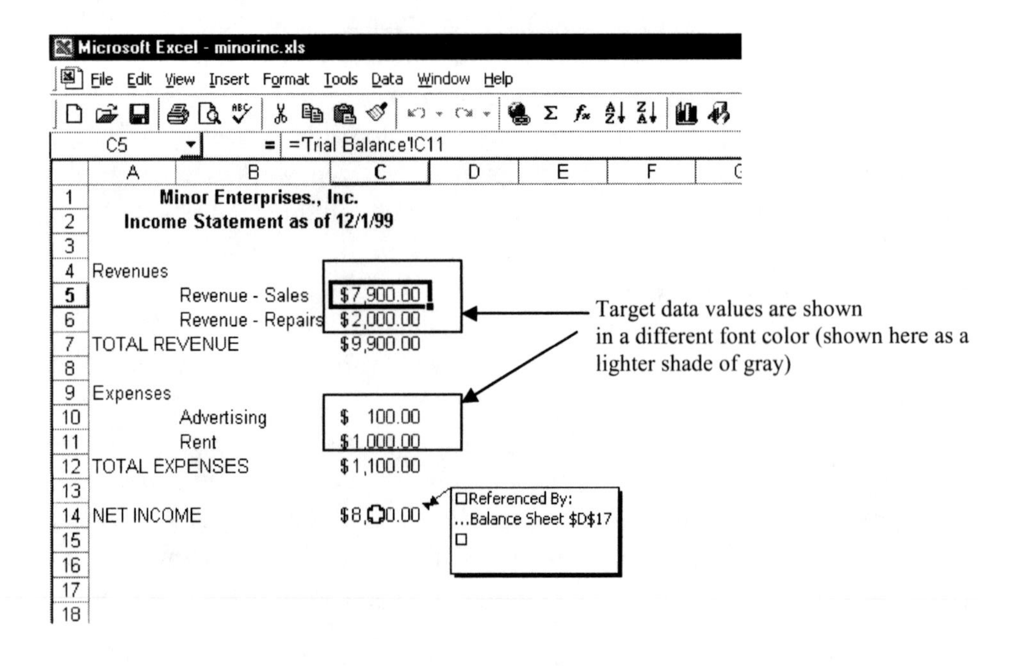

Link targets are highlighted by displaying the cell contents in a different-colored font. Figure 3 shows the Income Statement worksheet and Figure 4 shows the Balance Sheet, which both contain link targets. (The spreadsheet developer can choose any color for the target text, so the color-coding does not interfere with other colors used in the workbook.)

The Income Statement worksheet illustrates both a link source (Net Income) as well as link targets. By using different coding for the source and target cell links, the spreadsheet developer can more easily understand the workbook structure, and detect whether a link source or target error exists.

EVALUATION STUDY

To assess the validity of our approach, we performed a controlled experimental study. The following sections present our hypotheses, discuss the experimental study design and measures, and present and discuss the study results.

Figure 4: Balance sheet showing linked target cells (target cells are in a different font color, shown here are a lighter shade of gray)

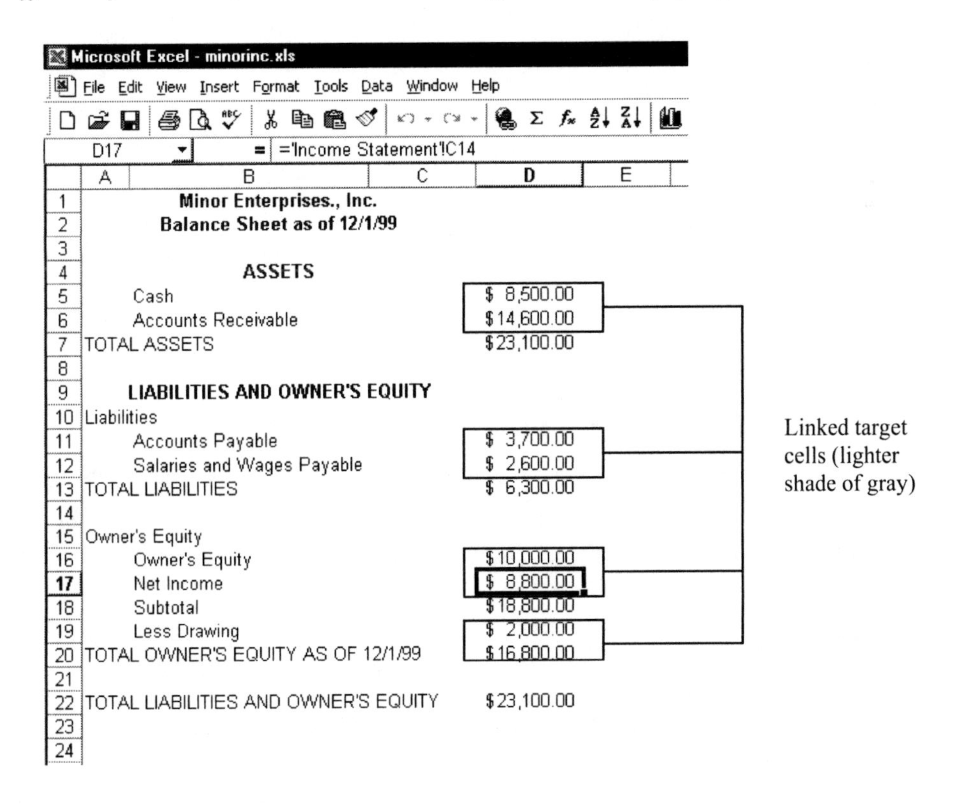

Hypotheses

For the visual code inspection approach to be valuable to spreadsheet users it should offer improved performance. Traditionally, performance in use of decision support systems, such as user-developed spreadsheets, is tied to system effectiveness (Turban & Aronson, 1998). Hypothesis 1 addresses the effects of the visual code inspection approach on accuracy in spreadsheet development, an important aspect of system effectiveness.

H1: Spreadsheets inspected using the visual code inspection approach are more accurate than unaided spreadsheets.

Studies of graphical data manipulation suggest that accuracy studies should include measures of performance speed in order to account for potential speed-accuracy trade-offs (Jarvenpaa, 1989; Wilson & Addo, 1993). Hypothesis 2 addresses speed of performance in spreadsheet development.

H2: Using the visual code inspection approach does not increase overall time needed to produce and maintain spreadsheets.

In addition, as Silver notes, "DSS users are often discretionary users, who may eschew systems they find not to their liking" (1990, p. 55). Thus, it is important that users be satisfied with the system or they will likely not use it, regardless of performance issues. Our final hypothesis addresses user satisfaction with the process of producing spreadsheets using this approach.

H3: Using the visual code inspection approach does not decrease satisfaction concerning spreadsheet production.

EXPERIMENTAL DESIGN

We conducted a between-groups experiment to test our hypotheses, using two sections of an undergraduate Information Systems course at a university in the United States Midwest. This experimental design is similar to spreadsheet development and error-finding studies conducted by Galletta et al. (1997) and Janvrin and Morrison (2000) in the regard that subjects were divided into control (traditional spreadsheet development) and experimental (spreadsheet development with different development and code inspection approaches) groups. The subjects had completed an eight-week spreadsheet tutorial sequence using Microsoft

Excel 97 spreadsheet software. In addition, all subjects received approximately one hour of training in use of the code inspection approach. The experiment was implemented as the final spreadsheet assignment for the course, which presumably motivated students to follow instructions and attempt to produce high-quality work. Due to the complexity of the assignment, students were given nine days to complete it. Similar studies have allowed subjects to work outside of the laboratory in an effort to add realism to the task (Panko and Halverson, 1994), and to facilitate more complex tasks that take more hours than are feasible for a laboratory experiment (Janvrin and Morrison, 2000). Although the length of the study and lack of laboratory controls could increase potential for experimental contagion, e.g., resulting from communication among subjects in different groups, we believe that this was mitigated by using separate course sections to make up control and experimental groups. From our observation, typical subjects were not aware that students in another section were using a different approach to the exercise, and this design enabled our subjects to perform a realistic, complex task requiring more time than they could reasonably spend in a controlled laboratory environment.

Both groups in the experiment developed a multiple-sheet budget-tracking spreadsheet in which instructor-supplied data were transferred to the following worksheets: Budget by Month, Expenses, and Income. These data were used as the source for links used in subsequent worksheets. Students produced the following linked worksheets: Cash Flows by Month, Budget by Month, Income by Category, Expenses by Category, and Summarized Expenses by Category. A correct solution had a total of 428 inter-worksheet links. Some of these links involved linking a range of cells rather than linking individual cells, leaving at least sixty-six distinct linking operations that had to be performed correctly. The experimental group was instructed to use Excel with the visual software inspection extensions, and the control group was instructed to use only Excel for producing these linked worksheets. Following initial creation of their budget-tracking spreadsheet, all students were instructed to make several modifications to the worksheets that required them to revise existing links and create new links. Once again, the experimental group was instructed to use Excel with the visual inspection extensions, and the control group was instructed to use only Excel for this activity. All subjects tracked the time they spent producing the worksheets in the assignment and completed a survey at the end of the assignment. The time sheet, survey, spreadsheet printouts, and spreadsheet computer files were handed in at completion of the assignment.

Measures

We measured accuracy by analyzing computer spreadsheet files to uncover three types of linking errors: missing links, incorrect links, and excess links. Each of these was coded as an error for each cell that was affected on the target sheet. To minimize the potential effects of repetitive errors on the results, error data were analyzed in two ways. First, spreadsheets were coded as low-error (zero to three errors) vs. high-error (four or more errors) based on the median observed value (four errors). Second, spreadsheets with no linking errors were coded separately from spreadsheets with any number of linking errors. Speed was measured through students' time-tracking reports. Satisfaction with the code inspection tools was measured against a baseline of satisfaction with the Excel application. This satisfaction *orientation* was calculated by summing survey data collected using a seven-position Likert scale that measured agreement with the following three statements (one indicates "Disagree Strongly" and seven indicates "Agree Strongly"):

- It was harder to create a worksheet while using the visual code inspection tools than using Excel by itself
- I enjoyed using Excel in this assignment
- I enjoyed using the visual code inspection tools in this assignment (reverse-coded)

Results were then compared against the midpoint of the scale, i.e., 10.5 of 21 possible rating points. Using this design, greater or lesser satisfaction with the code inspection tools may be expected to take the form of deviations away from the midpoint. Because these items measure satisfaction with both Excel and the code inspection tools, only data from the experimental group were collected for the satisfaction measure.

RESULTS

Data was screened prior to analysis to remove subjects who did not follow instructions as we intended (e.g., experimental subjects who did not use the visual code inspection tools) or whose responses could not be coded (e.g., left out one of the worksheets). As an additional control for systematic differences, a planned grouping (Cochran & Cox, 1992, pp. 37-43) was made between subjects in the two course sections on two control measures: reported experience in prior use of computers and desktop software packages (e.g., word processing, spreadsheet, presentation) and time reports for speed of setting up several initial screens. Data values were not used for subjects where there was no corresponding member found in the other group, resulting in 84 participants, i.e., 42 in the control condition and 42 in the experimental condition. An independent-groups *t*-test of grade point average (GPA) showed no significant differences between the conditions. Thus, we anticipate that the control and experimental groups observed in the present study have similar spreadsheet production capabilities. A summary of statistical analyses conducted for hypothesis testing is presented in Table 1.

Table 1: Summarized experimental study results

Measurement	Mean (S.D)	Statistical Test	Result
Proportion of high-error spreadsheets	Control: .614 (.277), n = 42 Experimental: .386 (.372), n = 42	Independent groups *t*-test $t = 3.180$, $p = .001$, one-tailed	Code inspection tool users made fewer errors
Proportion of spreadsheets with no linking errors	Control: .071 (.261), n = 42 Experimental: .452 (.504), n = 42	Independent groups *t*-test $t = 4.353$, $p < .001$, one-tailed	A higher proportion of code inspection tool users had no errors
Length of time (in minutes) to produce and revise linked worksheets	Control: 174.64 (61.16), n = 42 Experimental: 164.19 (58.13), n = 42	Independent groups *t*-test $t = 0.803$, $p = .424$, two-tailed	No significant difference between groups in speed of production and revision
Satisfaction with code inspection tool compared to Excel*	Experimental only: 10.69 (1.92), n = 42	Single-group *t*-test comparing orientation toward code inspection tools (scale value < 10.5) vs. Excel-only (scale value > 10.5) $t = 0.643$, $p = .524$, two-tailed	No significant difference in satisfaction using code inspection tools vs. using Excel alone

* *Calculated using a three-item instrument where each item was measured on 7-position Likert scale (1 indicates "Disagree Strongly," 4 indicates "Neither Agree nor Disagree," and 7 indicates "Agree Strongly")*

Hypothesis 1 predicts improved accuracy of code inspection tool users. We analyzed results to compare two different aspects of accuracy. First, we compared proportion of errors. Only 39% of spreadsheets in the experimental group had higher than median errors, vs. 61% in the control group (t=3.18, p=.001, one-tailed). Second, we compared the number of spreadsheets with no errors. In the experimental group 45% had no errors vs. 7% in the control group (t=4.35, p< .001, one-tailed). Hypothesis 1 is supported by both analyses.

Hypothesis 2 predicts that speed will not be adversely affected by using the visual code inspection approach. Reported time for completing the linking parts of the assignment averaged 164 minutes for the experimental group and 175 minutes for the control group (t=0.803, p = .424, two-tailed). Although the effect is not significant, subjects who used the code inspection tools averaged 11 minutes faster production of their spreadsheets than those who used Excel only. This finding supports Hypothesis 2.

Hypothesis 3 predicts that using the code inspection tools will not decrease satisfaction with the spreadsheet production process. Satisfaction orientation was biased toward Excel (10.69 vs 10.50 scale midpoint), but the effect is small and non-significant (t = 0.643, p=.542, two-tailed), supporting Hypothesis 3.

DISCUSSION

Our results show that the studied code inspection tools improve performance by reducing inter-worksheet linking errors as measured both by the number of errors and by the proportion of error-free worksheets. Importantly, no trade-off was observed between accuracy and speed of performance, indicating that the only performance costs involved in using the code inspection tools is the time spent initially learning how to use the tools. Even these fixed costs appear small, as only one hour was required for training in the present study. Thus, our results suggest that deployment of code inspection tools like this will provide near-immediate payback in accuracy performance benefits for user-developed spreadsheets.

Although no significant differences were seen in speed of performance in this study, interpretation of this finding is compromised by our collecting both spreadsheet production and revision activities as a single time measure. Thus, our findings do not rule out the possibility that between-conditions differences exist in speed of performance for the revision activities, separate from production. The code inspection approach is aimed towards aiding maintenance activities, including revisions, and it may be productive for future studies to implement finer-grained time measures than were collected in this study.

Other interesting implications also emerge from the performance results. First, it is possible that long-term use of the code inspection tools could increase spreadsheet accuracy further than we observed in our results, providing even greater benefits to adopting organizations. Second, subjects using the code inspection tools actually took less time to complete their spreadsheets than subjects using Excel only, despite their comparative lack of experience with the code inspection tools. Although this was not a significant relationship in the present study, it would be interesting to study whether the effect increases to significance over time, as users become more experienced in use of the code inspection tools. It is possible that subjects in the present study who did not use the tool were less confident about their solutions and spent additional time looking for errors, however they still made more errors. Our findings suggest that longitudinal studies of accuracy and speed performance comparing spreadsheet tool sets may provide important insights into the process of user spreadsheet development. Finally, clear potential exists to deploy additional methodologies for improving user-developed spreadsheets. Our results tend to confirm the prior research that has been conducted in this area, e.g., methodologies for choosing data displays (Wilson & Zigurs, 1999), and suggest that increased emphasis on new approaches will prove beneficial.

Our survey results show that subjects using the code inspection tools were similarly satisfied with the process as with using Excel alone. This is encouraging, as user perceptions of a system's restrictiveness (Silver, 1990) and the manner in which system's controls are framed (Wilson & Zigurs, 1999) can undermine its potential benefits. This finding implies that users will not tend to reject the code inspection tools following initial use, however, further research will be required to confirm this idea.

CONCLUSIONS

The current study tests the usefulness of the visual cues on the individual worksheets for finding linking errors. Future studies should examine the value of using the DFD view feature for documenting, auditing, and maintaining complex linked worksheets. Numerous studies show that spreadsheet errors are both costly and pervasive. To some extent, software manufacturers have responded to these problems, but our study suggests it is possible to go further in supporting end-user developers than is currently done. We have developed a viable visual code inspection approach for reducing inter-worksheet linking errors, and a tool that provides a working example of research that offers practical solutions to well-known problems in spreadsheet production.

REFERENCES

Brown, P. S. & Gould, J. D. (1987). An experimental study of people creating spreadsheets. *ACM Trans. on Office Information Systems* 5, 258-272.

Cragg, P. G. & King, M. (1993). Spreadsheet modeling abuse: An opportunity for OR? *Journal of the Operational Research Society, 44*(8), 743-752.

Davies, N. & Ikin, C. (1987). Auditing spreadsheets. *Australian Accountant,* 54-56.

Galletta, D. F., Abraham, D., El Louadi, M., Lekse, W., Pollailis, Y. A., & Sampler, J. L. (1993). An empirical study of spreadsheet error-finding performance. *Journal of Accounting, Management, and Information Technology* (3:2) April-June 1993, pp. 79-95.

Galletta, D. F., Hartzel, K. S., Johnson, S. E., Joseph, J. L., & Rustagi, S. (1997). Spreadsheet presentation and error detection: An experimental study. *Journal of MIS 13*(3), 45-63.

Jarvenpaa, S. L. (1989). The effect of task demands and graphical format on information processing strategies. *Management Science, 35*(3), 285-303.

Janvrin, D. & Morrison, J. P. (2000). Using a structured design approach to reduce risks in end user spreadsheet development. *Information & Management, 37*(1-12).

Lerch, F. J. (1988). Computerized financial planning: Discovering cognitive difficulties in knowledge building. Unpublished Ph.D. Dissertation, University of Michigan, Ann Arbor.

Panko, R. R. & Halverson, R P., Jr. (1994). Individual and group spreadsheet design: Patterns of Errors. *In Proceedings of the 27th HICSS,* Vol. IV, 4-10.

Panko, R. R. & Halverson, R. P., Jr. (1996). Spreadsheets on trial: A survey of research on spreadsheet risks. In J. F. Nunamaker, Jr. & R. H Sprague (eds.), *Proceedings of the Twenty-Ninth Annual Hawaii International Conference on System Sciences*, Vol. II (pp. 326-335). Washington, DC: IEEE Computer Press.

Panko, R. R. (1998). What we know about spreadsheet errors. *Journal of End User Computing 10*(2) (Spring), 15-21.

Panko, R. R. (2000). Two corpuses of spreadsheet errors. In J. F. Nunamaker, Jr. & R. H Sprague (eds.), *Proceedings of the Thirty-Third Annual Hawaii International Conference on System Sciences.* Washington, DC: IEEE Computer Press.

Panko, R. R. & Sprague, R. H., Jr. (in press). Hitting the wall: Errors in developing and code inspecting a 'simple' spreadsheet model. Accepted for publication in *Decision Support Systems.*

Parsons, J. J., Oja, D., & Auer, D. (1995). *Comprehensive Microsoft Excel 5.0 for Windows.* Cambridge, MA: Course Technology, Inc. IEX42.

Powell, J. (1999). Detecting errors is elementary. *Windows Magazine*, May 1999, 117.

Ronen, B., Palley, M. A., & Lucas, H. C. (1989). Spreadsheet analysis and design. *Communications of the. ACM* 32, 84-93.

Salchenberger, L. (1993) Structured development techniques for user-developed systems. *Information & Management. 24*(1), 41-50.

Silver, M. S. (1990). Decision support systems: Directed and nondirected change. *Information Systems Research, 1*(1), 47-70.

Simkin, M. G. (1987). How to validate spreadsheets. *Journal of Accountancy. 164*(5), 130-138.

Turban, E. & Aronson, J. E. (1998). *Decision Support Systems and Intelligent Systems, 5/e.* Upper Saddle River, NJ: Prentice-Hall.

Wilson, E. V. & Addo, T. B. A. (1994). An investigation of the relative presentation efficiency of computer-displayed graphs. *Information & Management, 26*(2), 105-115.

Wilson, E. V. & Zigurs, I. (1999). Decisional guidance and end user display choices. *Accounting, Management and Information Technologies,* 9, 49-75.

Section III:

Management Attitude, End User Education, and Training

Chapter X

Effectiveness of Systems Analysis and Design Education:
An Exploratory Study

Rajiv Kohli
University of Notre Dame, USA

Jatinder N.D. Gupta
The University of Alabama in Huntsville, USA

ABSTRACT

This paper reports the results of an exploratory study of student perceptions of the education and experiences of the Systems Analysis and Design (SA&D) course taught in the IS programs at academic institutions. An ex-ante *and* post hoc *empirical study of student perceptions in the SA&D courses was conducted. The results indicate that after taking the SA&D course and working with a real-life project, students' perceptions improved for the applicability of structured methodologies across industries, the importance of computer programming in systems analysis and design process, and the role of advanced technologies in SA&D. Respondents also perceived that when working as groups, SA&D team members did not do their fair share of the work. However, the importance of user involvement was recognized.*

INTRODUCTION

With frequent changes in existing information systems (IS) and the need to rapidly develop new systems, securing trained professionals in structured methodologies has become increasingly important. As computer technology evolves, the education of IS professionals will be expected to meet the skill set required by this changing business environment. To stay competitive, educational institutions have to be equipped to provide the necessary education and training to cater to business needs (Ahmadi & Brabson, 1998; Gill & Hu, 1999; Veneri, 1998).

The need for graduates trained in systems development methods was highlighted by managers in responses to a survey of topics for undergraduate Information Resource Management courses. The IS managers rated management of systems development as one of the most important topics (Doke, 1999). A joint academic-industry investigation of critical skills and knowledge requirements of information systems professionals found that, in the future, businesses will demand skills and knowledge in technology, management, business operations and interpersonal skills (Lee, Trauth, & Farwell, 1995). In addition to technical skills, businesses will also require skills to apply information technologies in solving business problems.

Practitioners have often expressed concerns that educational institutions do not adequately provide students with skills required to meet the changing needs of the business community. This is also evident from the results of the survey reported above in which the practitioners rated systems development as one of the most important topics. In another survey (Laribee, 1992), educators rated organizational issues as first and the management of systems development as the fourth most important topics. IS practitioners preferred graduates with relatively more technical skills than currently produced by academic institutions (Ahmadi & Brabson, 1998). This shows that educators share some responsibility for businesses' lack of competitiveness due to poorly educated managers (Runkle, 1991).

Given the changes in the IS discipline and a significantly increased demand for systems analysts projected by the Bureau of Labor and Statistics (Bureau of Labor and Statistics, 2000), educational institutions should frequently update their curricula. A proposal for updating skills and abilities of IS graduates includes: the selection and utilization of methodologies of SA&D; using tools and techniques to analyze, design and construct information systems; and assessing the feasibility and risk associated with such project implementation as part of the IS curriculum (Couger et al., 1995).

Although educational institutions strive to emphasize skills in the curriculum that are necessary to place IS graduates into current and future jobs (Farwell, Kuramato, Lee, Trauth, & Winslow, 1992), there are other reasons to improve effectiveness of Systems Analysis and Design courses. First, non-IS major students from disciplines such as accounting, finance, and marketing take IS courses to participate in the systems development process for inter-disciplinary applications. For integrated information systems development, the systems analyst has to work closely with information systems users in a multitude of disciplines (Blank & Barratt, 1988; Meissner, 1986). Second, the shift toward end-user systems development and information control requires that all SA&D students be exposed to problems and opportunities they might face while developing their own applications (Farwell, Kuramato, Lee, Trauth, & Winslow, 1992). End users' lack of technical knowledge can cause serious weaknesses in the system design. Errors made during the analysis and design phases of a project are most difficult and expensive to correct, especially after the application has been deployed (Bock & Joyner, 1992; Ruparel, 1991).

An SA&D course provides education and training to students in structured methodologies and prepares them to analyze and document user requirements, develop and test information systems, and educate users in the use of such information systems. In addition, students also learn communication and teamwork skills. Furthermore, the computer technologies applied in systems development have the optimum utility when they are backed by system analysts and developers, who are trained and experienced in the process of systems development. Therefore, the contents of the SA&D course is of significant importance for students as well as organizations (Misic & Rusoo, 2000; Misic & Rusoo, 1999).

With the rapid development of information systems applications and the use of Computer Assisted Systems Engineering (CASE) tools, the education and training in systems analysis and design (SA&D) has become increasingly important. While past studies have surveyed the course content offered by colleges and universities (Misic & Rusoo, 1999; Misic & Rusoo, 2000) and the expectations of practitioners about college graduates (Gill & Hu, 1999), the perceptions of students toward the education and experiences of the SA&D process has largely been overlooked. This paper investigates the effectiveness of an SA&D course in providing education and training as perceived by the students through an *ex-ante* (at the beginning of the SA&D course) and *post hoc* (at the end of the SA&D course) study.

The rest of the paper is organized as follows. First, we describe the SA&D course and review past SA&D studies reported in the literature. Then, we discuss the design of the exploratory study beginning with the demographics of the subjects, followed by the description of the SA&D course, the survey instrument used, and the statistical analyses conducted. The results of the exploratory study are presented and discussed. Next, the major conclusions and the implications of the study are provided. Finally, the limitations of the study and some directions for future research are discussed.

THE SYSTEMS ANALYSIS & DESIGN COURSE

Most undergraduate IS curricula have at least one course in SA&D. The American Assembly of Collegiate Schools of Business (AACSB), the accrediting agency for schools of business, also requires an SA&D course in the IS curriculum of business schools. While the contents of an SA&D course differ at various institutions, it is typical that students work on real-life projects and use computer-aided systems development (CASE) software to develop system prototypes (Richmond, 1992).

Colleges and universities increasingly require students to participate in field projects because they provide students with the opportunity to integrate their learning with practical applications, and to learn to work effectively with team members (Farwell, Kuramato, Lee, Trauth, & Winslow, 1992). Field projects also provide students the opportunity to interact with the users. Interaction with users allows the students to get comprehensive exposure to SA&D and complement their analytical learning with experience in systems development (Hass, 1992). The instructor is generally the project advisor, while the manager within the organization is the prospective customer of the student (or group). In several academic settings, the instructor and the practicing manager are the joint evaluators of the project (Gupta & Wachter, 1998).

The delivery of IS skills, including SA&D, can be outlined in a supply-commodity-demand model. Past studies to assess the effectiveness of IS education, and SA&D in particular, have focused on surveys of educators in universities i.e. the supply side (Gupta & Seeborg, 1989; Gupta, Wang, & Ravichandran, 1994; Misic & Rusoo, 1999). However, few studies have focused upon the effectiveness of programmer/systems analysts' skills and competencies and how the practitioners, forming the demand side, perceive the education of IS graduates (Laribee, 1992; Ruparel, 1991). Figure 1 outlines SA&D research topics and salient studies reported in the literature.

In a survey of information systems graduates, it was found that programming skills were perceived to be important. The survey also found that the top six job duties involved interacting with users of information systems (Padgett, Beise, & Ganoe, 1991). The importance of communication and interpersonal skills are also emphasized by other researchers and practitioners (Blank & Barratt, 1988;

Figure 1: Salient studies in systems analysis & design (SA&D) topics

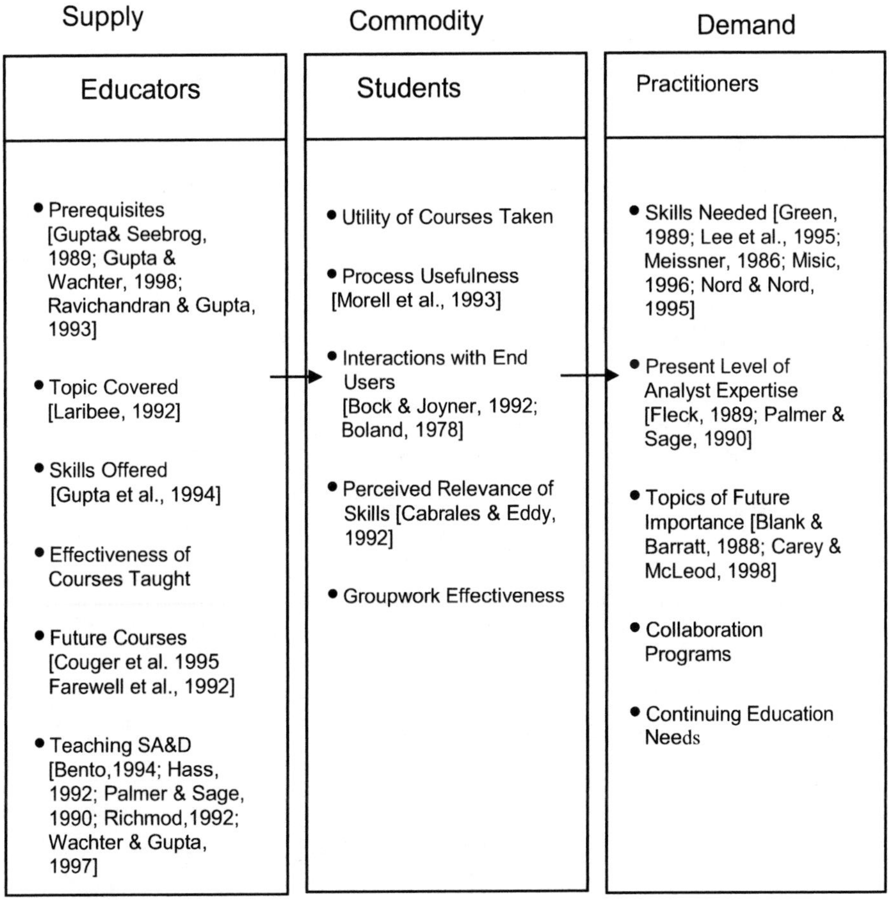

Supply	Commodity	Demand
Educators	Students	Practitioners
• Prerequisites [Gupta& Seebrog, 1989; Gupta & Wachter, 1998; Ravichandran & Gupta, 1993] • Topic Covered [Laribee, 1992] • Skills Offered [Gupta et al., 1994] • Effectiveness of Courses Taught • Future Courses [Couger et al. 1995 Farewell et al., 1992] • Teaching SA&D [Bento,1994; Hass, 1992; Palmer & Sage, 1990; Richmod,1992; Wachter & Gupta, 1997]	• Utility of Courses Taken • Process Usefulness [Morell et al., 1993] • Interactions with End Users [Bock & Joyner, 1992; Boland, 1978] • Perceived Relevance of Skills [Cabrales & Eddy, 1992] • Groupwork Effectiveness	• Skills Needed [Green, 1989; Lee et al., 1995; Meissner, 1986; Misic, 1996; Nord & Nord, 1995] • Present Level of Analyst Expertise [Fleck, 1989; Palmer & Sage, 1990] • Topics of Future Importance [Blank & Barratt, 1988; Carey & McLeod, 1998] • Collaboration Programs • Continuing Education Needs

Meissner, 1986). The manner in which analysts interact with users of the system can lead to well-defined systems that the users are more likely to use. In a traditional approach, the analyst conducts an interview with the user, while in an interactive approach, the analyst and the user share information, make suggestions, and then critique each other's suggestions. An empirical study found that the interactive approach produced higher quality designs with important implementation advantages over the traditional approach (Boland, 1978), especially for some ill-structured situations. Information systems students that participated in an interactive competitive bid among themselves to design an information system for an aerospace client reported their experience as challenging, rewarding and one that encouraged their learning of SA&D concepts in practice (Morrell, Freeman, Serrano, & Mock, 1993).

Lack of proper communication between analysts and users can lead to contrasting perceptions of each other's roles. A study of perceptual differences in job skills, job roles, and non-salary incentives found that analysts and users differ significantly in their perception of skills and roles expected from systems analysts. While analysts may recognize the importance of behavioral skills for effective development, the users often expect the analysts to exhibit technical skills where behavioral skills are required. This can lead to conflict between the analysts and the users of information systems (Green, 1989).

As educators and practitioners discuss the effectiveness of SA&D education and the approaches to deliver such education, it is important to understand student perception of the experience of SA&D process. The study reported in this paper attempts to answer the following questions:

- Do the students perceive the SA&D skills as valuable going into the course?
- Do the students find the course and the experience of value?
- Do the students change their perception of the SA&D process as a result of their hands-on experience of the SA&D projects?
- Do the students perceive working in a group SA&D project to be useful?

The Exploratory Study Description

We now describe the exploratory study, its contents, methods of data collection, and the statistical analysis used in obtaining the results.

Subjects

The subjects in the study were students enrolled in four sections of an undergraduate capstone course called *Structured Systems Analysis and Design*. Among the four sessions (A, B, C, and D), all except session C, were conducted at the university campuses. The on-campus programs support students who go to school full-time. These students have either taken a leave of absence or work part-time while being full-time students. Session C was conducted at an off-site location where the student population is comprised of primarily full-time government employees. Most students reported having between 5 and 10 years of work experience in disciplines other than information systems. Fewer than 10% of the surveyed students had less than one-year work experience. Table 1 presents the demographics of the students where the variable 'SESSION' summarizes the four offerings of the course from which data were collected.

Treatment

The treatment for the study was the *Structured Systems Analysis and Design* course including the project that required students to work on a real-life case. The course is a required course for students majoring in IS and an elective for non-IS majoring students. Students are recommended to take the course in the semester closest to graduation so they can apply the concepts from other courses taken in their curriculum.

The syllabus of the topics covered in the course complies with the DPMA and ACM-recommended curricula for a systems development course. The course prescribes a widely used textbook for SA&D and is accompanied by a project and cases handbook. The handbook provides a structure for conducting a systems analysis and design project by identifying expected deliverables at various stages of the SA&D process. Thus, the SA&D course used in this study is a traditional one, which emphasizes the complete system development life cycle using the structured analysis and design techniques. Contemporary topics like the use of web-based technologies and the use of the off-the-shelf software were not included in the course.

The data collected for this study covered four offerings of the SA&D course over a three-year period by two instructors. Both instructors used the same textbook, handbook, and syllabus. All offerings of the course required students to work as groups on a real-life project and submit deliverables periodically, per the handbook of projects and cases. The project accounted for 35% of the students' grade. The subjects also graded other group members on their level of participation in the project.

Instrument

The survey instrument was constructed based upon the issues in the literature, questions from the students and the industry experience of the authors. Based on

Table 1: Demographic variables of the SA&D students and the sessions of the course

Variable	Description	N	Mode
AGE	Age of Student	92	Between 20-25 years
FLD_EXP	Field of Experience	92	Other (Non IS)
FULTIME	Full time students	92	67% Full time
SEX	Sex of Student	90	57% Male
WORKEXP	Years of Work Experience	91	Between 5-10 years
MAJOR	Major in College	91	92% Information Systems
SESSION	Session of the Course		
	A	34	University campus Inst 1
	B	15	University campus Inst 2
	C	10	Off Campus Inst 1
	D	33	University campus Inst 2

Table 2: The variables and the corresponding statements

Variable	Statement
AI	Traditional SAD processes can benefit from the field of Artificial Intelligence.
ANALYST	The Analyst conducts the Systems Analysis and Design only, while programming and implementation is carried out by others.
ART	Development of computer systems is an art, and cannot be adequately taught in a classroom
ASSESS	There are scientifically tested ways to effectively assess the needs of users in organizations, and develop computer systems
C_SENSE	The so called SAD methodologies boil down to what is generally Common Sense.
COMMUN	Human communications skills are necessary for Systems Analysts.
DIFFER	SAD approaches differ for development of Transaction Processing Systems (TPS), Management Information Systems (MIS), and Decision Support Systems (DSS).
DIVERSE	SAD techniques are applicable across diverse industries such as healthcare, banking, insurance etc.
EXPERTS	Even experts disagree whether or not SAD is an effective way of developing systems, as compared to modification of systems as and when needed.
FORMAL	In the real world, many people have had no formal education in systems analysis and design methods and yet have successfully developed computer systems
GURANTEE	Even if SAD is conducted to it's best, it does not guarantee that the resulting system will be correctly designed.
INSTINCT	It is advantageous to learn about various methodologies for SAD given in books and then follow one's own instincts to develop computer systems
MONEY	If one is good at computer programming, she or he could make more money by becoming a Programmer than a Systems Analyst.
NEW_BUSI	It is imperative to conduct a systematic SAD before starting a new business.
ONE_TIME	SAD is a one time process for systems development, however future SAD will not be required until a new system is to be developed.
PROGRAMM	Programming skills are not required for Systems Analyst, but may be good to have.
REENGN	Business processes can be re-engineered as a result of conducting proper SAD.
ST_ORG	One has to have structured organizations to be able to apply structured methods for Systems Analysis and Design (SAD).
TESTING	Systems Analysis and Design (SAD) also includes executing and testing of Systems.
USER_SAD	With exposure to SAD, computer users can conduct their own SAD in the event of a future change.

these inputs, we formulated various issues in the form of questions and conducted a pilot. In addition, feedback from two instructors offering the same course was also solicited. As a result of the pilot test and the feedback from the instructors, several questions were clarified and some compound questions were either simplified or divided into two simple questions.

An ex-ante questionnaire consisted of six demographic variables shown in Table 1. The twenty (20) statements soliciting subjects' perception of the SA&D discipline and the skills required to successfully implement SA&D principles in practice are depicted in Table 2. The statements solicited students' perceptions on a Likert-scale of 1 to 5, where 1 was 'strongly disagree' and 5 was 'strongly agree'.

The post hoc instrument repeated the 20 statements of the ex-ante instrument to explore changes in the perceptions resulting from the course. In addition, the post hoc questionnaire consisted of nine questions asking the subjects' experiences about their team on a real-life SA&D project. The ex-ante instrument was administered prior to instruction on the first day of classes, and the post hoc instrument was administered on the last day of classes, after students submitted their term project. The instrument was completed anonymously. The students were identified by a four-digit number of their choice that was reused for the post hoc instrument.

Statistical Analysis

The following statistical analyses were conducted:

- Cross-tabulation between reported perceptions and reported demographics to identify relationships of respondents' demographics and their perceptions toward SA&D concepts,
- Wilcoxon Matched-Pairs Signed-Ranks test to study the pre- and post-course differences, and
- Kruskal-Wallis test of post hoc variables to investigate any differences among the sessions.

Given that the instrument measured positive and negative perceptions from technical, human and organizational perspectives, and that it did not measure any one perception or attitude, reliability was not an issue as it is among instruments designed to measure an attitude or a trait. For the purposes of data analysis and reporting, the post hoc variables were named by adding a '1' at the end of the ex-ante variable. For instance, the variable ASSESS (ex-ante) was labeled as ASSESS1 (post hoc).

STATISTICAL RESULTS

The statistical results of this study are presented in two categories: those that assess the changes in the student perceptions of the SA&D course between its beginning and the end, and those that measure the importance of group work on real-life SA&D projects.

Student Perceptions of the SA&D Course

Pearson's *R* correlation coefficient between the demographic variables and perception variables was obtained to identify the relationship between students' demographics and their perceptions. Table 3 lists the demographic and perception variables, their statistically significant correlations ($p < .05$), and the explanation of the correlation. The analysis indicates that older students, after taking the course, agreed with the statement that there are scientifically tested ways to assess user needs. One explanation for this correlation is that the maturity of the older students taking the course helped them gain a better understanding of the need-assessment process. Students may have misconceptions of user needs-assessment from their work experience that the hands-on course elucidated. However, the correlation was not found significant prior to their taking the course implying that age together with the experience of the course influenced the student perception of effectiveness of SA&D. Similarly, older students found that the communication skills are necessary and relevant for Systems Analysts. However, in this case, the correlation was found in the ex ante variable.

The correlation of perception variables AI, ART and DIFFER1 with the demographic variable 'Major of Student' was examined in detail. The correlation was found significant due to the majority of students belonging to the IS major. The perception of IS majors was not found to be significantly different from non-IS majors. Female students perceived that SA&D was no more than a common sense approach. A possible explanation for the female student perception that SA&D is

Table 3: Statistically significant ($p<.05$) demographic and perception variables with Pearson's R correlation coefficient and explanation of the correlation

Demographic Variable	Perception Variable	Pearson's R Significance	Explanation
Age	ASSESS1	.01	Higher the age, greater the ranking
	COMMUN	.03	Higher the age, greater the ranking
Major	AI	.00	Due to the high percentage of IS majors in the study these correlations were significant
	ART	.02	
	DIFFER1	.02	
	USER_SAD1	.02	
Sex	C_ SENSE	.00	Female respondents ranked higher
Work Experience	ART	.00	Greater the experience, lower the rating of SA&D as an art
	ART1	.02	Positions or ART hardened after the course was taken (see above)
	PROGRAMM	.03	Those with work experience between 5-10 years ranked programming as the highest

no more than common sense in ex ante is that they may have perceived it as conversational needs assessment. However, the exposure to the techniques of needs assessment in the course is likely to have changed their perception in the post hoc survey. Nevertheless, we refrain from reading too much into this correlation as it is likely that less variation among the smaller sample size of female students' leads to this statistically significant correlation.

We found the variable 'years of work experience' negatively correlated with the perception 'development of computer systems is an art and cannot be taught in the classroom'. This may indicate that the students with work experience between 5 and 10 years could have perceived that programming skills are not required by systems analysts. However, the compound nature of the question prohibits meaningful interpretation.

Table 4: Mean, median and standard deviation of variables before and after taking the course

Variables	Mean Before	Mean After	Median Before	Median After	Std Dev Before	Std Dev After
AI	3.64	3.78	4	4	0.77	1.07
ANALYST	2.84	2.62	3	3	1.18	1.23
ART_	2.49	2.84	2	3	1.07	1.24
ASSESS	3.63	4.02	4	4	0.85	1.02
C_SENSE	3.27	3.15	3	3	0.98	1.13
COMMUN	4.84	4.88	5	5	0.43	0.38
DIFFER	3.03	2.93	3	3	1.08	1.40
DIVERSE	4.57	4.71	5	5	0.70	0.65
EXPERTS	3.00	3.02	3	3	0.97	0.93
FORMAL	3.34	3.40	3	3.5	1.05	0.99
GURANTEE	4.01	3.88	4	4	0.80	1.04
INSTINCT	3.71	3.64	4	4	1.22	1.33
MONEY	2.41	2.40	2	2	1.08	1.12
NEW_BUSI	3.59	3.69	4	4	1.07	1.10
ONE_TIME	2.01	2.00	2	2	1.05	1.14
PROGRAMM	3.60	3.88	4	4	1.43	1.42
REENGN	4.14	4.24	4	4	0.81	0.82
ST_ORG	2.87	2.74	3	3	1.13	1.29
TESTING	4.60	4.41	5	5	0.80	1.03
USER_SAD	3.07	3.02	3	3	1.02	1.08

Table 4 summarizes the before and after mean, median, and standard deviation of the perception response variables of the study. Although not statistically significant (*p*=.*11*), there is some evidence of a change in the students' perception that SA&D can be adequately taught in the classroom. The reported median for the variable ART increased by one point on a 5-point scale before and after the course indicating that students perceived value in using SA&D tools and techniques. Similarly, although not statistically significant (*p*=.*11*), students' perception improved for the statement that business processes can be improved by applying SA&D.

Table 5 presents the chi-square values from the Kruskal-Wallis (KW) test indicating significant differences between the perceptions of respondents among the various groups. In this experiment, the KW test produced statistical differences among the four offerings of the course. The most significant difference was found among the students of session C. Session C students' perceptions ranked lowest among the four groups of students on the questions that SA&D can benefit from artificial intelligence; SA&D techniques are applicable among DIVERSE industries; the value of using INSTINCT in choosing SA&D methodologies; and SA&D also involves using TESTING of systems. Although further research is required to

Table 5: Kruskal-Wallis Test's Chi-Square values and statistical significance among the variables in four sessions of the study

Variable	Chi-Square	Sig.
AI	6.18	0.10
ANALYST	0.36	0.95
ART_	3.51	0.32
ASSESS	2.94	0.40
C_SENSE	3.91	0.27
COMMUN	1.27	0.74
DIFFER	0.17	0.98
DIVERSE	9.34	0.03
EXPERTS	6.01	0.11
FORMAL	5.56	0.13
GURANTEE	3.53	0.32
INSTINCT	13.08	0.00
MONEY	2.66	0.45
NEW_BUSI	3.38	0.34
ONE_TIME	1.78	0.62
PROGRAMM	3.33	0.34
REENGN	1.46	0.69
ST_ORG	0.86	0.84
TESTING	7.69	0.05
USER_SAD	2.49	0.48

analyze these differences, it can be hypothesized that a structured and specialized work environment can be a contributing factor.

We conducted the Wilcoxon Matched-Pairs test to investigate the differences between the perceptions of subjects before and after the course. Table 6 presents the z-score values and the significance from the test. As shown in the table, DIVERSE ($p < .05$) and AI, ANALYST, ASSESS ($p < .10$) show significant differences in the before and after surveys. The post-hoc scores indicate that students came to recognize the applicability of SA&D concepts across diverse industries. The results also show a higher ranking for the role of AI in SA&D, and confidence in scientifically tested ways to assess user requirements. As anticipated, fewer students believed that the analyst conducts only SA&D, while the programming and implementation are carried out by others. This indicates that prior to taking the course more students believed that the responsibility of a systems analyst is limited to analysis and design. However, after taking the course, the students realized that the systems analyst position may also include programming of applications.

Table 6: Z scores and significance of Wilcoxon Matched Pairs test indicating differences among the subjects before and after the SA&D course

Variables After-Before	**Z**	**Sig.**
AI1 - AI	-1.65	0.10
ANALYST1 - ANALYST	-1.84	0.07
ART1 - ART_	-1.58	0.11
ASSESS1 - ASSESS	-1.75	0.08
C_SENSE1 - C_SENSE	-0.42	0.67
COMMUN1 - COMMUN	-1.23	0.22
DIFFER1 - DIFFER	-0.14	0.89
DIVERSE1 - DIVERSE	-2.10	0.04
EXPERTS1 - EXPERTS	-0.47	0.64
FORMAL1 - FORMAL	-0.55	0.59
GURANTEE - GURANTE1	-0.87	0.38
INSTINCT - INSTINC1	-0.59	0.56
MONEY1 - MONEY	-0.75	0.45
NEW_BUSI - NEW_BUS1	-0.61	0.54
ONE_TIME - ONE_TIM1	-0.23	0.82
PROGRAMM - PROGRAM1	-0.91	0.36
RENGN1 - REENGN	-1.58	0.11
ST_ORG1 - ST_ORG	-1.09	0.28
TESTING-TESTING1	-0.65	0.51
USER_SAD - USER_SA1	-0.44	0.66

Effectiveness of Real-Life Projects

We now discuss the results of supplementary variables included in the post hoc survey only. These variables pertained to the experiences of working on the real-life hands-on projects. Given that the project is a significant part of the course grade and a defined learning objective, we solicited the perception of the students with regard to their experience of working on the group project. Due to logistical limitations, however, data for these supplementary post hoc variables were collected for the two largest sessions (A and D) only. Table 7 provides a list of these supplementary post hoc variables and the statements presented to the students.

Table 8 presents the chi-square values and the significance from the KW test to investigate the differences between the two sessions of the course. Session D students reported lower scores than students in session A. The difference in experiences in working on the project could have contributed to the differences. The areas where differences were found, listed in Table 8, are: (i) how the students were able to apply the skills from other courses to the SA&D, (ii) the experience of working with other group members while working in a team and the (iii) extent to which they could apply the skills of the SA&D course to the work environment.

On further analysis of the differences between the groups (Table 9), it is evident that the two groups had different experiences in working on the group projects. Students in session D found the hands-on experience more congenial than the

Table 7: Post hoc variables and the explanation of the statements

Variable	Statement
ALLOCAT	After being involved in the project, I feel I have a better understanding of how I should allocate work between myself and others, when working in a group
APPLY	I was able to apply what I learned in other courses, in the SAD course
EXPECT	Users expect too much from the outcome of SAD process
PRACTIC	Even though SAD teaches structured methods, one can only learn them through practice
PROJECT	The project was one of the most important learning of the SAD course
UNDUE	I feel that other members sometimes take undue advantage of your willingness to work as a team
USER_IN	Users' input in the SAD process is a key ingredient to the project's success
UTILIZE	I feel that I can utilize the structured techniques studied in the SAD course
WORK	It does not seem like a course in SAD was worth all the time and work I put in it

Table 8: Kruskal-Wallis Chi-Square values and significance of post hoc implementation variables

Variable	Chi-Square	Sig.
ALLOCAT	0.31	0.58
APPLY	7.15	0.01
EXPECT	0.01	0.92
PRACTIC	0.06	0.80
PROJECT	1.62	0.20
UNDUE	19.14	0.00
USER_IN	0.08	0.77
UTILIZE	7.73	0.01
WORK	0.27	0.60

experience of students in session A. This is evident from the mean and median scores of the variable UNDUE.

Session A students agreed with the statement that members of the team sometimes take undue advantage of their willingness to work as a team. On the other hand, fewer students of the D session perceived that to be the case (Table 9). Nevertheless, this appears to be an issue in both groups.

Two other variables indicating significant differences among the groups were (i) the ability of the students to apply the skills learned in other courses, such as database management and programming, to SA&D, and (ii) the skills from the SA&D course to the work environment. In these two variables, session A students, who had reported higher agreement with UNDUE, also reported greater agree-

Table 9: Post hoc variables, sample size, mean, median, and standard deviation of the perception rating of students in the sessions A and D

Session	A			D			Total
Variable	*Mean*	*Median*	*Std Dev*	*Mean*	*Median*	*Std Dev*	*Mean*
ALLOCAT	4.00	4.00	0.68	4.33	5.00	0.96	4.33
APPLY	4.48	5.00	0.64	3.90	4.00	0.84	4.18
EXPECT	3.37	3.00	0.97	3.37	3.00	1.07	3.37
PRACTIC	4.15	4.00	0.82	4.20	4.00	0.81	4.18
PROJECT	4.52	5.00	0.58	4.17	4.00	0.99	4.33
UNDUE	4.62	5.00	0.57	3.30	3.00	1.18	3.91
USER_IN	4.85	5.00	0.36	4.77	5.00	0.57	4.81
UTILIZE	4.56	5.00	0.64	4.03	4.00	0.72	4.28
WORK	1.70	1.00	0.91	1.83	2.00	0.99	1.77

ment with statements represented by these two variables. Conversely, session D students, who had reported congenial experience working with groups, report lower perception of the application of other skills to SA&D, and SA&D skills to work situations.

To investigate further, we conducted a chi-square cross-tabulation of the post hoc variables with the Pearson's correlation and found that the FLD_EXP (field of experience) was correlated with the UNDUE - group members take undue advantage - ($p=.04$) Further, a comparison of means with FLD_EXP as the control variable revealed that the Accounting/Finance and IS majors had rated UNDUE higher (4.80 and 4.06 respectively) than the those with majors - 'other', 'programming', and 'marketing' (3.75, 3.62, and 3.00 respectively). Further research into the perception of students and their background of experience may provide answers to this correlation.

Although there is no evidence, it could still be argued that the differences in the professors teaching the courses could have caused the above differences. We suggest that the differences in professors are unlikely to affect students' perceptions since the text, syllabus, and the project criteria for each session of the course were standardized by the department. Furthermore, since the analysis focused upon the difference between ex ante and post hoc perceptions of the course, the effect of professor differences, if any, would have been minimal.

CONCLUSIONS

The ex ante and post hoc analysis of the student perceptions of the SA&D course indicates that the students were somewhat misinformed about the requirements and capabilities of the SA&D course. Student perceptions after completing the SA&D course are summarized below.

- The students were more aware of the role of artificial intelligence (AI) technologies in supporting the SA&D process. Whereas they might have expected the analysis and design of systems to be a procedural exercise, after taking the course their perception of the integration of AI technologies changed. An exposure to other technologies can broaden the perspective of SA&D students and help them integrate skills acquired in other courses.
- The students had a greater appreciation of the role of computer programming in the systems analyst's career. Perhaps those students who were not well-versed in computer programming felt the need for programming skills while working on the projects. On the other hand, those with programming skills came to appreciate their value. Although computer programming is a required course in many IS and computer science programs, students with other majors

may not have had the same level of computer programming skills.

- The students felt that the SA&D course provided a more detailed understanding of the methods of developing information systems even though they may have held a cursory understanding of the methods of SA&D at the beginning the course. At the end of the course, educators often wonder whether the students finished the course with faith in the methods taught in the course. Educators may find it encouraging that the students in this study perceived the SA&D methodologies as relevant.
- The students believed that SA&D techniques are relevant across diverse professions and industries even though at the beginning some students had the impression that because SA&D is an information systems topic, it is useful only to the IS professionals. This study provides evidence of a change in this viewpoint.
- The students found the hands-on group project was valuable. However, support for (UNDUE) - team members take undue advantage of others - is disconcerting for both educators and practitioners. Perhaps the course curriculum should include team-building skills and businesses should enhance training in teamwork and communication of responsibilities among team members.
- The students firmly expressed the importance of users' involvement and feedback to the success of the SA&D project. This should be encouraging for users who sometimes complain that IS personnel are more interested in experimenting with the newest technology and less interested in users' business needs. However, there was a mixed response to the statement - users expect too much from the SA&D process. Perhaps businesses can educate potential IS users about the complexity of the systems development process.
- The students disagreed with the statement that the SA&D course was not worth the time and effort they put in.

Thus, the results of our exploratory study provide evidence that the students find the SA&D course and their experience of working in a group on a real-life IS project to be valuable. This is also demonstrated by significant changes in the students' perception of needs assessment, the role of programming, and whether computer systems development can be a taught as a discipline. This is consistent with the above discussion that the students found the SA&D process as scientifically tested and applicable across industries.

LIMITATIONS AND FUTURE RESEARCH DIRECTIONS

This study was conducted in one geographical area. Although there is no reason to believe that the responses from students in other geographical areas will differ from those in this study, a wider geographical area may present a wider applicability of the results. Further, this study considered a traditional design of the SA&D course, which includes computer programming. However, recent growth of the Internet-based technologies and alternate design of the information system programs are introducing SA&D courses that neither require nor use computer programming. In fact, systems are sometimes developed using Internet technology (Wachter & Gupta, 1997). It is possible that our conclusions about the importance of computer programming for such courses and programs will be different. However, as far as the importance of well-programmed systems is concerned, we think the conclusions will be the same. Nevertheless, future research should include such alternative SA&D course configurations in determining student perceptions of their experiences.

There are few studies that have empirically tested scales of SA&D effectiveness. Therefore, this study researched commonly found perceptions that the authors witnessed during their SA&D working, teaching, and consulting careers. Future studies should develop and test specific variables that measure student attitudes toward SA&D courses. Such studies should also develop measurement scales that reliably measure the effectiveness and applicability of such variables and their relevance to businesses. The Guttman approach, that has been shown to provide reasonably good convergent and discriminant validity to the development of job behavior rating scales for programmers and systems analyst, can be applied to the measurement of the effectiveness of SA&D topics and skills (Avery & Hoyle, 1974).

The study captured only two data points - beginning and ending of the course - in the SA&D education process. A longitudinal study where students' perceptions are captured at pre-determined intervals during the semester as well at the end can show in greater detail the points during the instruction and the analysis and design process at which perception changed. This could then be correlated with the topics covered in the course and the activities of the project at that point in the course. Similarly, the effectiveness of the SA&D tools can also be assessed during the course. This would also enable us to find the most appropriate course configuration and sequence of topics that should be covered at various phases of the SA&D course.

We encourage business practitioners as the 'demand' component of SA&D model (like the one shown in Figure 1) to express their expectations of SA&D students to educators. Educators as the 'supply' component should be more responsive to the needs of businesses. A joint forum for businesses and educators can ensure that students' skills or the 'commodity' are marketable. Researchers can then conduct periodic follow-up studies to assess how well the students are equipped with skills to meet the demand.

REFERENCES

Ahmadi, M. & Brabston, M. (1998). MIS education: Differences in academic practice and business managers expectations. *Journal of Computer Information Systems, 38*(2), 18-25.

Arvey, R. D. & Hoyle, J. C. (1974). A Guttman approach to the development of behaviorally based rating scales for systems analysts and programmer/analysts. *Journal of Applied Psychology, 59*(1), 61-68.

Bento, A. M. (1994). Systems analysis: A decision approach. *Information and Management, 27*(3), 185-194

Blank, M. M. & Barratt, D. (1988). Finding and selecting systems analyst and designers. *Journal of Systems Management, 39*(3), 8-11.

Bock, D. B. & Joyner, E. R. (1992). Combining socio-technical analysis with participative information systems design: A research case. *The Journal of Computer Information Systems, 32*(3), 60-66.

Boland, R. (1978). The process and product of system design. *Management Science, 24*(9), 887-898.

Bureau of Labor Statistics (2000). *Occupational Outlook Handbook*, 2000-2001 Edition, pp. 109-113 (see the web at URL: http://stats.bls.gov/oco/ocos042.htm).

Cabrales, E. J. & Eddy, J. P. (1992). Informatics education in Columbia: a study of the present situation and recommendations for the future. *Journal of Information Science, 18*(3), 217-224.

Carey, J. M. & McLeod, R. (1988). Use of system development methodology and tools. *Journal of Systems Management, 39*(3), 30-35.

Couger, J. D., Davis, G. B., Dologite, D. G., Feinstein, D. L., Gorgone, J. T., Jenkins, A. M., Kasper, G. M., Little, J. C., Longenecker, H. E., & Valacich, J. S. (1995). IS 95: Guideline for undergraduate IS curriculum. *MIS Quarterly, 19*(3), 341-359.

Doke, E. R. (1999). Knowledge and skill requirements for information systems professionals: An exploratory study. *Journal of Information Systems Education, 10*(1), 10-18.

Farewell, D. W., Kuramato, L., Lee, D., Trauth, E. M., & C. A. Winslow (1992). New paradigm for IS: The educational implications. *Information Systems Management, 9*(2), 7-14.

Fleck, R. A. (1989). Analyzing the analyst. *Journal of Systems Management, 40*(11), 7-9.

Gill, T. G. & Hu, Q. (1999). The evolving undergraduate information systems education: A survey of US institutions. *Journal of Education for Business, 74*(5), 289-295.

Green, G. I. (1989). Perceived importance of systems analysts job skills, roles, and non-salary incentives. *MIS Quarterly, 13*(2), 115-133.

Gupta, J. N. D., & Seeborg, I. S. (1989). The graduate MIS course in the schools and colleges of business. *Journal of Management Information Systems, 5*(4), 125-136.

Gupta, J. N. D., & Wachter, R. M., (1998). A capstone course in the information system Curriculum. *International Journal of Information Management, 18*(6), 427-441.

Gupta, J. N. D, Wang, P., & Ravichandran, R. (1994). An assessment of the information systems needs in Taiwan. *International Journal of Information Management, 14*(5), 369-384.

Haas, D. F., (1992). Teaching the structured design of interactive information systems. *IEEE Transactions on Education, 31*(4), 278-284.

Laribee, J. F. (1992). Building a stronger IRM curriculum: Views from IS managers and educators. *Information Systems Management, 9*(2), 22-28.

Lee, D. M. S., Trauth, E. M. & Farwell, D. (1995). Critical skills and knowledge requirements of IS professionals: a joint academic/industry investigation. *MIS Quarterly, 19*(3), 313-340.

Meissner, A. M. (1986). The changing role of the systems analyst. *Journal of Systems Management, 37*(11), 6-15.

Misic, M. The skills needed by today's systems analysts. *Journal of Systems Management, 47*(3), 34-40.

Misic, M., & Rusoo, N. L. (2000). Reading between the lines: An examination of systems analysis and design texts. *Journal of Systems and Software, 50*(1), 65-73.

Misic, M. & Rusoo, N. L. (1999). An assessment of systems analysis courses. *Journal of Systems and Software, 45*(3), 197-202.

Morrell, J. S., Freeman, J. L., Serrano, F., & Mock, R. (1993). Hands on experience for student in information systems design. *Journal of Applied*

Business Research, 9(4), 141-145.

Nord, G. D. & Nord, G. H. (1995). Knowledge and skill requirements important for success as a systems analyst. *Journal of Information Technology Management, 4*(3), 47-52.

Padgett, T. C., Beise, C. M., & Ganoe, F. J. (1991). Job preparation of IS graduates: Are they ready for the real world. *Journal of Systems Management, 42*(8), 17.

Palmer, J. D. & Sage, A. P. (1990). Information technology management of the university education: A methodology for information system design and development. *International Journal of Technology Management, 5*(2), 217-237.

Ravichandran, R. & Gupta, J. N. D. (1993). Information systems education issues: the US and European perspectives. In Khosrowpour, M. & K. Loch (eds.), *Global Information Technology Education Issues*. Idea Group Publishing.

Richmond, K. (1992). Information engineering, the James Martin way. *Information Strategy, 8*(2), 18-28.

Runkle, D. L. (1991). SMR Forum: Taught in America. *Sloan Management Review, 33*(1), 67-72.

Ruparel, B. (1991). A case study of systems analysis at the American Red Cross. *Journal of Systems Management, 42*(11), 13-17.

Sahraoui, S. (1998). Is information systems education neutral? *Journal of Computer Information Systems, 50*(3), 105-109.

Wachter, R. M. & Gupta, J. N. D. (1996). Teaching information systems via interactive television. *Computer Information Systems, 37*(1), 63-69.

Wachter, R. M. & Gupta, J. N. D., (1997). Distance education and the use of computers as instructional tools in systems development projects: A Case study of expert systems development. *Computers and Education, 29*(1), 13-23.

Veneri, C. (1998). Here today, jobs of tomorrow: Opportunities in information technology. *Occupational Outlook Quarterly, 50*(3), 45-57.

Chapter XI

A Framework for Cognitive Skill Acquisition and Spreadsheet Training in End-Users

S.E. Kruck
James Madison University, USA

John J. Maher
Virginia Tech University, USA

Reza Barkhi
Virginia Tech University, USA

ABSTRACT

It is well documented that electronic spreadsheet models utilized in many professions to enhance decision-making frequently contain errors that have negative effects on the ultimate quality of decisions. Limited research has been published that systematically identifies potential reasons for the causes of these errors, and what procedures can be taken to minimize or eliminate them. Our research provides initial evidence concerning this problem area by investigating how several important cognitive skills are affected by formalized spreadsheet training. Results indicate that one cognitive skill, logical reasoning, significantly increases after a six-week training period. Importantly, the greater the increase in logical reasoning skill, the more effectively the subject performed developing competent spreadsheet models. These findings provide a meaningful step in more perceptibly understanding and defining important cognitive changes that occur in individuals as they undergo formalized spreadsheet development training. Further extensions of this research should more clearly refine our understanding of the cognitive changes that occur in spreadsheet developers and eventually cultivate the development of more efficient and effective training methods for spreadsheet model designers.

INTRODUCTION

In a knowledge-based economy where end-user computing empowers the users to accomplish cognitively intensive tasks, cognitive skills play a critical role in how individuals perform their tasks. One of the first end-user computing tools to gain widespread popularity is the electronic spreadsheet. Effective electronic spreadsheet model development skills are considered vital for workers in a wide variety of occupations. Employers have identified competent spreadsheet skills as one of the most beneficial fundamental computer literacy skills a worker can possess following word processing skills (see Davis & Leitch, 1988; O'Leary, 1989; Coy & O'Grady, 1992; Heagy & Gallum, 1994; Davis, 1997; AAA, 2000). However, it has been well documented that spreadsheet models developed by end users contain surprisingly high error rates (e.g. Brown & Gould, 1987; Davis & Ikin, 1987; Cragg & King, 1993; Janvrin & Morrison, 1996; Panko & Halverson 1996; Panko & Havlerson 1997; Panko & Sprague 1998). Spreadsheet errors can have a dramatic effect on the performance and decision process of end users. Given the widespread use of spreadsheet models, it is critical to understand how spreadsheet training interacts with cognitive skills.

In this paper, we propose a framework that suggests spreadsheet training will influence four cognitive skills: logical reasoning, spatial visualization ability, mnemonic skill, and sequencing ability; and that these cognitive skills will influence the errors in spreadsheet models. We empirically test the framework to identify specific cognitive skills that influence errors in spreadsheet models developed by end users.

We use a block experiment (Cook & Campbell, 1979), where one group is the treatment group who will not receive spreadsheet training and another group will receive six weeks of spreadsheet training. We perform a pre-test and post-text analysis of the measures of the four components of cognitive skills in our framework (i.e., logical reasoning, spatial visualization, mnemonic skill, and sequencing). The results of the study lead us to modify the framework because only one of the cognitive skills, logical reasoning is found to possess the dominant effect while the other skills do not seem to have significant effects. Spreadsheet training enhances the logical reasoning ability of end users, which subsequently results in these users developing more effective spreadsheets that have substantially fewer errors. Spreadsheet training enhances the logical reasoning ability of end users and appears to do more for the end users than to merely teach them how to use another software package; it improves their logical reasoning ability.

The findings of this research can be a step in the right direction for developing better training modules for spreadsheet users by understanding the cognitive abilities that reduce errors and improve task performance. Ultimately, this could help enhance the correctness and productivity of end-user developed spreadsheet models, as well as influence the accuracy and proficiency of their decision-making process.

LITERATURE REVIEW

Cognitive Skills

Figure 1 illustrates a framework that suggests spreadsheet training influences cognitive skills, logical reasoning, spatial visualization, mnemonic skill, and sequencing skill of end users that will subsequently influence the error rate in spreadsheet models developed by the end users. Cognitive skills are related to how individuals acquire, store, retrieve, and utilize knowledge. Different types of cognitive skills are necessary to complete different tasks. When end-users develop spreadsheet models, they are highly engaged in problem solving, planning, and perceptual-motor functions. The demand on their working memory is high, as they have to remember the unit task structure and other task information that puts a high load on their memory. While the end user generally will not be putting much in long-term memory, he or she needs to retrieve information from long-term memory to design a spreadsheet model for a problem domain. Finally, accuracy is very important because a small error in the spreadsheet can have a chain effect leading to dramatically misleading numbers. Table 1 provides examples of required mental processes and memory capacities involved in various tasks to compare them on the above attributes with spreadsheet model development. This table was developed based on the "reasoned arguments" of Card, Moran, and Newell (1983) and Olson and Nilsen (1987). Table 1 illustrates that to complete typical everyday tasks requires various levels of alternative cognitive skills. A relatively high level of several different cognitive skills has been determined to be necessary for spreadsheet model development.

Figure 1: A framework for cognitive skills, spreadsheet training, and errors

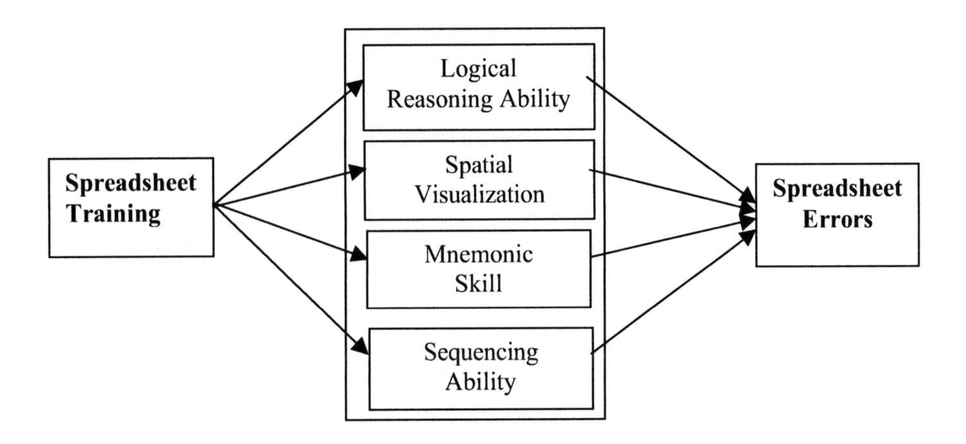

Training can influence various cognitive skills (e.g. Burnett & Lane, 1980; Galotti, Baron, & Savini, 1986; Kliegl, Smith, & Baltes, 1989; Baltes & Kliegl, 1992; Sein, Olfman, & Davis, 1993; Wenger & Payne, 1995; Wenger & Carlson, 1996; Johnson & Lawson 1998; Mackenzie 1999). Prior research has investigated various cognitive skills including logical reasoning ability, spatial visualization, mnemonic skill, and sequencing ability.

Table 1: Mental processes and memory capacities involved in specific tasks

	SKILL CHARACTER			WORKING MEMORY		LONG-TERM MEMORY		TASK DEMANDS	
Tasks	Problem Solving	Perceptual -motor	Planning	Unit task structure	Memory load	Input to LTM	Retrieval from LTM	Pacing	Accuracy
Typing	Low	High	Low	Low	Low	Low	Low	Low	Int.
Driving car	Low	High	Int.	Low	Int.	Low	Low	High	High
Mental multiplication	Int.	Low	Low	High	High	Low	Int.	Low	High
Balancing checkbook	High	Low	Int.	High	High	Int.	Int.	Low	High
Writing business letter	High	Low	High	High	Int.	Int.	Int.	Low	Int.
CPA doing income tax	High	Low	High	High	Int.	Int.	High	Low	High
Routine medical diagnosis	High	Low	High	High	High	High	High	Int.	High
Spreadsheet task	High	High	High	High	High	Low	High	Low	High

Card et al. 1983; Olson and Nilsen 1987-1988

The first cognitive skill proposed in Figure 1, logical reasoning ability, increases with training. Johnson and Lawson (1998) conducted an empirical study and they placed students into two groups: "expository" learning approach or "inquiry" learning approach. Logical reasoning ability explained significantly more variance in final examination scores for students that were provided with "expository" classes (18.8%) for the entire semester compared to those that were provided "inquiry" (7.2%) classes for the full semester. Interestingly, significant improvements in logical reasoning ability were found only in the inquiry-based classes, but not in the expository-based classes. The authors commented they felt more concern should be given to reasoning ability than to a broad range of specific concepts. There is more evidence to show the importance of logical reasoning to performance (Lawson, 1995, 1998). Logical reasoning can be improved as end users learn some software packages that require them to practice this ability. Even some educational games such as Minesweeper can increase the end-users logical reasoning skill (Mackenzie, 1999). Minesweeper is a standard accessory on all Windows-based personal computers. The player has to sequentially uncover all the squares in a rectangular grid that do not have 'land mines' assigned to them. The object is to 'flag' each square containing a land mine without ever stepping on one. Although few detailed statistics are provided in this short article, the author comments that Minesweeper can be utilized as an educational tool to help develop logical reasoning skills. Other studies also show that subjects can learn to improve their logical reasoning (Galotti et al., 1986). Logical reasoning is the first cognitive skill in the framework proposed in Figure 1.

A second cognitive skill that has been shown by established research to increase with specific training is spatial visualization. Spatial visualization is defined as the ability to manipulate or transform the image of spatial patterns into other arrangements (Ekstrom, French, & Harman, 1976). Individuals with strong spatial visualization ability can maintain multiple representations of objects and systems for manipulation (Pellegrino, 1985) and can outperform those with low spatial visualization ability for complex and creative tasks (Sein et al., 1993; Hutchins, Hollan, & Norman, 1985). An experimental study using a popular electronic spreadsheet package, Lotus 1-2-3©, found significantly better results for both comprehension score and task performance for those participants with high spatial visualization ability (Sein et al., 1993).

Electronic spreadsheets are basically two-dimensional matrices. The end-users ability to visualize patterns as row vectors and column vectors and the relationship between them and other cells can improve with spreadsheet training. A person trained in spreadsheet model development may find it easier to both rotate row and column vectors and visualize relative addressing as cell formulas are copied to other cells. Individuals can combine several cells into larger chunks that would help their short-term memory (Miller, 1956). If they cannot chunk data through spatial visualization, end users may find the massive amount of data in spreadsheet models hard to comprehend. There is evidence to suggest that spatial visualization ability of end users influences their use of databases and text editors. For example, database navigation performance can vary depending on the end user's spatial visualization ability (Vincente, Hayes, & Williges, 1987). Spatial visualization explained 55% of the variation in performance of subjects in retrieval from a news database (Dumais & Wright, 1986). Spatial ability of the end users influences their performance as they use a text editor (Klerer, 1984), and retrieve information (Greene, Gomez, & Devlin 1986). Hence, we use spatial visualization ability as the second cognitive skill in the framework shown in Figure 1.

The third type of cognitive skill in Figure 1 is mnemonic skill. Mnemonic skill is the ability or strategy to encode and organize knowledge as one learns so that it can be more easily retrieved later. One strategy to improve mnemonic skill is chunking (Miller, 1956). Individuals can be trained to increase their mnemonic skill (Kliegl et al., 1989; Baltes and Kliegl, 1992). In one study, subjects participated in 20 sessions (practice and training) and were trained to approximately double their mnemonic skill, as measured by the number of words recalled in serial order (Kliegl et al., 1989). Followup studies (Baltes & Kliegl, 1992) that extended previous research to allow participants to backtrack when performance fell below a specified criterion showed similar results: indicating significant increases achieved in the number of words recalled after training.

The fourth type of cognitive skill, sequencing ability, has also been identified as an important cognitive skill. Sequencing refers to the ability to put in the correct sequential order a number of individual operations that solve a problem. Wenger and Carlson (1996) conducted a series of four different experiments using certain arithmetic tasks in conjunction with sequencing of up to 12 steps. Some parts of the experiment were also designed with a sub-goal structure. This sub-goal requirement increased both the speed and the accuracy of the results. The researchers determined that these tasks did result in an increase in the efficiency of using working memory.

While previous studies have examined some of the cognitive skills in the framework proposed in this study, many of the previous studies have not been longitudinal. Longitudinal studies can be very insightful because changes in cognitive skills are likely to require a relatively long period of time, such as several weeks or months, rather than just a few short sessions. For example, to determine the effects of learning programming skills takes about a semester to result in a change in cognitive skills (VanLehan, 1996). Our current study attempts to add to the extant literature by determining which, if any, of several specific cognitive skills described in the framework in Figure 1 are increased during a semester course on end-user computing.

Using subjects from these classes, we test the framework proposed in Figure 1. We then try to identify the specific cognitive skills that are influenced by spreadsheet training. This should help end users focus on those cognitive skills and help develop a more efficient and effective training program. More efficient training programs can be developed by focusing on the cognitive skills that will result in reduced errors in spreadsheet models. This is important given that electronic spreadsheets are so widely utilized in many different professions.

Spreadsheet Errors

Spreadsheet models developed by end users can contain high error rates (Brown & Gould, 1987; Davies & Ikin, 1987; Cragg & King, 1993; Janvrin & Morrison, 1996; Panko & Halverson 1996; Panko & Havlerson 1997; Panko & Sprague, 1998). Spreadsheets are relied on for many business applications and undiscovered errors can be a serious problem due to the potential for a magnifying effect. In one highly publicized incident that occurred in a Fort Lauderdale construction company's bid for a job, the simple (and common) act of inserting a row into a working spreadsheet resulted in a large loss for the company on a $3 million job. The controller of Cummings Incorporated (the construction company) inserted a row to include additional overhead of $254,000 but failed to check whether or not this row was included in the formula that totaled the column. Cummings did win the bid but severely underestimated the cost of the project resulting in large financial losses to the firm (Gilman & Bulkeley, 1984; Ditlea 1987; Simkin, 1987; Kee, 1988; Hayden & Peters, 1989; Stone & Black, 1989).

A study by Cragg and King (1993) examined real spreadsheets from ten companies and discovered a 25% error rate. This is particularly surprising because all but one of the spreadsheets examined went through a formal testing process. Half of the spreadsheets had been used at least six months and averaged seven revisions. Two-thirds of the spreadsheets had been revised at least one time. This may have compounded the problem since modified spreadsheets tend to be more error prone than spreadsheets designed from scratch. Although a 25% error rate is substantial, it may actually understate the true error rate of the sample spreadsheets because the examination time was limited to two hours per spreadsheet. The actual size of the examined spreadsheets ranged from 150 to 10,000 cells.

Many companies are understandably reluctant to publicly admit or disclose the extant or even the existence of errors within their own spreadsheets. However, there has been a great deal of documented evidence provided from experimental studies conducted by researchers. Brown and Gould (1987) conducted an experiment involving experienced spreadsheet users and found that 44% of their end product contained errors. Furthermore, it was discovered that these experienced users spent little time planning the actual spreadsheet. The subjects were business professionals employed by IBM, each of whom had one to five years of experience and used spreadsheets about eight hours a week. Brown and Gould observed that the 44% error rate might well understate the true error rate found in practice. This is because the problems used in the experiment were well defined, while real-world problems are often ill defined and unstructured. The spreadsheets utilized in the experiment were simpler than those typically created at IBM by the participants.

Panko and Halverson (1996) conducted a study using groups of upper-division undergraduates and MBA students. One group of MBA's averaged 630 hours of experience developing and debugging spreadsheets while a second group of MBA students had little experience with spreadsheets. A third group was made up of upper-division undergraduates that did not include any accounting or finance majors. Subjects were given a clearly developed word problem to create a pro-forma income statement. As expected, the undergraduate students had the highest error rates in their spreadsheet models, 79%, with an average cell error rate of 5.6%. The spreadsheets developed by the two groups of MBA students were better than the undergraduates, but still contained errors in more than half (56%) of the templates with a cell error rate of 1%. Surprisingly, there were no significant differences in the error rates of MBA students with little spreadsheet experience when compared to the experienced MBAs.

In a second study, Panko and Halverson (1997) utilized MIS upper-division undergraduates. They allowed a group of subjects to work at home, hoping that it would add to the realism of the experiment. The authors found that 38% of the subjects who worked at home had errors in their spreadsheets, whereas only 27% of the subjects who worked in the PC lab had errors. The error rate again could have been kept artificially low since the participants worked on a clearly developed problem that was also "domain free." The use of a domain-free problem minimized any required specialized knowledge necessary to solve the problem.

These studies, taken as a whole, provide support for the existence of high error rates in end user developed spreadsheets. To date, no studies have been published (to our knowledge) that have determined why these errors occur or effectively how to reduce the errors. We hope that our current research will provide the first steps in helping to alleviate and reduce the amount of spreadsheet errors by identifying important cognitive skill changes involved in proper spreadsheet training procedures.

Table 2 provides a brief summary of representative studies that document unacceptably high error rates in spreadsheets for professionals in real-world applications, as well as for students in experimental studies (see Kruck & Maher, 1998, for a discussion of spreadsheet errors and proper design procedures). Most spreadsheet model research has primarily concentrated on documenting the existence of high error rates in completed models developed by end users in various situations. Our current research program begins to examine how cognitive skills are altered or modified after participants receive training in proper spreadsheet design methods.

HYPOTHESES

Figure 1 illustrates that we designed this research to determine if specific cognitive skills, logical reasoning ability, spatial visualization ability, mnemonic skill, and sequencing ability are influenced during formalized spreadsheet training. Logical reasoning can be described as "the ability to reason from premise to conclusion, or to evaluate the correctness of a conclusion" (Educational Testing Services (ETS) 1976). The Diagramming Relationships test developed by ETS is used to measure this cognitive skill. Logical reasoning ability has been shown as an important cognitive skill for developing spreadsheets by end users (Card et al., 1983; Olson & Nilsen, 1987). End users can improve their logical reasoning ability by practice and training (Johnson & Lawson, 1998; Lawson, 1995; Karplus, 1977; Mackenzie, 1999). The Diagramming Relationships test requires the participant to select the correct pictorial interrelationship among a set of three objects from five diagrams. This test minimizes the reading ability required to complete the test because of the pictorial representations of the relationships. This helps to ensure that logical reasoning is not confounded with verbal reasoning. We use the Diagramming Relationships test to measure the logical reasoning of end users. The end user must be able to use the pictorial relationship between cells to implement the spreadsheet solution. A completed spreadsheet can be considered a pictorial view of the solution to a problem. As a result of training in proper spreadsheet development, it is expected that performance on the Diagramming Relationships test will increase. This expected relationship leads to the first hypothesis, written in null form:

H1: There is no increase in logical reasoning skill of end users after spreadsheet training.

We measure spatial visualization by using the Choosing a Path Task (ETS, 1976). This task measures the subject's ability to determine a pattern or work from

Table 2: Summary of studies of spreadsheet errors

Author(s)	Year	Participants	% of Spreadsheets w/Errors
Brown & Gould	1987	IBM employees	44%
Davis & Ikin	1987	Live/real company spreadsheets	
		--major errors	21%
		--inadequate & extremely error prone	53%
Hassinen	1988	Novice students:	
		-- working on computer	48%
		-- working with paper & pencil	55%
Cragg & King	1993	Live/real company spreadsheets	25%
Panko & Halverson Jr.	1994	Business students:	
		-- working alone	81%
		-- working in groups of 2	71%
		-- working in groups of 4	50%
Panko & Halverson Jr.	1995	Accounting students	68%
		General business students working alone	82%
		General business students working in groups of 3	27%
Janvrin & Morrison	1996	Upper- & masters-level accounting & business administration students:	
		--ad hoc development group	14%*
		--structured systems group	7%*
Janvrin & Morrison	1996	Upper- & masters-level accounting & business administration students:	
		--ad hoc development group	18%**
		--structured systems group	9%**
Panko	1996	MIS upper-division undergraduates:	
		-- working at home	38%
		-- working in laboratory	30%
Panko & Halverson	1996	MBA students	57%
		Non-accounting & -finance upper-division undergraduates	79%
Panko & Halverson Jr.	1997	Business students:	
		-- working alone	79%
		-- working in groups of 2	78%
		-- working in groups of 4	64%
		Accounting & finance students	65%
Panko & Sprague Jr.	1997	Undergraduate students	37%
		Inexperienced MBA students	35%
		Experienced MBA students	24%

* paper template of solution provided
** check figure provided

a different direction. The specific factor measured is the "speed in exploring visually a wide or complicated spatial field" (ETS, 1976). The Choosing a Path Task requires the participant to follow a correct path, while rejecting false leads. Part of the requirement is planning, and "subjects may discover the simplifying strategy of searching from the goal rather than from the start" (ETS, 1976). The order of the test's layout actually forms a pattern in order to encourage comprehension of that pattern. This is often an important factor during spreadsheet construction. The solution to a problem may be more efficient and effective if one can determine the pattern or work from a different direction. Therefore, we expect that a participant's score on choosing a Path Task will increase after undergoing formalized training in spreadsheet model development. The second hypothesis is:

H2: There is no increase in spatial visualization skill of end users after spreadsheet training.

The third cognitive skill in the model is the mnemonic skill. Spreadsheet developers must determine what information is relevant to solve a particular problem. Real world problems are often vague, poorly defined, and have extraneous detail. The developer of spreadsheet models must determine which factors are important and organize the material to arrive at a solution to the specific problem. This type of mnemonic skill is related to general reasoning ability. We use the Necessary Arithmetic Operations Task test developed by ETS to measure this ability. The specific factor examined is "the ability to select and organize relevant information for the solution of a problem" (ETS, 1976). The Necessary Arithmetic Operations Task requires the participant to determine which numerical operations are required, as well as the proper order of these operations, to decipher the problem without actually solving the problem. This separation of the necessary arithmetic steps from the actual computations separates the confounding of numerical ability from the general reasoning required by this task. End users developing spreadsheet models have to retrieve relevant information and organize the problem in order to solve it. Therefore, it is expected that a participant's score on the Necessary Arithmetic Operations Task will increase after receiving formal spreadsheet training. This suggests the following hypothesis:

H3: There is no increase in mnemonic skills of end users after spreadsheet training.

In addition to the ability to use logical reasoning, spatial visualization, and mnemonic skill, spreadsheet developers must also possess sequencing ability. They must be able to correctly order the steps necessary to create a correct solution in solving problems using spreadsheets. This is potentially important because an incorrect order of steps can result in an erroneous spreadsheet model. To measure the sequencing ability of end users, we use the Nonsense Syllogisms task. The subject must generate enough examples to determine if the model is correct or incorrect. The Nonsense Syllogisms task requires the participant to read a nonsensical set of statements, consisting of a major and minor premise, perform a set of serial operations after ordering them and then decide whether the conclusion follows correctly from the premises. Spreadsheet developers must take a problem, determine a logical order to proceed so that the solution is correct, and then generate sufficient test cases to ensure that the model is accurate. Therefore, it is expected that a participant's score on the Nonsense Syllogisms task would increase after formalized spreadsheet training. This leads to the fourth hypothesis:

H4: There is no increase in sequencing ability of end users after spreadsheet training.

METHODOLOGY

Materials

The four tests we utilize to determine if there is a change in cognitive skills after formal spreadsheet training (Diagramming Relations, Choosing a Path, Nonsense Syllogisms, and Necessary Arithmetic Operations) are all part of Educational Testing Services' Kit of Factor-Referenced Cognitive Tests (1976). This kit consists of 72 marker tests for 23 cognitive factors. All the tests in the kit are suitable for participants with a minimum ninth-grade education. The tests have been updated from two earlier versions and represent the most recent cognitive tests developed by ETS. Each of the tests are considered "established," which means the construct underlying them has been found in at least three factor analyses performed by at least two different experiments or researchers (ETS, 1976).

The test packet distributed to each participant included a participant release, the actual tests, and a demographic questionnaire. The instructions for the tests were included in the packet and were also read aloud. There were several practice exercises with answers included for each of the tests. Following the instructions and practice exercises, participants worked the test within a prescribed time period (Diagramming Relationships – 4 minutes, Choosing a Path – 7 minutes, Necessary Arithmetic Operations – 5 minutes, and Nonsense Syllogisms – 4 minutes). Scores were based on the number of correct answers obtained minus a fraction of the number of incorrect answers. Participants were told in advance how their scores would be determined.

An observer was present during each experimental session to ensure that participants were conscientious in performing the pencil and paper tests. The conscientious performance standard was met if it appeared that the participant was making an effort to complete the test. All participants appeared to meet this criterion. Upon completion of the four cognitive tests, participants were given the demographic questionnaire to fill out.

We constructed a blocked design: one block was the control group and another was the treatment group. Subjects in the treatment group received six weeks of spreadsheet training. After the treatment group received the formalized spreadsheet training, both groups were administered the post-tests. The post-tests have been validated by ETS and are considered an equivalent test to the pre-test. The ETS tests indicate no significant learning effect between the pre- and post-test. The post-test followed the same basic steps as the pre-test, except the participants were not required to complete the demographics questionnaire.

Participants and Training Process

The participants in the experiment were undergraduate students enrolled in one of two courses conducted at a large land-grant university: Survey of Accounting (control group), or Personal Computers in Business (treatment group). A total of 42 subjects participated in both the pre- and post-test with 50% (n=21) in each of the treatment and control groups. We used a blocked controlled experiment (Cook & Campbell, 1979) where the students enrolled in the personal computer class received the treatment (i.e., spreadsheet training). The sample was composed of 48% males and 74% sophomores. Participants had a mean Grade Point Average of 2.76 (based on 4.00 scale) with a standard deviation of .45. Forty-eight percent have had no work experience involving computer usage. Ninety percent were full-time students (taking 12 or more credit hours/semester) and 70% were not working during the semester of the experiment. Students were free to discontinue participation in the experiment at any time. Seven participants failed to return for the post-test, and were removed from the sample, resulting in the final total of 42 participants.

The treatment group of participants received approximately 15 hours of formalized classroom spreadsheet training. The specific course, Personal Computers in Business, has been required of Business majors for more than ten years. The course has been constantly revised and updated to reflect state-of-the-art spreadsheet training. Because of the success rate of the students, as measured by examinations and projects, as well as the positive response received from multiple employers regarding our students' spreadsheet skills in the actual business world, we felt the spreadsheet training was effective and produced the result desired. The class was conducted in a computer laboratory in which the instructor developed a series of spreadsheets on a personal computer that was projected onto a large screen at the front of the room. Each student utilized a personal computer to complete classroom exercises along with the instructor. The teacher provided help when needed. The instructor frequently provided partially developed spreadsheet models, which allowed the student to focus on the desired skill while minimizing unnecessary data entry. Students were also required to complete content-related spreadsheet assignments outside the classroom that averaged approximately 10-15 hours of additional work.

The classroom training began with basic spreadsheet model design principles. Proper spreadsheet development techniques were stressed in each spreadsheet built or examined in the classroom. These techniques included properly organized layout, the use of descriptive names, and the practice of using separate and distinct sections for data input and formula calculations. The fundamental spreadsheet instruction also covered the essential area of formulas and functions (financial, statistical, logical, lookup, date and time). Students were encouraged and rewarded for using proper spreadsheet model construction.

Once the basic techniques of developing spreadsheet models were mastered, the training continued to more advanced topics which included graphs, data analysis, consolidation, and spreadsheet integration. The development of various types of graphs (charts) was covered including the appropriate structure related to each individual style of graph. The data analysis section covered the use of the solver tool, goal seek, alternative scenarios, and one- and two-input data tables. The students were taught to consolidate by position, by group, and by category. Various methods to integrate spreadsheets into word processing documents, database packages, and graphic software were covered using importing, pasting, embedding and linking techniques. The training concluded with a module teaching the incorporation of Visual Basic for Applications (VBA) into spreadsheet models. Formal structured design techniques were covered throughout the spreadsheet training sessions and documentation was further stressed when using VBA.

At the end of the training period, students were required to take a spreadsheet content examination using a personal computer in which they had to create, change, or comment on several spreadsheet models. This synchronous, on-site testing environment was considered the most appropriate way to evaluate what the students had actually learned from the spreadsheet training. The participants in the treatment group averaged 86% on the spreadsheet exam and averaged 86% on the projects indicating that they had obtained at least a reasonable degree of proficiency in the required concepts and tools of proper spreadsheet design and implementation. Both the exam and the projects required hands-on development at a personal computer. The students were required to create complete spreadsheet models in the projects and various sub-components of spreadsheet models during the exam. The purpose of the projects and exam was to reinforce and test topics learned during the spreadsheet training.

RESULTS

We used a two-factor *ANOVA* for each of the independent variables to determine statistical significance. Each *ANOVA* included one of the independent variables as an explanatory factor to examine the influence of each dependent variable. A comparison of the scores of the ETS developed pre-test and post-test indicates a significant difference exists in the improvement of the "Logical Reasoning" skills of the treatment group of subjects, but not the control group. Logical reasoning, as measured by the Diagramming Relationships test ($p < .004$, $F = 7.75$, $df = 39$, one-tailed) significantly increased for the treatment group. This important result indicates a substantial and measurable increase in logical reasoning skill occurred in the treatment group during the six-week period between tests. This finding allows rejection of the primary null hypothesis and provides support for the alternative that logical reasoning skill increased for the treatment group after six weeks of formalized spreadsheet training.

While the other three cognitive skills in Figure 1, spatial visualization, mnemonic skill, and sequencing ability were not significantly influenced by spreadsheet training, we found the greater the increase in a student's logical reasoning score, the lower the error rate in the spreadsheet that he or she developed ($p < .000$, $F = 4.015$). These empirical results are consistent with the explanation that there exists a significant positive association between increases in an end-user's logical reasoning score and his or her ability to develop effective spreadsheets. The results also show that teaching spreadsheets is more than just "learning how to hit the keys." As a result of spreadsheet training, the students improve their logical reasoning ability as measured by standard and validated tests.

The complete statistical analyses did not indicate significant changes in pre-test and post-test scores for any of the other three cognitive skills. In addition, there were no significant differences found in the pre-test and post-test scores of the control group (as expected) for any of the four cognitive skills. The results of all pre- and post-tests are tabulated in Table 3 and graphically illustrated in Figure 2.

These results are important because it provides preliminary evidence that a significant change occurs in one cognitive skill (logical reasoning ability) during the spreadsheet training process. The results also identify one cognitive change that influences error rates in spreadsheet models. Further research should explore other cognitive changes that occur during spreadsheet training and focus on cognitive skills that help minimize errors in spreadsheet models.

Several standard pre-analysis techniques were conducted to ensure data integrity. Pre-test data were analyzed to assure that participants not returning for the post-test were not significantly different than participants who did return. There was no significant difference found in the two groups ($p = .772$). Additional analysis was

Table 3: Summary of statistical analysis of test scores
Means, standard deviations, and significance levels for the tests

		Control (N=21)			Treatment (N=21)		
		Pre-test	Post-test	p-value	Pre-test	Post-test	p-value
Tests:							
Diagramming Relationships	Mean	9.05	10.16	0.860	8.05	10.87	0.004
	SD	3.21	3.28		3.29	3.28	
Choosing a Path	Mean	6.00	5.04	0.860	5.14	4.86	0.630
	SD	2.88	2.69		2.78	2.74	
Necessary Arithmetic Operations	Mean	8.76	9.08	0.350	8.61	9.08	0.250
	SD	2.12	3.06		2.60	1.85	
Nonsense Syllogisms	Mean	7.40	8.47	0.920	7.04	7.40	0.330
	SD	2.02	2.80		2.51	2.80	

performed to ensure that the treatment and control group means were not found to be significantly different prior to the treatment for each of the four tests. The two groups were not significantly different prior to the treatment based on a test of means for each of the four tests (Diagramming Relationships (testing logical reasoning ability): p = .323, Choosing a Path (testing spatial visualization): p = .334, Necessary Arithmetic Operations (testing mnemonic skill): p=.846, Nonsense Syllogisms (testing sequencing ability): p=.614).

Figure 2: Comparison of treatment groups scores

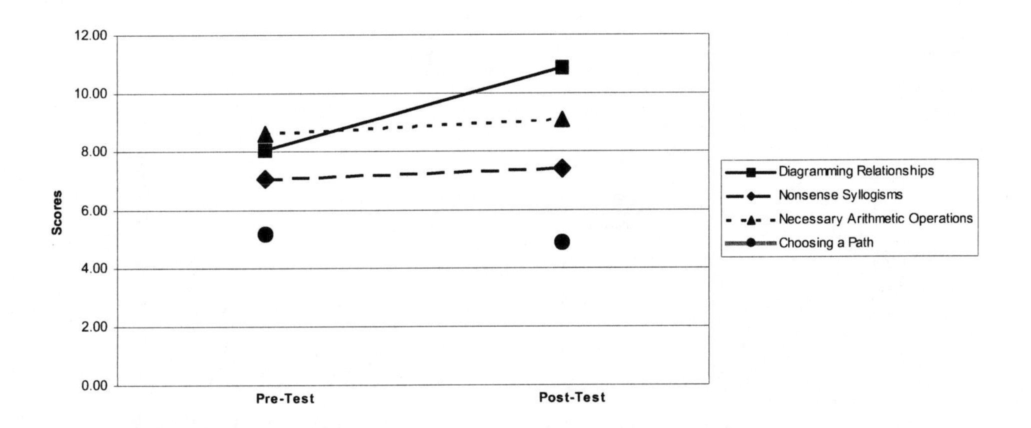

DISCUSSION

The research reported here examines the question of whether specific cognitive skills increase after students receive formalized training in structured spreadsheet model development. We proposed a framework, based on a study of the cognitive psychology literature, and tested it empirically. The results show that of the four cognitive skills proposed in the model, one of them was significantly influenced by spreadsheet training. Our study is the first that links spreadsheet training to a change in cognitive skill and subsequently to error rates in spreadsheets developed by end users. This critical result shows that spreadsheet training is more than just "learning to hit the keys" without any conceptual learning.

The empirical analyses indicate significant results for only one cognitive skill, logical reasoning, as measured by the ETS Diagramming Relationships test. Importantly, the greater the increase in a student's logical reasoning skill over the treatment period, the lower is the error rate in the spreadsheet, and hence, the better the students perform on the final spreadsheet examination. These findings have potentially meaningful implications for future spreadsheet training. The linkage between an increase in logical reasoning skills and effective spreadsheet development will need to be externally validated before a definitive association can be firmly established. However, our research has contributed interesting results providing an initial pathway for future exploration.

The other cognitive skills examined did not exhibit a significant increase. Although, as described earlier, the extant literature indicates that these three cognitive skills can be increased through training, no definitive link has been established specifically with spreadsheet training. Thus, we can only provide a preliminary explanation that increases in these particular cognitive skills are not significantly related to effective spreadsheet development. An alternative possibility is that the specific training methods utilized were not effective in increasing these particular cognitive skills and/or the training time period was not long enough to evoke a significant increase.

The literature contains numerous examples of specific training methods effectively increasing certain cognitive skills (e.g. Baltes & Kliegl, 1992; Galotti et al., 1986; Kleigl et al, 1989; Wenger & Carlson, 1996). The positive association we found between logical reasoning skills and effective spreadsheet development suggests that it would be fruitful to investigate and develop specific exercises that help increase the logical reasoning skill. This could save valuable training time and, possibly, result in better-prepared model developers. These spreadsheet developers, by extrapolation, should prepare more accurate spreadsheet models with fewer errors.

Future research could more precisely define the nature of the relationship between spreadsheet errors and logical reasoning skills. A clearer understanding of this relationship could help produce more efficient training methods for model builders. Additional research is also necessary to determine if there are other important cognitive skills that change during the spreadsheet model training process. Three of four cognitive skills examined in this study did not change significantly, but these skills may need a longer training period or more cognitively direct training to exhibit significant increases. The relationship between these various cognitive skills and the frequency of errors in spreadsheets also needs to be more thoroughly defined and investigated.

Potential limitations of this study include the possibility that there are uncontrolled variables that affect the outcome. Training and courses taken prior to the pre-test that affect the cognitive skills examined here could mask the effect because the treatment effect would be included in both the pre- and post-test measurements. This would bias the results against rejection of the null hypothesis of no change. This clearly did not occur for logical reasoning ability. However, the same cannot definitively be established for the other three cognitive skills. One possible interpretation is that the prior work experience of 52% of the participants that involved the computer to some degree was present to a significant extent and that it did lead to non-significant differences on three out of four cognitive skills tests. While we feel that it is unlikely that the control group effectively had received the equivalent of the treatment prior to undertaking the experiment, we cannot absolutely rule out this possibility. Another alternative is that students in the control group could be participating in other classes or activities that have the same affect as the treatment. This would bias the results in favor of rejecting the null of no change for the control group. However, the empirical results indicate there was no significant increase found in logical reasoning skills in the pre- and post-tests for the control group, which effectively minimizes the likelihood of this event.

While it is logical to infer that errors in spreadsheet models will decrease with proper spreadsheet training, this has not been definitively established in this study or in the literature. The difficulty found in empirically establishing this proposition is that no logical procedure is known to exist that would obtain a reliable spreadsheet model error rate for new users prior to learning something about spreadsheet construction. It would be best to establish that there exists a corresponding increase in logical reasoning skill and a decrease in the number of errors that occur in spreadsheet construction after receiving proper spreadsheet training, but this is prevented by the nature of the situation. Theoretically, it would be possible to test this at the beginning of the semester by asking students to complete a complex spreadsheet model the first day of class before they were given any formal training.

The inevitable result would be that the vast majority of new users would not know how to complete a complex model. This would likely prove to be a very frustrating exercise for everyone involved. Its sole purpose would be to prove the obvious, i.e. participants at the beginning of training make many more errors in spreadsheet model development than the same participants at the end of training. Thus, although entirely logical, this link has not been empirically established. What we have found is spreadsheet training leads to an observable increase in logical reasoning that subsequently leads to lower spreadsheet errors.

This study adds to the existing literature in several ways. Importantly, it establishes that an increase in logical reasoning skill takes place with formalized spreadsheet training. In addition, it also indicates that the greater the increase in logical reasoning skills, the better the student performs in developing spreadsheets and the lower the error rate. These results have potentially important implications for developing teaching and training modules for large numbers of future spreadsheet end users and developers. Finally, this is the initial step in a research program that attempts to determine *why* end user developed spreadsheets have high error rates in them. This program of research is substantially different from the existing spreadsheet literature that primarily establishes and confirms the existence of high error rates. Further study of the cognitive process may help to develop better training methods that result in spreadsheet models that have lower error rates.

Future research should extend this study by focusing on providing different forms of instruction and course material for subjects with different backgrounds and different levels of expertise. This would strengthen the results of this study to controllable variations. In addition, other forms of cognitive skills can be measured before and after spreadsheet training to a wider set of subjects to draw more meaningful conclusions with respect to external validity of the results to spreadsheet training and its impact on cognitive skill development.

REFERENCES

Albrecht, W. S. & Sack, R. J. American Accounting Association (AAA) (2000). Accounting education: charting the course through a perilous future. *Accounting Education Series,* Volume (16), American Accounting Association. Sarasota, FL.

Baltes, P. B. & Kliegl, R. (1992). Further testing of limits of plasticity: Negative age differences in a mnemonic skill are robust. *Developmental Psychology, 28*(1), 121-125.

Brown, P. & Gould, J. (1987). An experimental study of people creating spreadsheets. *ACM Transactions on Office Information Systems, 5*(3), 258-272.

Burnett, S. A. & Lane, D. M. (1980). Effect of academic instruction on spatial visualization. *Intelligence*, 4, 233-242.

Card, S. K., Moran, T. P., & Newell, A. (1983). *The Psychology of Human Computer Interaction*. Hillside, NJ: Lawrence Erlbaum.

Cook, T. D. & Campbell, D. T. (1979). *Quazi-Experimentation: Design & Analysis Issues for Field Settings*. Houghton Mifflin Company.

Coy, D. V. & O'Grady, W. (1992). Spreadsheet use on the increase. *Accountant's Journal, 71*(8), 69-73.

Cragg, P. G. & King, M. (1993). Spreadsheet modeling abuse: An opportunity for OR. *Journal of Operational Research Society, 44*(8), 743-752.

Davies, N. & Ikin, C. (1987). Auditing spreadsheets. *Australian Accountant,* 54-56.

Davis, J. R. & Leitch, R. A. (1988). Accounting information systems courses and curricula: New perspectives. *Journal of Information Systems, 3*(1), 153-166.

Davis, P. (1997). What computer skills do employers expect from recent college graduates? *Technological Horizons in Education Journal,* 74-78.

Ditlea S. (1987). Spreadsheets can be hazardous to your health. *Personal Computing,* 11 (January): 60-69.

Dumais, S. T. & Wright, A. L. (1986). Reference by name vs. location in computer filing system. *Proceedings of the Human Factors Society,* 824-828.

Educational Testing Service. (1976). *Manual for Kit of Factor-Referenced Cognitive Tests Educational Testing Service*. Princeton, NJ.

Ekstrom, R. B., French, J. W., & Harman, H. H. (1975). An attempt to confirm five recently identified cognitive factors. *Educational Testing Service,* PR-75-17.

Galotti, K. M., Baron, J., & Savini, J. (1986). Individual differences in syllogistic reasoning: Deduction rules or mental models? *Journal of Experimental Psychology,* 115, 16-25.

Gilman, H. & Bulkeley W. (1984, August). Can software firms be held responsible when a program makes a costly error? *The Wall Street Journal,* pp. 19.

Greene, S. L., Gomez, L. M., & Devlin S. J. (1986). A cognitive analysis of database query production. *Proceedings of the Human Factors Society,* 9-13.

Hassinen K., Sajaniemi, J., & Vaisanen, J. (1988). Structured spreadsheet calculation. *Proceedings of the IEEE Workshop on Languages for Automation*, pp. 129-133.

Hassinen, K. (1988). An experimental study of spreadsheet errors made by novice spreadsheet users. Department of Computer Science, University of Joensuu, PO Box 111, SF-80101 Joensuu, Finland.

Hayden R. L. & Peters R. M. (1989). How to ensure spreadsheet integrity. *Management Accounting,* (April) pp. 30-33.

Heagy, C. D. & Gallum, R. A. (1994). Recommended microcomputer knowledge for accounting graduates: A survey. *Journal of Accounting Education, 12*(3), 205-210.

Hutchins, E., Hollan, J., & Norman, D. (1986). Direct manipulation interfaces. *User Centered System Design.*

Janvrin, D. & Morrison, J. (1996). Factors influencing risks and outcomes in end-user development. *Proceedings of the Twenty-Ninth Hawaii International Conference on System Sciences*, pp. 346-355.

Johnson, M. A. & Lawson, A. E. (1998). What are the relative effects of reasoning ability and prior knowledge on biology achievement in expository and inquiry classes? *Journal of Research in Science Teaching, 35*(1), 89-103.

Karplus, R. (1977). Science teaching and the development of reasoning. *Journal of Research in Science Teaching,* 14, 169-175.

Kee, R. (1988). Programming standards for spreadsheet software. *CMA Magazine,* 62 (April): 55-60.

Klerer, M. (1984). Experimental study of a two-dimensional language vs. fortran for first course programmers. *International Journal of Man-Machine Studies* 20, 445-467.

Kliegl, R., Smith, J., & Baltes, P. B. (1989). Testing-the-limits and the study of adult age differences in cognitive plasticity of a mnemonic skill. *Developmental Psychology,* 25, 247-256.

Kruck, S. E. & Maher, J. J. (1998) Home mortgage analysis for cultivating crucial spreadsheet and model development skills, *Journal of Accounting Education.* 16, pp. 267-291.

Lawson, A. (1988) A Better Way to Teach Biology. *The American Biology Teacher,* 50, pp. 266-278.

Lawson A. (1995) *Science Teaching and the Development of Thinking.* Belmont, CA: Wadsworth.

Mackenzie, D. (1999) Addicted to logic. *American Scientist, 87*(3), pp 217-218.

Miller, G. A. (1956). The magical number seven, plus or minus two: Some limits on our capacity for processing information. *Psychological Review,* 63, 81-97.

O'Leary, D. E. (1989). Computer knowledge requirements for accountants: A survey of fortune 500 controllers. *Kent/Bentley Journal of Accounting and Computers,* 5, 64-73.

Olson, J. & Nilsen, E. (1987). Analysis of the cognition involved in spreadsheet software interactions. *Human-Computer Interaction,* 3, 309-349.

Panko, R. R. (1996). Hitting the wall: Errors in developing and debugging a "simple" spreadsheet model. *Proceedings of the Twenty-Ninth Hawaii International Conference on System Sciences,* 2 pp. 356-363.

Panko, R. R. & Halverson, Jr., R. P. (1994). Individual and group spreadsheet design: Pattern of errors. *Proceedings of the Twenty-Seventh Hawaii International Conference on System Sciences,* pp. 4-10.

Panko, R. R. & Halverson, Jr., R. P. (1997). Are two heads better than one? (at reducing errors in spreadsheet modeling). *Office Systems Research Journal, 15*(1).

Panko, R. R. & Sprague, R. H. Jr. (1998). Hitting the wall: Errors in developing and code inspecting a "simple" spreadsheet model. *Decision Sciences Journal, 22*(4), 337-353.

Pellegrino, J. W. (1985). Anatomy of analogy. *Psychology Today,* 49-54.

Sein, M. K., Olfman, L., Bostrom, R. P., & Davis, S. A. (1993). Visualization ability as a predictor of user learning success. *International Journal of Man-Machine Studies,* 39, 599-620.

Simkin, M. G. (1987). Micros in accounting: How to validate spreadsheets. *Journal of Accountancy,* 164, 130-138.

Stone, D. N. & R. L. Black (1989). Building structured spreadsheets. *Journal of Accountancy,* (October) 131-142.

VanLehn, K. (1996). Cognitive Skill Acquisition. *Annual Review of Psychology,* 47, 513-539.

Vincente, K. J, Hayes, C. D., & Williges, R. C. (1987). Assaying and isolating individual differences in searching a hierarchical file system. *Human Factors, 29*(3), 349-359.

Wenger, J. L. & Carlson, R. A. (1996). Cognitive sequence knowledge: What is learned? *Journal of Experimental Psychology: Learning, Memory & Cognition, 22*(3), 599-619.

Wenger, M. J. & Payne, D. G. (1995). On the acquisition of mnemonic skill: Application of skilled memory theory. *Journal of Experimental Psychology Applied 1*(3), 194-215.

Chapter XII

Attitude and Management Style Matter in IT Implementation: A Study of Small Business Owners

Elaine R. Winston
Frank G. Zarb School of Business, Hofstra University, USA

Dorothy G. Dologite
Baruch College, City University of New York, USA

ABSTRACT

According to previous studies, a positive attitude towards information technology (IT) among small business owners appears to be a key factor in achieving high quality IT implementations. In an effort to extend this stream of research, case studies were conducted with small business owners. A surprising finding of this study was that high quality IT implementations resulted with owners who had either a positive or a negative attitude towards IT. Another finding was that these owners also all had an entrepreneurial, or shared, management style. By contrast, owners who had an uncertain attitude about IT uniformly practiced a traditional (non-entrepreneurial) management style. This group also uniformly had low quality IT implementations. It is proposed, based on case study data, that small business owners with an uncertain attitude towards IT might experience higher quality IT results in their organizations through practicing a more entrepreneurial, or shared, management style. The study provides insights for both computer specialists and small business owners planning IT implementations.

INTRODUCTION

Most small business owners can find extensive support for the incorporation and continual upgrade of information technology (IT) into their businesses. The implementation of IT has been credited with significant cost reduction, productivity gains, and organizational effectiveness (Cooper & Zmud, 1990; Doukidis et al., 1994; Stair et al., 1989). One might have a difficult time finding the small business owner that would not at least acknowledge some benefit of using IT. Yet, it is interesting to note that while many small business owners readily commit to IT initiatives, many others delay and even avoid investing in IT (Maglitta, 1992; Nickell & Seado, 1986; Ray et al., 1994).

The small business owner's dominating role in any IT implementation is well documented (Cragg & King, 1993; Doukidis et al., 1994; Julien & Raymond, 1994; Thong & Yap, 1995). More specifically, some studies suggest that the owner's positive, negative, or uncertain attitude towards IT affects the quality of an IT implementation (Cragg & King, 1993; Delone, 1988). Additionally, the owner's management style influences the implementation process and has a direct impact on firm outcomes (Normann, 1971; Rogers & Shoemaker, 1971; Winston & Dologite, 1999). These characteristics, attitude and style, seem to play a key role in directing the small business owner's decisions regarding the technology to implement, the personnel that will manage the implementation, and the supporting managerial and human resource polices (Agarwal & Prasad, 1997; Cragg & King, 1993; Doukidis et al., 1994).

In this study, small business owners were interviewed to primarily explore their attitude towards IT and the quality of their IT. Management style, an expression of owner behavior and an integral aspect of the implementation process, became another significant dimension to investigate. A surprising finding of this study was that high quality IT implementations resulted with owners who had either a positive or a negative attitude towards IT. These positive and negative owners also all had an entrepreneurial, or shared, management style. By contrast, owners who had an uncertain attitude about IT uniformly practiced a traditional (non-entrepreneurial) management style. This group also uniformly had low quality IT implementations. These findings provide insights that can help IT practitioners as well as small business owners planning IT implementations.

The presentation of this qualitative study is organized as follows. In the next section, the research questions are developed. Literature that grounds the concept that attitude impacts the quality of an IT implementation is examined. Management styles are identified with a special focus on how they generally influence the implementation process. A description of methodology and the findings from the data analysis follows. The critical theme regarding the interaction between small business owners' attitude towards IT and their management style, which emerged during the interview and data analysis process, is then presented. Managerial and research implications are discussed in the concluding section of the paper.

DEVELOPMENT OF THE RESEARCH QUESTIONS

IT Implementation in Small Business

IT implementation is the process a business undertakes to diffuse IT within the organization (Rogers, 1983). To better understand this process it has been defined and described in six stages: initiation, adoption, adaptation, acceptance, routinization, and institutionalization (Kwon & Zmud, 1987; Coopers & Zmud, 1990). The process begins with scanning the environment for IT opportunities or solutions, adopting the appropriate IT, adapting it for the specific organization, and over time accepting and routinizing it into daily business activities (Cooper & Zmud, 1990; Kwon & Zmud, 1987; Rogers, 1983). The last stage, institutionalization, results in increased organizational efficiency, management effectiveness, and strategic advantages (Cooper & Zmud, 1990; Iivari & Ervasti, 1994; Venkatraman, 1991).

A recent survey of IT implementations in small businesses indicates that a relationship exists between the owner's attitude towards IT implementation quality (Winston & Dologite, 1999). Owners with positive attitudes toward IT were found to be more likely to implement IT in support of strategic goals (Bergeron & Raymond, 1992; Malone, 1985) than owners with negative or uncertain attitudes. The positive owners were also more inclined to use IT as a device for transforming the way work is done in order to achieve business effectiveness (Julien & Raymond, 1994; King, 1996).

A common approach to examining IT implementation problems and solutions has been the identification of factors leading to the success or failure of IT implementation (Kwon & Zmud, 1987; Pare & Elam, 1997; Winston & Dologite, 1999). Such an attempt may neglect any relationship that may exist among the factors. This study focuses on three issues from the factor studies and explores their relationship—the interaction of attitude, management style, and implementation quality. A better understanding of any interaction should assist the computer specialist, as well as small business owner, in choosing appropriate strategies to maximize the quality of an IT implementation.

Attitude Towards IT

Previous studies suggest that small business owners with negative attitudes towards IT implementation generally avoid investing in IT because they fail to understand the strategic impact of IT on their business (Cragg & King, 1993; Delone, 1988). Only when faced with the threat of closing do these entrepreneurs seek the short-term solution of implementing IT for survival (Agarwal & Prasad, 1997; Quinn, 1979).

Some small business owners who perceive IT implementation as risky and uncertain become immobilized by indecision and hesitation. As a result, they handicap any potential increased business earnings that could be achieved from using IT (Quinn, 1979).

Even after approving an investment, owners with a negative or uncertain attitude towards IT often have difficulty sustaining commitment through an implementation. This results in reducing resources allocated to a project, inhibiting organizational changes required to achieve benefits, and preventing the use of IT to its fullest potential. These problems persist regardless of the complexity level of the IT application (Cragg & King, 1993; Malone, 1985).

Small business owners with positive attitudes towards IT, on the other hand, often have a deep knowledge about IT and find it easy to commit to an IT implementation (Cheney et al., 1986; Cragg & King, 1993; Nickell & Seado, 1986; Ray et al., 1994; Thong & Yap, 1995; Winston & Dologite, 1999). Consequently, owner knowledge of IT and commitment are believed to increase the likelihood that a business will effectively incorporate IT. More specifically, a positive attitude will likely help the owner endure the frustration and effort of overcoming the technical and organizational obstacles that frequently confront innovative initiatives (Harrison et al., 1997; Quinn, 1979).

Management Style

Management style influences various aspects of the implementation process in small businesses, such as IT strategy, owner commitment and involvement, and timing (Cooley et al., 1987; Cragg & King, 1993). Yet, IT implementation studies often do not explore the owner's management style. Perhaps this is because of the confusion that style is connected to personality, and therefore not likely to change. Management style, however, is demonstrated by work role and by patterns of actions (Waterman et al., 1995; Lawler & Mohrman, 1989). A small business owner's management style, then, is essentially manageable. Management style can be generally classified as either entrepreneurial or traditional (Jelinek & Litterer, 1995; Senge, 1990; Waterman et al., 1995).

- *Entrepreneurial* - employees are encouraged to make use of distracting data, embrace ambiguity as a source of opportunity, present new ideas, and initiate action in new directions.
- *Traditional* - employees are encouraged to ignore data that do not fit existing frames of reference, focus only on the job at hand, and comply with established reporting relationships and rules.

An entrepreneurial style suggests that an owner's policies support shared management and collaboration (Jelinek & Litterer, 1995; Senge, 1990). Where this style exists, employees accept responsibility for guiding the affairs of the organization (Quinn, 1979). They collaborate to share information and responsibility, to define and solve information problems, as well as to fulfill a common vision (Jelinek & Litterer, 1995; Senge, 1990).

An entrepreneurial policy enhances the capacity of a business to address and reduce any risk and uncertainty connected with a new IT implementation (Jelinek & Litterer, 1995). An entrepreneurial policy greatly affects the support and commitment a work force has to an IT implementation (Cragg & King, 1993). In addition, employees tend to rely on one another to make the IT implementation successful and to keep others informed of its progress (Cooley et al., 1987).

By contrast, a traditional management style reflects an owner's policies that support bureaucracy and clearly identified boundaries of responsibility (Jelinek & Litterer, 1995). The basis of the traditional management style is to establish order, exercise control and achieve efficiency in the work force. Small business owners supporting a traditional style organize their own responsibilities into a hierarchy of specialized roles supported by a top-down allocation of authority (Walton, 1985).

The small business owner who practices a traditional style typically attempts to reduce the uncertainty surrounding the use of IT by retaining control of the problem as well as its solution (Herbert & Bradley, 1993; Thong & Yap, 1995). Further, policies may not exist or be clearly defined for hearing end users' opinions (Walton, 1985).

Quality of IT Implementation

Studies of IT implementations have identified specific outcomes of success and find such indicators as increased profits, greater market share, or improved return on investment (ROI) performance (Byrd, 1995; Cooper & Zmud, 1990; Iivari & Ervasti, 1994). At a more operational level, the results of a high-quality IT implementation process include increased internal organizational performance and efficiency, better customer service, and a higher quality working life within the organization (Doukidis et al., 1994; Julien, 1995; Schafer, 1995; Serwer, 1995). It is these added considerations of a high quality IT implementation, at the operational level, that can lead to an organization's increased profits, greater market share, or improved ROI performance. This is the level of analysis that concerns this study.

There is support for the idea that a user of IT evaluates the implementation in terms of its perceived benefits to them (Bailey & Pearson, 1983; Ives et al., 1983; Szajna & Scamell, 1993). Research on the quality of an IT implementation lends support to user evaluation of IT in terms of benefits realized, such as routine use of the IT and increased decision quality (Bailey & Pearson, 1983; Ives et al., 1983; Szajna & Scamell, 1993). In this study, small business owners' statements reflecting, for example, improvement in employee performance, increased operational efficiency, and the development of new work processes are used to evaluate implementation quality (Doukidis et al., 1994; Julien, 1995).

In this context, exploring the relationship between the owner's attitude and quality as well as management style and quality seems appropriate. The relationship of an owner's attitude and actions during an IT implementation process and their impact on operational-level outcomes has not yet been examined in the literature. This will be the central focus of this study.

Based on the above review of literature on IT implementation and user evaluation of perceived IT quality, the following questions guided this research:

- How does the small business owner's attitude towards IT influence the quality of an IT implementation?
- How does the small business owner's management style influence the quality of an IT implementation?

METHODOLOGY

Qualitative methodologies are used for this multiple case study research. They include using open-ended interviews, which can provide valuable insights into IT use in small businesses. Through an open-ended interview, for example, the researcher elicits responses to open-ended questions that frequently yield answers that could not have been predefined. The unusual and surprising nature of data gathered in this way often is difficult to gain from some of the more common methodologies such as the survey. As an example, a survey might be designed to find out if location is a concern of a small business owner who is considering an IT implementation. A "yes-no" answer or a rank on a Likert scale may not give the true reason for not implementing IT at a 90-year-old company: the old factory is infested with rats that eat the wires to the computer equipment.

The open-ended questions are derived from the literature and ask small business owners about their attitude towards IT and their perception about the quality of the IT implementation in their organization. The questions are available in the Interview Guide found in Appendix 1 and are discussed below in the Findings section. In addition, owners were asked to describe, in free-form fashion, their situations and perceptions of IT. These interview techniques resulted in a bank of rich and detailed data for analysis (Lofland & Lofland, 1995; Marshall & Rossman, 1995).

Thirteen small business owners were chosen at random from an initial pool of 30. Selected by accessibility and convenience, the pool of candidates was formed from a list supplied by the Small Business Development Center, Baruch College, City University of New York, along with business contacts of the investigators. Of the 13, four were family owned. The average number of employees was 27, and the mean number of years in business was 25. Table 1 contains data about each participant's type, size, and age of business, founding characteristics, and type of IT implementation.

Data Collection

Each small business owner was interviewed for about three hours by the first author. Each was asked to discuss their most current IT implementation. Typed reports were produced from interview notes that were used for within and cross-case analysis. The reports were shared with participants to fill in gaps of the text or correct interpretation of interview responses.

To facilitate within and cross-case analysis, responses were filed both by participant and by question into an Excel workbook. The use of a worksheet

Table 1: Characteristics of owner businesses and IT implementations

Business Owner ID	Type of Business	Size of Business (# Employees)	Age of Business (years)	Founding Characteristics	Type of IT Implementation
PE1	Textile Broker	21	10	Purchased ownership	Communications Supply linkage Database Management
PE2	Writer/Actor	3	10	Founder	Communications Desktop Publishing
PE3	Telecommunications software developer	10	11	Founder	Financial and Accounting Communications Database Management
PE4	Real estate consulting	3	15	Founder	Communications Office Productivity Supply linkage
PE5	Engineering	90	26	Purchased ownership	Communications Financial and Accounting Graphic Design
PE6	Telephone time reseller	18	3	Founder	Communications Database Management Financial and Accounting
NE1	Accounting	6	15	Founder	Financial and Accounting
NE2	Insurance broker	25	40	Son of Founder	Communications Supply Linkage Vertical market
NE3	Promotion	10	12	Founder	Communications Desktop Publishing
UT1	Furniture manufacturer	100	83	Daughter of Founder	Financial and Accounting
UT2	Mail order catalogue for established retail specialty food business	20	6	Founder (Daughter of Founder of retail specialty food business)	Database Management Financial and Accounting
UT3	Real estate managing agent	38	42	Son of Founder	Communications Database Management Financial and accounting Supply Linkage
UT4	Accounting	9	51	Purchased ownership	Communications Financial and Accounting Office Productivity

format enabled immediate organization of the data and visually aided the analysis process (Miles & Huberman, 1994). Additionally, a relational database was developed. The integration of the worksheets with the database enabled the researchers to build queries, sort data, and join tables of information, which further supported the emerging category coding and interpretation process.

Data Analysis

Within-case analysis and cross-case pattern coding were used to explore the data gleaned from the interviews (Eisenhardt, 1989; Marshall & Rossman, 1995; Miles & Huberman, 1994; Pare & Elam, 1997). These methods enabled the investigators to look beyond first impressions of the data and made it possible to detect replication existing across cases. A category coding scheme, which generally resulted in the data given in Table 2, was developed that divided the data into broad categories: attitude towards IT, management style, and implementation quality criteria. Coding allowed the rapid retrieval and clustering of all segments related to a particular question, construct, or theme (Pare & Elam, 1997; Rubin & Rubin, 1995).

Each researcher coded and interpreted the transcripts. Themes that emerged were compared among cases. The themes were supported by the data, refined, or not supported and discarded because of a lack of sufficient data (Pare & Elam, 1997). Related themes were used to develop descriptions and general findings. The researchers' use of a "devil's advocate," or a non-involved domain expert who checked the data for possible rival hypotheses, helped strengthen the dependability of the study findings.

FINDINGS

This section discusses the four main findings that emerged from this study: (1) attitude towards IT, (2) management style, (3) the emergence of the attitude/style profiles, and (4) implementation quality. Table 2 presents a summary of these findings discussed here.

Attitude Toward IT

A study of the interview transcripts with small business owners revealed consistent statements that reflected three types of attitudes toward IT: positive, negative, and uncertain. These attitudes are consistent with those found in earlier studies (Cheney et al., 1986; Cragg & King, 1993; Nickell & Seado, 1986; Ray et al., 1994). Table 2 shows that six owners reported positive, three owners reported negative, and four reported uncertain attitudes. Excerpts from the interviews that support these categories are provided in Appendix 2.

In this study, attitude refers to the feelings that owners attach to IT and the beliefs they have about IT (Cook & Selltiz, 1970). Indicators of a positive attitude reflect feelings and beliefs that computers, for example, make daily routine more productive, have many uses in a firm, and enable better decisions

Table 2: Case comparison of small business owner's attitude, management style, and IT implementation quality

Business Owner ID (A Combination of *Attitude* and *Style* with Sequence Number)	***Attitude*** **Towards IT**	**Management** ***Style***	**Implementation Quality**
PE1	Positive (P)	Entrepreneurial (E)	High
PE2	Positive	Entrepreneurial	High
PE3	Positive	Entrepreneurial	High
PE4	Positive	Entrepreneurial	High
PE5	Positive	Entrepreneurial	High
PE6	Positive	Entrepreneurial	High
NE1	Negative (N)	Entrepreneurial	High
NE2	Negative	Entrepreneurial	High
NE3	Negative	Entrepreneurial	High
UT1	Uncertain (U)	Traditional (T)	Low
UT2	Uncertain	Traditional	Low
UT3	Uncertain	Traditional	Low
UT4	Uncertain	Traditional	Low

(Ray et al., 1994). Negative and uncertain attitudes reflect feelings and beliefs that computers, for example, diminish the human side of the office, make employees feel uncomfortable, create an overwhelming pressure to automate, and increase the possibility that valuable information could be lost (Ray et al., 1994).

Positive owners reported that they personally use the IT in their organization and find the technology fascinating. They unreservedly acknowledge that implementing IT will increase their organizations' efficiency and effectiveness. These owners also indicated that using IT improved the speed and accuracy of decision-making, as well as the quality of work life, in their organizations.

In contrast, negative owners revealed a tendency to resist suggestions that IT can improve business efficiency and effectiveness. They argued that IT will not have any conclusive positive effect on their businesses mainly because of high investment and maintenance costs. All negative owners reported being annoyed at having to rely on IT to remain in business and having to be dependent on external personnel for IT maintenance.

Owners who were neither positive nor negative remained uncertain about IT. They reported conflicting attitudes and feelings towards IT. Three out of four owners who reported uncertain attitudes towards IT inherited forty-plus (40+) year-old family businesses, as indicated in Table 1. Given a long tradition of sole proprietorship, these owners indicated that they felt most comfortable controlling all decisions and keeping things exactly as they always were. These small business owners perceive IT in general as an unfavorable force in an organization because it enables employees to have access to more information than a closely held business owner would want.

Management Style

In addition to attitude, the small business owner's management style surfaced as a related category when considering the achievement of a high or low quality IT implementation. We found that the findings in this category closely link into the categories — owner's attitude towards IT and the quality of the organization's IT implementation.

Management style was derived from statements the small business owners made in response to inquiries that came from Part II of the Interview Guide. The inquiries concern actions taken, or policies developed, concerning IT in their organization. In this study, as identified in Table 2, nine owners indicated that their management style is entrepreneurial and four indicated that it is traditional. Excerpts from the interview data that support these categories are provided in Appendix 2.

Employees in an entrepreneurial oriented organization often make decisions about hardware and software purchases. Participation in decision-making usually depends on an employee's area of expertise and proximity to the implementation. Employees tend to rely on one another to help ensure that the IT is effectively used and routinized in business activities.

The traditional style manager tends to establish policies that set managerial and operational jurisdiction over IT. Employee input on the implementation is frequently constrained and employees are not encouraged to work together on any IT effort.

In general, the data show that all uncertain owners follow a traditional style while all positive as well as negative owners follow an entrepreneurial style. This major finding, along with support from the literature, suggests how management style may influence an IT implementation. It provokes another research question:

> *How does the interaction of a small business owner's attitude towards IT and their management style affect the quality of an IT implementation?*

ATTITUDE/STYLE PROFILES

Distinct attitude/style profiles evolved from the data analysis: Positive-Entrepreneur (PE), Negative-Entrepreneur (NE) and Uncertain-Traditionalist (UT). Support for classifying small business owners in this study into these three profiles was provided by a consistent pattern of data that describes attitude towards IT and management style.

The researchers also searched the data for patterns that could characterize alternative profiles, such as positive-traditionalist, negative-traditionalist, or uncertain-entrepreneur. These alternative attitude/style profiles were not identified in this study. Table 3 indicates the data clusters and sample supporting statements for the three identified attitude/style profiles.

The owners' attitude/style profile for each case is given in Table 2. To increase the validity of the profiles that were identified, more detailed descriptions and quotes from the business owners are offered.

Positive-Entrepreneur (PE)

A small business owner classified as a positive-entrepreneur (PE) has a positive attitude towards IT and actively seeks applications of IT to enhance his or her business. The following statements exemplify the proactive strategies of PE owners:

> *I'm fascinated at how things change because of IT and often investigate how change can impact my business. (PE1)*

> *We put in the latest IT to remain competitive. We know the technology because we develop software for it. (PE3)*

Table 3: Attitude/style profiles of small business owners towards IT implementation

	Positive-Entrepreneur (PE)	Negative-Entrepreneur (NE)	Uncertain-Traditionalist (UT)
Attitude	**Positive:** Expresses a positive perception about IT, identifies opportunities for innovative use of new IT.	**Negative:** Expresses a negative perception about IT, hesitation to invest in IT, implements IT out of necessity.	**Uncertain:** Expresses indecisive perception about IT, hesitation to invest in IT, anxiety about using IT.
Management Style	**Entrepreneurial:** Identifies the use of policies that encourage collaboration and shared management.	**Entrepreneurial:** Identifies the use of policies that encourage collaboration and shared management.	**Traditional:** Uses policies that support power, authority, and status; suggests the inability to adopt tactics to decipher overwhelming data, conflicting suggestions, and numerous alternatives regarding IT.

It gives me the image that I've got a huge organization behind me. I learned about the IT that was available and I knew exactly what I wanted from it in terms of my business. (PE4)

In addition, PE owners exhibit an entrepreneurial management style determined by the following statements:

I have employees I can trust to make decisions in my business. Even though I am stuck with a key person who limits the amount of technology I can use, what I do have I used—and it made me in the hundred of thousands. (PE4)

We provide lots of employee training and even let the employees decide when they could use a computer specialist for additional help. (PE1)

Employees tell us how to do things more effectively. (PE3)

Negative-Entrepreneur (NE)

Small business owners classified as negative-entrepreneurs (NE) reflect negative attitudes towards IT and invest in IT primarily to remain in business. As a group, they indicate that a barrier to investing in IT is their lack of knowledge. Eventually they become like PE owners when they take actions about IT that characterize an entrepreneurial style; however, they consistently report reactive rather than proactive strategies:

> *We are purchasing a major IT system that's costing over $100,000, and by the time we pay it off, we will need a new system. The cost of the IT [in relation to its] longevity is ludicrous—what we are buying now will be obsolete in five years, but we have no other choice. No one knew anything about enterprise software, only that we had to purchase a package just to remain competitive in business. (NE2)*

> *We go to accounting shows and are bombarded by advertisements for information technology products. I didn't know what would change when I brought IT into the business. (NE1)*

> *I invest in IT to keep pace with my clients' use of technology in their businesses. We used an outside consultant to set up a local area network (LAN), and he'll show us how to use it and train us if we beg and plead. (NE3)*

Interestingly, all NE owners have developed practices that might assist them to overcome their negative attitudes towards IT. Displaying an entrepreneurial management style and the desire to remain competitive in the marketplace, NE owners rely on young, IT-current employees for IT recommendations. The following statements made by small business owners provide supporting evidence:

> *We use young employees right out of college to show us how to use some of the new IT required by law. They tell me what we need. (NE1)*

> *Employee suggestions are tremendously important. We asked the employees what they wanted, and their suggestions were taken seriously. (NE2)*

> *I definitely listen to and rely on my employees for their knowledge. They're young and less scared of IT because they grew up with it. (NE3)*

Uncertain-Traditionalist (UT)

Small business owners classified as uncertain-traditionalist (UT) have uncertain attitudes towards IT. They take actions about IT that characterize a traditional style of management. These owners state that they actively learn about IT, but they do not have the capability to interpret all the information. Consequently, they rely on traditional practices, as evidenced in the following statements:

> *Using a computerized order entry system would require that we change the way we do business. The order entry system will interrupt things that would mess us up. (UT1)*
>
> *I know Microsoft Word but I don't know anything else and if the IT is going to be used in my company, I've got to know it. My father's still running the retail store, and he doesn't even want a computerized cash register. He's very comfortable with the way things are done. (UT2)*
>
> *For us to put in a voice mail system would cost over $5,000 and it's not necessary. We like the personal touch that comes from a person actually picking up the telephone. (UT4)*

UT owners are technologically aware:

> *When I was setting up the accounts receivable and accounts payable software, I was particularly good in getting all the necessary information. (UT1)*
>
> *I look to model other companies. I go into stores and ask a lot of questions. I'm very inquisitive that way. (UT2)*
>
> *I go to seminars to find out what's in the market. I stay abreast of what's going on in the industry. (UT4)*

IT information overload, however, appears to have aggravated the uncertainty of the UT business owners:

> *Every consultant tells me to use different software and to buy different hardware. I'm shaking in my boots. I know I've got to get started with this (IT) in a few weeks. (UT2)*

I spent a lot of time and got a lot of information on systems, but I still don't know much about any of them. (UT1)

IT is coming too quickly. Technology is coming at us in a frantic way. (UT4)

A different perspective on the uncertain attitudes of small business owners towards IT emerged from case UT3, perhaps because it involved telephony technology implementation. It illustrates how conflict arising in the outside environment creates ambiguity, as illustrated by both incentive and deterrent:

Incentive: We are looking into telephony where we can track telephone calls in the system. When I get a call, a list of the last five conversations . . . will come up. I can get an idea of the last conversation the customer had with our company and say, "Yes, I know so and so, whom you spoke with on this date is doing this." (UT3)

Deterrent: The technology moves people beyond wanting information in one minute. Now they want it this second. They assume everything is on-line and that we have instant access to it. (UT3)

In the case of UT3, the customers and their satisfaction drive the business and supply both the incentive and the deterrent for IT implementation. The implementation that resulted, in this case, was of a low quality. The quality issue is covered next.

Implementation Quality

The small business owners reported the impact of IT implementation on their businesses. Their statements to questions in the section of the interview guide titled *Implementation Quality* indicate both high-quality and low-quality implementations. Table 2 shows the findings for each case concerning IT implementation quality. Excerpts from the interviews that support the classifications of high and low quality are provided in Appendix 2.

Positive-entrepreneurs perceived that their investment in IT had a beneficial effect on their business, ranging from increased operational effectiveness and efficiency to cultural changes that help to improve the quality of work life for their employees:

I am able to hold on to more information previously lost in the past. Many of the notes I jotted down on paper for a project were thrown away when the project was completed. Those notes could have been very useful in later projects. (PE1)

The IT implementation changed the style of doing business and enriched the quality of working conditions. (PE5)

An uncertain-traditionalist, on the other hand, found that IT investments that require a significant outlay of resources do not provide any overall benefits:

IT does not save time or money. Our one employee that knows how to use the network spends 30% of her time as a network administrator instead of doing her primary responsibilities. Plus the cost of the network, the hardware and the software, adds up. (UT4)

Another uncertain–traditionalist identified a significant benefit that IT could provide to his business and employees. He realized and acknowledged that he must engage in a fundamental rethinking of his business and its organization and policies:

IT makes the employee's job easier . . . then they deal with clients in a more beneficial manner. We are a client-oriented business. Yet, in order to make an employee's job easier, real business process change must take place. (UT3)

This owner also reported that his employees do not understand the enterprise-level IT implemented in the organization and, further, they cannot properly use it.

On the other hand, owners with negative attitudes about IT invested in IT and achieved results that exceeded their expectations. Their statements indicate the positive impact on their businesses from IT use:

What's happened in the business has gone way beyond what I thought would happen. (NE1)

The IT does allow us to produce much more professional looking business proposals and memos. (NE3)

One NE owner made a large IT investment that resulted in reducing business risk and in helping to salve the substantial resources expended:

> *The IT makes us more efficient and helps bring in more clients. We can budget our expenses and get an accurate financial picture. This is particularly important because the family owns the business and we were all drawing cash from it without checking out how the business was actually doing. (NE2)*

These comments provide valuable insight into the IT attitudes of negative-entrepreneur business owners. It evidences that such owners can metamorphosize into positive owners of IT. It also evidences that negativity does not paralyze the plunge into IT. As long as the owner has an entrepreneurial management style, the main ingredient is in place to make the plunge and eventually experience a successful IT implementation.

DISCUSSION

The findings center on the emergence of the three different types of attitudes and three different types of profiles that surfaced in the data, as evident in Table 3. The biggest surprise to surface, however, concerns the negative-entrepreneur type of small business owner. Although an NE owner invested in new IT primarily as a reactive strategy to avoid going out of business, he or she still experienced a high quality IT implementation. This finding was a surprise because the literature suggests that owners with negative attitudes towards IT would most likely achieve poor quality IT implementations (Agarwal & Prasad, 1997; Quinn, 1979).

Another interesting finding was that the uncertain traditionalist type of small business owner was unable to initiate a forward-looking approach for guidance through an IT implementation process. Based on previous research (Cragg & King, 1993; Malone, 1985), the investigators expected that the uncertain owner would seek advice and information from employees, or other more technical sources, about which type of IT is an appropriate investment. The data suggested, however, that the uncertain-traditionalist owners became immobilized, typically from an information overload in their pursuit of IT knowledge.

The finding that was most expected was the small business owner with a positive attitude toward IT who, in turn, also had a high-quality IT implementation. The interesting aspect that surfaced here was that the positive attitude was coupled with an entrepreneurial management style in all cases. This type of owner reported a collection of proactive strategies when dealing with an IT implementation, such as:

- Engaging the support and input of employees.
- Making a concerted effort to learn about IT.
- Becoming involved in the IT implementation process.
- Using IT to attain competitive advantages for the business.
- Finding benefits from an IT implementation in operational areas much before they appear in financial areas.

Unlike the uncertain owner, the positive entrepreneur takes advantage of a deep knowledge of the business as well as knowledge of IT to resolve ambiguous issues that might otherwise impede the successful and creative use of IT in the organization (Winston & Dologite, 1999).

IMPLICATIONS AND FUTURE RESEARCH

The findings of this study have implications for small business owners as well as IS practitioners and researchers. The responses in this study have a uniformity of relationships that enable the investigators to offer some propositions mainly for the benefit of raising the awareness of small business owners. They focus on the possibilities for fostering quality IT implementations. They also suggest an agenda for further research to corroborate the findings in this study.

Negative-Entrepreneur (NE) Small Business Owners

Proposition #1: Small business owners who have a negative attitude towards IT and who practice an entrepreneurial management style will be more likely to achieve a high quality IT implementation than small business owners who have a negative attitude and who do not practice an entrepreneurial management style.

In this study, owners with negative attitudes towards IT reduced the risk associated with IT by using supportive, collaborative, and shared management policies and practices in their organizations. They not only depended on employee input, but they also acted on recommendations of employees. This practice was reported to be a significant influence when contending with changes that occurred as a result of an IT implementation.

Uncertain-Traditionalist (UT) Small Business Owners

Proposition #2: Small business owners with an uncertain attitude toward IT implementation who practice a traditional management style will likely experience a low quality IT implementation unless they adjust their management style.

The uncertain-traditionalist owners' preference for a high level of control and bureaucracy, which is very much a part of their business climate, inhibits innovation and theoretically reduces the chance for a quality IT implementation. It was the UT owners in this study who evaluated IT primarily on a financial basis. They easily calculated the cost of the IT as well as the additional employee time required to maintain it.

It is difficult for a UT owner, on the other hand, to calculate productivity increases that arise from, for example, more accurate reports or faster processing time. Such operational benefits of IT are elusive to them. Further, as a result of an overload of IT information, they do not wish to become heavily involved in the IT adoption and implementation process.

Management Style

Proposition #3: Small business owners who practice an entrepreneurial management style with supportive shared management and/or collaborative policies are more likely to achieve higher quality IT implementations than those who endorse a traditional management style exemplified by hierarchies and defined boundaries of operational responsibility.

In small businesses, management style directs the climate of the organization. Generally, an entrepreneurial climate increases the capability of a business to contend with and temper any uncertainty connected with a new IT implementation. During an IT implementation, employees become involved in areas well beyond their normal scope of responsibility and consider such fundamental IT implementation issues as hardware and software purchases and training. In other words, in organizations with a shared management style, employees accept responsibility for guiding the affairs of the organization.

Some implications of this study are especially relevant for IT practitioners. For example, it appears that early in an implementation process, an IT practitioner should recognize a small business owner's attitude/style profile and be aware of how the profile potentially can influence implementation quality. Additionally, the following suggestions may help IT practitioners improve the likelihood of achieving a high quality IT implementation.

- Consider that a small business owner with a negative attitude toward IT might improve the likelihood of achieving a high quality IT implementation by practicing and endorsing entrepreneurial management policies.
- Work to help change a small business owners' traditional management style, rather than try to change an owners' negative attitude towards IT, which is probably a more complex issue to deal with.
- Encourage owners with traditional management styles to employ policies that require employee participation and collaboration in IT decisions.
- Help uncertain-traditional small business owners identify and solicit support from employees in their businesses who know and understand the IT and how it can be applied to the business.

Some issues surfaced in this study that deserve future research attention. One concerns the possibility that differences in the quality of an IT implementation in a small business may be impacted by the quality of the sources and type of IT information obtained by an owner (Julien, 1995). In most cases, both internal and external collaborators helped owners in this study adapt IT information to their small business. It may be that filtered information helps reduce uncertainty surrounding the use of IT and as a result enables a high quality IT implementation (Jelinek & Litterer, 1995).

Other research opportunities present themselves. An especially intriguing one concerns a qualitative investigation that focuses on creative problem solving techniques (CPS) (Couger, 1995). Such a study may shed light on how IT practitioners could more productively interact with Uncertain-Traditionalist small business owners to achieve high quality IT implementations

This study has acknowledged limitations that necessitate more research. First, the qualitative nature of the study develops propositions that require

Table 4: Summary of findings

Small Business Owner		**Quality of IT Implementation**	**Contributors of IT Implementation Quality**
Attitude Towards IT	**Management Style**		
Positive	Entrepreneurial (open, collaborative)	High	Attitude and style
Negative	Entrepreneurial (open, collaborative)	High	Reliance on employees
Uncertain	Traditional (closed, hierarchical)	Low	Bureaucracy and feeling of being overwhelmed

future studies to generalize the findings to larger populations. Second, qualitative design, by nature, is not conducive to statistical analysis to determine significance of findings. In order to overcome these limitations, additional research using attitude and management style surveys that can be quantified are required.

Also, because this study focused on attitude, style, and IT implementation quality, it consciously allocated dealing with other related, and relevant, issues for future studies. Issues that are on a future agenda include how type of IT influences the small business owner's attitude towards IT and the quality of an IT implementation. Other issues that need special investigation include, among others, the relationship of an owner to the business, and the business' prior experience with IT. All these issues and more could extend our understanding of IT implementation in small businesses.

SUMMARY

Table 4 displays a summary of the findings of this study. To review, the categorization of small business owners' attitudes towards IT and their management style was determined from data collected during multiple case study interviews. Using qualitative methods, an interesting relationship emerged between attitude and management style when considering the achievement of a high or low quality IT implementation. Main contributors to IT implementation quality were also identified, and business owners were classified as Positive-Entrepreneur, Negative-Entrepreneur, and Uncertain-Traditionalist. Only the Uncertain-Traditionalist experienced a low quality IT implementation.

The results concerning how attitudes towards IT and management style affect the quality of an IT implementation can guide the small business owner and information expert concerned with the design and plan of the implementation process. This also suggests that IS work should increasingly address combined managerial and technical issues. In small business, the owner's feelings and organizational policies, rather than the technology, may be most important in determining an IT initiative's success.

REFERENCES

Agarwal, R. & Prasad, J. (1997). The role of innovation characteristics and perceived voluntariness in the acceptance of information technologies. *Decision Sciences 28*(3), 557-582.

Bailey, J. E. & Pearson, S. W. (1983). Development of a tool for measuring and analyzing computer user satisfaction. *Management Science, 29*(5), 530-545.

Bergeron F. & Raymond L. (1992). Planning of information systems to gain a competitive edge. *Journal of Small Business Management, 30*(1), 21-26.

Byrd, T. A., Sambamurthy, V., & Zmud, R. W. (1995). An examination of it planning in a large diversified public organization. *Decision Sciences, 26*(1), 49-73.

Cheney, P. H., Mann, R. I., & Amoroso, D. L. (1986). Organizational factors affecting the success of end-user computing. *Journal of Management Information Systems, 3*(1), 65-80.

Cook, S. & Selltiz, C (1970). A multiple-indicator approach to attitude measurement. In G. F. Summers, (ed.), *Attitude Measurement* (pp. 1-5). Chicago: Rand McNally and Company.

Cooley, P. L., Walz, D. T., & Walz D. B. (1987). A research agenda for computers and small business. *American Journal of Small Business,* 31-42.

Cooper, R. B. & Zmud, R. W. (1990). Information technology implementation research: A technology diffusion approach. *Management Science, 36*(2), 123-139.

Couger, J. D. (1995). *Creative Problem Solving and Opportunity Finding,* Melbourne, Australia: Boyd and Fraser.

Cragg, P. B. & King, M. (1993). Small-firm computing: Motivators and inhibitors. *MIS Quarterly, 17*(1), 47-60.

Delone, W. H. (1988). Determinants of Success for Computer Usage in Small Business, *MIS Quarterly, 12*(1), 51-61.

Doukidis, G. I., Smithson, S., & Lybereas, T. (1994). Trends in information technology in small businesses. *Journal of End User Computing, 6*(4), 15-25.

Eisenhardt, K. M. (1989). Building theories from case study research. *Academy of Management Review, 14*(4), 532-550.

Harrison, D. A., Mykytyn, P. P., & Riememschneider, C. K. (1997). Executive decisions about adoption of information technology in small business: Theory and empirical tests. *Information Systems Research, 8*(2), 171-195.

Herbert, F. J. & Bradley, J. H. (1993). Expert systems development in small business: A managerial perspective. *Journal of Small Business Management, 31*(3), 23-34.

Iivari, J. & Ervasti, I. (1994). User information satisfaction: IS implementability and effectiveness. *Information and Management, 27*(5), 205-220.

Ives, B., Olson, M. H., & Baroudi, J. J. (1983). The measurement of user information satisfaction. *Communications of the ACM, 26*(10), 785-793.

Jelinek, M. & Litterer, J. A. (1995). Toward entrepreneurial organizations: Meeting ambiguity with engagement. *Entrepreneurship Theory and Practice, 19*(3), 137-168.

Julien, P. (1995). New technologies and technological information in small businesses. *Journal of Business Venturing, 10*(6), 459-475.

Julien, P. & Raymond, L. (1994). Factors of new technology adoption in the retail sector. *Entrepreneurship Theory and Practice,* Summer, 79-90.

King, W. R. (1996). Strategic issues in groupware. *Information Systems Management,* Spring, 73-75.

Kwon, T. H. & Zmud, R. W. (1987). Unifying the fragmented models of information systems implementation. In J. Boland & A. Hirchheim (eds.), *Critical Issues in Information Systems Research.*, New York: John Wiley.

Lawler III, E. & Mohrman, S. (1989). High involvement management. *Organizational Dynamics,* April, 27-31.

Lofland, J. & Lofland, L. H. (1995). *Analyzing Social Settings: A Guide to Qualitative Observation and Analysis* (3rd ed.) New York: Wadsworth Publishing Company.

Maglitta, J. (1992). That tap tap is your boss. *Computerworld, 25*(17).

Malone, S. C. (1985). Computerizing small business information systems. *Journal of Small Business Management, 23*(2), 10-16.

Marshall, C. & Rossman, G. B. (1995). *Designing Qualitative Research* (2nd ed.), Newbury Park, CA: Sage Publications.

Miles, M. B. & Huberman, A. M. (1994). *Qualitative Data Analysis: An Expanded Sourcebook.* Beverly Hills, CA: Sage Publications.

Nickell, G. S. & Seado, P. C. (1986). The impact of attitudes and experience on small business computer use. *American Journal of Small Business, 10*(4), 37-47.

Normann, R. (1971). Organizational innovativeness: Product variation and reorientation. *Administrative Science Quarterly,* 16, 203 - 215.

Pare, G. & Elam, J. J. (1997). Using case study research to build theories of IT implementation. In A. S. Lee, J. Liebenau, & J. I. DeGross, (eds.), *Information Systems and Qualitative Research.* New York: Chapman and Hall.

Quinn, J. B. (1979). Technological innovation, ownership, and strategy. *Sloan Management Review, 20*(2), 19-30.

Ray, C. M. H., Thomas, M., & Dye, J. L. (1994). Small business attitudes toward computers. *Journal of End User Computing, 6*(1), 16-25.

Rogers, E. M. (1983). *Diffusion of Innovation*. New York: The Free Press.

Rogers, E. & Shoemaker, F. (1971). *Communications of Innovations: A Cultural Approach*. New York: The Free Press.

Rubin, H. & Rubin, I. (1995). *Qualitative Interviewing: The Art of Hearing Data*. Beverly Hills, CA: Sage Publications.

Schafer, S. (1995). How information technology is leveling the playing field. *Inc. Technology, 17*(4), 92-96.

Senge, P. M. (1990). *The Fifth Discipline*. New York: Doubleday.

Serwer, A. E. (1995). Paths to wealth: in the new economy. *Fortune*(20), February, 57-62.

Stair, Jr., R., Crittenden, W., & Crittenden, V. (1989). The use, operation, and control of the small business computer. *Information and Management,* 16, 125-130.

Szajna, B. & Scamell, R. W. (1993). The effects of information system user expectations on their performance and perceptions. *MIS Quarterly, 17*(4), 493-515.

Thong, J. Y. L. & Yap, C. S. (1995). CEO characteristics, organizational characteristics and information technology adoption in small businesses. *Omega, 23*(4), 429-442.

Venkatraman, N. (1991). IT-induced business reconfiguration. In M. S. S. Morton (ed.), *The Corporation of the 1990s: Information Technology and Organizational Transformation* New York: Oxford Press.

Walton R. E. (1985). From control to commitment in the workplace. *Harvard Business Review,* March-April, 77-84.

Waterman, Jr., R. H., Peters, T., & Phillips, J. (1995). The 7-S framework. In H. Mintzberg, J. Quinn, & J. Voyer (eds.), *The Strategy Process*. Englewood Cliffs, NJ: Prentice Hall.

Winston, E. R. & Dologite, D. G. (1999). Achieving IT infusion: A conceptual model for small businesses. *Information Resources Management Journal, 12*(1), 26-38.

APPENDIX 1
Interview Guide

Part I Date _______

Interview Guide # ________________ Owner __________________

Type of Business ______________________________________

Age of Business ________________ # of Employees ____________

Does this business use (check all that apply):

_____ MIS system _____ Data base management systems

_____ EDI _____ Groupware (Lotus Notes)

_____ Internet _____ Other

What is the newest IT used in your business? ________________________

Part II

Attitudes Towards IT:

1. Are any funds budgeted for new IT?
2. How did your ideas about how IT might impact your business develop? (Probe: magazines, training classes, contacts...)
3. What did you think would change when you brought the technology into the business?
4. What is the worst thing about IT?
5. What is the best thing about IT?

IT Actions and Policies:

6. How was the decision reached to purchase the IT and who participated in the decision?
7. How did you go about introducing IT into the business? (Probe: How was it set up? If you used a consultant, how did you locate the consultant? What kind of relationship do you have with the consultant?)
8. In what ways is employee input useful? (Probe: If owner does not mention a way.)

Implementation Quality:

9. How has what actually happened in the business differed from what you thought would happen? (Probe: What kinds of problems did you think IT would solve but didn't?)
10. How does IT affect your relationships with other companies? (Probe: Do you depend on these other companies for anything—business information, technology, sales...?)

11. How do you judge the success of IT? How do you know IT is being used successfully in your business? (Probe: What about the costs?)
12. What kinds of problems have you experienced with IT? (Probe: Who helps you with these problems?
13. What has been the overall effect of IT? (Probe: How has it impacted productivity in terms of output per worker, job satisfaction, work quality, increased revenue, quality of work life . . . ?)

APPENDIX 2

Excerpts from Interviews

Attitude Towards IT	
Positive	
PE1	I'm personally fascinated at how things change because of IT and I'm excited to see it.
PE2	The IT saves me a dramatic amount of time and information gathering is much better.
PE3	IT allows you to do things faster and more accurately. It's fun. Great advantage you can do it at 2:00AM.
PE4	It works. It gives me the image I need.
PE5	IT is a service for human beings. Technology is fantastic.
PE6	IT allows us to exist.
Negative	
NE1	I go to accounting shows and advertisers bombard me. Couldn't hide from IT even if you wanted to. Have to be very computer literate to manipulate the IT. It's terrible if it goes down and we don't know what the heck to do. Lose a day sometimes.
NE2	The cost involved compared to the longevity … is ludicrous. By the time we pay off the loan for the IT we will need a new system.
NE3	We had to put in a system to keep pace with our clients technologically our business is the entertainment industry. I used an outside consultant … when we have a problem he will help us but I have to beg ...
Uncertain	
UT1	I thought our records would be streamlined and less prone to error, but they are only as accurate as the data you put in. We have not really gotten involved in the heart of IT because that would mean we have to change the way we do business.
UT2	I'm shaking in my boots. I've got to start this business and I have to know the technology. I decided on the IT by modeling other companies. I know the computer system has to be very flexible. The consultants are the biggest problem. The first was horrible, the second satisfactory.
UT3	I started the process begrudgingly realizing we had to computerize. Even if you buy the best IT it's like stereo equipment…buy the best on Monday by Friday it's outdated. IT has given us the ability to be much more organized and function … as a team. IT moves people beyond wanting the information in 1 minute now they want it this second.
UT4	In our business using IT is essential. The IT is coming at us in a frantic way. Every time you turn around you need to upgrade …
Management Style	
Entrepreneurial	
PE1	Employees are responsible for functional tasks and the system they use. We have a very liberal policy. Funds are budgeted for IT as needed.
PE2	I relied on a network of friends and colleagues to help direct me.
PE3	Employees tell us how to do thing more efficiently. We have an employee suggestion system. Decisions are informal … an employee will say we need one of those.
PE4	A guy came to sell me stolen a computer before they were popular. I got lucky because IBM became the popular computer. I have a keen ability to get other people to share their information and in one case their … database. I do a lot of networking.
PE5	Employees are involved in all levels depending on how comfortable they feel with the topic or area requiring support.
PE6	Employees keep us to date on what s happening and this helps improve the process. … hands on schooling keeps interfering with my education.
NE1	Employees are very computer literate. IT decisions are made by the employees. They understand how to do things better. I follow through on their suggestions ...
NE2	Employee input is tremendously useful. We ask employees what they wanted and their requests are taken seriously. They provide us with many good ideas that we did not think of.
NE3	I definitely listen to my employees. I rely on their information and knowledge. They are younger and less scared and grew up with the technology.

Management Style Continued	
Traditional	
UT1	Most of the employees are computer illiterate and cannot use the system properly. We never take advantage of employee input.
UT2	Employees are not useful. They don't have the knowledge about IT. That's the basic theme in the fast food business.
UT3	I try to keep up with the clients basically, not the employee.
UT4	I primarily rely on one or two vendors. The decision to implement IT was driven by our client's needs. I stay informed of what going on in the industry and the media helps.
Quality of IT Implementation	
High	
PE1	Increase personal job satisfaction. The employees can provide more accurate reports … faster.
PE2	Client relations have improved. I have increased the amount of work I can do. The IT has easily improved every aspect, from writing to information gathering. … quality of working life has improved. The IT gives me more time to be creative.
PE3	Productivity gain. I speak with end-users and they tell me that a new way of doing business (enabled by the IT) is much better.
PE4	It gives me the image … I am a much larger company.
PE5	We obtain economic benefits … improvements in the quality of work life.
PE6	The costs of the IT are always much less than the benefits. With the IT we are able to differentiate ourselves from the competitors.
NE1	Increase in productivity. I am lucky to have very computer literate employees so that the learning curve is not very big.
NE2	The IT enables us to be more efficient so that we can bring in more clients. … now have the ability to budget our expenses.
NE3	The IT is tremendous … increase in employee happiness. The employees work much more efficiently.
Low	
UT1	Most of the employees are computer illiterate and cannot use the system properly.
UT2	We implemented the database system and many things did not work. The computer system was not flexible and it became unusable for business.
UT3	IT is only as good as its ease of use. My problem is that the employees cannot use the system. They don't understand it and cannot get out the information they need.
UT4	The system is not helping us save time or money.

Chapter XIII

A Three-Tier Technology Training Strategy in a Dynamic Business Environment

Albert H. Huang
University of the Pacific, USA

ABSTRACT

As end-user training becomes increasingly important in today's technology-intensive business environment, progressive companies remain alert to find ways to provide their end users with timely training and resources. This paper describes an innovative training strategy adopted by one midsize organization to provide its end users with adequate, flexible, and responsive training. The paper then compares the three-tier strategy with other models described in technology training literature. Managers who supervise technology end users in organizations comparable to the one in the study may find the three-tier strategy workable and may want to use it in their own training programs to facilitate training and improve end-user skills. Researchers and scholars may find that the idea of three-tier training generates new opportunities for research.

INTRODUCTION

Existing studies on end-user technology training emphasize the training process: Research efforts have focused on needs assessment (Nelson et al., 1995), trainee learning styles (Bostrom et al., 1990), and delivery methods (Sein & Bostrom, 1989; Compeau & Higgins, 1995). Although such studies are important in understanding the operational issues of the training process, they do not address higher-level strategic concerns. Without a training strategy, it will prove difficult for trainers and organizations to devise an effective program to support end users and meet business objectives, because employers and trainers will only be able to design training programs based on their personal experiences (Sein et al., 1999).

In a dynamic business environment, business organizations need to address issues such as: How much training is enough? Should organizations blanket-train all end users on every application, or should they be selective? How often should an organization train its end users? Because employees' productive work time in a highly competitive market is too precious to be lavished on unjustified training, organizations also need to determine the cost-benefit ratio of training time to productive work time. Thus, employers face related issues such as: Can organizations justify the hiring of employees without adequate technology skills and then provide them training and how will they train employees with little or no technical know-how? To answer these questions, employers desperately need a training strategy.

The purpose of this paper is to show how one company developed a training strategy that would answer these questions. The paper first describes the challenges modern businesses face in supplying technology users with adequate training. It then describes some unique difficulties that one midsize financial organization faced and the three-tier approach they adopted to solve their training problems. The following section discusses the advantages of the study strategy and compares it to other models described in literature. Finally, it proposes further opportunities for research using the three-tier training model.

Definition and Scope of Technology Training

Traditionally, technology training has been an important part of end-user support. Technology training is defined as the process of transferring required knowledge and operational skills to users of information technology. The fundamental purpose of technology training is to produce users with practical skills that enable them to use technology applications. A more ambitious goal of technology training is to create motivated users who can apply learned skills and knowledge to their jobs, and who can continue to learn as skill and technology requirements change (Sein et al., 1999).

The value of technology training is clear: It ensures end users' success in operating computers, as emphasized by previous research (Bostrom et al., 1990; Davis & Bostrom, 1993). End-user technology training is a necessary component in the successful implementation of new information systems and operational procedures; it plays a critical part in quality assurance and continuous total quality improvement (White & Christy, 1987); and it should be viewed as a form of investment in human capital rather than as an expense (Becker, 1992).

Technology Training Needs

Recent decades have seen the demand for technology training increase steadily until it has come to be regarded as a necessary component of doing business (Compeau et al., 1995). Today, even routine business activities—hiring new employees, implementing new systems, changing computing platforms—require training to facilitate the transition. Because what each organization regards as "current technology" changes frequently, technology training has become an ongoing activity. Organizations that are successful in highly competitive environments understand that technology training is vital, and so adopt continuous training programs to create a culture of learning (Pitman, 1994).

Challenges Facing Technology Training

Not only has technology training become a constant feature of today's typical business experience, its complexity has deepened in proportion to the need for it. Many business organizations find it a daunting task to provide adequate technology training to end user populations whose membership is constantly becoming more demographically diverse and who are already under serious resource and time constraints.

Finding a supply of training materials to cover a proliferating list of subjects is another challenge. Some years ago, when it first became popular for consumers to buy personal computers, the free software that came bundled with those computers often could have been said to suffice as "training material" for those novice technology users (Fitzgerald & Caster-Steel, 1995). But current software applications are significantly more varied and more complex than their bulky and simplistic ancestors. End users are now far more sophisticated, and commonly participate in activities such as systems development and using client-server applications—things that would previously have been considered "advanced" (Kappelman & Guynes, 1995).

The process of selecting just the right training method from the plethora of candidates is frequently bewildering. Many business organizations have decided to rely primarily on computer-based training (CBT) as a way of minimizing overall training costs; but when they attempt to combine traditional instruction methods with CBT, they may need to sift through a confusing array of formats, delivery methods, and interaction modes before making their choice (Huang, 1996-97).

The need to ensure that a business's chosen technology training program will accomplish its business objectives exerts pressure on everyone involved in the training process, because no training objectives are more crucial than meeting business objectives. After all, training is a means to an end. Companies only agree to finance training for their end users when they have some assurance that the users will be able to apply their newly acquired skills to improving productivity and quality. Thus, businesses expect technology training to improve user performance and, ultimately, to help meet organizational goals.

Prior Research on Technology Training

The body of extant research on technology training contains a large number of both empirical and theoretical studies on end-user training. Drawing from studies on end-user training, this section briefly reviews selected studies of three types—those addressing user issues, those addressing methodological issues, and those addressing training objectives and needs assessment.

Creating an effective training program requires taking these three issues into account and addressing them concurrently and with equal emphasis. The section below, "Case Study—SVF Company," which follows the discussion of research issues, describes a real-world training program that considers these issues.

Research Addressing User Issues

End-user characteristics have been a popular subject of study. Sein et al. (1999) suggests that the most effective way to classify end users is by their job functions, abilities, learning styles, and motivation. Aside from these categories, trainees have also been grouped according to prior knowledge, demographics, cognitive styles, and learning preferences. Sometimes they have been classified as transactional, casual, or power users. "Transactional" users are defined as those who use tools to carry out a transaction; "casual" users are those who use tools to retrieve information; and "power" users are those who are able to provide an interface between end users and development teams (Sein et al., 1999).

Research Addressing Methodological Issues

Training methods may be classified as conceptual or procedural (Santhanam & Sein 1994, Olfman & Manddiwalla 1994); as behavioral modeling (Compeau & Haggins 1995); as exploratory learning; or as collaborative learning. There is also an abundance of studies comparing CBT to instructor-led training (Huang 1996-97).

Research Addressing Business Objective Issues and Needs Assessment

One attempt to ensure that technology training meets business objectives is called the "lifecycle approach." According to this view, a complete end-user training process normally includes three stages: initiation, delivery, and post-training (Compeau et al., 1995). The initiation stage emphasizes identifying training needs and then designing training to fill these needs. The delivery stage focuses on actual teaching and learning activities. Post-training aims to provide outcome assessment and end-user support. Implementing a training program with these three stages can ensure that an organization has chosen the right training, has provided it to the right people, and has achieved the right outcomes.

Case Study—SVF Corporation

In the following section, an actual corporate training strategy is described and discussed. The strategy qualifies as a suitable model because the midsize corporation that implemented it has been using it for several years with good success.

Company Profile

"SVF" is the pseudonym (the actual name is concealed as requested by the company) of a West Coast corporation that is thriving in the highly competitive financial services industry. The company routinely handles sensitive financial information and serves individual and corporate clients with a wide range of financial services including mortgage, personal, and business loans; investments; securities brokering; financial planning; and related services. In recent years, because of an economic boom in the region, the company has enjoyed significant growth in its client base and cash flow and has expanded the list of financial products it offers. (The author of this paper is not affiliated with the company.)

End-User Profiles

SVF employs over 200 employees to perform a variety of jobs; the majority of these are technology users including managers, account representatives, customer service agents, financial advisors, accountants, office staff, and systems technicians. Although most of the technology users are college graduates, their

Table 1: Distribution of end users' education levels

Degrees	Percentage
High school diploma	6%
Associate degree	8%
Bachelor's degree	77%
Graduate degree	7%
Other	2%

educational backgrounds and technology skills vary widely. Tables 1 and 2 show the distribution of these technology users' educational backgrounds.

Technology Platforms & Applications

SVF Corporation uses Windows NT-based networks with PC client workstations as its primary technology platform—there are no Macintosh or other personal computers. Each of its branch locations has its own local area network plus several NT servers to provide file storage, applications, messaging, printing, and Internet services. Branch offices are linked by a Virtual Private Network (VPN). Dial-up networks are also used to connect SVF with wholesalers of financial products. About five years ago, SVF started to use portable computers loaded with analytical software. When visiting their current and prospective clients, account representatives use these portable computers to analyze financial positions and portfolios. They even have a small portable printer that can produce legal forms on site to complete a business transaction immediately.

The majority of SVF's personnel use word processors, spreadsheets, and database management systems daily. The predominant software package is Microsoft Office, although a few employees still use WordPerfect applications.

Table 2: Distribution of education backgrounds of users with college degrees

Education Background	Percentage
Business and related	42%
Engineering, Computer Science, etc.	10%
Liberal Arts, Social Sciences, etc.	35%
Other	13%

They also use e-mail for internal and client communication. Commonly used forms, memorandums, and other internal documents are stored in a simple Intranet. Proprietary systems allow account representatives and financial consultants to access the databases of financial product suppliers.

Training Challenges Facing SVF Corporation

Because its rapidly changing business environment led to growth and increased hiring, SVF needed to greatly increase its technology training. In addition to the common training challenges described earlier, SVF faced several unique situations that increased the difficulty of providing this training.

Their first challenge was to provide users with adequate training without severe interference to primary business activities. This balance was particularly difficult for SVF because its employees were already carrying large workloads and maintaining busy schedules due to a years-long shortage of qualified workers in that labor market. Because many of their employees were already working overtime and enduring long commutes, the corporation realized that it would be unrealistically demanding to expect them to spend additional time on technology training, especially if the training sessions were long and concerned applications that the employees may or may not need.

The second challenge was to provide a training program with enough flexibility to meet the demands of its diverse users—SVF users are highly diversified in terms of educational background, age, ethnicity, and other factors. In recent years, a rapid turnover of employees had compounded the difficulty of providing training, because new employees were always found to be under-trained. The systems manager, who is also responsible for technology training, stated that the number of employees in training programs had increased steadily in the past few years, and that employee backgrounds had become increasingly diverse.

Third, SVF found that, though it had enjoyed the rewards of having a larger and wealthier client base, it had not been able to provide the more intelligent level of customer service that these new clients demanded. Some clients had become highly impatient when dealing with employees who appeared to be unfamiliar with their own computer system, and SVF management had received numerous complaints from clients regarding the inadequate training of its employees. Thus, technology training came to bear the responsibility for ensuring that users could properly use technology to increase customer satisfaction.

Training Strategy

Early in 1997, SVF adopted an in-house training program to cope with its technology training challenges. Their training program divided technology training into three tiers based on the timing of the training in relation to the use of technology applications (Figure 1). This three-tier strategy is especially suitable for use in a dynamic, even hectic business environment. (Management admitted that, in the past, there never seemed to be a right time to conduct training at SVF.)

The first tier of the strategy is General Technology Education, an ongoing effort to impart basic general knowledge and basic technical knowledge. The timing of General Education Training does not include learning to use a specific technology application or accomplish a specific task. The second tier of the strategy is Business Application Training, which is designed and conducted specifically to teach the use of business applications. Business Application Training is usually given before an employee is expected to learn to use an application, or when a new employee without sufficient training is hired. The third tier is Just-In-Time (JIT) Training, and occurs at the exact time an employee needs to use an unfamiliar or complicated technology application. The three tiers of technology training are described in detail below.

First Tier: General Technology Education

Regardless of how fast or how dramatic technological changes have been or may become, certain fundamentals of information technology will remain nearly constant: For example, the basic functions of a computer network will remain the same regardless of its platform. The architectures of computers will remain similar

Figure 1: The three-tier end-user technology training strategy

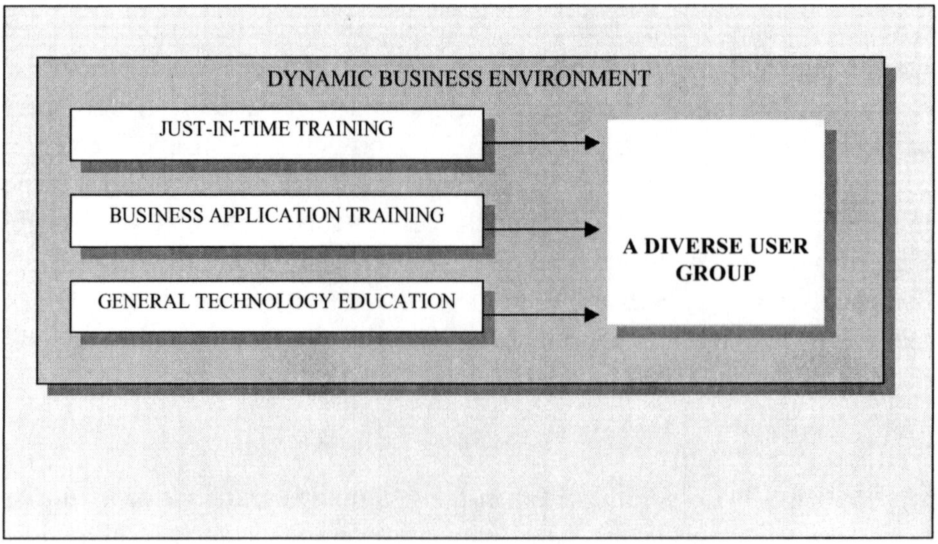

DYNAMIC BUSINESS ENVIRONMENT

JUST-IN-TIME TRAINING

BUSINESS APPLICATION TRAINING

GENERAL TECHNOLOGY EDUCATION

A DIVERSE USER GROUP

despite differences in operating systems and application software. So, businesses will always be able to conduct user training on general technology topics without fear that the knowledge imparted will quickly become obsolete. Using this principle, SVF designed and implemented a general technology education program for its employees. The purpose was to give employees without adequate technology backgrounds an overall understanding of technology and of SVF's technological infrastructure.

General Technology Education thus provides SVF's end users with a fundamental understanding of information technology and its applications. Its focus is to promote better understanding of technology and to foster related skills, although its content is neither application-specific nor task-specific. It emphasizes knowledge and skills that are applicable to a wide range of applications and situations. The objectives of General Technology Education are: to give users a general knowledge base that will permit them to learn more specific technology applications as they progress (Sein et al., 1999); to increase user acceptance of new technology (Lee et al., 1995); to increase users' ability to evaluate technology applications; and to help users apply technology to solve problems.

General Technology Education should be an ongoing activity that is provided in installments to enhance long-term retention, and should take into account changes in user behavior (Baddeley & Longman, 1978; Bahrick, 1979; Melton, 1970). SVF offers a General Technology Education session once a month for new employees or for anyone who needs a refresher. A special session is scheduled if many new employees are hired at the same time.

In their General Technology Education sessions, SVF covers basic concepts of hardware, software, networking protocols, and telecommunication concepts, with primary emphasis on their chosen technology platform. Non-technical topics such as security awareness, file backup requirements and procedures, and government regulations are also prominent. Because the corporation performs so many financial transactions, security awareness and backup procedures are particularly important.

Some employers may not agree with SVF's emphasis on General Technology Education. They may argue that General Technology Education is more correctly the function of educational institutions, and that employees should have obtained such knowledge and skills in high school or college. While this argument may be theoretically correct, the reality is that new graduates often lack sufficient technical knowledge and skills because colleges and universities simply turn out too few graduates with adequate technical skill to meet the demands of the employment market (Alavi et al., 1995). In a tight job market, employers often have few options—to remain competitive and to continue growing, they simply have to shoulder the responsibility of teaching their users the basics. SVF has been hiring employees with non-business backgrounds for some time now because of the difficulty of finding enough workers with the right skill sets.

The audience for General Technology Education is largely made up of end users with non-technical backgrounds. SVF realized that they could obtain basic course content material for their General Technology Education program from one of the many providers of commercially produced education programs. Sources of these instructional materials include traditional academic institutions, college extension programs, professional trainers, CBT programs, Web-based training, video lessons, and other self-guided study materials.

Because General Technology Education is neither task-specific nor application-specific, *where* it is held—in-house or outside—is unimportant. But it must be timed to be completed before application training or JIT Training, because it provides foundational knowledge that students will use in other types of training programs. Because of its importance, General Technology Education should be repeated at intervals to improve retention. At SVF, employees without a technical background are required to take a technology education course when they are hired. Repeat training is encouraged, but not mandated. The company also maintains a library of books, manuals, videotapes, and interactive CD ROMs for the use of its employees.

Due to resource constraints at SVF, the systems manager also serves as General Technology Education instructor. Because this individual has been with SVF for six years and is knowledgeable about both the technical and business operations of the company, there seems to be no significant drawback to his continuing as both systems manager and instructor, except that his workload has increased.

Second Tier: Business Application Training

End users in a complex environment need more than general technical knowledge to work productively. At SVF Corporation, end users need further specific knowledge to adopt and use technology applications that vary widely in their user interfaces, operational procedures, and functions. Due to the rapid advances in technology applications and the changes in business environments, training on special applications has become a constant chore for many organizations, including SVF.

The goal of Business Application Training is to train end users to use a specific application or applications, and to focus on imparting enough depth to give its users a thorough understanding of the application. Besides understanding an application, Business Application Training should explain the logic behind an application's functioning rather than merely providing step-by-step instructions tailored to specific tasks. This in-depth and background-wealthy approach to learning allows the application's users to "think through" and then perform unforeseen tasks without further training. In other words, Business Application Training needs to be application-specific rather than task-specific.

Topics for application training may vary depending on the type of organization doing the training. At SVF, common business applications such as productivity tools, communication tools, and proprietary business applications are the main topics for application training. The contents of an application-training program normally include an overview of the application, its terminology, structures, operations, and functional procedures. Users practice sample tasks during the training session.

The content of application training is specific to a single application, so it should provide knowledge about only that application. To conserve resources (especially user time), SVF employees only receive training on applications that are potentially useful to them. Ideally, the corporation tries to conduct application training *after* general technology education but *before* the use of an application. In actual practice, some new employees do not receive General Technology Education before Business Application Training because of the timing of their hiring, but are able to schedule General Technology Education sometime in the first month. New hires are also provided with instructional videos and independent study guides to make up any deficiency.

Application training should not take place so long before actual use of the application that the employee forgets the instruction and needs to be retrained. Learners should be given the opportunity to apply the knowledge and skills they have gained to the task at hand shortly after training concludes. At SVF, when employees are expected to learn a newly installed application, or when the principal application changes, special training sessions are usually held within a week of the change, except in unusual circumstances.

Depending on which application is being trained, companies may choose to develop the training materials themselves or to purchase packaged training tools. Tutorials, online training, video training tapes, and study guides are available for many popular applications. Professional training services and traditional academic institutions also provide training classes on popular applications. For unusual and custom-designed applications, the cost will be higher because a custom training program will be needed. Due to its relatively small size, SVF Corporation does not maintain an in-house training staff. Instead it hires professional instructors from a consulting company to conduct most of its application training on general office productivity tools. For specialized or proprietary systems, the vendors who developed the systems usually provide the application training. This is another reason why SVF needs to provide general technology education—because application vendors usually cover only knowledge specific to the software applications they sell.

As an adjunct to General Education Training, SVF maintains a library of independent study guides and videotapes on generic office productivity tools, and user manuals for special applications. According to the systems manager at SVF, the manuals for specialized systems are usually not well written and are little help to users who want to train at their own pace; and video and CBT programs are usually superficial in content and offer no feedback method to address users' questions. An instructor is usually required for Business Application Training.

The Third Tier: Just-In-Time (JIT) Technology Training

The purpose of Just-In-Time (JIT) technology training is to provide users with the instructions they need to use a technology application *while* they are actually using the application. Its focus is on task performance, rather than on learning the application. Thus, JIT Training does not emphasize long-term retention of knowledge or skills. Instead, it provides detailed, step-by-step, easy-to-follow instructions that show exactly how to use an application. This type of training is suitable for end users who only need to retain the information long enough to complete a task, or even to complete a single step of a task. Theoretically, end users may or may not need prior application training. When an employee has to use a more complex application, second-tier application training may be needed beforehand to provide foundation knowledge about the application. JIT Training will then provide assistance in performing its more complicated procedures. For simple applications, previous application training may be omitted, and JIT Training will be sufficient. At SVF, the main objective of JIT Training is not to enable employees to use a technology application without previous application training, but to complement application training.

There are several reasons for using JIT Training as an adjunct to regular application training. First, end users may not have had sufficient time to receive application training in anticipation of a new system's adoption or an unexpected system changeover. Like SVF, most businesses do not receive sufficient notice of systems changes from their suppliers. JIT Training, by definition, requires no lead-time before the use of an application; so it is a particularly suitable training method for businesses that operate in a highly competitive or dynamic environment. Second, some services and financial products are infrequently used; so the applications that support them remain unfamiliar to employees. It would be counterproductive and expensive to conduct special training on these applications because end users tend to forget the process because they rarely use it (Baddeley & Longman, 1978; Bahrick, 1979; Melton, 1970). Third, JIT Training, with its step-by-step instructions, can be used in conjunction with application training to help ensure correct use of more complex applications. (This is how SVF uses it.)

The content of JIT Training differs from the content of regular application training in that it is tailored to fit user tasks. Its short, precise, easy-to-follow instructions are similar to the tutorials that come with some packaged software that has been customized to meet the special needs of users, or to help users perform certain tasks.

JIT Training is an ideal training method for some groups of end users. At SVF, JIT Training is available on applications used by account representatives and customer-call operators. It is also suitable for temporary employees who may not have had the opportunity to receive regular application training. However, JIT Training is not appropriate for all applications, particularly analytical applications that require a deeper understanding of the logic behind the operation.

The nature of JIT Training requires that it be conducted on site. Therefore, the training format is normally a computer-based program that can be loaded onto a portable computer or stored on portable media such as a CD-ROM. SVF Corporation provides two types of JIT Training for its users: The first is a small booklet that contains specific steps to follow in handling common tasks. These booklets are available to call operators to help them find the correct information requested by customers. The second type of JIT Training information is loaded on a CD-ROM that account representatives can use with their portable computers. The CD-ROM contains more than 100 step-by-step procedures that help the account representatives answer tax or financial questions using specialized software programs. Users may access these aids through a standard Web browser.

Summary of the Three-Tier Training Strategy

The technology training strategy used by SVF Corporation can be summarized in the following table that shows their scheduling, emphases, trainees, subjects, and training methods.

Qualitative Benefits of the Three-Tier Training Model

Using the three-tier technology training strategy has benefited SVF in several ways: It has helped the corporation to more systematically identify its technology training needs, has made the training program more responsive to changing needs, and has improved the employees' overall understanding of technology and applications.

Table 3: Summary of three-tier training strategy

	SCHEDULING	EMPHASES	TARGET TRAINEES	SUBJECTS AND TOOLS OF TRAINING	TRAINING METHODS	TRAINERS
GENERAL TECHNOLOGY EDUCATION	Ongoing activity, when new employees are hired	General, non-application-specific	Users without technical backgrounds	General technology knowledge, company technology platform	Instructor, manuals, tutorials, videos, books, etc.	System administrator or user managers
BUSINESS APPLICATION TRAINING	Shortly before implementation; hiring of new employees	Application-specific	Users of specific applications	Business applications and proprietary systems provided by wholesalers	Instructor, manuals, tutorials, videos, books, etc.	Vendors, contracted instructors, or consultants
JIT TRAINING	Same time as task performance	Application-specific and task-specific	Call operators, temporary workers, users of complicated applications	Complicated applications, rarely used applications, unanticipated applications, software upgrades	CBT, booklets	None

Systematic Identification of Training Needs: By using the three-tier strategy, SVF can systematically identify training needs for each tier, rather than viewing "Training" as a single, generalized subject. General Technology Education needs are determined by considering the overall competency of employees, the technology platforms currently in use, and new technology development trends. Business Application Training needs are determined based on implementation of the applications used and planned changes in those applications. JIT Training is needed mostly for rarely used or more complicated applications, and is prompted by feedback from the systems support technicians who notice more operator errors. As long as SVF uses this systematic approach to identify its training needs, it is unlikely that it will miss an important subject for training or provide unnecessary training.

Using the strategy also makes it easier to define the scope and content of training. Because training is separated into tiers, users receiving Business Applications Training can focus on learning a specific application without having to repeat the fundamentals. Conversely, General Technology Education can focus on imparting basic technical knowledge without the confusion of getting into specific applications. JIT Training only needs to focus on assisting with detailed procedures and ease of use.

Flexibility and Responsiveness: The three-tier strategy is flexible. First, it facilitates the use of different training methods at different tiers. For General Technology Education and Business Application Training, the method of choice is usually instructor-led sessions in classrooms. For JIT Training, the choices are CBT or booklets. The strategy also allows SVF to react to changes in technology and business objectives quickly, without dramatically modifying its training plans. Roughly speaking, the General Technology Education tier should remain relatively stable over time, and should be modified only to reflect significant changes in the technology platform at SVF. (Changes in application training would be needed only if SVF discarded a major technology application and replaced it with another.) Changes in JIT Training would only be made when the systems support manager permanently modified the training software because user feedback indicated it was necessary.

Saving User Time: The strategy also allows end users to choose training programs that are important to them. For example, users with technology backgrounds do not need to attend General Technology Training; and they only participate in Business Application Training to learn about specific systems. Users who lack basic technical knowledge derive far more benefit more from General Technology Education. Employees who use an application only rarely can still use it to perform tasks correctly with JIT Training support that comes at the moment they need it.

Better-Trained End Users: Although SFV does not have quantitative data to support the improvement they see in user knowledge and productivity; anecdotal evidence shows that users are more knowledgeable about technology than before the training program was implemented. The manager of one branch attributes these successes especially to General Technology Education. She believes that foundation knowledge gives users a better understanding of how technology works, and thus improves users' knowledge of business applications.

Fringe Benefits: Increased technology literacy also helps SVF employees conduct their primary business activity—providing financial services. This has been especially true in recent years because the corporation's clients have grown more sophisticated and now show increased interest in technology stocks. As a result of their General Technology Education at SVF, account representatives and investment advisors are able to more intelligently answer their clients' technology-related questions.

Training Strategies Compared

In this section, the three-tier training model is compared with other training models, and the downside of the strategy is discussed.

The three-tier strategy versus the hierarchical strategy: In a recent article, Sein, Bostrom, and Olfman (1999) proposed a training strategy framework to guide the development and research of end-user training. The framework contains four major components: Types of IT Tools, Types of Trainees, Training Methods, and Levels of Knowledge achieved. They suggest that a variety of users who need to learn a variety of applications may need a variety of types of training to achieve the desired level of software knowledge. (See Table 4.) Additionally, they argue that a training strategy should answer questions such as which users should be trained on which tools and which training methods are better for obtaining what levels of knowledge. In other words, they say a training strategy should be able to match appropriate tools with appropriate users and appropriate methods of training to achieve an appropriate level of knowledge.

The three-tier strategy described in this paper seems to be able to meet some of these criteria—it has already helped SVF Corporation to provide training programs according to applications and users, while allowing different delivery methods at each of the three tiers. However, the three-tier model does not address the six recognized levels of software knowledge shown in the table. It covers only the first four levels, from the command-based to the tool-conceptual level of software knowledge. Further, the three-tier model has not been empirically tested. Thus, the appropriate mix of users, training methods, and training subjects has not been determined.

Table 4: Sein, Bostrom, and Olfman's illustration of the six levels of software knowledge

Knowledge Level	Example
Command-based	Know the keystrokes and mouse movements to delete a sentence
Tool-procedural	Know how to create a table
Business-procedural	Know how to create a form letter to be sent to multiple customers
Tool-conceptual	Know how to use a tool to solve a business problem
Business-motivational	Know what technology tools can do to improve performance
Meta-cognition	Provide learners with the ability to learn well in the future

The three-tier strategy versus the lifecycle model: The lifecycle model of user training starts with the initiation stage, follows with the training stage, and ends with post-training activities (Compeau et al., 1995). In the lifecycle model, although the types of trainees in the program are a factor at each stage, the model focuses mainly on the training process. The three-tier training approach described in this paper focuses on trainees and organizations. With this approach, training starts with providing General Technology Education to new end users to establish a knowledge foundation. Users then receive Business Application Training on selected subjects depending on their existing skill sets, job assignments, and organizational needs. JIT Training is provided whenever they need it to assist them with more complicated procedures or with rarely used applications. (See Figure 2.)

Other strengths and weaknesses: In addition to the qualitative benefits mentioned earlier, the three-tier training method seems an improvement over other approaches because it is practical and workable. Although the method's effectiveness has yet to be tested empirically, it easily gains user acceptance in a dynamic business environment like that of SVF Corporation. From the company's perspective, the three-tier strategy makes sense economically because it provides essential training to users at the right time without wasting either precious training resources or users' time.

Figure 2: The timeline of the three-tier training strategy

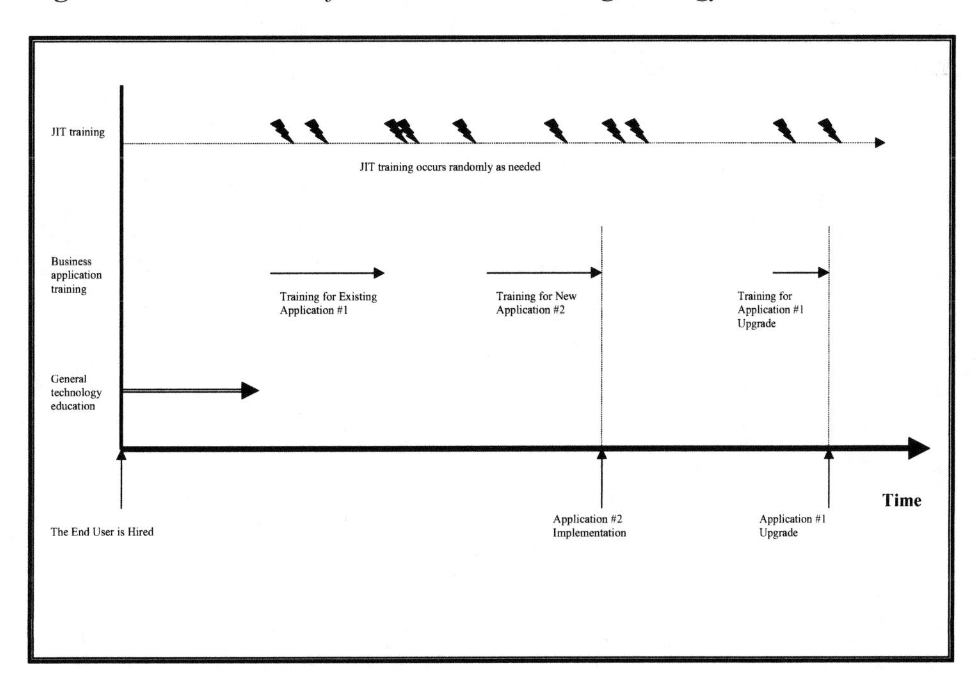

Although SVF Corporation reports no negative outcomes from using the three-tier strategy, the author observes several possible drawbacks. First, the strategy is designed primarily to mold to a dynamic business environment and to avoid overtaxing training resources—thus it may not be the best choice for achieving long-term training outcomes. Second, if communication among those responsible for implementing the three tiers is inadequate, some efforts may be duplicated while other areas may remain unaddressed. Third, users may try to skip General Technology Education if they cannot see an immediate correlation between it and their work; and this attitude, in turn, may reduce their ability to do well in Business Application Training and JIT Training.

CONCLUSION

End-user training has always been and will continue to be important for businesses using computer information systems. Nevertheless, no amount of progress in making information technology user-friendly will dismiss the challenges to providing meaningful end-user training, because the real-world obstacles stated in this paper will remain. Despite an abundance of research on technology training, actual solutions are still rare, so user managers will continue to search for practical and effective training programs to meet the demands of an increasingly dynamic business environment.

This case study of SVF Corporation's training strategy is a valuable lesson for practitioners and academics alike because it shows how companies can adapt to meet end-user needs in such an environment. For practitioners who are searching for workable solutions to their training challenges, it offers a workable real-world model that can be modified for use in their organizations. For academics, the study generates new ideas and opportunities for research. Although the strategy has worked well for this company, it may not be applicable to others. The three-tier training strategy needs more work to transform it from a company-specific approach to a workable strategy usable by other organizations with similar needs. To achieve this, empirical studies in the following areas are suggested:

1. Determine appropriate subjects to be included in General Technology Education.
2. Determine appropriate technology applications to be included in JIT Training.
3. Determine the impact of General Technology Education on the effectiveness of application training.
4. Determine the impact of JIT Training on user task performance.

The results of these studies will validate the three-tier training strategy used at SVF as a general strategy that can help similar organizations to cope with their training challenges. Meanwhile, companies that face challenges similar to those of SVF Corporation may wish to adapt and modify the three-tier strategy to their specific business environments and objectives.

REFERENCES

Alavi, M., Wheeler, B. C., & Valacich, J. S. (1995). Using IT to reengineer business education: An exploratory investigation of collaborative telelearning, *MIS Quarterly, 19*(3), 293–311.

Baddeley, A. D. & Longman, D. J. A. (1978). The influence of length and frequency of training session(s)? On the rate of learning to type, *Ergonomics,* 21, 627–635.

Bahrick, H. P. (1979). Maintenance of knowledge: questions about memory we forgot to ask, *Journal of Experimental Psychology: General,* 108, 627–635.

Becker, G. S. (1992). Human Capital—A Theoretical and Empirical Analysis with Special Reference to Education. Chicago: University of Chicago Press

Bostrom, R. P., Olfman, L., & Sein, M. K. (1990). The importance of learning style(s)? In end-user training. *MIS Quarterly, 14*(1), 101–119.

Compeau, D. R. & Haggins, D. A. (1995) Computer self-efficacy: development of a measure and initial test. *MIS Quarterly, 19*(2), 189-211.

Compeau, D., Olfman, L., Sei, M., & Webster, J. (1995). End-user training and learning. *Communications of the ACM, 38*(7), 24-26.

Davis, S. A. & Bostrom, R. P. (1993). Training end users: an experimental investigation of the role of computer interface and training methods. *MIS Quarterly, 17*(1), 61-85.

Fitzgerald, E. P. & Caster-Steel, A. (1995). Champagne training on a beer budget. *Communications of the ACM, 38*(7), 49–60.

Huang, A. H. (1996-97). Challenges and opportunities of online education. *Journal of Educational Technology Systems, 25*(3), 229–247

Kappelman, L. A. & Guynes, C. S. (1995). End-user training and empowerment, *Journal of Systems Management, 46*(5), 36–41.

Lee, S. M., Kim, Y. R., & Lee, J. (1995). An empirical study of the relationships among end-user information systems acceptance, training, and effectiveness. *Journal of Management Information Systems, 12*(2), 189-202.

Melton, A. W. (1970). The situation with respect to the spacing of repetitions and memory, *Journal of Verbal Learning and Verbal Behavior,* 9, 596–606.

Nelson, R. R., Whitener, E. M., & Philcox, H. H. (1995). The Assessment of end-user training needs. *Communications of the ACM, 38*(7), 27–39.

Olfman, L. & Mandviwalla, M. (1994). Conceptual versus procedural software training for graphical user interfaces: a longitudinal field experiment. *MIS Quarterly, 18*(4), 405-426.

Pitman, B. (1994). How to build a learning culture to cope with rapid change. *Journal of Systems Management*, 27.

Santanam, R. & Sein, M. K. (1994). Improving end user efficiency: effects of conceptual training and nature of interaction. *Information Systems Research, 5*(4), 378-399.

Sein, M. K. & Bostrom, R. P. (1989). Individual differences and conceptual models in training novice users. *Human-Computer Interaction,* 4, 197-229.

Sein, M. K., Bostrom, R. P., & Olfman, L. (1999). Rethinking end-user training strategy: applying a hierarchical knowledge-level model. *Journal of End User Computing, 11*(1), 32-39.

White, C. E. Jr. & Christy, D. P. (1987). The information center concept: A normative model and a study of six installations. *MIS Quarterly, 11*(4), 451–458.

Comprehensive Bibliography

The contents of this bibliography by no means represent an exhaustive list of references in the end user computing area. These, however, provide a cross-section of some of the significant research studies conducted in the areas of organizational commitments toward end user computing, business environments conducive to end user computing, and end user systems. This is true in spite of the fact that most of the research studies listed in the bibliography came from the chapters included in this book. We believe that these references will be immensely helpful to researchers who are interested in conducting research in these areas. We also believe that these references will be helpful to end user managers who are interested in using end user computing technology to help end users accept and understand information technology better.

REFERENCES

Abdul-Gader, A. (1990). End-user computing success factors: Further evidence from a developing nation. *Information Resources Management Journal, 3*(1), 1-13.

Ackerman, M. S. (1994) Augmenting the Organizational Memory: A Field Study of Answer Garden. In R. Furuta & C. Neuwirth, (ed.), *CSCW'94,* New York: ACM Press, 243-252.

Ackerman, M. S. & Palen, L. (1996) The Zephyr Help Instance: Promoting ongoing activity in a CSCW system. In M. J. Tauber et al., (eds.) *The Proceedings of CHI 96,* New York: ACM Press, 268-275.

Agarwal, R. & Prasad, J. (1998) The antecedents and consequents of user perceptions in information technology adoption. *Decision Support Systems, 22,* 15-29.

Agarwal, R. & Prasad, J. (1997). The Role of Innovation Characteristics and Perceived Voluntariness in the Acceptance of Information Technologies, *Decision Sciences 28*(3), 557-582.

Agarwal, R., Prasad, J., & Zanino, M. C. (1996) Training experiences and usage intentions: A field study of a graphical user interface, *International Journal of Human Computer Studies*, *45*(2), 215-241.

Aggarwal, A. K. (1998). End user training - revisited. *Journal of End User Computing, 10*(3), 32-33.

Aggarwal, A. & Mirani, R. (1999). DSS model usage in public and private sectors: Differences and implications. *Journal of End User Computing, 11*(3), 20-28.

Ahmadi, M. & Brabston, M. (1998) MIS Education: Differences in Academic Practice and Business Managers Expectations. *Journal of Computer Information Systems, 38*(2), 18-25.

Ajzen, I. & Fishbein, M. (1980). *Understanding Attitudes and Predicting Social Behavior*. Englewood Cliffs, NJ: Prentice-Hall.

Al-Jabri, I. M. & Al-Khaldi, M. A. (1996). Effects of end user characteristics on computer attitude among undergraduate business students. *Journal of End User Computing, 9*(2), 16-22.

Al-Shawaf, A.-R. H. (1993). *An Investigation of the Design Process for End-user Developed Systems: An Exploratory Field Study.* Unpublished Ph.D., Virginia Commonwealth University.

Alavi, M. & Leidner, D. E. (1999). Knowledge Management Systems: Issues, Challenges, Benefits, *Communications of AIS, 1*(7), 2-41.

Alavi, M., Wheeler, B. C., & Valacich, J. S. (1995). Using IT to Reengineer Business Education: An Exploratory Investigation of Collaborative Telelearning, *MIS Quarterly*, 19(3), 293–311.

Alavi, M., Nelson, R. R., & Weiss, I.R. (1988). Managing End-User Computing as a Value-Added Resource. *Journal of Information Systems Management,* Summer 1988, 26-35.

Amoroso, D. L. (1992). Using end user characteristics to facilitate effective management of end user computing. *Journal of End User Computing, 4* (4), 5-15.

Amoroso, D. & Cheney, P. (1991). Testing a causal model of end-user application Effectiveness. *Journal of MIS,* 8, 63-89.

Amoroso, D. L. & Cheney, P.H. (1991). Testing a causal model of end user application effectiveness. *Journal of Management Information Systems, 8*(1), 63-89.

Amoroso, D. L. (1986). *Effectiveness of End-user Developed Applications in Organizations: An Empirical Investigation.* Unpublished Ph.D., University of Georgia.

Amoroso, D. L. & Cheney, P. H. (1991). Testing a causal model of end-user application effectiveness. *Journal of Management Information Systems, 8*(1), 63-89.

Angle, H. & Perry, J. (1981). An Empirical Assessment of Organizational Commitment and Organizational Effectiveness, *Administrative Science Quarterly*, 26, 1-14.

Antonioni, D. (1998). Relationship between the big five personality factors and conflict management styles. *International Journal of Conflict Management,* 9, 336-355.

Armstrong, J. S. & Overton, T. S. (1977). Estimating nonresponse bias in mail surveys, *Journal of Marketing Research,* (XIV: August), 396-402.

Arvey, R. D. & Hoyle, J. C. (1974) A Guttman approach to the development of behaviorally based rating scales for systems analysts and programmer/analysts. *Journal of Applied Psychology*, *59*(1), 61-68.

Babbitt, T. G., Galletta, D. F., & Lopes, A. B. (1998). Influencing the Success of Spreadsheet Development by Novice Users. *Proceedings of the Nineteenth International Conference on Information Systems*, 319-324.

Baddeley, A. D. & Longman, D. J. A. (1978). The influence of length and frequency of training session(s)? On the rate of learning to type, *Ergonomics,* 21, 627–635.

Bahrick, H. P. (1979). Maintenance of knowledge: questions about memory we forgot to ask, *Journal of Experimental Psychology: General,* 108, 627–635.

Bailey, J. E. & Pearson, S. W. (1983). Development of a Tool for Measuring and Analyzing Computer User Satisfaction, *Management Science, 29*(5), 530-545.

Baker, E., Geirland, J., Fisher, T., & Chandler, A. (1999) Media Production: Towards Creative Collaboration Using Communication Networks. *Computer Supported Cooperative Work,* 8, 303-332.

Bandura, A. (1986). *Social Foundation of Thought and Action: A Social Cognitive Theory*, New Jersey: Prentice-Hall.

Bandura, A. (1982). Self-efficacy mechanism in human agency. *American Psychologist,* 37, 122-147.

Bandura, A. (1977). *Social Learning Theory*. Englewoods, NJ: Prentice-Hall.

Bandura, A. (1982). Self-Efficacy Mechanism in Human Agency, *American Psychologist,* 37, 122-147.

Bardram, J. E. (1997) I Love the System - I Just Don't Use It. In S. C. Hayne & W. Prinz, (eds.), *Proceedings of Group '97,* New York: ACM Press, 251-260.

Barker, V. & O'Connor, D.E. (1989). Expert Systems for Configuration at Digital: XCON and Beyond. *Communications of the ACM, 32*(3), 298-318.

Barrick, M. R. & Mount, M. K. (In press). Select on conscientiousness and emotional stability. Chapter to appear in E. A. Locke (ed.), *Basic Principles of Organizational Behavior: A Handbook.* Blackwell Publishers.

Barrick, M. R. & Mount, M. K. (1993). Autonomy as a moderator of the relationship between the Big Five personality dimensions and job performance. *Journal of Applied Psychology,* 78, 111-118.

Barrick, M. R. & Mount, M. K. (1991). The Big Five personality dimensions and job performance: A meta-analysis. *Personnel Psychology,* 44, 1-26.

Barrick, M. R., Mount, M. K., & Judge, T. A. (In press). The FFM personality dimensions and job performance: Meta-Analysis of meta-analyses. Invited submission to a special "selection" issue of *International Journal of Selection and Assessment.*

Baster, G., Konana, P., & Scott, J.E. (2001). Business Components: A Case Study of Bankers Australia Limited Trust. *Communications of the ACM, 44*(5), 92-98.

Becker, G. S. (1992). *Human Capital—A Theoretical and Empirical Analysis with Special Reference to Education.* Chicago: University of Chicago Press

Behshtian, M. & VanWert, P.D.(1987). Strategies for Managing User Developed Systems. *Information and Management,* 12, 1-7.

Bell, L. G., Wicklund, R. A., Manko, G. & Larkin, C. (1976). When Unexpected Behavior Is Attributed to the Environment. *Journal of Research in Personality,* 10, 316-327.

Benham, H., Delaney, M., & Luzi, A. (1993). Structured techniques for successful end user spreadsheets. *Journal of End User Computing* (Spring), 18-25.

Bentley, R., Hughes, J. A., Randall, D., Rodden, T., Sawyer, P., Shapiro, D. & Sommerville, I. (1992) Ethnographically-informed systems design for air traffic control. In (ed.), *Proceedings of the ACM Conference on Computer Supported Cooperative Work (CSCW'92),* Toronto, Ontario: ACM Press, 123-129.

Bento, A. M. (1994) Systems Analysis: A decision approach. *Information and Management,.27*(3), 185-194

Bergeron, F. & Berube, C. (1990). End users talk computer policy. *Journal of Systems Management* (December), 14-16, 32.

Bergeron, F. & Berube, C. (1988). The management of the end-user environment: An empirical investigation. *Information & Management,* 14, 107-113.

Bergeron, F. & Berube, C. (1988). The management of the end-user environment: An empirical investigation. *Information & Management,* 14, 107-113.

Bergeron F. & Raymond L. (1992). Planning of Information Systems to Gain a Competitive Edge, *Journal of Small Business Management, 30*(1), 21-26.

Bikson, T. K. & Eveland, J. D. (1996) Groupware Implementation: Reinvention in the Sociotechnical Frame. In M. S. Ackerman, (ed.), *Proceedings of CSCW '96,* New York: ACM Press, 428-437.

Billings, R. & Wroten, S. (1978). Use of path analysis in industrial/organizational psychology: Criticisms and suggestions. *Journal of Applied Psychology,* 63, 677-688.

Blackler, F. & Brown, C. (1985). Evaluation and the Impact of Information Technologies on People in Organizations, *Human Relations, 38*(3), 213-231.

Blank, M. M. & Barratt, D. (1988) Finding and selecting systems analyst and designers. *Journal of Systems Management, 39*(3), 8-11.

Blegen, M. A. (1993). Nurses' Job Satisfaction: a Meta-Analysis of Related Variables, *Nursing Research, 42*(1), 36-41.

Blili, S., Raymond, L., & Rivard, S. (1998). Impact of Task Uncertainty, End-User Involvement and Competence on the Success of End-User Computing. *Information and Management*, 33, 137-153.

Blili, S., Raymond, L., & Rivard, S. (1996). Definition and Measurement of End User Computing Sophistication. *Journal of End User Computing, 8*(2), 3-10.

Bloom, A. J. & Hautaluoma, J. E. (1990). Anxiety management training as a strategy for enhancing computer user performance. *Computers in Human Behavior*, 6, 337-349.

Bluestone, I. (1983). The Human Factor: Some Effects of the Computer Revolution on Labor, *Computers and People,* 32, 12-14.

Blythin, S., Hughes, J. A., Kristoffersen, S., Rodden, T., & Rouncefield, M. (1997) Recognising 'success' and 'failure': evaluating groupware in a commercial context. In S. C. Hayne & W. Prinz, (eds.), *Proceedings of Group '97,* New York: ACM Press, 39-46.

Bock, D. B. & Joyner, E. R. (1992) Combining Socio-Technical Analysis with Participative Information Systems Design: A research case. *The Journal of Computer Information Systems*, *32*(3), 60-66.

Bohlen, G. R. & Ferratt, T. W. (1997). End user training: An experimental comparison of lecture versus computer-based training. *Journal of End User Computing, 9* (3), 14-27.

Boland, R. (1978) The process and product of system design, *Management Science*, *24*(9), 887-898.

Bostrom, R. P., Olfman, L., & Sein, M. K. (1990). The importance of learning style in end user computing. *MIS Quarterly, 14*(1), 100-119.

Bowers, J. (1994) The Work to Make a Network Work: Studying CSCW in Action. In R. Furuta & C. Neuwirth, (eds.), *Proceedings of CSCW'94,* New York: ACM Press, 287-298.

Bowman, B. J., Grupe, F. H., & Simkin, M. G. (1995). Teaching end user applications with computer-based training: Theory and an empirical investigation. *Journal of End User Computing, 7*(2), 12-18.

Brancheau, J. C. & Brown, C. V. (1993). The management of end-user computing: Status and directions. *ACM Computing Surveys, 25*(4), 450-482.

Bretschneider, S. & Wittmer, D. (1993). Organizational adoption of microcomputer technology: The role of sector. *Information Systems Research,* 4, 88-108.

Briggs, R. O., Balthazard, P. A., & Dennis, A. R. (1996). Graduate business students as surrogates for executives in the evaluation of technology. *Journal of End User Computing, 8*(4), 11-17.

Brown, M. E. (1969). Identification and Some Conditions of Organizational Involvement, *Administrative Science Quarterly,* 14, 346-355.

Brown, K. A. (1984). Explaining group poor performance: An attributional analysis. *Academy of Management Review, 9*(1), 54-63.

Brown, A. D. & Jones, M. R. (1998). Doomed to failure: Narratives of inevitability and conspiracy in a failed IS project. *Organization Studies, 9*(1), 73-88.

Brown, P. S. & Gould, J. D. (1987). An experimental study of people creating spreadsheets, *ACM Transaction on Office Information Systems 5,* 258-272.

Buchanan, D. A. & Bessant, J. (1985). Failure, uncertainty, and control: The role of operators in a computer integrated production system. *Journal of Management Studies,* 22, 292-308.

Butcher, J. N., & Rouse, S. V. (1996). Personality: Individual differences and clinical assessments. *Annual Review of Psychology,* 47, 87-111.

Bureau of Labor Statistics (2000) *Occupational Outlook Handbook*, 2000-2001 Edition, pp. 109-113 (see the web at URL: http://stats.bls.gov/oco/ocos042.htm).

Burn, J., Marshall, P., & Wild, M. (1999). Managing Knowledge for Strategic

Advantage in the Virtual Organisation. *Proceedings of the 1999 ACM SIGCPR Conference on Computer Personnel Research,* 19-26.

Byrd, T. & Marshall, T. (1997). Relating information technology investment to organizational performance: A causal model analysis. *Omega,* 25, 43-56.

Byrd, T. A., Sambamurthy, V., & Zmud, R. W. (1995). An Examination of IT Planning in a Large Diversified Public Organization, *Decision Sciences, 26*(1), 49-73.

Cabrales, E. J. & Eddy, J. P. (1992) Informatics education in Columbia: a study of the present situation and recommendations for the future. *Journal of Information Science, 18*(3), 217-224.

Cale, E. G. (1994). Quality issues for end-user developed software. *Journal of Systems Management* (January), 36-39.

Carey, J. M. (1992). Job satisfaction and visual display unit (VDU) usage: An explanatory model, *Behaviour & Information Technology, 11*(6), 338-344.

Carey, J. M. & McLeod, R. (1988) Use of system development methodology and tools. *Journal of Systems Management, 39*(3), 30-35.

Chan, Y. E. & Storey, V. C. (1996). The use of spreadsheets in organizations: Determinants and consequences. *Information & Management, 31*, 119-134.

Cheney, P. Mann, R., & Amoroso, D. (1986). Organizational factors affecting the success of end-user computing. *Journal of MIS,* 3, 65-80.

Cheney, P. H., Mann, R. I., & Amoroso, D. L. (1986). Organizational factors affecting the success of end-user computing. *Journal of Management Information Systems*, 3, 65-80.

Cheney, P. H., Mann, R. I., & Amoroso, D. L. (1986). Organizational Factors Affecting the Success of End-user Computing, *Journal of Management Information Systems, 3*(1), 65-80.

Churchill, E. F. & Bly, S. (1999) It's all in the words: Supporting work activities with lightweight tools. In S. Payne (ed..) *Proceedings of Group '99*, New York: ACM Press, 40-49.

Ciborra, C. (1994). The Grassroots of IT and Strategy. In *Strategic Information Systems: A European Perspective*, (eds.) Ciborra, C & Jelassi, T. New York: John Wiley, 3-24.

Clement, A. (1994) Considering Privacy in the Development of Multi-media Communications, *Computer Supported Cooperative Work*, 2, 67-88.

Coenen, F. & Bench-Capon, T. (1993). *Maintenance of Knowledge-Based Systems.* London: Academic Press.

Cohen, J. & Cohen, P. (1983). *Applied multiple regression/correlation analysis for the behavioral sciences*. Hillsdale, NJ: Lawrence Erlbaum Associates.

Colbert, A. E. & Kwon, I. G. (2000). The Factors Related to the Organizational Commitment of College and University Auditors, *Journal of Managerial Issues, 12*(4), 484-492.

Colville, I. D., Waterman, R. H., & Weick, K. E. (1999). Organizing and the search for excellence: Making sense of times in theory and practice. *Organization, 6*(1), 129-148.

Compeau, D. R. & Higgins, C. A. (1995). Application of social cognitive theory to training for computer skills. *Information Systems Research, 6*(2), 118-143.

Compeau, D. R. & Haggins, D. A. (1995) Computer self-efficacy: development of a measure and initial test. *MIS Qaurterly*, *19*(2), 189-211.

Compeau, D., Olfman, L., Sei, M., & Webster, J. (1995) End-user training and learning. *Communications of the ACM*, *38*(7), 24-26.

Concord Communications (1999). Concord Network Rage Survey. [Online] Available: http://www.concord.com/library/network_rage/ [Aug.16].

Cook, J. & Wall, T. D. (1980). New Work Attitude Measures of Trust, Organizational Commitment, and Personal Need Non-Fulfillment, *Journal of Occupational Psychology*, 53, 39-52.

Cook, S. & Selltiz, C (1970). A multiple-indicator approach to attitude measurement. In Summers, G. F. (ed.), *Attitude Measurement*. Chicago: Rand McNally and Company, 1-5.

Cook, T. D. & Campbell, D. T. (1979). *Quasi-Experimentation*. Boston, MA: Houghton Mifflin Company. 28-30.

Cooley, P. L., Walz, D. T., & Walz D. B. (1987). A Research Agenda for Computers and Small Business, *American Journal of Small Business*, 31-42.

Cooper, R. B. & Zmud, R. W. (1990). Information Technology Implementation Research: A Technology Diffusion Approach, *Management Science*, *36*(2), 123-139.

Costa, P. T. & McCrae, R. R. (1988). From catalog to classification: Murray's needs and the Five-Factor Model. *Journal of Personality and Social Psychology,* 55, 285-265.

Costa, P. T., McCrae, R. R., & Holland, J. L. (1984). Personality and vocational interests in an adult sample. *Journal of Applied Psychology,* 69, 390-400.

Cotter, R. V., & Fritzche, D. J. (1995). *The Business Policy Game*. Englewood Cliffs, NJ: Prentice-Hall.

Couger, J. D. (1995). *Creative Problem Solving and Opportunity Finding*, Melbourne, Australia: Boyd and Fraser Publishing Company.

Couger, J. D., Davis, G. B., Dologite, D. G., Feinstein, D. L., Gorgone, J. T., Jenkins, A. M., Kasper, G. M., Little, J. C., Longenecker, H. E., & Valacich, J. S. (1995) IS 95: Guideline for undergraduate IS curriculum. *MIS Quarterly*, *19*(3), 341-359.

Counte, M. A., Kjerulff, K. H., Salloway, J. C., & Campbell, B. (1985). Implementing computerization in hospitals: A case study of the behavioral and attitudinal impacts of a medical information system, *Journal of Organizational Behavior Management,* 6, 109-122.

Cousins, P. (1981). Closing the gap between technology and the people who use IT, *Training and Development Journal*, 10, 45-52.

Cragg, P. B. & King, M. (1993). Small-firm computing: Motivators and inhibitors, *MIS Quarterly, 17*(1), 47-60.

Cragg, P. G. & King, M. (1993). Spreadsheet modelling abuse: An opportunity for OR? *Journal of the Operational Research Society, 44*(8), 743-752.

Crawford, J. B. (1986). *An Investigation of Strategies for Supporting and Controlling User Development of Computer Applications.* Unpublished Ph.D., University of California, Irvine.

Crosby, P. (1984) *Quality without Tears: The Art of Hassle Free Management.* New York: McGraw-Hill.

Czara, S. J., Hammond, K., Blascovich, J. J., & Swede, H. (1989). Age related differences in learning to use a text-editing system. *Behavior and Information Technology*, *8*(4), 309-319.

Dambrot, F. H., Silling, S. M., & Zook, A. (1988). Psychology of computer use: Sex differences in prediction of course grades in a computer language course. *Perceptual and Motor Skills*, 66, 627-636.

Date, C. J. (1990). *An Introduction to Database Systems* (5th edition). Reading: Addison-Wesley.

Davenport, T. H. (1994). Saving IT's soul: Human centered information management. *Harvard Business Review,* March-April 1994, 119 - 131.

Davenport, T. H., Long, D. W. D., & Beers, M. C. (1998). Successful Knowledge Management Projects, *Sloan Management Review*, Winter, 43-57.

Davenport, T. H. & Marchand, D. A. (1999). Is KM Just Good Information Management? *Financial Times*, March 3, 2-3.

Davies, N. & Ikin, C. (1987). Auditing Spreadsheets. *Australian Accountant,* 54-56.

Davis, F. D. (1989) Perceived usefulness, perceived ease of use, and user acceptance of information technology, *MIS Quarterly*, *13*(3), 319-340.

Davis, S. A. & Bostrom, R. P. (1993) Training end users: An experimental investigation of the role of computer interface and training methods. *MIS Quaretrly, 17*(1), 61-85.

Davis, B. L., Skube, C. J., Hellervik, L. W., Gebelein, S. H., & Sheard, J. L. (1992). *Successful Manager's Handbook.* Minneapolis: Personnel Decisions, Inc.

Davis, D. L. & Davis, D. F. (1990). The effect of training technique and personal characteristics on training end users of information systems. *Journal of Management Information Systems,* 7, 93-110.

Davis, F. D., Bagozzi, R. P., & Warshaw, P. R. (1989). User acceptance of computer technology: A comparison of two theoretical models. *Management Science,* 35, 982-1003.

DeLone, W. & McLean, E. (1992). Information systems success: The quest for dependent variable. *Information Systems Research,* 3, 60-95.

Delone, W. H. (1988). Determinants of Success for Computer Usage in Small Business, *MIS Quarterly, 12*(1), 51-61.

DeRaad, B. & Doddema-Winsemius, M. (1999). Instincts and personality. *Personality and Individual Differences,* 27, 293-305.

Devargas, M. (1989). *Introducing the Information Center.* NCC Blackwell.

Digman, J. M. (1990). Personality structure: Emergence of the Five Factor Model. *Annual Review of Psychology,* 41, 417-440.

Digman, J. M. & Takemoto-Chock, N. K. (1981). Factors in the natural language of personality: Re-analysis, comparison and interpretation of six major studies. *Multivariate Behavioral Research,* 16, 149-170.

Doke, E. R. (1999) Knowledge and skill requirements for information systems professionals: An exploratory study. *Journal of Information Systems Education, 10*(1), 10-18.

Doll, W. J., & Torkzadeh, G. (1989). A discrepancy model of end-user computing involvement. *Management Science, 35*(10), 1151-1171.

Doll, W. & Torkzadeh, G. (1988). The measurement of end-user computing satisfaction. *MIS Quarterly,* 12, 259-274.

Doll, W. & Weidong, X. (1997). Confirmatory factor analysis of the end-user computing satisfaction instrument: A replication. *Journal of End User Computing, 9*(2), 24-31.

Dologite, D, Mockler, R. J., Ragusa, J. M., Lobert, B., & Banavara, N. (1994). Is There a Successful Knowledge-Based System Developer Profile? *Heuristics, 15*(2), 73-83.

Doukidis, G. I., Smithson, S., & Lybereas, T. (1994). Trends in Information

Technology in Small Businesses, *Journal of End User Computing*, *6*(4), 15-25.

Duncan, O. (1966). Path analysis: Sociological examples. *American Journal of Sociology,* 72, 1-16.

Dunn, W. S., Mount, M. K., Barrick, M. R., & Ones, D. S. (1995). Relative importance of personality and general mental ability in managers' judgements of applicant qualifications. *Journal of Applied Psychology,* 80, 500-509.

Edberg, D. T. & Bowman, B. J. (1996). User-developed applications: An empirical study of application quality and developer productivity. *Journal of Management Information Systems, 13*(1), 167-185.

Eisenhardt, K. M. (1989). Building Theories from Case Study Research, *Academy of Management Review*, *14*(4), 532-550.

Etezadi-Amoli, J. & Farhoomand, A. F. (1996). A structural model of end user computing satisfaction and user performance. *Information & Management,*30, 65-73.

Evans, G. E. & Simkin, M. G. (1989). What best predicts computer proficiency? *Communications of the ACM, 32*(1), 1322-1327.

Eveland, J. D., Blanchard, A., Brown, W., & Mattocks, J. (1994) The Role of "Help Networks" in Facilitating Use of CSCW Tools. In R. Furuta & C. Neuwirth, (eds.) *CSCW'94,* New York: ACM Press, 265-274.

Eyob, E. (1995). Managing the Motivation of Information Technology Staff for Higher Organizational Productivity and Employee Job Satisfaction, *Journal of International Information Management, 3*(1), 27-33.

Fahy, M. & Murphy, C. (1996). From End-User Computing to Management Developed Systems. Proceedings of the *4th European Conference on Information Systems*, Ed, Coelho, J.D., Jelassi, T., Konig, W., Krcmar, H., & O'Callaghan, R., 127 - 142.

Farewell, D. W., Kuramato, L., Lee, D., Trauth, E. M., & Winslow, C. A. (1992) New paradigm for IS: The educational implications. *Information Systems Management*, *9*(2), 7-14.

Feigenbaum, E., McCorduck, P., & Nii, H.P. (1988). *The Rise of the Expert Company*. New York: Times Books.

Finley, M. (1996). What's your techno type – and why you should care? *Personnel Journal*, January, 107-109.

Fiske, D. W. (1949). Consistency in the factorial structures of personality ratings from different sources. *Journal of Abnormal and Social Psychology,* 44, 329-344.

Fitzgerald, E. P. & Caster-Steel, A. (1995) Champagne training on a beer budget. *Communications of the ACM*, 38(7), 49–60.

Fleck, R. A. (1989) Analyzing the analyst. *Journal of Systems Management, 40*(11), 7-9.

Ford, J. K., Quinones, M., Sego., & Speer, J. (1991). Factors affecting the opportunity to use trained skills on the job. Paper presented at the *Annual Conference of the Society of Industrial and Organizational Psychology,* St. Louis, Missouri.

Fornell, C. & Larcker, D. F. (1981). Evaluating structural equation models with unobservable variables and measurement error. *Journal of Marketing Research*, (XVIII), 39-50.

Fowler, J. (1999). Understanding IT: A perspective. *Target Marketing,* 22, 68-71.

Francioni, J. M. & Kandel, A. (1988). A software engineering tool for expert system design. *IEEE Expert*, 33-41.

Gaines, B. R. (1987). An overview of knowledge-acquisition and transfer. *International Journal of Man-Machine Studies,* 26, 453-472.

Gaines, B. R. & Shaw, M. L.G. (1999) Embedding formal knowledge in active documents. *Communications of the ACM, 42*(1), 57-63.

Gallagher J. P. (1988) *Knowledge Systems for Business*. Englewood Cliffs, NJ: Prentice Hall.

Galletta, D. F., Abraham, D., El Louadi, M., Lekse, W., Pollailis, Y. A., & Sampler, J. L. (1993). An Empirical Study of Spreadsheet Error-Finding Performance. *Journal of Accounting, Management, and Information Technology, 3*(2) April-June 1993, pp. 79-95.

Galletta, D. F., Hartzel, K. S., Johnson, S. E., Joseph, J. L., & Rustagi, S. (1997). Spreadsheet presentation and error detection: An experimental study. *Journal of MIS 13*(3), 45-63.

Galliers, R. D., Merali, Y. & Spearing, L. (1994). Coping with information technology? How British executives perceive the key information systems management issues in the mid-1990s. *Journal of Information Technology, 9*(3), 223-238.

Gatewood, R. D. & Field, H. S. (1998). *Human Resource Selection* (4th edition). Fort Worth, Texas: The Dryden Press.

Gelderman, M. (1998). The relation between user satisfaction, usage of information systems and performance. *Information & Management,* 34, 11-18.

Georgantzas, N. C. & Acar, W. (1995). *Scenario-Driven Planning: Learning to Manage Strategic Uncertainty*. Quorum Books.

George, J. (1992). The role of personality in organizational life: Issues and evidence. *Journal of Management,* 2, 185-213.

Gibson, R. & McDonough, M. (1996). A comparison of foreign government computing policies. *Journal of End User Computing, 8*(3), 3-9.

Gill, T. G. & Hu, Q. (1999) The evolving undergraduate information systems education: A survey of US institutions. *Journal of Education for Business, 74*(5), 289-295.

Gist, M. E., Schwoerer, C. E., & Rosen, B. (1989). Effects of alternative training methods on self-efficacy and performance in computer software training. *Journal of Applied Psychology*, 74, 884-891.

Glass, C. R. & Knight, L. A. (1988). Cognitive factors in computer anxiety, *Cognitive Therapy and Research,* 12, 351-366.

Goldberg, L. R. (1992). The development of markers for the Big Five factor structure. *Psychological Assessment,* 4, 26-42.

Goodhue, D. (1988). IS attitudes: Toward theoretical and definition clarity. *Data Base,* 19(3/4), 6-15.

Goodhue, D. (1995). Understanding user evaluations of information systems. *Management Science, 41*(12), 1827-1844.

Goodhue, D. (1988). I/S attitudes: Toward theoretical and definitional clarity. *Data Base,* Fall/Winter, 6-15.

Govindarajulu, C. & Reithel, B.J. (1998). Beyond the information center: An instrument to measure end-user computing support from multiple sources. *Information and Management*, 33, 241-250.

Govindarajulu, C. (1998). The status of end-user computing support: An empirical study. *Proceedings of the 1998 IRMA International Conference*, pp. 376-381.

Govindarajulu, C. & Crews, R. (1997). End-user computing support and user attitudes: An empirical study. *Proceedings of the 28th Annual Meeting of the DSI*, pp. 720-725.

Granger, M. & Lippert, S. (1998). Preparing future technology users. *Journal of End User Computing, 10*(3), 27-31.

Green, G. I. (1989) Perceived importance of systems analysts job skills, roles, and non-salary incentives. *MIS Quarterly, 13*(2), 115-133.

Green, S. & Mitchell, T. R. (1979). Attributional Processes of Leaders in Leader-Member Interactions. Organizational Behavior and Human Performance, 23, 429-458.

Greenberg, S. & Rounding, M. (2001) The Notification Collage: Posting Information to Public and Personal Displays. In J. A. Jacko, A. Sears, M. Beaudouin-Lafon & R. J. K. Jacob (eds.) *Proceedings of CHI 2001*. New York: ACM Press, 514-521.

Greenhaus, J. H. & Pasuraman, S. (1993). Job Performance and Career Advancement Prospects: An Examination of Gender and Race Effects. *Organizational Behavior and Human Decision Processes,* 55, 273-297.

Griesser, J. & Tubalkain, T. (1992). Building a Distributed Expert System Capability. In Turban, E. & Liebowitz, J. (eds.) *Managing Expert Systems.* Hershey, PA: Idea Group Publishing.

Grinter, E. (2000) Workflow systems: Occasions for success and failure. *Computer Supported Cooperative Work,* 9, 189-214.

Grinter, R. E. (1997a) Doing software development: Occasions for automation and formalisation. In J. A. Hughes *et al.*, (eds.) *ECSCW'97 - Proceedings of The Fifth European Conference on Computer Supported Cooperative Work,* Dordrecht, Kluwer, 173-187.

Grinter, R. E. (1997b) From workplace to development: What have we learned so far and where do we go. In S. C. Hayne & W. Prinz, (eds.) *Proceedings of Group'97,* New York: ACM Press, 231-240.

Grudin, J. (1994) Groupware and social dynamics: Eight challenges for developers. *Communications of the ACM* 37, 93-105.

Grudin, J. (1988) Why CSCW applications fail: Problems in the design and evaluation of organization interfaces. In *Proceedings of CSCW '88,* New York: ACM Press.

Grudin, J. & Palen, L. (1995) Why groupware succeeds: Discretion or mandate. In H. Marmolin, Y. Sundblat & K. Schmidt, (eds.) *Proceedings of ECSCW'95,* Dordrecht, Kluwer, 263-278.

Grudin, J. & Poltrock, S. E. (1997). Computer-supported cooperative work and groupware. In M. V. Zelkowitz, (ed.) *Advances in Computing.* New York: Academic Press, 269-320.

Guimaraes, T., Yoon, Y., & Clevenson, A. (1996). Factors important to expert systems success: A field test. *Information & Management,* 30, 119-130.

Guion, R. (1998). Some virtues of dissatisfaction in the science and practice of personnel selection. *Human Resource Management Review,* 8, 351-365.

Gunton, T. (1988). *End User Focus.* Prentice Hall.

Gupta, J. N. D. & Seeborg, I. S. (1989) The graduate MIS course in the schools and colleges of business. *Journal of Management Information Systems,* *5*(4), 125-136.

Gupta, J. N. D. & Wachter, R. M., (1998) A capstone course in the information system Curriculum. *International Journal of Information Management,* *18*(6), 427-441.

Gupta, J. N. D, Wang, P., & Ravichandran, R. (1994) An assessment of the information systems needs in Taiwan. *International Journal of Information Management, 14*(5), 369-384.

Haas, D. F., (1992) Teaching the structured design of interactive information systems. *IEEE Transactions on Education. 31*(4), 278-284.

Hackney, R. & McBride, N. K. (1995). The efficacy of information systems in the public sector: Issues of context and culture. *International Journal of Public Sector Management, 8*(6), 17 - 29.

Hair, J. F., Anderson, R. E., Tatham, R. L., & Black, W. C. (1992). *Multivariate Data Analysis with Readings* (3rd edition). New York: MacMillian Publishing Company.

Hair, J. F. Jr., Anderson, R. E., Tatham, R. L., & Black, W. C. (1992). *Multivariate Data Analysis with Readings*, third edition. New York: Macmillan Publishing Company.

Harper, R. H. R. (1996) Why People Do and Don't Wear Active Badges: A Case Study, *Computer Supported Cooperative Work*, 4, 297-318.

Harper, R. H. R. & Carter, K. (1994) Keeping People Apart, *Computer Supported Cooperative Work*, 2, 199-207.

Harrington, K. V., McElroy, J. C., & Morrow, P. C. (1990). Computer anxiety and computer based training: A laboratory experiment. *Journal of Educational Computing Research, 6* (3), 343-358.

Harrison, A.W. & Rainer, R.K. (1992). The influence of individual differences on skill in end user computing. *Journal of Management Information Systems, 9* (1), 93-111.

Harrison, D. A., Mykytyn, P. P., & Riememschneider, C. K. (1997). Executive Decisions about Adoption of Information Technology in Small Business: Theory and Empirical Tests, *Information Systems Research, 8*(2), 171-195.

Harrison, P. D., West, S. G. & Reneau, J. H. (1988). Initial Attributions and Information Seeking by Superiors and Subordinates in Production Variance Investigations. *Accounting Review, 63*(2), 307-320.

Hatcher, L., Prus, J. S., Englehard, B., & Farmer, T. M. (1991). A measure of academic situational constraints: Out-of-class circumstances that inhibit college student development. *Educational and Psychological Measurement,* 51, 953-962.

Havill, V. L., Besevegis, E., & Mouroussaki, S. (1998). Agreeableness as a diachronic personality trait. In G. A. Kohnstamm & C. F. Halverson, Jr. (eds.), *Parental Descriptions of Child Personality: Developmental Antecedents of the Big 5*. The LEA series in personality and child psychology (pp. 49-64). Mahwah, NJ: Lawrence Earlbaum.

Hawk, S. R. & Aldag, R. J. (1990). Measurement Biases in User Involvement Research.OMEGA, *International Journal of Management Science, 18*(6), 605-613.

Hayek, L.M. & Stephens, L. (1989). Factors affecting computer anxiety in high school computer science students. Journal of Computers in Mathematics and Science Teaching, 8, 73-76.

Hayes-Roth, F., Waterman, D.A., & Lenat, D. (1983). *Building Expert Systems*. Reading: Addison-Wesley.

Hebert, M. & Benbasat, I. (1994) Adopting information technology in hospitals: The relationships between attitudes/expectations and behavior, *Hospital and Health Services Administration, 39*(3), 369-383.

Heider, F. (1958). *The Psychology of Interpersonal Relations.* New York:.John Wiley & Sons

Heneman, H. G., Judge, T. A., & Heneman, R. L. (2000). *Staffing Organizations*. Boston: Irwin McGraw-Hill.

Henry, J. W. & Stone, R. W. (1999). End-user perceptions of the impacts of computer self-efficacy and outcome expectancy on job performance and patient care when using a medical information system, *International Journal of Healthcare Technology Management,* 1, 103-124.

Henry, J. W. & Martinko, M. J. (1997). An attributional analysis of the rejection of information technology. *Journal of End User Computing,* Fall, 3-17.

Henry, J. W. & Stone, R. W. (1995). A structural equation model of job performance using a computer-based order entry system, *Behaviour and Information Technology, 14*(3), 163-173.

Henry, J. W. & Stone, R. W. (1994). A structural equation model of end-user satisfaction with a computer-based medical information system, *Information Resources Management Journal, 7*(3), 21-33.

Hepsø, V. (1997) The social construction and visualiation of a new Norweigan offshore installation. In J. A. Hughes *et al.*, (eds.), *ECSCW'97 - Proceedings of The Fifth European Conference on Computer Supported Cooperative Work,* Dordrecht, Kluwer, 109-124.

Herbert, F. J. & Bradley, J. H. (1993). Expert systems development in small business: A managerial perspective, *Journal of Small Business Management, 31*(3), 23-34.

Herik, K. W. v. d. & Vreede, G.-J. d. (1997) GSS for cooperative policymaking: No trivial matter. In S. C. Hayne & W. Prinz, (eds.) *Proceedings of Group'97,* New York: ACM Press, 148-157.

Hewstone, M. (1989). *Causal Attribution*. Cambridge: Basil Blackwell Inc.

Hicks, R. C. (1994-95). Deriving appropriate rule modules for rule-based expert systems. *Journal of Computer Information Systems,* 20-25.

Hiltz, S. & Johnson, K. (1990). User satisfaction with computer-mediated communication systems. *Management Science,* 36, 739-764.

Hindus, D., Ackerman, M. A., Mainwaring, S., & Starr, B. (1996) Thunderwire: A field study of and audio-only media space. In M. S. Ackerman, (ed.) *Proceedings of CSCW '96,* New York: ACM Press, 238-247.

Hogan, R. T. & Briggs, S. R. (1984). Noncognitive measures of social intelligence. *Personnel Selection & Training Bulletin*, 5, 184-190.

Holsapple, C. W. & Raj, V.S. (1994). An exploratory study of two KA methods. *Expert Systems, 11*(2), 77-87.

House, R., Shane, S., & Herold, D. (1996). Rumors of the death of dispositional research are vastly exaggerated. *Academy of Management Review*, 21, 203-224.

Huang, A. H. (1996-97) Challenges and opportunities of online education. *Journal of Educational Technology Systems, 25*(3), 229–247

Hughes, C.T. & Gibson, M.L. (1987). An attribution model of decision support systems (DSS) Usage. *Information and Management,* 13, 119-124.

Hunter, J. E. (1989). *The Wonderlic Personnel Test as a Predictor of Training Success and Job Performance*. E. F. Wonderlic Personnel Test, Inc.

Hunter, J. E. (1983). A causal model of cognitive ability, job knowledge, job performance, and supervisor ratings. In F. Landy, S. Zedeck, & J. Cleveland (eds.) *Performance Measurement and Theory* (pp. 257-266). Hillsdale, NJ: Lawrence Erlbaum.

Hunter, J. E. & Hunter, R. F. (1984). Validity and utility of alternative predictors of job performance. *Psychological Bulletin, 96,* 72-98.

Huntington, D. (1989). Real time process control expert system implementations. *AI Review*, Menlo Park: American Association for Artificial Intelligence.

Hurtz, G. M. & Donovan, J. J. (2000). Personality and job performance: The Big Five revisited. *Journal of Applied Psychology,* 85, 869-879.

Igbaria, M. (1990). End-user computing effectiveness: A structural equation model. *OMEGA, 18*(6), 637-652.

Igbaria, M. & Baroudi, J.J. (1995). The impact of job performance on career advancement prospects: An examination of gender differences in the workplace. *MIS Quarterly*, March, 107-123.

Igbaria, M. & Chakrabarti, A. (1990). Computer anxiety and attitudes towards microcomputer use. *Behaviour & Information Technology,* 9, 229-241.

Igbaria, M. & Greenhaus, J. H. (1992). Determinants of MIS employee's turnover intentions: A structural equation model, *Communications of the ACM*, (35), 35-49.

Igbaria, M. & Iivari, J., & Maragahh, H. (1995). Why do individuals use computer technology? A Finnish case study. *Information and Management*, 29, 227-238.

Igbaria, M. & Nachman, S. (1990). Correlates of user satisfaction with EUC. *Information and Management, 19*(2), 73-82.

Igbaria, M. & Tan, M. (1997). The consequences of information technology acceptance on subsequent individual performance. *Information & Management,* 32, 113-121.

Igbaria, M. & Toraskar, K. (1994). Impact of end-user computing on the individual: An integrated model. *Information Technology & People,* 6, 271-292.

Igbaria, M. & Wormley, W.M. (1995). Race differences in job performance and career success. *Communications of the ACM, 38*(1), 82-92.

Igbaria, M. & Zviran, M. (1996). Comparison of end-user computing characteristics in the US, Israel and Taiwan. *Information & Management,* 30, 1-13.

Iivari, J. & Ervasti, I. (1994). User information satisfaction: IS implementability and effectiveness, *Information and Management*, *27*(5), 205-220.

Irgon, A., Zolnowski, J., Murray, K.J., & Gersho, M. (1990). Expert system development: A retrospective view of Five Systems. *IEEE Expert*, 25-40.

Ives, B., Olson, M. H., & Baroudi, J. J. (1983). The measurement of user information satisfaction, *Communications of the ACM, 26*(10), 785-793.

Jain, R. (1997). A diffusion model for public information systems in developing countries. *Journal of Global Information Management, 5*(1), 4-15.

Jancke, J. Venolia, G. D., Grudin, J., Cadiz, J. J. & Gupta, A. (2001) Linking public spaces: Technical and spatial issues. In J. A. Jacko, A. Sears, M. Beaudouin-Lafon & R. J. K. Jacob (eds.) *Proceedings of CHI 2001*. New York: ACM Press, 530-537.

Janvrin, D. & Morrison, J. P. (2000). Using a structured design approach to reduce risks in end user spreadsheet development. *Information & Management, 37* (1-12).

Janvrin, D. & Morrison, J. (2000). Using a structured design approach to reduce risks in end user spreadsheet development. *Information & Management, 37*(1), 1-12.

Jarvenpaa, S. L. (1989). The effect of task demands and graphical format on information processing strategies. *Management Science, 35*(3), 285-303.

Jawahar, I. M. (in press). The influence of dispositional factors and situational constraints on end user performance: A replication and extension. *Journal of End User Computing*.

Jawahar, I. M., & Elango, B. (1988). Predictors of performance in software training: Attitudes toward computers versus attitudes toward working with computers. *Psychological Reports*, 83, 227-233.

Jawahar, I. M., & Elango, B. (2001). The effects of attitudes, goal setting and self-efficacy on end user performance. *Journal of End User Computing, 13* (2), 40-45.

Jawahar, I. M., Stone, T. H., & Cooper, W. H. (1992). Activating resources in organizations. In R.W. Woodman & W. A. Pasmore (eds.), *Research in Organizational Change and Development,* 6, 153-196. JAI Press.

Jeffries, R. (1999). Extreme testing. *Software Testing and Quality Engineering.* 23-26.

Jelinek, M. & Litterer, J. A. (1995). Toward entrepreneurial organizations: Meeting ambiguity with engagement, *Entrepreneurship Theory and Practice, 19*(3), 137-168.

Jex, S. M. & Bliese, P. D. (1999). Efficacy beliefs as a moderator of the impact of work-related stressors: A multilevel study, *Journal of Applied Psychology, 84*(3), 349-361.

John, O. P., & Srivastava, S. (1999). The "Big Five" trait taxonomy: History, measurement, and theoretical perspectives. In L. Pervin & O. P. John (eds.), *Handbook of personality: Theory and research* (Second edition; pp. 102-138). New York: Guilford.

Johnson, P. E. (1983). What kind of expert should a system be. *Journal of Medicine and Philosophy,* 8, 77-97.

Jones, E. E. & Nisbett, R. E. (1972). The actor and observer: Divergent perceptions of the causes of behavior. Chapter 5 in Jones et al. (eds.) *Attribution: Perceiving the Causes of Behavior.* Morristown, NJ: General Learning Press.

Joshi, K. (1992). Interpersonal skills for cooperative user-analyst relationships: Some research issues. *Data Base,* Winter, 23-25.

Judge, T. (1992). The dispositional perspective in human resource research. In G.R. Ferris & K.M. Rowland (eds.), *Research in Personnel and Human Resource Management* 10, pp. 31-72). Greenwich, CT: JAI Press.

Judge, T. A., Locke, E. A., Durham, C. C., & Kluger, A. N. (1998). Dispositional effects on job and life satisfaction: The role of core evaluations. *Journal of Applied Psychology,* 83, 17-34.

Julien, P. (1995). New technologies and technological information in small businesses, *Journal of Business Venturing, 10*(6), 459-475.

Julien, P. & Raymond, L. (1994). Factors of new technology adoption in the retail sector, *Entrepreneurship Theory and Practice,* Summer, 79-90.

Kaplan, S. E. & Reckers, P. (1985). An examination of auditor performance evaluation. *Accounting Review, 60*(3), 477-487.

Kappelman, L. A. & Guynes, C. S. (1995) End-user training and empowerment, *Journal of Systems Management, 46*(5), 36–41.

Karahanna, E., Straub, D., & Chervany, N. (1999). Information technology adoption across time: A cross-sectional comparison of pre-adoption and post-adoption. *MIS Quarterly,* 23, 183-213.

Katz, D. & Kahn, R. L. (1978). *The Social Psychology of Organizations.* Chichester: John Wiley.

Keisler, S. (1983). New technology in the workplace, *Public Relations Journal,* 39, 12-14.

Kelley, H., Compeau, D. & Higgins, C. (1999). Attribution analysis of computer self-efficacy. *Proceedings of the 1999 Americas Conference of Information Systems*, 782-784

Kelley, H. H. (1973). The processes of causal attribution. *American Psychologist,* 28, 107-128.

Kelley, H. H. & Michela, J. L. (1980). Attribution theory and research. *Annual Review of Psychology,* 31, 457-501.

Kennedy, T. C. S. (1975). Some behavioral factors affecting the training of naïve users of an interactive computer system. *International Journal of Man-Machine Studies*, 7, 817-834.

Kent, R. L. & Martinko, M. J. (1995). The measurement of attributions in organizational research. In Martinko, M. (ed.) *Attribution Theory: An Organizational perspective,* 17-33. Delray Beach, FL: St. Lucie Press.

Kernaghan, K. & Siegel, D. (1991). *Public Administration in Canada.* Scarborough, Ontario: Nelson Canada.

Kernan, M. C. & Howard, G. S. (1990). Computer anxiety and computer attitudes: An investigation of construct and predictive validity issues. *Educational and Psychological Measurement*, 50, 681-690.

Khan, E. H. (1992). The effects of information centers on the growth of end-user computing. *Information & Management,* 23, 279-289.

Khosrowpour (ed.), *Proceedings of the 1998 IRMA Conference* (pp. 352-357). Boston, USA: Idea Group Publishing.

King, W. R. (1996). Strategic Issues in Groupware, *Information Systems Management*, Spring, 73-75.

Koch, J. L. (1974). Need environment congruity and self-investment in organizational roles, *Sociology of Work and Occupations,* 1, 175-196.

Konvalina, J., Stephens, L., & Wileman, S. (1983). Identifying factors influencing computer science aptitude and achievement. *AEDS Journal, 16*(2), 106-112.

Kraut, R. E., Cool, C., Rice, R. E. & Fish, R. S. (1994) Life and death of new technology: Task, utility and social influences on the use of a communication medium. In R. Furuta & C. Neuwirth, (eds.) *Proceedings of CSCW'94,* New York: ACM, 13-21.

Kroenke, D. (1992). *Management Information Systems*. Watsonville, CA: McGraw-Hill.

Kwon, T. H. & Zmud, R. W. (1987). Unifying the fragmented models of information systems implementation. In *Critical Issues in Information Systems Research*, J. Boland & A. Hirchheim (eds.) New York: John Wiley.

Lalljee, M. (1981). Attribution theory and the analysis of explanations. In Antaki, C. (ed.) *The Psychology of Everyday Explanations*, 119-138. London: Academic Press.

Laribee, J. F. (1992) Building a stronger IRM curriculum: Views from IS managers and educators. *Information Systems Management*, *9*(2), 22-28.

Lawler III, E. & Mohrman, S. (1989). High involvement management, *Organizational Dynamics*, April, 27-31.

Lee, R. S. (1970). Social attitudes and the computer revolution. *Public Opinion Quarterly,* 34, 53-59.

Lee, A., Girgensohn, A. & Schlueter, K. (1997) NYNEX portholes: Initial user reactions and redesign implications. In S. C. Hayne & W. Prinz, (eds.) *Proceedings of Group'97,* New York: ACM Press, 385-394.

Lee, D. M. S., Trauth, E. M. & Farwell, D. (1995) Critical skills and knowledge requirements of IS professionals: A joint academic/industry investigation. *MIS Quarterly*, *19*(3), 313-340.

Lee, S. M., Kim, Y. R. & Lee, J. (1995). An empirical study of the relationships among end-user information systems acceptance, training, and effectiveness. *Journal of Management Information Systems*, *12*(2), 189-202.

Lerch, F. J. (1988). *Computerized Financial Planning: Discovering Cognitive Difficulties in Knowledge Building.* Unpublished Ph.D. Dissertation, University of Michigan, Ann Arbor.

Lewicky, P., Hill, T., & Bizot, E. (1988). Acquisition of procedural knowledge about a pattern of stimuli that cannot be articulated. *Cognitive Psychology*, 20, 24-37.

Lewicky, P., Czyzewska, M., & Hoffman, H. (1987). Unconscious acquisition of complex procedural knowledge. *Journal of Experimental Psychology: Learning, Memory, and Cognition,* 13, 523-530.

Lin, F. Y. & McClean, S. (2001). A data mining approach to the prediction of corporate failure. *Knowledge Based Systems, 14*(1), 189-195.

Locke, E. A. & Latham, G. P. (1990). *A Theory of Goal-Setting and Task Performance.* Englewoods, NJ: Prentice-Hall.

Locke, E. A., Shaw, K. N., Saari, L. M., & Latham, G. P. (1981). Goal-setting and task performance:1969-1980. *Psychological Bulletin,* 90, 125-152.

Lofland, J. & Lofland, L. H. (1995). *Analyzing Social Settings: A Guide to Qualitative Observation and Analysis* (3rd ed.), New York: Wadsworth Publishing Company.

Loh, L. & Ong, Y.-S. (1998) The adoption of Internet-based stock trading: A conceptual framework and empirical results. *Journal of Information Technology,* 13, 81-94.

Longmate, E. & Baber, C. (2002) A comparison of text messaging and email support for digital communities. In X. Faulkner, J. Finlay & F. Détienne (eds.) *Proceedings of HCI 2002*, London, Springer, 69-87.

Losada, M., Sanchez, P. & Noble, E. E. (1990) Collaborative technology and group process feedback: Their impact on interactive sequences in meetings. In *Proceedings of the Conference on Computer Supported Cooperative Work (CSCW '90),* Los Angeles, California: ACM Press,

Lucas, H. (1978). Empirical evidence for a descriptive model of implementation. *MIS Quarterly,* 2, 27-41.

Lum, L., Kervin, J. Clar, K. Reid, F. & Sirola, W. (1998). Explaining nursing turnover intent: Job satisfaction, pay satisfaction, or organizational commitment? *Journal of Organizational Behavior, 19*(3), 305-320.

Maddern, S. (2000). High-tech brain drain. *America's Network,* 104, 70-72.

Magal, S. R. & Snead, K. C. (1993). The role of causal attributions in explaining the link between user participation and information system success. *Information Resources Management Journal,* Summer, 8-19.

Maglitta, J. (1992). That tap tap is your boss, *Computerworld, 25*(17).

Mahmood, M. & Swanberg, D. (1999). Factors affecting information technology usage: A meta-analysis of the experimental literature. *Proceedings of the 1999 IRMA International Conference*, pp. 359-364.

Mahmood, A. A., Burn, J. M., Gemoets, L. A., & Jacquez, C. (2000). Variables affecting information technology end-user satisfaction: A meta-analysis of the empirical literature. *International Journal of Human-Computer Studies,* 52, 751-771.

Mahurin, R. K. (1992). Review of the computer programmer apptitude battery. In J. J. Kramer & J. C. Conoley (eds.), *The Eleventh Mental Measurements*

Yearbook (p. 225-227). Lincoln, NE: The Buros Institute of Mental Measurements, University of Nebraska.

Mallach, E.G. (1994). *Understanding Decision Support Systems and Expert Systems*. Boston: McGraw-Hill.

Malone, S. C. (1985). Computerizing Small Business Information Systems, *Journal of Small Business Management, 23*(2), 10-16.

Mambrey, P. & Robinson, M. (1997) Understanding the role of documents in the hierarchical flow of work. In S. C. Hayne & W. Prinz, (eds.), *Proceedings of Group '97,* New York, ACM Press,

Marcoulides, G. A. (1988). The relationship between computer anxiety and computer achievement. *Journal of Educational Computing Research, 4*, 151-158.

Mark, G. (1997) Merging multiple perspectives in groupware use: Intra- and intergroup conventions. In S. C. Hayne & W. Prinz, (eds.) *Proceedings of Group '97,* New York, ACM Press, 19-28.

Mark, G., Fuchs, L. & Sohlenkamp, M. (1997) Supporting groupware conventions through contextual awareness. In J. A. Hughes *et al.*, (eds.), *ECSCW'97 - Proceedings of The Fifth European Conference on Computer Supported Cooperative Work,* Dordrecht, Kluwer, 253-268.

Mark, G., Haake, J. M. & Streitz, N. A. (1996) Hypermedia structures and the division of labor in meeting room collaboration. In M. S. Ackerman, (ed.) *Proceedings of CSCW '96,* New York: ACM Press, 170-179.

Markus, M. (1983). Power, politics, and MIS implementation. *Communications of the ACM,* 26, 430-444.

Markus, M. L. (1987) Towards a "critical mass" theory of interactive media: Universal access, interdependence and diffusion, *Communication Research, 14*, 491-511.

Marsh, R. M. & Mannari, H. (1977). Organizational commitment and turnover: A prediction study, *Administrative Science Quarterly,* 22, 57-75.

Marshall, C. & Rossman, G. B. (1995). *Designing Qualitative Research* (2nd ed.), Newbury Park, CA: Sage Publications, Inc.

Martinko, M. J. & Gardner, W. L. (1987). The leader/member attribution process. *Academy of Management Review, 12*(2), 235-249.

Mathews, R. C., Buss, R. R., Chinn, R., Stanley, W. B., Blanchard-Fields, F., Cho, R.-J., & Druhan, B. (1989). The role of implicit and explicit processes in learning from examples: A synergistic effect. *Journal of Experimental Psychology: Learning, Memory, and Cognition*, 15, 1083-1100.

Mawhinney, C. H. & Saraswat, S. P. (1991). Personality type, computer anxiety, and student performance. *Journal of Computer Information Systems,* 8, 110-123.

McAuley, E., Duncan, T. E. & Russell, D. W. (1992). Measuring causal attributions: The Revised Causal Dimension Scale (CDSII). *Personality and Social Psychology Bulletin, 18*(5), 566-573.

McBride, N., Lander, R., & McRobb, S. (1997). Post-modernist information management. *Proceedings of the 7th Annual Business Information Technology Conference,* Manchester Metropolitan University, November 5-6 1997.

McCall, J. A., Richards, P. K., & Walters, G.F. (1977). Factors in software quality assurance. *RADC-TR-77-369,* Rome Air Development Center, Rome.

McCrae, R. R. & Costa, P. T. (1987). Validation of the five-factor model of personality across instruments and observers. *Journal of Personality and Social Psychology*, 52, 81-90.

McCrae, R. R. & Costa, P. T. (1987). Validation of the Five Factor Model of personality across instruments and observers. *Journal of Personality and Social Psychology,* 52, 81-90.

McCrae, R. R. & Costa, P. T. (1991). The Neo personality-inventory using the 5-Factor Model in counseling. *Journal of Counseling Development,* 69, 637-372.

McCrae, R. R. & Costa, P. T., Jr. (1999). A five-factor theory of personality. In L. Pervin & O. P. John (eds.), *Handbook of Personality: Theory and Research* (Second edition; pp. 139-153). New York: Guilford.

McCrae, R. R. & John, O. P. (1992). An introduction to the five-factor model and its applications. *Journal of Personality,* 60, 175-216.

McGill, T. J., Hobbs, V. J., Chan, R., & Khoo, D. (1998). User satisfaction as a measure of success in end user application development: An empirical investigation.

McLean, E. R., Kappelman, L. A., & Thompson, J. P. (1993). Converging end-user and corporate computing. *Communications of the ACM, 36*(12), 79-92.

McNeese-Smith, D. K. (2001). A nursing shortage: Building organizational commitment among nurses, *Journal of Healthcare Management, 46*(3), 173-186.

McNurlin, B. (1987). A Three Year Strategy for Expert Systems. *EDP Analyzer, 25*(3).

Meier, S. T. (1985). Computer aversion. *Computers in Human Behavior,* 1, 171-179.

Meissner, A. M. (1986) The changing role of the systems analyst. *Journal of Systems Management*, *37*(11), 6-15.

Melton, A. W. (1970). The situation with respect to the spacing of repetitions and memory, *Journal of Verbal Learning and Verbal Behavior*, 9, 596–606.

Miles, M. B. & Huberman, A. M. (1994). *Qualitative Data Analysis: An Expanded Sourcebook*, Beverly Hills, CA: Sage Publications.

Miller, M. D., Rainer, R. K. & Harper, J. (1997) The unidimensionality, validity and reliability of Moore and Benbasat's relative advantage and compatibility scales. *Journal of Computer Information Systems,* 1, 38-46.

Mirani, R. & King, W. (1994). The development of a measure for end-user computing support. *Decision Sciences,* 25, 481-498.

Misic, M. The skills needed by today's systems analysts. *Journal of Systems Management*, *47*(3), 34-40.

Misic, M. & Rusoo, N. L. (2000) Reading between the lines: An examination of systems analysis and design texts. *Journal of Systems and Software, 50*(1), 65-73.

Misic, M. & Rusoo, N. L. (1999) An assessment of systems analysis courses. *Journal of Systems and Software, 45*(3), 197-202.

Monk, A.F. & Watts, L. (1999) Telemedical consultation in primary care: A case study in CSCW design. In M.A. Sasse & C. Johnson (eds.) *Proceedings of Interact '99.* Amsterdam: IOS Press, 367-374.

Moore, G. C. & Benbasat, I. (1991) Development of an instrument to measure the perceived characteristics of adopting an information technology innovation. *Information Systems Research*, *2*(3),192-222.

Moran, T. P., Chiu, P., Harrison, S., Kurtenbach, G., Minneman, S. & Melle, W. v. (1996) Evolutionary engagement in an ongoing collaborative work process: A case study. In M. S. Ackerman, (ed.) *Proceedings of CSCW '96,* New York: ACM Press, 150-159.

MORI-Market and Opinion Research International (1999). Compaq Survey: Rage Against the Machine. [Online] Available: http://www.compaq.co.uk/rage/ [Aug 16].

Morrell, J. S., Freeman, J .L., Serrano, F. & Mock, R. (1993) Hands on experience for student in information systems design. *Journal of Applied Business Research, 9*(4), 141-145.

Morris, J. & Sherman, J. D. (1981). Generalizability of an organizational commitment model, *Academy of Management Journal*, 24, 512-526.

Morris, A., Shinn, M., & DuMont, K. (1999). Contextual factors affecting the organizational commitment of diverse police officers: A levels of analysis perspective, *American Journal of Community Psychology, 27*(1), 75-78.

Mosier, J. N. & Tammaro, S. G. (1997) When are group scheduling tools useful? *CSCW*, 6, 53-70.

Mount, M. K. & Barrick, M. R. (1995). *Manual for the Personal Characteristics Inventory*. Libertyville, IL: Wonderlic Personnel Test, Inc.

Mount, M. K. & Barrick, M. R. (1998). Five reasons why the "Big Five" article has been frequently cited. *Personnel Psychology,* 51, 849-857.

Mount, M. K., Barrick, M. R., & Stewart, G. L. (1998). Five-factor model of personality and performance in jobs involving interpersonal interactions. *Human Performance,* 11, 145-165.

Mount, M. K., Witt, L. A. & Barrick, M. R. (2000). Incremental validity of empirically keyed biodata scales over GMA and the five factor personality constructs. *Personnel Psychology,* 53, 299-323.

Mowday, R. T., Porter, L. W., & Steers, R. M. (1982). *Employee-Organization Linkages.* San Diego: Academic Press, Inc.

Munro, M. C., Huff, S. L., Marcolin, B. L., & Compeau, D. R. (1997). Understanding and measuring user competence. *Information and Management,* 33, 45-57.

Myers, G. J. (1978). *Composite/Structured Design.* New York: Van Nostrad Reinhold.

Nardi, B., Whittaker, S., & Bradner, E. Interaction and outeraction: Instant messaging in action. In W. Kellogg & S. Whittaker (eds.) *Proceedings of CSCW'00,* New York: ACM Press, 79-88.

Nelson, R. R. (1991). Educational needs as perceived by IS and end-user personnel: A survey of knowledge and skill requirements. *MIS Quarterly, 15*(4), 503-525.

Nelson, R. R., & Cheney, P. H. (1987). Training end users: An exploratory study. *MIS Quarterly,* 11, 547-559.

Nelson, R. R., Whitener, E. M., & Philcox, H. H. (1995) The assessment of end-eser training Needs. *Communications of the ACM, 38*(7), 27–39.

Nelson, D. L. (1990). Individual adjustment to information-driven technologies: A critical review, *MIS Quarterly,* 14, 79-98.

Nelson, D. L. & Kletke, M. G. (1990). Individual adjustment during technological innovation: A research framework, *Behaviour & Information Technology, 9*(4), 257-271.

Neuman, G. A. & Wright, J. (1999). Team effectiveness: Beyond skills and cognitive ability. *Journal of Applied Psychology,* 84, 376-389.

Ngwenyama, O. K. (1993). Developing end-user's systems development competence. *Information & Management,* 25, 291-302.

Nickell, G., & Pinto, J. (1986). The computer attitude scale. *Computers in Human Behavior,* 12, 301-306.

Nickell, G. S. & Seado, P. C. (1986). The impact of attitudes and experience on small business computer use, *American Journal of Small Business, 10*(4), 37-47.

Nidumolu, S., Goodman, S., Vogel, D., & Danowitz, A. (1996). Information technology for local administration support: The governorates project in Egypt. *MIS Quarterly, 20,* 197-224.

Nonaka, I. & Takeuchi, H. (1995). *The Knowledge Creating Company: How Japanese Companies Create the Dynamics of Innovation.* New York: Oxford University Press.

Nord, G. D. & Nord, G. H. (1995) Knowledge and skill requirements important for success as a systems analyst. *Journal of Information Technology Management, 4*(3), 47-52.

Norman, W. T. (1963). Toward an adequate taxonomy of personality attributes: Replicated factor structure in peer nomination personality ratings. *Journal of Abnormal and Social Psychology,* 66, 574-583.

Normann, R. (1971). Organizational innovativeness: Product variation and reorientation, *Administrative Science Quarterly,* 16, 203 - 215.

Nunnally, J. C., & Bernstein, I. H. (1994). *Psychometric Theory* (3rd edition). New York: McGraw-Hill.

Nunnally, J. (1978). *Psychometric Methods* (2nd ed.). New York: McGraw-Hill.

O'Connor, M., Cosley, D., Konstan, J. A. & Riedl, J. (2001) PolyLens: A recommender system for groups of users. In W. Prinz, M. Jarke, Y. Rogers, K. Schmidt & V. Wulf (eds.) *Proceedings of ECSCW 2001.* Dordrecht, Kluwer, 199-218.

O'Neill, B. S. & Mone, M. A. (1998). Investigating equity sensitivity as a moderator of relations between self-efficacy and workplace attitudes, *Journal of Applied Psychology, 83*(5), 805-816.

Odedra, M. (1993). Critical factors affecting success of CBIS: Cases from Africa. *Journal of Global Information Management, 1*(3), 16-31.

Offodile, O.F. & Acar, W. (1993) Comprehensive situation mapping for robot evaluation and selection. *International Journal of Operations and Production Management, 13*(1), 71-80.

Okamura, K., Fujimoto, M., Orlikowski, W. & Yates, J. (1994) Helping CSCW applications succeed: The role of mediators in context of use. In R. Furuta & C. Neuwirth, (eds.) *CSCW'94,* New York: ACM Press, 55-66.

Olfman, L. & Mandviwalla, M. (1994). Conceptual versus procedural software training for graphical user interfaces: A longitudinal field experiment. *MIS Quarterly, 18*(4), 405-426.

Olson, M. H. (1982). New information technology and organizational culture. *MIS Quarterly*, 6, 71-99.

Olson, D. L., Schellenberger, R. E., & Mechitov, A. I. (1995). Teaching knowledge base consistency and completeness. *Journal of Computer Information Systems*, 7-12.

Olson, J. S. & Teasley, S. (1996) Groupware in the wild: Lessons learned from a year of virtual collaboration. In M. S. Ackerman, (ed.) *Proceedings of CSCW '96,* New York: ACM Press, 419-427.

Olsten Corporation (1993). Survey of changes in computer literacy requirements for employees as reported in "Computer skills are more critical, but training lags," *HR Focus, 70*(5), 18.

Orlikowski, W. J. (1992) Learning from notes: Organizational issues in groupware implementation. In J. Turner & R. Kraut, (eds.) *Proceedings of the ACM Conference on Computer Supported Cooperative Work (CSCW'92),* Toronto, Ontario: ACM Press, 362-369.

Orlikowski, W. J. & Gash, D. C. (1994) Technological frames: Making sense of information technology in organisations. *ACM Transactions on Information Systems, 12*(2), 174-207.

Otten, K. (1989). A changing information environment challenges public administrations. *Information Management Review, 4*(4), 9-16.

O'Quin, K., Kinsey, T. G., & Beery, D. (1987). Effectiveness of microcomputer-training workshop for college professionals. *Computers in Human Behavior,* 3, 85-94.

Padgett, T. C., Beise, C. M., & Ganoe, F. J. (1991) Job preparation of IS graduates: Are they ready for the real world. *Journal of Systems Management, 42*(8), 17.

Palen, L., Salzman, M. & Youngs, E. (2000) Going wireless: Behavior and practice of new mobile phone users. In W. Kellogg & S. Whittaker (eds.) *Proceedings of CSCW'00*, New York: ACM Press, 201-210.

Palmer, J. D. & Sage, A. P. (1990) Information technology management of the university education: A methodology for information system design and development. *International Journal of Technology Management*, *5*(2), 217-237.

Palvia, P. (1991). On end user computing productivity. *Information and Management*, 21, 217-224.

Pan, C. S., Shell, R. L., & Schleifer, L. M. (1994). Performance variability as an indicator of fatigue and boredom effects in a VDT data-entry task, *International Journal of Human-Computer Interaction 6*(1), 37-45.

Panko, R. R. & Halverson, R. P. (1996). Spreadsheets on trial: A survey of research on spreadsheet risks. *Proceedings of the Twenty-Ninth Hawaii International Conference on System Sciences, 2*, 326-335.

Panko, R. R., & Halverson, R. P., Jr. (1994). Individual and group spreadsheet design: Patterns of Errors. In *Proceedings of the 27th HICSS, 4*, 4-10.

Panko, R. R. & Halverson, R. P., Jr. (1996). Spreadsheets on trial: A survey of research on spreadsheet risks. In J. F. Nunamaker, Jr. & R. H Sprague (eds.), *Proceedings of the Twenty-Ninth Annual Hawaii International Conference on System Sciences,* 2 (pp. 326-335). Washington, DC: IEEE Computer Press.

Panko, R. R. (1998). What we know about spreadsheet errors. *Journal of End User Computing 10*(2) (Spring), 15-21.

Panko, R. R. (2000). Two corpuses of spreadsheet errors. In J. F. Nunamaker, Jr. & R. H Sprague (eds.), *Proceedings of the Thirty-Third Annual Hawaii International Conference on System Sciences.* Washington, DC: IEEE Computer Press.

Panko, R. R. & Sprague, R. H., Jr. (in press). Hitting the wall: Errors in developing and code inspecting a 'simple' spreadsheet model, accepted for publication in *Decision Support Systems.*

Panko, R. (1998). What we know about spreadsheet errors. *Journal of End User Computing*, 10, 15-21

Pankoke-Babatz, U. & Syri, A. (1997) Collaborative workspaces for time deferred electronic collaboration. In S. C. Hayne & W. Prinz, (eds.) *Proceedings of Group '97,* New York: ACM Press, 187-196.

Pare, G. & Elam, J. J. (1997). Using case study research to build theories of IT implementation. In A. S. Lee, J. Liebenau, & J. I. DeGross (eds.), *Information Systems and Qualitative Research*, . New York: Chapman and Hall.

Parnas, D. L. (1972). On the criteria to be used in decomposing systems into modules. *Communications of the ACM, 15*(12), 1053-1058.

Parsons, J. J., Oja, D., & Auer, D. (1995). *Comprehensive Microsoft Excel 5.0 for Windows.* Cambridge, MA: Course Technology, Inc. IEX42.

Paunonen, S. V., Jackson, D. N., Trzebinski, J., & Forsterling, F. (1992). Personality structure across cultures: A multi-method evaluation. *Journal of Personality and Social Psychology,* 62, 447-456.

Pedhazur, E. J. & Schmelkin, L. P. (1991). *Measurement, Design and Analysis:*

An Integrated Approach. Hillsdale, New Jersey: Lawrence Erlbaum Associates.

Pentland, B. T. (1989). The learning curve and the forgetting curve: The importance of time and timing in the implementation of technological innovations. Paper presented at the Annual Academy of Management Meetings, Washington, DC.

Peppard, J. & Ward, J. (1999). 'Mind the Gap': Diagnosing the relationship between the IT organization and the rest of the Business. *Journal of Strategic Information Systems,* 8, 29 - 60.

Perruchet, P., Gallego, J., & Savy, I. (1990). A critical reappraisal of the evidence for unconscious abstraction of deterministic rules in complex experimental situation. *Cognitive Psychology,* 22, 493-516.

Peters, L. H., Chassie, M. B., Lindholm, H. R., O'Connor, E. J., & Kline, C. R. (1982). The joint influence of situational constraints and goal setting on performance and affective outcomes. *Journal of Management, 8*(2), 7-20.

Peters, L. H. & O' Connor, E. J. (1980). Situational constraints and work outcomes: The influence of a frequently overlooked construct. *Academy of Management Review*, 5, 391-397.

Peters, L. H., O' Connor, E. J., & Rudolf, C. J. (1980). The behavioral and affective consequences of performance-relevant situational variables. *Organizational Behavior and Human Performance,* 25, 79-96.

Pitman, B. (1994). How to build a learning culture to cope with rapid change. *Journal of Systems Management*, 27.

Plowman, L., Rogers, Y. & Ramage, M. (1995) What are workplace studies for? In H. Marmolin, Y. Sundblad & K. Schmidt, (eds.) *Proceedings of ECSCW'95,* Kluwer,

Powell, J. (1999). Detecting errors is elementary. *Windows Magazine,* May 1999, 117.

Prescott, M. B. & Conger, S. A. (1995) Information technology innovations: A classification by IT locus of impact and research approach, *Data Base Advances*, *26*(2 & 3), 20-41.

Prinz, W. & Kolvenbach, S. (1996) Support for workflows in a ministerial environment. In M. S. Ackerman, (ed.) *Proceedings of CSCW '96,* New York: ACM Press, 199-208.

Quinn, J. B. (1979). Technological innovation, ownership, and strategy, *Sloan Management Review*, 20(2), 19-30.

Rafaeli, A. (1986). Employee attitudes toward working with computers. *Journal of Organizational Behavior*, 1, 89-106.

Rafaeli, A. & Sutton, R. I. (1986). Word processing technology and perceptions of control among clerical workers, *Behaviour and Information Technology* (5), 31-37.

Rainer, R. K., Jr. & Harrison, A. W. (1993). Toward development of the end user computing construct in a university setting. *Decision Sciences Journal, 24*(6), 1187-1202.

Ravichandran, R. & Gupta, J. N. D. (1993) Information systems education issues: the US and European Perspectives. In Khosrowpour, M. & K. Loch (eds.) *Global Information Technology Education Issues*, Hershey: Idea Group Publishing.

Ray, C. M. H., Thomas, M., & Dye, J. L. (1994). Small business attitudes toward computers, *Journal of End User Computing, 6*(1), 16-25.

Raymond, L. & Bergeron, F. (1992). Personal DSS success in small enterprises. *Information & Management, 22*, 301-308.

Reber, A. S. & Lewis, S. (1977). Toward a theory of implicit learning: The analysis of the form and structure of a body of tacit knowledge. *Cognition*, 5, 333-361.

Reber, A. S., Kassin, S. M., Lewis, S., & Cantor, G. W. (1980). On the relationship between implicit and explicit modes in the learning of a complex rule structure. *Journal of Experimental Psychology: Human Learning and Memory*, 6, 492-502.

Ree, M. J., Earles, J. A., & Teachout, M. S. (1994). Predicting job performance: Not much more than g. *Journal of Applied Psychology,* 79, 518-524.

Regan, D. T. & Totten, J. (1975). Empathy and attribution: Turning observers into actors. *Journal of Personality and Social Psychology, 32*(5), 850-856.

Rice, R. E. & Tyler, J. (1995) Individual and organisational influences on voice mail use and evaluation, *Behaviour and Information Technology*, 6, 329-341.

Richmond, K. (1992) Information engineering, the James Martin way. *Information Strategy, 8*(2), 18-28.

Rivard, S. & Huff, S. (1988). Factors of success for end-user computing. *Communications of the ACM,* 31, 552-561.

Rivard, S., & Huff, S.L. (1988). Factors of success for end user computing. *Communications of the ACM, 31*(5), 552-561.

Rivard, S., Poirier, G., Raymond, L., & Bergeron, F. (1997). Development of a measure to assess the quality of user-developed applications. *The DATA BASE for Advances in Information Systems, 28*(3), 44-58.

Rivard, S. & Huff, S. L. (1988). Factors of success for end-user computing. *Communications of the ACM,* 31, 552-561.

Sadri, G. & Robertson, I. T. (1993). Self-efficacy and work-related behaviour: A review and meta-analysis, *Applied Psychology: An International Review,* 42, 139-152.

Robey, D., Farrow, D. L. & Franz, C. R. (1989). Group process and conflict in system development. *Management Science, 35*(10), 1172-1191.

Robson, W. (1997). *Strategic Management and Information Systems*. London: Pitman.

Rocco, E. (1998) Trust breaks down in electronic contexts but can be repaired by some face-to-face contact. In C.-M. Karat *et al.*, (eds.) *The Proceedings of CHI'98,* New York: ACM Press, 469-502.

Rockart, J. F., & Flannery, L. S. (1983). The management of end user computing. *Communications of the ACM, 26*(10), 776-784.

Rogers, E. M. (1983) *Diffusion of Innovations.* New York: The Free Press.

Rogers, E. & Shoemaker, F. (1971). *Communications of Innovations: A Cultural Approach.* New York: The Free Press.

Rogers, Y. (1994) Exploring obstacles: Integrating CSCW in evolving applications. In R. Furuta & C. Neuwirth, (eds.) *CSCW'94,* New York: ACM Press, 67-78.

Ronen, B., Palley, M. A., & Lucas, H. C. (1989). Spreadsheet analysis and design. *Communications of the ACM, 32*(1), 84-93.

Rosen, L.D., Sears, D.C., & Weil, M.M. (1987). Computer phobia. *Behavior Methods, Instruments and Computers*, 19, 167-179.

Roszkowski, M. J., Devlin, S. J., Snelbecker, G. E., Aiken, R. M., & Jacobsohn, H. G. (1988). Validity and temporal stability issues regarding two measures of computer aptitudes and attitudes. *Educational and Psychological Measurement*, 48, 1029-1035.

Rubin, H. & Rubin, I. (1995). *Qualitative Interviewing: The Art of Hearing Data*, CA: Sage Publications.

Ruggles, R. (1998) The state of the notion: Knowledge management in practice, *California Management Review, 40*(3), 80-89.

Runkle, D. L. (1991) SMR forum: Taught in America. *Sloan Management Review, 33*(1), 67-72.

Ruparel, B. (1991) A case study of systems analysis at the American Red Cross. *Journal of Systems Management, 42*(11), 13-17.

Russell, C. (1999). New technologies improve selection. *HR Focus: Special Report on Recruitment & Retention*, S5-S6.

Russell, D. (1982). The causal dimension scale: A measure of how individuals perceive causes. *Journal of Personality and Social Psychology, 42*(6), 1137-1145.

Sahraoui, S. (1998) Is information systems education neutral? *Journal of Computer Information Systems*, *50*(3), 105-109.

Salancik, G. R. (1977). Commitment and the control of organizational behavior and belief. In B. M. Staw & G. R. Salancik (eds.) *New Directions in Organizational Behavior*. Chicago, IL: St. Clair Press.

Salchenberger, L. (1993) Structured development techniques for user-developed systems. *Information & Management 24*(1), 41-50.

Salgado, J. (1997). The Five Factor Model of personality and job performance in the European community. *Journal of Applied Psychology*, 30-43.

Sanderson, D. (1994) Mediating collaborative research? *Computer Supported Cooperative Work*, 2, 41-65.

Sankar, C. S. & Marshall, T. E. (1993). Database design support: An empirical investigation of perception and performance. *Journal of Database Management, 4*(3), 4-14.

Santanam, R. & Sein, M. K. (1994). Improving end user efficiency: Effects of conceptual training and nature of interaction. *Information Systems Research*, *5*(4), 378-399.

Schafer, S. (1995). How information technology is leveling the playing field, *Inc. Technology*, *17*(4), 92-96.

Schmidt, F. L. & Hunter, J. E. (1998). The validity and utility of selection methods in personnel psychology: Practical and theoretical implications of 85 years of research findings. *Psychological Bulletin,* 124, 262-274.

Schmidt, F. L., Hunter, J. E., & Outerbridge, A. N. (1986). Impact of job experience and ability on job knowledge, work sample performance, and supervisory ratings of job performance. *Journal of Applied Psychology, 71*, 432-439.

Schneider, B. (1978). Person-situation selection: A review of some ability-situation interaction research. *Personnel Psychology*, 31, 281-297.

Seligman, M. E. P. (1990). *Learned Optimism*. New York: Alfred A. Knopf, Inc.

Sein, M. K. & Bostrom, R. P. (1989). Individual differences and conceptual models in training novice users. *Human-Computer Interaction*, 4, 197-229.

Sein, M. K., Bostrom, R. P., & Olfman, L. (1999) Rethinking end-user training strategy: applying a hierarchical knowledge-level model. *Journal of End User Computing, 11*(1), 32-39.

Seneviratne, S. (1999). Information technology and organizational change in the public sector. In G. D. Garson (ed.), *Information Technology and Computer Applications in Public Administration: Issues and Trends* (pp. 41-61). Hershey, PA: Idea Group Publishing.

Senge, P. M. (1990). *The Fifth Discipline*, New York: Doubleday.

Serwer, A. E. (1995). Paths to wealth: In the new economy, *Fortune* (20), February, 57-62.

Shah, H. U. & Lawrence, D. R. (1996). A study of end user computing and the provision of tool support to advance end user empowerment. *Journal of End User Computing, 8*(1), 13-21.

Shayo, C., Guthrie, R., & Igbaria, M. (1999). Exploring the measurement of end user computing success. *Journal of End User Computing, 11*(1), 5-14.

Silver, M. S. (1990). Decision support systems: Directed and nondirected change. *Information Systems Research, 1*(1), 47-70.

Simkin, M. G. (1987). How to validate spreadsheets. *Journalof Accountanc, 164*(5), 130-138.

Sims, H. P. & Gioia, D. A. (1984). Performance failure: Executive response to self-serving bias. *Business Horizons,* Jan/Feb, 64-71.

Snyder, M. & Swann, W.B. (1978). Hypothesis-testing in social interaction. *Journal of Personality and Social Psychology, 36*(11), 1202-1212.

Snyder, M. & White, P. (1981). Testing hypotheses about other people: Strategies of verification and falsification. *Personality and Social Psychology Bulletin, 7*(1), March, 39-43.

Spellman, P. J., Mosier, J. N., Deus, L. M., & Carlson, J. A. (1997) Collaborative virtual workspace. In S. C. Hayne & W. Prinz, (eds.) *Proceedings of Group'97,* New York: ACM Press, 197-203.

Stair, Jr., R., Crittenden, W. & Crittenden, V. (1989). The use, operation, and control of the small business computer, *Information and Management,* 16, 125-130.

Stajkovic, A. D. & Luthans, F. (1998). Self-efficacy and work-related performance: A meta-analysis. *Psychological Bulletin, 124* (2), 240-261.

Star, S. L. & Ruhleder, K. (1994) Steps towards an ecology of infrastructure: complex problems in design and access for large-scale collaborative systems. In R. Furuta & C. Neuwirth, (eds.), *CSCW'94,* New York: ACM Press, 253-264.

Steel, R. P. & Mento, A. J. (1986). Impact of situational constraints on subjective and objective criteria of managerial job performance. *Organizational Behavior and Human Decision Processes*, 37, 254-265.

Steers, R. M. (1977). Antecedents and outcomes of organizational commitment, *Administrative Science Quarterly*, 22, 46-56.

Steers, R. M. & Spencer, D.G. (1977). The role of achievement motivation in job design, *Journal of Applied Psychology*, 62, 472-479.

Stevens, J. M., Beyer, J., & Trice, H. M. (1978). Assessing personal role, and organizational predictors of managerial commitment, *Academy of Management Journal,* 21, 380-396.

Steves, M. P., Morse, E., Gutwin, C., & Greenberg, S. (2001) A comparison of usage evaluation and inspection methods for assessing groupware usability. In C. Ellis & I. Zigurs (eds.) *Proceedings of Group '01*, New York: ACM Press, 125-134.

Stewart, G. L. (1996). Reward structure as a moderator of the relationship between extraversion and sales performance. *Journal of Applied Psychology,* 81, 619-627.

Stockdale, A. & Wood, M. (1992). Building a small expert system for a routine task. *Management Decision, 30*(3), 46-49.

Stone, R. W. & Henry, J. W. (1998). Computer self-efficacy and outcome expectations and their impacts on behavioral intentions to use computers in non-volitional settings, *Journal of Business and Management, 6*(1), 45-58.

Straub, D., Keil, M., & Brenner, W. (1997) Testing the technology acceptance model across cultures: A three country study, *Information & Management*, 33, 1-11.

Suchman, L. A. & Trigg, R. H. (1991). Understanding practice: Video as a medium for reflection and design. In J. Greenbaum & M.Kyng, (eds.) *Design at Work: Cooperative Design of Computer Systems*. Hillsdale, NJ: Lawrence Erlbaum Associates, 65-89.

Szajna, B. & Scamell, R. W. (1993). The effects of information system user expectations on their performance and perceptions, *MIS Quarterly*, *17*(4), 493-515.

Szajna, B. (1994). An investigation of the predictive validity of computer anxiety and computer attitude. *Educational and Psychological Measurement, 54* (4), 926-934.

Szajna, B. & Mackay, J. M. (1995). Predictors of learning performance in a computer-user training environment: A path-analytic study. *International Journal of Human-Computer Interaction, 7*(2), 167-185.

Tammaro, S. G., Mosier, J. N., Goodwin, N. C., & Spitz, G. (1997) Collaborative writing is hard to support: A field study of collaborative writing, *CSCW*, 6, 19-51.

Tang, J. C. & Isaacs, E. (1993) Why do users like video? *CSCW*, 1, 163 - 196.

Tang, J. C., Isaacs, E. A., & Rua, M. (1994) Supporting distributed groups with a montage of lightweight interactions. In R. Furuta & C. Neuwirth, (eds.) *CSCW'94,* New York: ACM Press, 23-34.

Tannenbaum, S. I. & Yukl, G. (1992). Training and development in work organizations. *Annual Review of Psychology,* 43, 399-441.

Tapscott, D. & Caston, A. (1993). *Paradigm Shift.* New York: McGraw-Hill.

Taylor, M. J., Moynihan, E .P & Wood-Harper, A. T. (1998). End-user computing and information system methodologies. *Information Systems Journal*, 8, 85-96.

Terborg, J. R. (1981). Interactional psychology and research on human behavior in organizations. *Academy of Management Review,* 6, 569-576.

Thong, J. Y. L. & Yap, C. S. (1995). CEO characteristics, organizational characteristics and information technology adoption in small businesses, *Omega, 23*(4), 429-442.

Tollmar, K., Sandor, O. & Schömer, A. (1996) Supporting social awareness @ work, design and experience. In M. S. Ackerman, (ed.), *Proceedings of CSCW '96,* New York: ACM Press, 298-307.

Tomer, J.F. (1998). Organizational capital and joining-up: Linking the individual to the organization and society, *Human Relations, 51*(6), 825-846.

Tornatzky, L. G. & Klein, K. J. (1982) Innovation characteristics and innovation adoption-implementation: A meta-analysis of findings. *IEEE Transaction on Engineering Management*, *29*(1), 28-45.

Tupes, E. C. & Christal, R. E. (1958). *Stability of Personality Trait Factors Obtained Under Diverse Donditions* (USAF WADC Tech. Note No. 58-61). Lackland Air Force Base, TX: U. S. Air Force.

Turban, E. & Aronson, J. E. (1998). *Decision Support Systems and Intelligent Systems, 5/e.* Upper Saddle River, NJ: Prentice-Hall.

Turner, S. & Turner, P. (1996) Expectations and experiences of CSCW in an Engineering Environment. *Collaborative Computing, 1*(4), 237-254.

Tversky A. & Kahneman D. (1974). Judgment under uncertainty: Heuristics and biases. *Science*, 185, 1124-1131.

Ugbah, S. & Umeh, O. (1993). Information resources management: An examination of individual and organizational attributes in state government agencies. *Information Resources Management Journal, 6*(1), 5-13.

Ullman, J. (1980). *Principles of Database Systems.* Stanford: Computer Science Press.

Van de Ven, A. H. & Delbecq, A. L. (1976) Determinants of coordination modes within organizations. *American Sociological Review*, 41 (April), 322-338.

Veneri, C. (1998) Here today, jobs of tomorrow: Opportunities in information technology. *Occupational Outlook Quarterly*, *50*(3), 45-57.

Venkatraman, N. (1991). IT-induced business reconfiguration. In *The Corpora-*

tion of the 1990s: Information Technology and Organizational Transformation, M. S. S. Morton (ed.), New York: Oxford Press..

Vroom, V. H. (1964). *Work and Motivation*. New York: Wiley.

Wachter, R. M. & Gupta, J. N. D. (1996) Teaching information systems via interactive television. *Computer Information Systems*, *37*(1), 63-69.

Wachter, R. M. & Gupta, J. N. D., (1997) Distance education and the use of computers as instructional tools in systems development projects: A case study of expert systems development. *Computers and Education*, *29*(1), 13-23.

Wagner, C. (2000). The illusion of knowledge. In *Intellectics and Computational Logic*, Steffen Hölldobler (ed.), Kluwer Academic Publishers, 347-359.

Walton, R. E., (1982). Social choice in the development of advanced information technology, *Human Relations* (35), 1073-1084.

Walton R. E. (1985). From control to commitment in the workplace, *Harvard Business Review,* March-April, 77-84.

Ward, J. & Peppard, J. (1996). Reconciling the IT/ business relationship: A troubled marriage in need of guidance. *Journal of Strategic Information Systems*, 5, 37-65.

Warner, L. & Smith, T. (1990). Computer training: Necessity not luxury. *Management Accounting, 68*(3), 48.

Warnock-Matheron, A. & Plummer, C. (1980). Introducing nursing information systems in the clinical setting. In M. J. Ball, K. J. Hannah, U. Gerdin Jelger, & H. Peterson (eds.) *Nursing Informatics: Where Caring and Technology Meet.* New York: Brunner/Mazel, 115-127.

Waterman, Jr., R. H., Peters, T., & Phillips, J. (1995). The 7-S framework. In *The Strategy Process* H. Mintzberg, J. Quinn, & J. Voyer (eds.), NJ: Prentice Hall.

Waterman, D. A. (1986). *A Guide to Expert Systems*. Reading: Addison-Wesley.

Watson Dugan, K. (1989). Ability and effort attributions: Do they affect how managers communicate performance feedback information? *Academy of Management Journal, 32*(1), 87-114.

Watson, H. & Wood-Harper, A. T. (1996). Deconstructing contexts in interpreting methodology. *Journal of Information Technology*, *11*(1), 36-51.

Watts, J., Woods, D. D., Corban, J., Patterson, E. S., Kerr, R. L., & Hicks, L. C. (1996). Voice loops as cooperative aids in space shuttle mission control. In M. S. Ackerman, (ed.), *Proceedings of CSCW '96,* New York: ACM Press, 48-56.

Weary, G., Stanley, M. A., & Harvey, J. H. (1989). *Attribution.* New York: Springer-Verlag.

Weary Bradley, G. (1978). Self-serving biases in the attribution process: A reexamination of the fact or fiction question. *Journal of Personality and Social Psychology,* 36, 56-71.

Weick, K. (1979). *The Social Psychology of Organizing.* New York: McGraw-Hill.

Weiner, B. (1985). An attributional theory of achievement motivation and emotion. *Psychological Review, 92*(4), 548-573.

Whittaker, S. & Schwarz, H. (1999) Meetings of the board: The impact of scheduling medium on long term group coordination in software development. *Computer Supported Cooperative Work, 8,* 175-205.

Whittaker, S. (1996) Talking to strangers: An evaluation of the factors affecting electronic collaboration. In M. S. Ackerman, (ed.) *Proceedings of CSCW '96,* New York: ACM Press, 409-418

White, C. E. Jr. & Christy, D. P. (1987). The information center concept: A normative model and a study of six installations. *MIS Quarterly, 11*(4), 451–458.

Wilson, E. V. & Addo, T. B. A. (1994). An investigation of the relative presentation efficiency of computer-displayed graphs. *Information & Management, 26*(2), 105-115.

Wilson, E. V. & Zigurs, I. (1999). Decisional guidance and end user display choices. *Accounting, Management and Information Technologies, 9,* 49-75.

Winston, E. R. & Dologite, D. G. (1999). Achieving IT infusion: A conceptual model for small businesses, *Information Resources Management Journal, 12*(1), 26-38.

Wonderlic Personnel Test, Inc. (1992). *Wonderlic Personnel Test and Scholastic Level Exam: User's Manual.* Lilbertyville, IL: Wonderlic Personnel Test, Inc.

Wood, R. E. & Bandura, A. (1989). Impact of conceptions of ability on self-regulatory mechanisms and complex decision-making. *Journal of Personality and Social Psychology*, 56, 407-415.

Yaverbaum, G. J. & Nosek, J. (1992). Effects of information system education and training on user satisfaction. *Information & Management, 22,* 217-225.

Yoon, Y., Guimaraes, T., & O'Neal, Q. (1995). Exploring the factors associated with expert systems success. *MIS Quarterly,* 19, 83-106.

Zack, M. H. (1999a). Competing on knowledge. In *2000 Handbook of Business Strategy.* Faulkner & Gray, 81-88.

Zack, M. H. (1999b). Developing a knowledge strategy. *California Management Review. 41*(3) 125-145.

Zimmerman, B. J., Bandura, A., & Martinez-Pons, M. (1992). Self-motivation for academic attainment: The role of self-efficacy beliefs and personal goal setting. *American Educational Research Journal, 29* (3), 663-676.

Zinatelli, N., Cragg, P.B. & Cavaye, A. L. M. (1996). End-user computing sophistication and success in small firms. *European Journal of Information Systems,* 5, 172-181.

Zuboff, S. (1998) *In the Age of the Smart Machine.* Oxford: Heinemann.

Zuckerman, M. (1979). Attribution of success and failure revisited, or: The motivational bias is alive and well in attribution theory. *Journal of Personality,* 47, 245-287.

About the Authors

M. Adam Mahmood is Professor of Computer Information Systems in the Department of Information and Decision Sciences. He also holds the Ellis and Susan Mayfield Professorship in the College of Business Administration at the University of Texas at El Paso. He is a visiting professor at the Helsinki School of Economics and Business Administration in Finland and a visiting scholar at the University of Canterbury in New Zealand. Dr. Mahmood's research interests center on the utilization of information technology including electronic commerce for managerial decision making and strategic and competitive advantage, group decision support systems, and information systems success as it relates to end user satisfaction and usage. On this topic and others, he has published three books and 78 technical research papers in some of the leading journals and conference proceedings in the information technology area including *Management Information Systems Quarterly, Decision Sciences, Journal of Management Information Systems, European Journal of Information Systems, INFOR — Canadian Journal of Operation Research and Information Processing, Journal of Information Systems, Information and Management, Journal of End User Computing, Information Resources Management Journal, Journal of Computer-Based Instruction, Data Base*, among others. Dr. Mahmood's scholarly and service experience includes a number of responsibilities. He is presently serving as Editor in Chief of the *Journal of End User Computing*. He has recently been appointed as Guest Editor of the *International Journal of Electronic Commerce* and the *Journal of Management Information Systems*. He has also recently served two one-year terms as President of the Information Resources Management Association. In 1997, former Governor of Texas and present President of the United States of America George Bush appointed him to a Texas State Board. In

1998 and again in 2002, he has been recognized by American Men & Women of Science "as being among the most distinguished scientists in the United States and Canada." In 2001, the International Biographical Centre of Cambridge, England named him as one of the 2000 Outstanding Scientists of the 20th Century. Also in 2001, Governor Perry appointed him to the Texas State Board that oversees the Department of Information Resources.

* * *

Reza Barkhi is an Associate Professor of Information Systems in the Department of Accounting and Information Systems, Pamplin College of Business, at Virginia Polytechnic Institute & State University. His current research interests are in the areas of collaborative technologies and managerial problem-solving, and Application of Artificial Intelligence Techniques to Organizational problems. Dr. Reza has published in journals such as *Journal of Management Information Systems, Location Science, Computers & Operations Research, Journal of Educational Technology Systems, Information Resource Management Journal, International Journal of Information Technology and Decision Making, Journal of Advanced Manufacturing Systems,* and *European Journal of Operational Research*. He has also presented his research at major national and international conferences. He received a B.S. in Computer Science, an M.B.A., M.A., and a Ph.D. in Information Systems and Decision Sciences from The Ohio State University.

Lisa A. Burke (Ph.D., Indiana University) is an associate professor of management at Louisiana State University in Shreveport, teaches general management, organization theory, staffing, and training to undergraduates and MBAs. Her email address is lburke@pilot.lsus.edu.

Dorothy Dologite is a Professor of Computer Information Systems at the Zicklin School of Business, Baruch College, City University of New York. She wrote 12 books and many articles related to computer information and knowledge-based systems. Her 15 years of computer industry experience, before becoming an educator, includes positions with computer hardware and software firms. She lectured and conducted workshops on computers in China, Russia and other countries. She did a Fulbright Scholar project on strategic information systems in Malaysia. Her current research interests include diffusing IT in developing countries, exploring IS-driven change in organizations, and applying knowledge-based and other intelligent systems technology to business and educational environments.

Jatinder N. D. Gupta is currently an Eminent Scholar of Management, Professor of Management Information Systems, and Chairperson of the Department of Accounting and Information Systems in the College of Administrative Science at the University of Alabama in Huntsville, Huntsville, Alabama. Most recently, he was Professor of Management, Information and Communication Sciences, and Industry and Technology at the Ball State University, Muncie, Indiana. He holds a Ph.D. in Industrial Engineering (with specialization in Production Management and Information Systems) from Texas Tech University. Co-author of a textbook in Operations Research, Dr. Gupta serves on the editorial boards of several national and international journals. Recipient of the Outstanding Faculty and Outstanding Researcher awards from Ball State University, he has published numerous papers in such journals as *Journal of Management Information Systems*, *International Journal of Information Management*, and *Mathematics of Operations Research*. His current research interests include information technology, scheduling, planning and control, organizational learning and effectiveness, systems education, and knowledge management. Dr. Gupta is a member of several academic and professional societies including the Production and Operations Management Society (POMS), the Decision Sciences Institute (DSI), and the Information Resources Management Association (IRMA).

John W. Henry is a Professor Emeritus of Management at Georgia Southern University in Statesboro, Georgia. His research and teaching interests are information systems implementation, end-user acceptance/rejection of information systems, and computer ethics. Dr. Henry has published numerous research works, some of which have appeared in the *Journal of Business Ethics, Computers in Human Behavior, Behaviour and Information Technology, Executive Development, Information Resources Management Journal, Journal of End-User Computing* and many national and regional Proceedings.

Albert Huang is an Assistant Professor of Management Information Systems of the Eberhardt School of Business at the University of the Pacific, Stockton, California. He received his doctorate in Business Computer Information Systems from the University of North Texas. Before joining the University of the Pacific, Dr. Huang spent several years on the faculty of the School of Business at the University of Hawaii-Hilo, USA. Dr. Huang has authored or co-authored many papers in the areas of user interface, end-user training and empowerment, Internet applications, and organizational learning. His work has been published in *Information & Management*, *Communications of the ACM*, *Journal of End User Computing*, and many other academic journals. He is also a Certified Novell Engineer.

I.M. Jawahar is an Associate Professor of Management in the College of Business at Illinois State University. He received his Ph.D. from Oklahoma State University. Dr. Jawahar has published numerous articles in journals including *Personnel Psychology, Journal of Applied Psychology, Academy of Management Review, Journal of Management* and *Journal of End User Computing*. Currently, Dr. Jawahar serves on the Editorial Boards of *Journal of Management*, and *Journal of End User Computing*. He is a recipient of the Dale Yoder and Herb Heneman Research Award (SHRM Research Award) for his research in the area of performance appraisal. His areas of research include performance appraisal, organizational justice, social issues in management, and behavioral aspects of technology management.

Rex Karsten received his Ph.D. in Management Information Systems from the University of Nebraska-Lincoln. He is currently an Associate Professor of Management Information Systems at the University of Northern Iowa, where he teaches business programming, information systems development, and MIS policy. His research interests include all aspects of end user-systems professional interaction, computer self-efficacy, and information systems pedagogy. He has published articles in a variety of journals, including the *Journal of End User Computing, Informing Science*, the *Journal of Research on Computing in Education*, the *Journal of Computer Information Systems*, *Computers & Education*, the *Journal of Decision Systems*, and *Total Quality Management*.

Rajiv Kohli is an assistant professor in the Mendoza College of Business at the University of Notre Dame. He was recently an internal Consultant and Project Leader - Decision Support Services at the corporate office of Trinity Health in South Bend, Indiana. Dr. Kohli received his Ph.D. from the University of Maryland, Baltimore County. He has taught at Lehigh University, University of Maryland College Park, and University of Maryland University College where he was awarded the Teaching Recognition Award. Dr. Kohli has worked or consulted with Cisco Systems, MCI Telecommunications, and Westinghouse Electronics, in addition to several healthcare organizations. Dr. Kohli's research is published or is forthcoming in *Information Systems Research, Communications of the ACM, Journal of Management Information Systems, Decision Support Systems*, and *Information & Management* among other journals. He is also a co-author (with Sarv Devaraj) of the book *The IT Payoff: Measuring the Business Value of Information Technology Investments* (Financial Times Prentice Hall, 2002). Dr. Kohli's research interests include Organizational Impacts of Information Systems, Process Innovation, and Enhanced Decision Support Systems.

S. E. Kruck is an Assistant Professor in the College of Business at James Madison University and teaches in the Computer Information Systems/Operations Management Program. Dr. Kruck earned a Ph.D. from the Department of Accounting and Information Systems at Virginia Polytechnic and State University and has published articles in *Journal of Computer Information Systems; Journal of End User Computing; Journal of Information Systems Education; Information Management and Computer Security; Journal of International Information Management; Information Technology, Learning , and Performance; and Journal of Accounting Education*. Dr. Kruck is also a CPA in the state of Virginia and has more than twelve years of professional experience as a corporate accountant.

John J. Maher is Mahlon Harrell Research Fellow and Associate Professor in the Department of Accounting & Information Systems, Pamplin College of Business, Virginia Polytechnic Institute and State University. His current research interests involve the modeling of decision makers in business, the use of information systems for decision-making purposes, and the use of Web-based relational databases to improve business systems. Dr. Maher earned his Ph.D. in Accounting and Management Information Systems from the Pennsylvania State University. He has published his research in the *Accounting Review*, the *International Journal of Intelligent Systems in Accounting, Finance & Management*, the *Journal of Accounting, Auditing & Finance, Journal of Accounting Education, Review of Quantitative Finance and Accounting, Review of Business Information Systems, Journal of End User Computing* and many others.

Neil McBride is the Director of the Centre for IT Service Management Research at De Montfort University. His research interests include the management of help desks, IT service strategy and information systems evaluation. His publications have appeared in several journals such as the *European Management Journal*, *Information Systems Journal* and the *Communication of the AIS.*

Tanya McGill is a Senior Lecturer in the School of Information Technology at Murdoch University in Western Australia. She has an M.B.A. from the University of Western Australia and a Ph.D. from Murdoch University. Her research interests include end user computing and information technology education. Her work has appeared in various journals including *the Journal of Research on Computing in Education, European Journal of Psychology of Education, Journal of the American Society for Information Science* and *Journal of End User Computing.*

John Melrose is a Professor in the Department of Management Information Systems at the University of Wisconsin-Eau Claire where he has served since 1970. His current teaching emphasis is the introductory MIS undergraduate course and an on-line MIS graduate course in the M.B.A. program. Primary research interests include computing skills of incoming business college students, teaching pedagogy for on-line Internet-based graduate courses, and project management. His primary business experience is with a major financial institution in the Eau Claire area.

Joline Morrison is an Associate Professor in the Department of Management Information Systems at the University of Wisconsin-Eau Claire. Her teaching emphasis is in the area of client-server database management and administration. Her research interests include software engineering topics, with emphasis on knowledge management and organizational memory.

Mike Morrison is an Associate Professor in the Department of Management Information Systems at the University of Wisconsin-Eau Claire. His teaching emphasis is in the area of distributed systems and Web database integration, and his research focuses on Web oriented software engineering, Web database integration, distributed systems development and application integration.

Robert W. Stone is currently a Professor of Information Systems at the University of Idaho in Moscow, Idaho. His teaching interests are Information Systems and Quantitative Methods. His research interests include organizational impacts from information system use and user acceptance of information systems. Dr. Stone has published numerous research works, some of which have appeared in *Information & Management, International Journal of Technology Management, Review of Accounting Information Systems, Behavior, Research Methods, Instruments, & Computers*, *Journal of Business Research*, *Behaviour & Information Technology*, and *Information Resources Management Journal*, and many national and regional proceedings. He has also served as the Proceedings Editor for the International Academy for Information Management and is an Associate Editor of the *Information Resources Management Journal.* He is also on the editorial review boards of the *Southern Business Review* and the *Journal of Business Ethics.*

Phil Turner's research interests centre on the application of activity theory to user-centred design. He is also an active member of the Social Computing research group at Napier, where he is a senior lecturer. He has managed many commercial and academic projects in the domain of end user computing, most recently as

Napier manager for the European-funded project DISCOVER, which concerned the design of virtual environments for practising emergency management, and is now also part of the Napier BENOGO project team.

Susan Turner is a lecturer and researcher in the Social Computing research group in the School of Computing at Napier University, Edinburgh. She has over 15 years of experience in user-centred design projects in industry, research and academia, much of it focusing on Computer Supported Cooperative Work. Her current research interests are aspects of narrative in user-centred design and design for a sense of place and presence in virtual environments. She is currently working on the latter topic for the European project BENOGO, which aims to replicate the experience of real places in virtual environments.

Christian Wagner is Acting Head and Associate Professor at the Department of Information Systems at the City University of Hong Kong. Wagner's research interest lies at the integration area between technology and managerial application. His research has largely focused on the development of information systems and their application to improve decision making performance. The resulting publications have appeared in journals such as *IEEE Transactions on Knowledge and Data Engineering, Communications of the ACM, Decision Support Systems, Management Science*, the *Journal of Management Information Systems, Journal of End User Computing*, and the *Journal of Product Innovation Management*. In total, Wagner has authored or co-authored about 40 referenced articles. Wagner maintains close ties with industry. In 2000, he took a one-year leave from City U to work as Chief Technology Officer and VP of Engineering for a software start-up company in California. Wagner obtained his Ph.D. from the University of British Columbia in 1989.

Vance Wilson is an Assistant Professor of Management Information Systems at the University of Wisconsin-Milwaukee. His research focuses on organizational aspects of human-computer interaction, including study of asynchronous healthcare communication, computer-mediated communication, computer-based decisional guidance, and support technology for software engineering teams.

Elaine Winston is an Assistant Professor of Information Systems at Hofstra University. She earned her Ph.D. from Baruch College, City University of New York. Her fifteen years of computer industry experience includes consulting at large and small global businesses. Her current research interests include the implementation of technology in small businesses, the IS change agent role, and knowledge-based system development. She has presented papers at conferences and has published papers in a variety of journals, including *Information Resources Management Journal* and *Journal of End User Computing*.

L. A. Witt (Ph.D., Tulane University) was formerly a private sector human resources director with client groups including information technology professionals. He is currently an associate professor of management at the University of New Orleans. His research interests include person-culture and person-job fit, social skill, and organizational politics. His email is lwitt@uno.edu.

Trevor Wood-Harper is the Foundation Chair of Information Systems and Director of the Information Systems Research Institute at the Information Systems Institute, University of Salford. With 36 academic staff it is the largest IS school in the U.K. He is also Professor of Management Information Systems at the University of South Australia, Adelaide and held visiting chairs at University of Oslo, Copenhagen Business School and Georgia State University. He has co-authored 15 books and monographs and over 200 research articles in a wide range of topics including the Multiview Methodology, Software Maintenance, Project Management, Electronic Commerce, Web-Based Systems Development, Action Research, Business Process Re-engineering, Ethics in Systems Development, Fundamentals of Information Systems and Doctoral Education.

Index

U

V

W